Victorian America and the Civil War examines the relationship between American Victorian culture and the Civil War. Anne C. Rose argues that at the heart of American Victorian culture was romanticism, the impulse to search in secular pursuits for answers to questions once settled by traditional religion. By studying the biographies of seventy-five middle-class men and women who lived in the Civil War era, Rose identifies elements of disequilibrium, passion, and intellectual excitement in American Victorian culture, in contrast to prevailing interpretations of Victorianism that emphasize self-control and moral assurance. The Civil War was a central event in the cultural life of American Victorians, Rose concludes, since the war provided the intellectual means to reassess the value of human effort and hence some resolution to this generation's relentless questioning.

Victorian America and the Civil War

Victorian America
and
the Civil War

ANNE C. ROSE

The Pennsylvania State University

CAMBRIDGE
UNIVERSITY PRESS

PUBLISHED BY THE PRESS SYNDICATE OF THE UNIVERSITY OF CAMBRIDGE
The Pitt Building, Trumpington Street, Cambridge CB2 1RP, United Kingdom

CAMBRIDGE UNIVERSITY PRESS
The Edinburgh Building, Cambridge CB2 2RU, United Kingdom
40 West 20th Street, New York, NY 10011-4211, USA
10 Stamford Road, Oakleigh, Melbourne 3166, Australia

© Cambridge University Press 1992

First published 1992
First paperback edition 1994
Reprinted 1995, 1997

Printed in the United States of America

Typeset in Garamond

A catalogue record for this book is available from the British Library

Library of Congress Cataloguing-in-Publication Data is available

ISBN 0-521-41081-9 hardback
ISBN 0-521-47883-9 paperback

To the memory of
Virginia and Helen,
and for Adam, whose love sustains me

Contents

Contents

Illustrations

Preface

Historians, as the very nature of their work reveals, are fascinated by change over time. It is intriguing for me to consider how much intellectual circumstances have altered since I began this book a decade ago and how new developments have affected my approach. A few articulate voices challenged historians in the early 1980s to examine the relationships between long-term trends, the principal concern of social history, and public events, the subject of traditional political history. Among American historians, this call encouraged efforts to restore the Civil War to a central place in analyses of nineteenth-century society. My own attempt to address this problem has been enriched by the flourishing condition of current scholarship on the culture of the Civil War era. During the past decade historians have also given renewed attention to questions surrounding the interpretation of language and other symbols created by human beings. Writing in the midst of enthusiastic debate on the meanings of texts and their contexts, I could not help but benefit from the interest and indeed legitimacy this dialogue has brought to cultural history. Words, customs, and gestures may now be explored in a spirit that recognizes their importance, along with social and political forces, to any historical explanation. The study of religion also achieved impressive strength during the 1980s. Perhaps vital discussions of religion have emerged in response to scholarly concern with the products of consciousness. At least as influential, the appearance of fervent religious movements in the contemporary world impelled many historians to take another look at the social implications of spiritual issues. This book's argument – that American Victorians faced, most essentially, a religious dilemma – is intimately related to the interpretative possibilities opened up by this modern awareness.

Probably few authors write exactly the books they anticipated, and the excitement of rethinking a subject is one of the most engaging aspects of doing research. In the process of producing *Victorian America and the Civil War*, I have moved toward an appreciation of the complex interconnections of culture and war, toward greater patience in probing the meanings of language and actions, and toward increased sensitivity to the power of religious motives in history. To the extent that I offer a new view of a much-studied era, I have been invaluably aided by the changing intellectual temper of our own time.

This book has been organized to allow different kinds of reading. I wish to explain the logic behind my arrangement of the text, footnotes, and bibliography. I have left the text relatively free of historiographic discussion in order to make my presentation as clear a window as possible on the lives and thoughts of American Victorians. I have provided notes beneath the text, however, for readers who would like to follow my commentary on the relationship of my argument to contemporary scholarship. Entries in the bibliography have been grouped under categories that generally correspond to the themes of the book's chapters. Thus sections that list publications on Victorian religion, work, leisure, family, politics, and on the Civil War follow two introductory sections composed, respectively, of sources on the individual Victorians studied and of broad analyses of nineteenth- and early twentieth-century American culture. Readers who want to pursue sources mentioned in the notes may find full information on manuscripts, articles, and books in the bibliography.

This study could not have been completed without the generous assistance provided by many institutions and people. Several fellowships have supplied the time and resources needed for research, including a National Endowment for the Humanities Fellowship for Independent Study and Research, a Huntington Library–Exxon Fellowship, and a stipend from the Carnegie Mellon Faculty Development Fund. The staffs of a number of libraries and archives have facilitated my work: the library systems of Carnegie Mellon University, the University of Pittsburgh, and Penn State University; the Henry E. Huntington Library; the North Carolina State Archives; the Indiana State Historical Society; Beinecke Library, Yale University; and the archives of the United States Military Academy. Illustrations have been provided by several archives. I am grateful to the staffs of the National Portrait Gallery, Smithsonian Institution, especially Pamela Kirschner and Vandy Cook; the South Caroliniana Library, University of South Carolina, especially Eleanor Richardson; Houghton Library and the Harvard University Art Museums, Harvard University; the New-York Historical Society; and the Library of Congress. I wish to thank Elisabeth Muhlenfeld and William H. Armstrong for their helpful advice on locating photographs. I am grateful to Shelley Giordano, Laura Gordon–Murnane, and Susan Shirk for their excellent work as research assistants and to Lynn Kile for her much-needed expertise in computing.

The manuscript has benefited from the careful and critical readings of a number of scholars. I wish to extend special thanks to Jean Baker and Johanna Shields, who read the entire manuscript and offered many excellent suggestions. Those who criticized individual chapters often pushed me to think about my material in new and productive ways. I am grateful to Andrew Achenbaum, John Andrew, Nancy Cott, David Brion Davis, Daniel Walker Howe, Jackson Lears, William McFeely, R. Lawrence Moore, Richard Schoenwald, Peter Stearns, and Bertram Wyatt-Brown. Karen Halttunen, in her capacity as a reader for Cambridge University Press, challenged me to probe the implications of my argument. Several other anonymous readers made astute observations that helped with final revisions. I have not been able to incorporate the comments of all of these readers. But I have tried to listen carefully to their ideas, and I thank them for sharing their views.

The support of colleagues and friends has been invaluable. I particularly thank Andy Achenbaum, Gary Cross, Gary Gallagher, Chuck Grench, David Kaiser, Adele Lindenmyer, Kate Lynch, and Robert Rosenstone, for their intangible but very real contributions to this book. Several all-too-brief conversations with Richard Fox have helped me to see Victorianism from the perspective of twentieth-century culture. My friendship with Johanna Shields has grown along with frequent discussions of this project. Her intelligence and warmth have been wonderful.

My deepest intellectual debts are to David Brion Davis and the late Sydney Ahlstrom. I am grateful for David Davis's kindness over many years, but even more for his lesson that ideas play a crucial role in history and may represent the determination of human beings not only to understand but to better their world. I think Sydney Ahlstrom would have been tremendously excited by contemporary debate about historical trends in American religion. It is my hope that this study honors his vision of religious experience as a central component of individual and social identity in the American past and contributes to the dialogue about American religion that he wished so much to forward.

Frank Smith of Cambridge University Press was interested in this book when only a fragment had been written. His appreciation of my goals and his commitment to the project have been critical to its completion. I thank him for his generosity and expertise. Katharita Lamoza skillfully supervised the book's production. I am grateful for her flexibility and candor.

Since I am a mother as well as a scholar, I could not have worked without the assurance that my children were being cared for with the combination of affection, patience, and discipline that children deserve. My family has been fortunate to have had caregivers who possess that nearly impossible set of traits: Kylie Barto, Tommie Anne Dumm, Susan Guisto, Pam Hamm, Jen Hart, Nancy Lofquist and the staff of Westminster Child Care, Debby Morrison, Tonya Skirpan, and, most especially, Dolores Dungee. I hope they know how important their contribution to this book has been.

My family is only mildly interested in what my four-year-old son calls "the old-fashioned times," but they have always believed in me. Their love makes my work possible. My children, Eleanor and Jonathan, have grown with this book, and they have brought me the inexpressible joy of loving them. I am saddened that my mother and my grandmother, to whom the book is dedicated in part, did not live to see it finished. My own determination to understand and appreciate the historical experience of individuals owes a profound debt to their thoughtfulness, caring, and personal strength. The book is dedicated, too, to Adam, my husband. His love, freely given, is my greatest possession.

Introduction

"For many reasons," James Garfield of Ohio wrote home from Camp Buell, Kentucky, in 1862, "I have been feeling that I would be glad to be out of the perplexities of war and enter again the pursuits of peace." Still, he told his wife, Crete, reflecting on his divided mind, "I am perfectly aware that a few weeks of quiet would make me desirous of being in the strife again."[1] Poised between the mixed attractions and torments of both civilian and army life, Garfield saw that peace offered opportunities for active "pursuits" along with often tedious "quiet," much as war appealed by its vigorous "strife" yet also posed strategic and moral "perplexities." The center of Garfield's awareness, however, was that the experiences of peace and war were equally part of his identity, strands woven in a complex pattern of aspirations, decisions, and reflections. For historians, Garfield's insight raises the larger question of the relationship of American Victorian culture to the Civil War. Did the values of the mid-nineteenth-century middle classes predispose them to accept war as a solution to society's problems as well as shape their specific decisions for conducting the conflict? Did the war transform their lives and, more crucial from a cultural standpoint, change the way they judged their experience? In the case of James Garfield, military service was a decisive interlude in his career as a rising politician. Garfield held back from accepting a commission in 1861 in hopes of securing a rank commensurate with his ambition. In 1863, he left the Union army and entered Congress, eager to confront the "new questions and new dangers," as he wrote to his brother, that the war posed for the nation.[2] Through study of individual histories such as Garfield's, this book aims to explore the connections between culture and war in Victorian America.

The task of investigating the meaning of the Civil War in relation to its surrounding society has increasingly engaged the energies of historians in

---

[1] James Garfield to Lucretia Garfield, Feb. 15, in *The Wild Life of the Army: Civil War Letters of James A. Garfield*, ed. Williams (1964), p. 68.
[2] James Garfield to Austin Garfield, June 25, 1862, in ibid., p. 118.

I

recent years. Scholars have worried that the intellectual success of analytical methods that measure long-term trends affecting private life, an approach represented most commonly by social history, has deflected attention from public events. At the same time, the taste of many modern readers for able narratives of battle has sustained military history as a distinct historical genre, yet its insights have been integrated only partly into discussions of wartime culture.[3] Since the early 1980s, a tacit determination among historians to unite these perspectives and to remedy their shortcomings has produced a growing body of work on war and society in the Civil War era. Readers now may better comprehend the roles of ideology, institutions, and communities in the nation's most profound internal crisis.[4] Even so, most of these analyses focus narrowly in terms of subject and time. Writers tend to concentrate on soldiers rather than civilians and to define the war's relevant context as the society of the 1860s. These choices obscure the essential fact that there were many Civil Wars. There was the war that soldiers encountered and the war that touched civilians. There was the war of immediate experience, the war of memory, and even the elusive war of anticipation, as images of portended disorder informed late antebellum society. In 1965, George Fredrickson offered an ambitious interpretation of the Civil War as a turning point in American history, a moment when northern intellectuals rejected the romantic idealism of the antebellum period for the bureaucratic pragmatism of the century's last decades.[5] My study takes issue with *The Inner Civil War* on a number of points. Most important, it asserts the power of culture to shape war as well as to be changed by combat, and it argues for the persistence of romanticism. Nonetheless, *Victorian America and the Civil War* aspires to follow Fredrickson's work in the sense that my intention is to place the war in a culture conceived broadly enough to contain both military and civilian experiences that were connected through time with enduring questions of value.

This book examines the Civil War as one event in the experience of a generation of middle-class men and women whose lives spanned much of

---

[3] Two essays that call attention to some of these problems are Eric Foner, "Introduction" to his *Politics and Ideology in the Age of the Civil War* (1980), pp. 3–12, and Maris A. Vinovskis, "Have Social Historians Lost the Civil War? Some Preliminary Demographic Speculations," in Vinovskis, ed., *Toward a Social History of the American Civil War: Exploratory Essays* (1990), pp. 1–30.

[4] Among many excellent works, some of the most innovative are Moorhead, *American Apocalypse: Yankee Protestants and the Civil War, 1860–1869* (1978); Goen, *Broken Churches, Broken Nation: Denominational Schisms and the Coming of the American Civil War* (1985); Shattuck, *A Shield and Hiding Place: The Religious Life of the Civil War Armies* (1987); Foster, *Ghosts of the Confederacy: Defeat, the Lost Cause, and the Emergence of the New South, 1865–1913* (1987); Linderman, *Embattled Courage: The Experience of Combat in the American Civil War* (1987); Paludan, *"A People's Contest": The Union and the Civil War* (1988); Mitchell, *Civil War Soldiers* (1988); Jimerson, *The Private Civil War: Popular Thought during the Sectional Conflict* (1988); Rable, *Civil Wars: Women and the Crisis of Southern Nationalism* (1989).

[5] *The Inner Civil War: Northern Intellectuals and the Crisis of the Union* (1965).

the nineteenth century and sometimes extended into the twentieth. They may be introduced first in terms of their social traits and second by the common pattern of their inward strivings. This pair of opening descriptions will be followed by discussion of a number of key, yet intellectually problematic, concepts on which this analysis depends.

From a social perspective, *Victorian America and the Civil War* centers on the lives of seventy-five men and women who were born between the end of the War of 1812 in 1815 and the beginning of the first major American depression in 1837.[6] The dates were selected in order to identify a group of Americans who lived through the Civil War as adults and whose outlook was shaped by common events. During the slightly more than two decades during which these individuals were born, the revivalism of the Second Great Awakening peaked in intensity and the urban industrial revolution entered its so-called take-off phase. These were the formative events of their childhoods. On the whole, these individuals represented a coherent generation of people who came to terms with their experience in a frame of mind that may be distinguished from the perspectives of their parents and children. Even so, the attitudes of older and younger members of this broad-based cohort at times diverged, and the values of people born outside these temporal bounds sometimes resembled the outlook of those within the period. This study documents the extent to which Americans born between 1815 and 1837 shared a unique perspective, yet also explains cases in which their worldview was neither internally unified nor restricted to themselves.

Within this generation, the selected group was chosen to achieve diversity in terms of geographic region of residence, occupation (within the middle classes), and gender. The seventy-five people studied came from all parts of the country: twenty-four spent most of their lives in the Midatlantic states, fifteen in the South, fifteen in New England, thirteen in the Midwest, and eight in the Far West. From the viewpoint of careers, the occupations most often represented included politician, entrepreneur, attorney, writer, minister, reformer, agricultural employer, professional soldier, journalist, engineer, educator, and actor. All were middle class in the sense that they pursued white-collar occupations. More specifically, they were sufficiently wealthy, educated, and prominent to be considered community leaders, whether the community composed a town, city, or the nation. With respect to gender, sixty-one men and fourteen women are principal figures.

Religion was not a central issue of this study when I began. As it turned out, I argue that the religious dilemma of the men and women in this generation provided the critical dynamic of their culture. Although these

---

[6] The information about these individuals presented in the following paragraphs summarizes the contents of four appendixes, A through D. The appendixes contain tabulated data on their religious affiliations and views (A), occupations (B), residences (C), and political affiliations and views (D).

seventy-five people were selected with less thought to their religious beliefs than to their social characteristics, it has proved important to know their childhood faiths. Of the sixty-four whose religious nurture can be traced, thirty-eight were raised in churches of the Protestant mainstream (Congregational, Presbyterian, Methodist, Baptist, and Disciples of Christ), and the remainder may be grouped as follows: nine Episcopalians, seven Unitarians and Universalists, three Roman Catholics, two Swedenborgians, one Dutch Reformed, one Quaker, and three who had either no religious training or a background of an unconventional kind. In the course of their lives, these individuals engaged in many odysseys, some involving changes of place, work, and political loyalty. But the most fundamental transformation occurred within consciousness, as they moved away from inherited religious definitions of meaning to answers to questions of life's purposes that they devised themselves.

This book offers the collected biographies of these seventy-five individuals as a window on the struggles of middle-class Victorians to define satisfying values in times of both peace and war. Although seventy-five is a small number of people in the grand scheme of things, the group was composed with careful attention to social traits that allow use of their example in an effort to comprehend the culture of the most prosperous and educated members of the middle classes. What the accomplishments of each person were, including whether he or she was famous, was much less important to me than how that individual's selection contributed to the social balance of the group overall. To say that they represent a statistically valid sample of middle-class society would be too strong a claim. Yet these are a set of substantially documented biographies brought together deliberately to explore the private dimensions of middle-class life.

What were the motives and goals, the perplexities and longings of American Victorians? The central interest of *Victorian America and the Civil War* is the inner life of sensibility and intelligence grasped through individuals' language and actions. What were the Victorians like, and how did the Civil War figure in their experience?

American Victorian culture was informed by the spiritual dilemma of the mid-nineteenth-century middle classes. Often without rejecting doctrines critically or leaving churches socially, the Victorians no longer found traditional Christian concepts of personal and common purpose compelling. Poised between the anxiety and exhilaration inherent in their transitional stance, they set out to recover in secular pursuits the gratifications once provided by religion. They sought careers that shaped identities, leisure that engaged imagination, family life that evoked resonant feeling, and a political process that explored ideals. Thus the Victorians were romantics, not only in their search for intense experience, but in the stricter sense that made them a generation whose members approached society with questions raised

4

by problems with faith. As they moved intellectually from a vertically structured universe focused on the possibility of transcendence to an expansive, horizontal world that invited the expression of human potential, they grasped the promise of the Civil War as a field, a cultural as well as physical space, for recasting ideals. The Victorians were not unaware of the trials and horrors of war. They felt keen disappointment at the failure of the founders' republicanism and saw clearly the suffering of soldiers and civilians alike. But the war's prospects of personal glory and shared idealism contested their soberer judgment, drew them powerfully toward the conflict, and came to dominate their recollections of war. To the extent that the Victorians' relentless search for meaning in secular activities finally achieved resolution, it was the Civil War, conceived as a struggle over profound issues, that convinced them that human effort even without clear supernatural references still had value.

This thesis about the connection between American Victorianism and the Civil War may be stated simply, but it depends on a number of ideas much debated among contemporary scholars. For the sake of clarity, it is essential to give my position on the meaning of these principal terms: culture, Victorianism, romanticism, secularization, and middle class or middle classes. These discussions will help to explain my use of language as well as my substantive judgments. The relationship of my approach to current issues in Civil War scholarship will also be considered in this explanation of the study's design.

This book is preeminently an evaluation of culture, and it rests on the premise that culture grows from the efforts of individuals to interpret their experience in ways that clarify their lives' purposes. My position diverges from at least two major trends in current discussions of culture. On the one hand, many scholars focus on the power over consciousness of symbols, not simply language but also customs, rituals, and crafted material objects. In the view of these critics, the roots of culture lie in the prerational impulses and interests of social groups rather than in the intentions of individuals. Culture thus generated influences society more or less autonomously of rational designs. On the other hand, the role of culture in assertions of social and political domination has received much attention from talented thinkers. Scholars committed to this position assume that ideas cannot be comprehended fully outside the context of struggles over social power between competing interests such as classes, races, or sexes.[7]

---

[7] One discussion that helps to explain how symbols may function as complex and autonomous sources of meaning is John E. Toews, "Intellectual History after the Linguistic Turn: The Autonomy of Meaning and the Irreducibility of Experience," *American Historical Review* 92 (1987): 879–907. For varied perspectives on the role of language and texts in the interpretation of culture, see also Dominick LaCapra and Steven L. Kaplan, eds., *Modern European Intellectual History: Reappraisals and New Perspectives* (Ithaca: Cornell University Press, 1982); Dominick LaCapra, *Soundings in Critical Theory* (Ithaca: Cornell University Press, 1989), esp. pp. 182–209; David A. Hollinger, "Historians and the Discourse of Intellectuals," in Hollinger, *In the American Province: Studies in the History and Historiography of Ideas* (Bloomington:

Both of these voices in debate rightly push historians to think about culture as something more than the deliberate creation of intellectuals, and I share their determination to probe culture's prerational origins, to see its articulate producers as part of social networks, and to appreciate its formative role in society. Still, I cannot omit individuals from consideration even if their motives are elusive and their decisions are informed by collective interests. My work assumes that cultural dilemmas are experienced most fundamentally by individuals and that personal impulses to achieve resolution give force to symbols in society. The dynamics of cultural change, in other words, come from people capable of reflection and choice. My approach presupposes, too, that private issues of power are as important as public contests. No doubt American Victorian culture served the white middle classes in their relations with social subordinates and evolved through clashes of interest. But there was an anterior and, I think, distinguishable question of power, how the Victorians reached for self-mastery by seeking terms to allay their own profound doubts. I wish to explore this inner crisis in order to lay a firmer groundwork for future study of the public ambitions of the mid-nineteenth-century middle classes.

In light of the emphasis that some cultural historians now place on the dense meanings and internal contradictions of texts, it is necessary to ask if the private mood of individuals may indeed be grasped through available historical evidence.[8] *Victorian America and the Civil War* depends on the usual resources of cultural history, including journals, letters, published works (and particularly reminiscences), and biographies. None of the primary writings are transparent, but neither do they forbid analysis. This interpretation draws mainly on the private records of people who were educated and articulate. Yet most were not intellectuals in the sense that working with ideas was their principal occupation. To the extent that they were complicated individuals, their prose is nuanced by ambivalence and tension. Still, most of my evidence does not pose the same level of interpretative difficulty as do major literary works. In addition, the book's biographical technique allows the words of these Victorians to be scrutinized in relation to their life choices. Language and actions form a patchwork of evidence where meanings emerge as much from contradictions as from consistency in a person's experience. The varied sources of collective biography allow an observer to see individuals

Indiana University Press, 1985), pp. 130–51; Bryan D. Palmer, *Descent into Discourse: The Reification of Language and the Writing of Social History* (Philadelphia: Temple University Press, 1990); and Anne C. Rose, "Interdisciplinary Perspectives on American Culture," *University of Chicago Law Review* 55 (1988): 396–411. Two recent and subtle interpretations of how culture may serve the consolidation of social power are Lears, *No Place of Grace: Antimodernism and the Transformation of American Culture, 1880–1920* (1981), and Ginzberg, *Women and the Work of Benevolence: Morality, Politics, and Class in the Nineteenth-Century United States* (1990).

[8] On the difficulties of interpreting texts, see Dominick LaCapra, "Rethinking Intellectual History and Reading Texts," in LaCapra and Kaplan, eds., *Modern European Intellectual History*, pp. 47–85.

from within the texts they created and from outside them. These two perspectives work together to check misimpressions and to open channels for understanding.

Just as it is helpful in assessing the possibilities of interpretation to shift discussion from the nature of texts in general to the materials used in this study, so may the larger question about the workings of culture be narrowed to focus on nineteenth-century America. It might be argued that the centrality of the individual to my concept of culture is justified in speaking of a comparatively modern bourgeois society but is less appropriate to social systems neither as ideologically committed nor as socially organized to encourage selfhood. Perhaps that is true. Yet in the end I am less concerned with discerning the abstract dynamics of culture than in devising an approach able to cast light on American Victorianism in particular.

Why should the word "Victorian" be applied to the mid-nineteenth-century American middle-class experience? Part of a historian's task is to evaluate the usefulness of available concepts, judging how much their conventional meaning should be retained or revised if the words are to open dialogue between new and existing scholarship. In the case of "Victorian," this study covers roughly the same period and social strata commonly associated with British and American Victorianism.[9] But to see how the Victorianism of this analysis at once resembles and contests current images of Victorian culture, it is necessary to look beyond dating to the system's inner contours.

Despite numerous studies that highlight the irrational, violent, and passionate aspects of Victorian culture, a view of Victorianism centering on its commitment to self-control, social order, and absolute values remains dominant among scholars. In a recent essay on modernism, for example, Daniel Singal characterized the preceding culture of Victorianism by its "belief in a predictable universe presided over by a benevolent God and governed by immutable natural laws, a corresponding conviction that humankind was capable of arriving at a unified and fixed set of truths about all aspects of life, and an insistence on preserving absolute standards based on a radical dichotomy between that which was deemed 'human' or 'civilized' and that regarded as 'animal.' "[10] My interpretation of Victorianism incorporates two

---

[9] The standard studies of British and American Victorianism, respectively, are Houghton, *The Victorian Frame of Mind, 1830–1870* (1957), and Howe, ed., *Victorian America* (1976), esp. Howe's introductory essay, "Victorian Culture in America," pp. 3–28. A recent overview of American Victorian society and culture is Schlereth, *Victorian America: Transformations in Everyday Life* (1991). Although there are a number of studies of mid-nineteenth-century American values, few use the term "Victorian," perhaps because of the elusiveness of the concept. Some thoughtful exceptions are Halttunen, *Confidence Men and Painted Women: A Study of Middle-Class Culture in America, 1830–1870* (1982); Smith-Rosenberg, *Disorderly Conduct: Vision of Gender in Victorian America* (1985); and McDannell, *The Christian Home in Victorian America, 1840–1900* (1986).

[10] "Towards a Definition of American Modernism," *American Quarterly* 39 (1987):9. Nearly all cultural histories that focus on later challenges to Victorianism define Victorianism in terms similar to Singal's

components of definitions such as Singal's, the Victorians' affinities for temporal order and unchanging truth. But this analysis recasts their role in a culture now dynamically conceived. The wealth, privilege, and predictability of middle-class society was less important to the Victorians as an ideal, in my view, than as the social precondition for exploring in a passionate, determined, and sometimes desperate mood the possible gratifications of life on earth. The reliable routines of middle-class conventionality made possible a quest that rarely was socially disruptive, but often was radical in the expansive range of feeling and imagination cultivated within outwardly respectable lives. In this redefined context of cultural striving, immutable values were no longer an intellectual possession but a disturbingly elusive ideal, still persistently sought, however, by a generation eager to find spiritual rest from temporal flux. Over time, the Victorians grew to savor the intense variety of human activity. But unlike later modernists, they never lost their wish to escape the disequilibrium induced by the displacement of Christianity as a vital ideal.

A rationale for this book's use of "Victorian" thus centers on the importance of middle-class order and intellectual certainty to these nineteenth-century Americans. Even so, the "Victorianism" of *Victorian America and the Civil War* is significantly different from the complacent outlook still widely pictured in scholarship. The Victorianism described in this study was marked by restless experimentation, excessive indulgence, and immersion in process as a substitute for identifiable goals. It was a culture impatient of limitations and hospitable to luxuriant sensations. There are two reasons why this Victorianism has been largely ignored. First, assessments that have followed the modernists' critique of their forebears focus on the verbal resolutions of the Victorians' questioning rather than the troubled state of mind from which their writings arose. In the rebellion of a younger intellectual generation against the elders' authority, modernists had no motive to try to appreciate the complexity of Victorianism's evolution. Second, the Victorians' formal prose has been read as a simple record of values instead of a tool for the solution of cultural problems. When public statements are set beside letters, diaries, and personal choices described in biographies, however, it is clear that the Victorians used language in a functional as much as in a representational way. This book's argument about Victorianism has grown from

assessment. Consider May, *The End of American Innocence: A Study of the First Years of Our Own Time, 1912–1917* (1959); Higham, "The Reorientation of American Culture in the 1890s," in Weiss, ed., *The Origins of Modern Consciousness* (1965), pp. 25–48; Lears, *No Place of Grace*; Singal, *The War Within: From Victorian to Modernist Thought in the South, 1919–1945* (1982); and Coben, *Rebellion against Victorianism: The Impetus for Cultural Change in 1920s America* (1991). Works that have highlighted the irrational and disorderly aspects of Victorianism are Marcus, *The Other Victorians: A Study of Sexuality and Pornography in Mid-Nineteenth-Century England* (1964); Gay, *The Bourgeois Experience:.From Victoria to Freud*, vol. 1, *The Education of the Senses* (1984), and vol. 2, *The Tender Passion* (1986); and Reynolds, *Beneath the American Renaissance: The Subversive Imagination in the Age of Emerson and Melville* (1988).

reflection on the tensions between public and private writings, language and action, and explicit and tacit values. Purpose, control, and idealism did emerge as articulated norms, particularly through the vehicle of Civil War reminiscences. But the background of their expression was metaphysical uncertainty mixed with excitement at the prospect of intellectual and spiritual freedom. The Victorianism of this study is not a thing but a process through which the middle classes established a new cultural order designed to answer unavoidable questions of life's significance.

At the risk of confusion of language, I allude at times to this transition in consciousness as "romanticism." "Victorianism" refers broadly to the motives, assumptions, and initiatives whereby the middle classes reinvented their culture. "Romanticism" connotes more narrowly the intellectual task of recasting sacred meanings in secular terms. The aspiration of the English romantics, M. H. Abrams has written, was "to save traditional concepts, schemes, and values which had been based on the relation of the Creator to his creature and creation, but to reformulate them within the prevailing two-term system of subject and object, ego and non-ego, the human mind or consciousness and its transactions with nature."[11] In *Natural Supernaturalism,* Abrams analyzed this impulse among major English writers of the early nineteenth century. It is possible that the Second Great Awakening delayed romanticism in America or that the middle classes came to sense the problematic relation of sacred and secular later than did intellectuals. Either way, American Victorianism of the mid-nineteenth century contained strong romantic elements of anxiety, striving, and indulgence in temporal opportunities, all set in motion by religious crisis.

Far more than to highlight a mood, however, the word "romanticism" serves to describe the spiritual transformation at the heart of this study more precisely than the more common and controversial term "secularization." In recent years, the widespread revival of religious interest in America and abroad has provoked useful skepticism among scholars about whether secularization really occurred and, if so, what its characteristics were and how they should be measured. Did secularization involve the civil disestablishment of religious institutions, the desacralization of consciousness, the reduction of religion to socially marginal functions, or some combination of these developments? Should the vitality of religion be judged in statistical terms (by counting sacred buildings, memberships, and contributions), in psychological terms (by reading documents produced by articulate people), or in social terms (by evaluating the extent of influence of religious values in secular society)?[12]

---

[11] *Natural Supernaturalism: Tradition and Revolution in Romantic Literature* (1971), p. 10.

[12] For a discussion of the difficulty of finding appropriate terms to analyze secularization, see Daniel Bell, "The Return of the Sacred?: The Argument on the Future of Religion," *British Journal of Sociology* 28 (1977): 419–49. The most recent major interpretations of American religious history tend either to

Victorian America and the Civil War should help to answer these questions. But as the record of the experience of a single generation of the American middle classes, this analysis can best serve as an illustration of one part of a long, complex process rather than as a model for the possible decline of the sacred. In contrast to "secularization," "romanticism" typically refers to a spiritual and intellectual change associated with the nineteenth century. Probably some characteristics of the Victorians' religious experience do pertain to people in other times and places. These common patterns might include the availability of personal choice on such basic issues as accepting Christian metaphysics, emotional distance from doctrines and institutions never formally abandoned, and competition between sacred and secular concepts and habits. As a matter of opinion, I am inclined to believe that secularization did take place in America in the sense that religion is no longer as spontaneous and influential a part of culture as it once was. Even modern Americans of strong religious commitments must be aware that a relative, friend, or neighbor might choose to be irreligious. They must accommodate, too, to a general inattentiveness to religion in such basic areas of social activity as education, leisure, and business. But whatever my view of long-term trends, the essential cautionary fact that informs this study is that Victorianism was succeeded in time not only by modernism but by Protestant fundamentalism. At the same time that midcentury romanticism was a prelude to modernists' more profound doubts about cosmic order, it also invited fundamentalists' determined resistance to the Victorians' spiritual slackness.[13] Victorian romanticism may best be seen as a secularizing interlude in the history of American spirituality. It was not part of a simple linear progression to a self-sufficient temporal world.

Social historians have grown increasingly interested during the past decade in the ways that culture, a perspective such as Victorianism, might contribute to class formation, and this line of inquiry invites preliminary comment on the goals of *Victorian America and the Civil War* with respect to discussion of social classes. The intent of this study must be distinguished from the

---

contest the notion of secularization or to change the terms of analysis so that religion's persistence is presumed. See Butler, *Awash in a Sea of Faith: Christianizing the American People* (1990), and Hatch, *The Democratization of American Christianity* (1989). But historians of both religion and society who perceive secularizing trends also continue to be active and influential. Among them are Turner, *Without God, Without Creed: The Origins of Unbelief in America* (1985), and Ginzberg, *Women and the Work of Benevolence.*

[13] The most comprehensive work on Protestant fundamentalism is Marsden, *Fundamentalism and American Culture: The Shaping of Twentieth Century Evangelicalism, 1870–1925* (1980). Although modernism had many irreligious expressions, there was also a distinctly religious modernism. See Hutchison, *The Modernist Impulse in American Protestantism* (1976). In the twentieth century, Protestant neoorthodox thinkers, like earlier fundamentalists, took issue with the mood of self-confident humanism that the Victorians evolved to answer their religious doubts, and they called for reemphasis of traditional Christian doctrines such as the reality of human sinfulness and the transcendence of God. For the neoorthodox critique, see, e.g., Reinhold Niebuhr, *Moral Man and Immoral Society: A Study in Ethics and Politics* (New York: Scribner's, 1930), esp. chs. 1–3, and Ahlstrom, *A Religious History of the American People* (1972), ch. 55.

focus of historians of class. The book's principal interest is the inward responses of individuals of a particular social background rather than the way their consciousness informed their collective behavior as a class. That is not to deny intimate connections between class and culture. The Victorians' privileges facilitated cultural experimentation, and private achievement of a degree of peace of mind must have supported public ambitions for power. Still, to be concerned with a mental world common to people who shared social traits is a different enterprise than to investigate how values affected class cohesion.[14]

Perhaps like any intensely studied social phenomenon, the nineteenth-century middle class of the scholarly imagination has been shown by recent analyses to be diverse internally and dynamic temporally, to the point that it seems a truer reflection of social conditions to refer to "middle classes" rather than to a single "middle class." Distinctions could be made among multiple middle classes on the basis of terms of measurement, so that a middle class defined by wealth might be differentiated from a middle class distinguished by values. Yet my decision to refer to plural middle classes depends on the simpler observation that variations introduced by wealth, region of residence, and size of home community made a hypothetical "middle class" consist more accurately of converging groups. I began this study with a rudimentary criterion of middle-class status, the performance of white-collar work. The need to secure sufficient biographical information and literary documentation to write a history of consciousness led me to choose comparatively well-to-do and well-known individuals. Viewed in terms of their ultimate accomplishments, they might be considered members of an elite. But the image cast by biographies that extend through time underscores their kinship with the broader middle classes. These Victorians were children of parents who made their mark near the turn of the nineteenth century in the nation's scattered cities and towns. Few of the Victorians looked back at lineages of prominent forebears, few rose without industry of their own, and few chose to leave provincial communities to live in large cities until near the end of their lives. Upward mobility from modest roots and persistent localism were the attributes of their experience that kept them in touch with their neighbors of middling fortunes. Within communities, they were often perceived as leaders, and from place to place there were differences in the implicit requirements demanded by citizens for those permitted to exercise influence. A man of modest wealth who helped to found a western town

---

[14] Exemplary histories concerned with the importance of values in the consolidation of class power in America are Johnson, *A Shopkeeper's Millennium: Society and Revivals in Rochester, New York, 1815–1837* (1978); Ryan, *Cradle of the Middle Class: The Family in Oneida County, New York, 1790–1865* (1981); and Ginzberg, *Women and the Work of Benevolence.* Historians of Europe have also emphasized the importance of shared language and ideas in class formation. See, e.g., Gareth Stedman Jones, *Languages of Class: Studies in English Working Class History, 1832–1982* (Cambridge University Press, 1983).

might gain prestige in Topeka but not in Boston. Once established as a person of privilege, however, an individual might hopscotch from one circle of leaders to another. Mid-nineteenth-century America seemed to contain a cluster of middle classes who were beginning to sense their kinship.[15]

The question of how representative the ideas of this stratum of people were of middle-class opinion overall must finally be answered equivocally if it is be addressed honestly. The characteristics of social mobility, geographic immobility, and acquired reputation suggest that the views of these Victorians recurred more deeply within the middle classes. The language of this book asserts the continuity of their perspective with the outlook of the middle classes in general: their values are called "middle class." Yet in the end, only further study of middle-class Americans less prominent than these can settle how socially encompassing the cultural process documented here was.

So much discussion of definitions and assumptions pertaining to nineteenth-century society and culture must make readers wonder how this analysis circles back to the other half of the original question, the role of the Civil War in a Victorian setting. This study's intent to see the Civil War as part of lives that stretched through time leaves a diminished impression of the conflict's historical importance in comparison to the implicit assertion of the war's centrality found in the large body of literature on the sectional crisis. No matter how influential the war was in a person's life, it was inevitably one event among many. Each of the following chapters concludes with discussion of the relationship of the Civil War to a particular aspect of culture. Despite my determination to bring into focus how the middle classes experienced the war, wartime developments remain to an extent one phase of an intricately textured and enduring Victorianism. Perhaps this is simply a shortcoming of the book. But perhaps, too, the reduced image of the Civil War's significance created by a biographical perspective should be accounted an additional and valid point of view, one that highlights the war's episodic role in the private lives of citizens.

Collective biography is more than a series of individual stories, however, and as a method it has the capacity to discern broad trends connected with the Civil War that somewhat restore a sense of the war's historical importance. *Victorian America and the Civil War* addresses two overall questions: what

[15] The most ambitious study of the nineteenth-century middle-class experience is Blumin, *The Emergence of the Middle Class: Social Experience in the American City, 1760–1900* (1989). Among other works on the middle classes, see Bledstein, *The Culture of Professionalism: The Middle Class and the Development of Higher Education in America* (1976); Halttunen, *Confidence Men and Painted Women;* Gilkeson, *Middle-Class Providence, 1820–1940* (1986); and Aron, *Ladies and Gentlemen of the Civil Service: Middle-Class Workers in Victorian America* (1987). Whether the South had middle classes like those of the North is part of the larger question of southern social and cultural distinctiveness. In the midst of much controversial literature on the subject, recent works that stress the capitalist entrepreneurship of at least some white southerners, a trait that might link them to northern middle classes, are Oakes, *The Ruling Race: A History of American Slaveholders* (1982), and from a more critical perspective, Hahn, *The Roots of Southern Populism: Yeoman Farmers and the Transformation of the Georgia Upcountry, 1850–1890* (1983).

meaning did the Victorians ascribe to the war, and did the war decisively change culture? The first issue shifts attention from the war as a social fact to the war as an imaginative construction. On that level, the Civil War was a cornerstone in the Victorians' redefinition of sacred values in secular terms. The second question asks about transition in time and, more deeply, about the relative power of ideas, social developments, and political events. This book argues that the most decisive social and intellectual trends of the midcentury period were in place before the war and were not transformed fundamentally by the conflict. Socially, bureaucracy and individualism were already making many communities more routinized and anonymous by the 1850s.[16] Intellectually, religious disaffection was challenging the availability of belief that had anchored culture in earlier decades, while at the same time imagination was invigorating experience with new languages and rituals. The war encouraged bureaucratic organization, personal autonomy, and the expansion of experimental mental and sentimental frames of reference. But it did not cause the central dilemma of the Victorians to be redefined.

It might be argued that this approach to the Civil War too widely skirts the political and moral issues that historians commonly believe produced the crisis.[17] Is it possible to understand the war without attention to disagreements between North and South over republicanism and the morality of slavery? If, as Lincoln said in his second inaugural address, slavery was "somehow" the war's cause, can an interpretation of the conflict be offered without sustained discussion of relationships between whites and blacks? If analysis of culture may be disengaged from these questions, should values be seen as influencing but not finally causing political events?

Study of the Civil War involves many overlapping histories, and though in reality they may have interpenetrated in intimate ways, scholars habitually disentangle one issue from another in order to read each one's meaning closely. Probably historians are more skeptical about interpreting culture without politics than vice versa because of the widely held opinion that attitudes are tangential to society. But anyone who takes ideas seriously will be able to imagine disengaging thoughts from events temporarily in order

[16] Most historians of nineteenth-century America have assumed that individualism and bureaucracy were inimical to one another. Individual freedom, the common argument assumes, was restricted by tightening social structures as the century progressed. In contrast, this book judges both routinization and personal autonomy to have been consequences of the replacement of insular traditional communities by a society made up of complex and socially diverse urban places with mobile populations. To an extent, it is true that individual liberty was curtailed increasingly by rigid rules, tight professional communities, and social pressures toward mediocrity exercised by mass culture. But at least as often, the mechanisms evolved to run a dynamic society opened opportunities to individuals by expanding their choices, while at the same time exposing them to the wearying impersonality of a culture where self-creation was the norm.

[17] The most recent major syntheses of issues that concern historians of the Civil War era are McPherson, *Battle Cry of Freedom: The Civil War Era* (1988), and Foner, *Reconstruction: America's Unfinished Revolution* (1988).

to comprehend history's subjective dimension. Despite contemporary uncertainty about causality among scholars arising from intellectual challenges to empiricism, I argue that culture, when reintegrated into a full view of the war, should be considered one of its causes.[18] On the most elemental level, the various historical forces become "causes" only through human choices. Cultural assumptions help to determine the outcome of individual decisions as much as do economic, political, and social interests. In my text, I tend to use language other than terms associated with linear, impersonal causality because my view of historical movement admits multiple influences on choices and assumes that decisions may be mutually contradictory, either with reference to diverse groups of people within a social setting or over time. Still, it is helpful to place this book's thesis in the context of debate about the Civil War's causes to emphasize that culture does not simply offer commentary on events but works as a force of central importance.

Victorian America and the Civil War also engages long-standing questions about the Civil War through discussion of sectional cultures. Whether the societies of the antebellum North and South were essentially different and whether southern whites can be understood without reference to blacks, slave and free, are matters of intense scholarly interest and little accord.[19] This book's argument has grown from the premise that consideration of social class may usefully inform comment on sectionalism. Perhaps distinctive regional orientations were less pronounced among cosmopolitan members of the prosperous middle classes, because community leaders were the first to participate in national systems of enterprise, communication, and voluntary organization. Analysis of the seventy-five individuals studied here on the whole confirmed this presupposition. But I also came to appreciate how much southern Victorianism was located in a comparatively traditional society, marked by informal community, scarcity of bureaucracy, and the

---

[18] Doubts about empiricism have been raised particularly by theories of interpretation that stress the epistemological difficulty of penetrating historical evidence in order to grasp history's "true" direction. Two such approaches influential in recent decades have centered, first, on the idea of successive interpretative "paradigms," a theory first proposed by Thomas Kuhn in *The Structure of Scientific Revolutions* (Chicago: University of Chicago Press, 1962), and, second, on the multiple possible meanings of cultural symbols that supply historical evidence, a point made initially by semiotic theorists. On these respective developments, see Gene Wise, *American Historical Explanations: A Strategy for Grounded Inquiry* (Homewood, Ill.: Dorsey Press, 1973), and Toews, "Intellectual History after the Linguistic Turn." These two positions have not been uncontested, however, especially by social historians. For a strong theoretical defense of historical materialism, see Palmer, *Descent into Discourse.*

[19] Probably the most compelling argument for the distinctiveness of southern white culture is Wyatt-Brown, *Southern Honor: Ethics and Behavior in the Old South* (1982). Historians who have made a strong case that southern whites and blacks may only be understood in relation to each other are Genovese, *Roll, Jordan, Roll: The World the Slaves Made* (1972), and Fox-Genovese, *Within the Plantation Household: Black and White Women of the Old South* (1988). For an overview of the issue, see Edward Pessen, "How Different from Each Other Were the Antebellum North and South?" *American Historical Review* 85 (1980): 1119–49.

persistence of patriarchy, as well as by slavery. Prominent southerners and northerners shared romanticism's religious reserve and secular passions, and the determination to create a new culture centered in temporal opportunities and strivings impelled them all. Their social materials were essentially the same. Career choices, leisure time, family sentiment, and political involvement were available to people of means without respect to section to be crafted into lives rich in inner satisfaction. To the extent that I imply in my narrative that Victorianism as a process was more advanced in the North, I do not mean that the southern middle classes were either cultural borrowers or backward cousins. Rather, the sense of cosmic disequilibrium at the heart of Victorianism grew increasingly pronounced as people were pressured by the competing claims and difficult choices of modern society. Overall, the rise of a national middle-class culture is the focus of this study. The formation of sectional Victorianisms, including the importance of slavery to southern Victorianism, is a secondary theme, not because of the subject's insignificance but as a pragmatic decision concerning which story must logically be told first.

This discussion of the language and assumptions of *Victorian America and the Civil War* underscores how much the writing and reading of history depend on some measure of agreement between author and audience on the meaning of words and concepts within a text. Not all of the readers of this book will approve my use of controverted terms. But if this narrative is to provide a window on the determination of individuals within a historical community to reestablish their sense of order and self-worth, readers must at least be informed about the intentions behind the words. Through this language, I offer this study as an interpretation of mid-nineteenth-century American culture. By calling it an "interpretation," I do not mean that I am uncertain whether the experience I report actually occurred. Yet I think that different angles of vision on the same themes would most likely produce conclusions that in part would supplement and in part contest my analysis. More attention to public culture, gender differences, and comparisons to British Victorianism, a few of the subjects that receive limited or no consideration here due to decisions about how to shape a manageable study, might well shift the balance in identifying the nature of American Victorianism and the meaning of the Civil War in relation to culture. I do not seek to write a definitive work. I aim to present a coherent thesis that serves to provoke further dialogue among historians.

My immediate and indeed principal goal, however, is to use the Victorians' words and actions to approach their private thoughts and feelings. Their generation was neither the first nor the last to struggle with religion. But when they found themselves spiritually bereft of the accustomed certainties of traditional Christianity, they behaved with resolve and creativity. The

Civil War, the nation's far more visible collective trial, offered an unexpected cultural solution to the Victorians' inner crisis. This convergence of inward and outward strands of the experience of American Victorians is the point toward which this narrative tends.

Religion

Organizations are splitting asunder, institutions are falling into decay, customs are becoming uncustomary, usages are perishing from neglect, sacraments are decried by the multitude, creeds are decomposing under the action of liberal studies and independent thought.

Octavius Brooks Frothingham, 1865

The central religious experience of American Victorians was the quiet erosion of inherited patterns of feeling, belief, and practice in the course of their adult lives. Nurtured as children in churches, few were confronted with conversion crises, nor did they contend with infidelity acutely, but surprised themselves, as time went on, by how secular they had imperceptibly become. Tolerant and practical, even the most pious had small use for theology. The Bible still served as an essential point of reference for understanding their world, but a firm hold of its meaning increasingly gave way to an aesthetic role for Scripture as a source of consoling allusions and personal uplift. At the same time, the languages of science and social science moved onto religion's weakened intellectual ground. Many Victorians continued childhood habits of church attendance, and laymen took responsibility for church government. Yet institutional ties gained strength as much from a taste for civic organization as from deep conviction, and public observance did not always match private practice.

Two key reasons, one social and one institutional, explain the Victorians' disengagement from their religious tradition. The first, paradoxically, was the successful integration of piety and society that their parents aimed to achieve. If the Second Great Awakening's basic message was the duty to explore Christianity's social applications, the Victorians, who grew up in this evangelical setting, discovered how hazardous an intimacy of faith and worldly enterprise might be. Religion did condition a flourishing culture, but secular values keenly competed with spiritual priorities as well. Second, the combination of growing church bureaucracies and more educated and hence thoughtful parishioners accentuated both impersonality and individualism that weakened religious communities. Moreover, the inclination to cope with this fragmentation by emphasizing toleration in efficient churches compounded the difficulties of religious bodies and their members. With less effective dialogue inside institutions, Victorians on their own were more vulnerable to divergence from childhood beliefs.[1]

Thus Victorian religion was marked by the diminished intellectual clarity and uncertain emotional commitment commonly associated with secularization, yet this transformation must be assessed with care. The faith of this generation was troubled, but belief adapted at times to demands made upon it in unconventional ways. Victorians who were unmoved by traditional Christian practices drew close to the invisible world by communing with spirits in seances and by observing, and half-willingly savoring, the superstitious credulity of simpler people. More profoundly, as the Victorians embraced the secular, they did so with nearly religious awe of the tangible world's potential for gratifications that seemed as inexhaustible as those offered by spiritual gifts. Wonder once evoked by thoughts of salvation was simulated by dreams of material gain, individual glory, and perfect love. Romantic impulses thus edged aside traditional faith. Yet there were continuities of feeling, despite changed objects of aspiration, that remind us that movement toward an inner world marked by temporal boundaries was not a simple journey to spiritual indifference.[2]

---

[1] For an overview of the Awakening's social consequences, see Walters, *American Reformers, 1815–1860* (1978), although Walters correctly warns in his "Introduction," pp. 3–19, that religion was not the only moving force behind antebellum reform. The most synthetic treatment of such themes as skepticism and individualism in religion is Weisenburger, *Ordeal of Faith: The Crisis of Church-Going America, 1865–1900* (1959), esp. chs. 1–3. Recent studies that explore the consequences of the individualistic focus of nineteenth-century Protestantism include Lears, *No Place of Grace: Antimodernism and the Transformation of American Culture, 1880–1920* (1981), esp. p. xiv, and Goen, *Broken Churches, Broken Nation: Denominational Schisms and the Coming of the American Civil War* (1985), esp. pp. 153–64; Goen also discusses the growing institutional concerns of mainstream Protestant denominations, esp. p. 180. On the development of religious bureaucracies, see also Gregory H. Singleton, "Protestant Voluntary Associations and the Shaping of Victorian America," in Howe, ed., *Victorian America* (1976), pp. 47–58, and my "Social Sources of Denominationalism Reconsidered: Post-Revolutionary Boston as a Case Study," *American Quarterly* 38 (1986): 243–64.

[2] Studies of nineteenth-century religious change that emphasize continuities between sacred and secular attitudes include Abrams, *Natural Supernaturalism: Tradition and Revolution in Romantic Literature* (1971), esp. pp. 11–16; Chadwick, *The Secularization of the European Mind in the Nineteenth Century* (1975), esp. pp. 1–18; Houghton, *The Victorian Frame of Mind, 1830–1870* (1957), esp. chs. 4, 6, and 11; Reynolds, *Faith in Fiction: The Emergence of Religious Literature in America* (1981), esp. pp. 1–6; Turner, *Without God, Without Creed: The Origins of Unbelief in America* (1985), esp. ch. 9; Kuklick, *Churchmen and Philosophers: From Jonathan Edwards to John Dewey* (1985), esp. pp. 256–60; Stevenson, *Scholarly Means to Evangelical Ends: The New Haven Scholars and the Transformation of Higher Learning in America, 1830–1890* (1986), esp. ch. 1; and Rabinowitz, *The Spiritual Self in Everyday Life: The Transformation of Personal Religious Experience in Nineteenth-Century New England* (1989). For a brilliant exposition of the adaptation of traditional belief to modernizing conditions, see Clifford Geertz, *Islam Observed: Religious Development in Morocco and Indonesia* (Chicago: University of Chicago Press, 1968). Jan C. Dawson cautions against idealizing a foregoing age of faith by suggesting that nineteenth-century liberal Christianity at least allowed adherents to escape the determinism of Calvinism. See her intriguing book on the manipulation of images of Puritanism, *The Unusable Past: America's Puritan Tradition, 1830 to 1930* (1984), esp.

Indeed, the Victorians approached the Civil War as an opportunity to find ideals as enlivening as faith at full tide. As the Victorians strove in war as in peace to replicate religious intensity, they saw the war as an occasion for personal testing, shared adventure, and the resolution of political goals. They were not so far removed from Christianity that secular motives displaced religious objectives altogether. The war was an event of such monumental proportions that it revived apocalyptic hopes and, as the killing continued, sober theories of God's retributive justice. Yet in the end, this Christian frame of reference competed with conceptions of war unconcerned with religion, to the point that pious allusions became one set of symbols among several. In the course of the Victorians' lives, Christianity's power to determine choices lost ground to its capacity to offer explanations and consolation for events beyond its sphere. Just so, the Civil War recalled religion for support in a time of crisis, but could not restore faith's former influence.[3]

Many Americans of the middle classes who were otherwise divided by section, gender, and creed shared this Victorian religious experience. Instances to support this chapter's conclusions involve southerners as well as northerners, women as well as men, and Catholics as well as Protestants. Yet there were also subtle differences between each of these respective groups. One consequence of the comparative traditionalism of southern culture was the informal integration into daily life of religious customs and language, to the extent that routinized churchgoing was less valued. Victorian women at times contended more strenuously and self-consciously than men with Christian images that had been used through much of history to limit women's role. Catholics, caught between Protestant romanticism and nativism that made them ambiguous objects of special attraction and scorn, escaped some of the spiritual dislocation felt by Protestants because of their marginal status.[4]

ch. 1. Other major studies of broad trends in mid-nineteenth-century American religion include Saum, *The Popular Mood of Pre–Civil War America* (1980), pt. 1; Holifield, *The Gentlemen Theologians: American Theology in Southern Culture, 1795–1860* (1978); Smith, *Revivalism and Social Reform: American Protestantism on the Eve of the Civil War* (1965); Carter, *The Spiritual Crisis of the Gilded Age* (1971); Hutchison, *The Modernist Impulse in American Protestantism* (1976); and Marsden, *Fundamentalism and American Culture: The Shaping of Twentieth Century Evangelicalism, 1870–1925* (1980).

[3] The most comprehensive recent interpretations of the relationships of nineteenth-century religion to the Civil War are Moorhead, *American Apocalypse: Yankee Protestants and the Civil War, 1860–1869* (1978); Goen, *Broken Churches, Broken Nation;* Shattuck, *A Shield and Hiding Place: The Religious Life of the Civil War Armies* (1987); Faust, *The Creation of Confederate Nationalism: Ideology and Identity in the Civil War South* (1988), chs. 2–3; and Paludan, *"A People's Contest": The Union and the Civil War, 1861–1865* (1988), ch. 14. See also Wiley, *The Life of Billy Yank: The Common Soldier of the Union* (1951) and *The Life of Johnny Reb: The Common Soldier of the Confederacy* (1943), reprinted in *The Common Soldier in the Civil War* (n.d.), 1: ch. 10, 2: ch. 10; Barton, *Goodmen: The Character of Civil War Soldiers* (1981), esp. ch. 2; and Linderman, *Embattled Courage: The Experience of Combat in the American Civil War* (1987), pp. 252–6.

[4] The most convincing explanation of the nature and sources of the more community-oriented, less bureaucratized culture of the South is Wyatt-Brown, *Southern Honor: Ethics and Behavior in the Old South* (1982). For a view of southern religion not incompatible with Wyatt-Brown's interpretation, see Shattuck,

Overall, Victorian religion was characterized by intellectual and emotional retreat from Christian doctrines and rituals, even though religious symbols still helped to demarcate the boundaries of middle-class life. As the members of this generation lost hold of inherited insights, they tried to replace religion's assurances with temporal rewards, striving to invest their work, leisure, families, politics, and particularly their war with enduring meaning. In the process, they created a culture rich in possibilities for human experience that is the subject of this book's subsequent chapters. Here the Victorians' religious dilemma is explained from three perspectives: characteristic changes in the course of individuals' lives, broad patterns of belief and practice, and the relationship of religious trends to the Civil War.

RELIGION AND PERSONAL GROWTH

When Horace Bushnell published *Christian Nurture,* a seminal critique of revivalism issued in 1847 that called for the rearing of Christians from childhood, he spoke less as a daring reformer than as an eloquent voice for religious customs already in place. Perhaps not even Bushnell could see how much conversion-oriented religion had already waned, but thorough Christian socialization was one consequence of the Second Great Awakening. The Victorians studied here were exposed from their earliest years to an aggressive Christian culture. Yet the intelligence of antebellum America was by no means exclusively religious, and secular books, music, and learning competed for the Victorians' attention. As a result, their entry into the Christian community, whether by sudden awakening or gradual nurture, was rarely smooth and almost never complete.[5]

Shield and Hiding Place, esp. pp. 1–11. Lori D. Ginzberg has examined the growing secularism during the midcentury decades of middle-class women involved in benevolence, in *Women and the Work of Benevolence: Morality, Politics, and Class in the Nineteenth-Century United States* (1990). On the religious orientation of nineteenth-century middle-class women, see also Cott, *The Bonds of Womanhood: "Woman's Sphere" in New England, 1780–1835* (1977), ch. 4; Ryan, *Cradle of the Middle Class: The Family in Oneida County, New York, 1790–1865* (1981), ch. 2; Smith-Rosenberg, "The Cross and the Pedestal: Women, Anti-Ritualism, and the Emergence of the American Bourgeoisie," in her *Disorderly Conduct: Visions of Gender in Victorian America* (1985); and McDannell, *The Christian Home in Victorian America, 1840–1900* (1986). Recent interpretations of Catholicism that present contrasting views of Catholic assimilation in Protestant culture are Gardella, *Innocent Ecstasy: How Christianity Gave America an Ethic of Sexual Pleasure* (1985), and Taves, *The Household of Faith: Roman Catholic Devotions in Mid-Nineteenth-Century America* (1986).

[5] See *Christian Nurture* (New Haven: Yale University Press, 1947). Although James Turner emphasizes intellectual trends in contrast to my focus on middle-class experience, he presents a similar argument that modernity damaged religion's ability to enable individuals to achieve a clear view of transcendent objects, in *Without God, Without Creed,* esp. p. xiii. Anne M. Boylan shows how Protestants very gradually accepted the sufficiency of Christian nurture without conversion, a change completed by 1880, in her study of the evolution of the Sunday schools as an institution, *Sunday School: The Formation of an American Institution, 1790–1880* (1988), esp. ch. 5.

Home, church, and school taught mutually reinforcing religious lessons as they had for two centuries, but with an intensity enhanced by the Awakening's fervor. Like many of her contemporaries, Lucy Larcom was born into a family where religion, along with the necessities of domestic economy, structured the weekly routine. In addition to daily prayers in her parents' household in Beverly, Massachusetts, Saturdays were devoted from noontime on to the baking and cleaning needed to free the Sabbath from labor. Sunday worship was followed by instruction by her father at home, where the Bible along with the Westminster and Shorter Catechisms supplied his questions. Southerners left less evidence than did the Larcom family of regular church attendance, but parents and guardians still insisted on children's religious habits. As an old woman living near Huntsville at the turn of the twentieth century, Virginia Clay looked back on her Alabama upbringing to say that "from my earliest girlhood three lessons had been taught me religiously, viz.: to be proud alike of my name and blood and section; to read my Bible; and, last, to know my 'Richmond Enquirer.' "[6]

Clay may have exaggerated the equal stature of Scripture and newspaper retrospectively, but her list underlines the ambiguous effect of rising literacy on religion. Children conscientiously taught to read in response to the conviction that educated citizens must sustain the republic encountered the Bible firsthand. But they gained access to popular literature, too, in growing quantities that by sheer mass could challenge religion's preeminence. When the family of Priscilla Cooper Tyler in Pennsylvania read aloud to one another in the 1820s, her mother's account to an absent son suggests how nearly interchangeable sacred and secular prose had become: "We have read several of Walter Scott's novels and some better books Sundays. If [the girls] can't go to evening church I read them a couple of sermons."[7] Similarly, the popularity of hymns issued in cheap editions enhanced pious feeling, yet as easily overshadowed the message of such conventional religious forms as the Bible and sermons. Larcom devoted an entire chapter of her memoirs to "The Hymn-book," more space than she gave to her father's lessons and to churchgoing combined. She betrayed their comparative personal value when she wrote that she knew one hundred hymns by heart by the time she was five. Charlotte Cushman, the daughter of a Boston merchant who became an actress, as unwittingly revealed the risk that religious music would blur

[6] Larcom, *A New England Girlhood: Outlined from Memory* (1889), pp. 24, 48–56; Clay, quoted in Wiley, *Confederate Women* (1975), p. 76. For an analysis of the traditional Puritan theory of the religious obligations of families, see Edmund S. Morgan, *The Puritan Family: Religion and Domestic Relations in Seventeenth-Century New England* (1944; reprint, New York: Harper and Row, 1966), esp. chs. 1, 6.

[7] Mary Cooper to James Cooper, ca. 1827–28, quoted in Coleman, *Priscilla Cooper Tyler and the American Scene, 1816–1889* (1955), p. 19. David D. Hall discusses the way fiction, children's literature, and journalism gradually displaced religious books, in "Introduction: The Uses of Literacy in New England, 1600–1850," in Joyce et al., eds., *Printing and Society in Early America* (1983), pp. 1–47.

the bounds of the secular when she recalled that she learned to sing in public by joining church choirs.[8] The ability of these young people to read prose and music fostered their intimacy with religion but opened secular doors as well.

Despite the chances for individual exploration in a culture where sacred and profane opportunities flourished side by side, Victorians required to attend church as children were still subject to institutional controls. Church-going was especially routinized in New England. Edward Everett Hale, who grew up to become a minister, looked back nostalgically in his memoirs of 1893 to the 1820s and 1830s when no one took Sunday drives. Bostonians of all ages spent mornings and afternoons in church, Hale recalled, with Sunday school for children after services. Outside New England, people of Puritan heritage took regular worship most seriously. Jay Cooke, the financier, went as a boy to the Methodist church in Sandusky, Ohio, built in 1828. His parents had migrated from eastern New York a decade before, but his father traced his family back to early settlers of Salem, Massachusetts.[9]

Loyal church attendance cannot be the sole measure of childhood piety, however, because conscientious teaching was not the only reason that religious lessons were learned. As Hale observed in his reminiscences, Boston churches during his youth stood vacant all week, until Lyman Beecher began daily services to stir up a revival to win souls from congregations that Beecher judged so routinized as to be spiritually dead. Just so, scarce mention of Sunday worship in the records of southerners' childhoods as reasonably indicates their attention to the irregular spiritual outpourings of protracted revivals as their weak initiation into Christian culture. Moncure Conway wrote in 1904 that Virginia's once-established Episcopal churches were nearly defunct when he was a boy in the 1830s and 1840s. His father instead found religion at a Methodist camp meeting. Although church services never figured largely enough in Conway's family routine to draw comment in his autobiography, Methodism dictated so coherent a set of precepts on the treatment of slaves, acceptable literature, and appropriate education that it drew children toward the Christian community.[10] Whether the strength of

[8] Larcom, *New England Girlhood*, ch. 3; Stebbins, *Charlotte Cushman: Her Letters and Memories of Her Life* (1879), p. 19.

[9] Hale, *A New England Boyhood* (1893), pp. 129–31; Larson, *Jay Cooke: Private Banker* (1936), pp. 3–4, 10, 13. Evidence on church attendance in later decades of the nineteenth century is problematic. Weisenburger states that America remained a churchgoing nation after the Civil War and cites the fact that even liberal Harvard required daily prayers and Sunday services until 1886, in *Ordeal of Faith*, pp. 1, 3. But he also devotes an entire chapter to "Why Some Church Pews Were Empty" (ch. 3). Turner argues that church membership and attendance increased throughout the century, despite the simultaneous decline of assurance in the truth of traditional beliefs, in *Without God, Without Creed*, p. 262. My analysis attempts to explain a similar incongruity between institutional activity and individual reserve.

[10] Hale, *New England Boyhood*, pp. 133–4; Conway, *Autobiography, Memories and Experiences of Moncure Daniel Conway* (1904), 1:16, 19, 23, 28, 34, 43. Studies of antebellum revivalism include Miller, *The Life of the Mind in America: From the Revolution to the Civil War* (1965), bk. 1; Mathews, *Religion in the*

Figure 1. Edward Everett Hale (1822–1909). Unitarian minister and author. Photographed at the George K. Warren Studio, Boston, possibly by Sumner B. Heald, ca. 1871. National Portrait Gallery, Smithsonian Institution.

religion grew from the attentiveness to Sunday ritual prevalent in the North, from the daily repetition of precepts recalled in the South, or from both, the Victorians were taught as children to heed religious authority.

Yet some parents unwittingly taught them, too, that religious customs could with impunity be ignored or, more insidiously, be stretched to accommodate secular interests. As a boy growing up in New Hampshire,

Old South (1977); Johnson, *A Shopkeeper's Millennium: Society and Revivals in Rochester, New York, 1815–1837* (1978); Ryan, *Cradle of the Middle Class;* and Bilhartz, *Urban Religion and the Second Great Awakening: Church and Society in Early National Baltimore* (1986).

Franklin Benjamin Sanborn understood the tacit rule that churchgoing was mainly for women, a trend so well documented by historians that his awareness must have been widely shared.[11] Edward Everett Hale acknowledged that Sunday evening religious concerts had begun to encroach on the traditional Sabbath during his childhood. Methodists proscribed novel reading, Conway recalled, but his parents loved Dickens nonetheless.[12] Probably through most of American history irreligious habits competed with pious observance. But the comments of Hale and Conway on music and fiction indicate the rise of a sensuous and often secular culture of unprecedented range and depth, whose pleasures might be cautiously indulged at the same time that a person considered himself or herself to be a good Christian. Thus apostasy blossomed in the shadow of piety. To the extent that the Victorians made similar choices as adults, how to mix spiritual and temporal desires was a lesson they learned from their parents.

Beyond formal religious instruction, education conveyed Christian lessons during the Victorians' childhoods. Schools exercised an unprecedented influence over young people, as an evangelical drive for a Christian society built on a republican commitment to an enlightened public and a traditional Protestant belief in literacy to produce new common schools, academies, and colleges. How much evangelical objectives focused schooling varied in this rapidly changing setting. To have boys who were bound for college instructed by ministers was a practice with colonial roots, because clergymen were often the most educated men in communities. Religious assumptions pervaded teaching, but conversion was not an explicit goal. When Frederick Law Olmsted was sent to board with successive Connecticut ministers around 1830, his parents' choice conformed to this traditional pattern.[13] In North Carolina, Zebulon Vance attended an academy housed in a Baptist church and later Washington College, run by a minister, before entering the University of North Carolina in 1851. Without precisely stated evangelical goals, his schools represented a middle ground between traditional clerical instruction and aggressive proselytizing. More typical of deliberate efforts to further Christian education was the experience in Ohio of James Garfield. Garfield attended Geauga Seminary, established by the Free Will Baptists and, after his conversion in 1850, Western Reserve Eclectic Institute (later Hiram College), sponsored by the Disciples of Christ. The blend of secular and sacred

---

[11] Sanborn, *Recollections of Seventy Years* (1909), 1:20. Nancy Cott argues that women were the majority of Protestant church members in New England from the seventeenth century on, in *Bonds of Womanhood*, pp. 126–7.

[12] Hale, *New England Boyhood*, p. 135; Conway, *Autobiography*, 1:34.

[13] Roper, *FLO: A Biography of Frederick Law Olmsted* (1973), pp. 7–9. Daniel Calhoun explains the colonial practice of instruction by ministers, in *The Intelligence of a People* (1973), p. 42. Another study useful for understanding why eighteenth-century ministers, in contrast to their more professionally oriented nineteenth-century counterparts, offered education as a kind of community service is Scott, *From Office to Profession: The New England Ministry, 1750–1850* (1978), ch. 1.

themes in Garfield's journal during his years at school, 1849 to 1854, reveals precisely the kind of Christian character such academies hoped to create.[14]

Alongside this concern with spiritual nurture, however, there were other opportunities for schooling that grew from motives besides religion. The middle classes were keenly interested in cultivation, and many institutions defined their student bodies and selected their curricula in ways that ignored questions of faith. Virginia Clay attended a female academy in Nashville, Tennessee (1839–40), William Potter went to normal school in Bridgewater, Massachusetts (1847–48), and Moncure Conway studied at a classical academy in Fredericksburg, Virginia (1842).[15] To be sure, public worship and religious instruction still figured in the schedule of most schools, however they conceived their goals. But the balance between secular and sacred, as well as the interpretation of the sacred, was no longer clearly defined, and the imprecision occasioned disputes. Illinois College in Jacksonville, staffed by Yale graduates, offered William Herndon excellent instruction in the mid-1830s. But he came home to Springfield after a year, when his father, a southern-born Democrat, apparently took issue with the school's religious liberalism and abolitionist leanings.[16] Probably there was more contention about the kind of values taught than how thoroughly morals should dominate learning. Either way, though the Victorians as children encountered Christianity in schools, as they did in families and churches, in no setting did they see religion's authority unquestioned.

It is striking that Christian families, churches, and schools produced so few conversions among these Victorians as young people. Despite Bushnell's view of religious nurture as an acceptable alternative to spiritual crisis, a change of heart was still seen by most Protestants during the Victorians' childhoods as the preferred way to make Christians. Yet only ten of the seventy-five individuals studied left clear evidence of a religious experience that evolved through stages of doubt, resolution, and profession of faith. The small number might be less surprising if many grew up in denominations critical of conversion. But there were only seven Unitarians and Universalists,

---

[14] Tucker, *Zeb Vance: Champion of Personal Freedom* (1965), pp. 30–7; *The Diary of James A. Garfield*, ed. Brown and Williams (1967), 1:xvii–xix. On the religious impetus behind educational expansion, see Ahlstrom, *A Religious History of the American People* (1972), p. 425. For a dramatic instance of how one woman transformed her father's evangelical message into a task for education, see Sklar, *Catharine Beecher: A Study in American Domesticity* (1973), esp. ch. 12.

[15] On Clay, Potter, and Conway, see, respectively, Wiley, *Confederate Women*, p. 41; Diaries, 1847–48, 1849, William Potter Papers; and Conway, *Autobiography*, 1:32.

[16] Donald, *Lincoln's Herndon* (1948), pp. 9–14. Almost none of these Victorians attended public common schools, one sign of their prosperous backgrounds. Even so, the modest role of religion in the common-school movement epitomizes the uncertain blend of spiritual and social concerns in some new educational endeavors. Carl F. Kaestle explains that republicanism, capitalism, and Protestantism equally contributed to the ideology of common-school reform, and though morality was consistently taught, its social utility was often the dominant motive. See *Pillars of the Republic: Common Schools and American Society, 1780–1860* (1983), esp. p. 76.

three Catholics, and one Quaker in this group, in contrast to thirty-eight who went as children to churches in the evangelical mainstream (Congregational, Presbyterian, Methodist, Baptist, and Disciples of Christ) and twelve more who belonged to churches that either approved conversion at times or in an unusual form, including nine Episcopalians, one Dutch Reformed, and two Swedenborgians. Perhaps at no time and place in American history after the earliest days of Puritan settlement did more than a minority of the population experience a decisive change of heart. But the Victorians were raised by churchgoing parents in an era unique in its attention to the multiplication of devices for the transmission of faith, and thus their spiritual difficulties are arresting. Because no religious awakening of the social scope and cultural fertility of that of their youth occurred thereafter, moreover, the Victorians' inability to fulfill the adult expectations imposed by their childhood training signaled a disaffection from the Christian tradition more enduring than the ebb and flow of enthusiasm inherent in evangelical revivalism. Rather than have conversion anchor the spiritual experience of most of the Victorians as adults, four patterns of religious transition emerged in addition to a single awakening: recurrent questioning and redirection, steady church loyalty, gradual loss of faith, and vocal subversion of tradition. Most of those modes of spiritual passage were protracted and inconclusive, and none effectively guarded piety from the challenge of secular interests.[17]

[17] The individuals who experienced conversion as young adults were John Wesley North, George Atkinson, Charles Maclay, Frederick Law Olmsted, Jabez Curry, Oliver Otis Howard, James Garfield, Moncure Conway, Lyman Abbott, and Rebecca Felton. Several additional people were converted in middle or old age, including John Hood, Zebulon Vance, James Guignard, and John Guignard. See Appendix A for childhood and adult religious affiliations of this group. Because I have tried to work with individuals where some records exist for all periods of their lives, the eleven people for whom I have found no evidence of childhood practice may not have had any long-term involvement with a religious group. In categorizing individuals, I have counted those with more than one childhood affiliation in the group most influential during their youth. Although the Victorians with evangelical backgrounds constituted the largest single block of the total (thirty-eight of sixty-four, 59.4 percent), religious minorities may be represented more strongly in this sample than in the nation. If 1830 may be considered a fairly central date in the generation's childhood, in that year Protestant denominations were ranked by the American Education Society in the following order: Calvinist Baptist (2.7 million members), Methodist (2.6 million), Presbyterian (1.8 million), Congregational (1.2 million), Episcopal (240,000), with smaller denominations following (cited in Winthrop Hudson, *American Protestantism* [Chicago: University of Chicago Press, 1961], p. 99). The significant number of Unitarians, Universalists, Swedenborgians, and Quakers in this study (ten altogether) may make it appropriate to see this group as more religiously liberal than the nation as a whole, though nonetheless representative of the prosperous middle classes. The balance in a liberal direction is probably due less to simple regional bias, since only fourteen of seventy-five were from New England (see Appendix C on "Residences"), than to the combination of class and place of origin. In other words, the upper-middle-class roots of most of my individuals from New England made them more likely to belong to progressive Protestant denominations. Due to scarce and unreliable estimates, it is difficult to get a comparative perspective on the number of conversions among the Victorians vis-à-vis the frequency of personal spiritual awakenings in other eras. The proportion of Victorians (ten of seventy-five) who were converted more or less matches the figure of one in eight Americans who Winthrop Hudson proposes were church members in 1835, presumably entering congregations by conversion, and the figure of one in seven he cites for 1850. Both proportions represent an increase over the one in fifteen he argues were in churches in 1800. See ibid., p. 96. Because most

The Victorians who came by crisis to spiritual maturity adhered most closely to the evangelical tradition, yet their conversions were rarely conventional. On first glance, the experience of Lyman Abbott, the son of a minister and religious writer who chose the same vocations himself, conformed to a pattern long established for American young people. Closer scrutiny of Abbott's history suggests, however, why other boys and girls bound less firmly than Abbott to the religious community met with repeated seasons of doubt. Looking back in his autobiography, Abbott told a story of faith successfully sustained, describing how childhood certainties broke down in religious anxieties that were overcome in the end, first by a flawed conversion and then by a true one. Yet unlike classic conversions, Abbott's doubts were not personal but intellectual. Rather than question his worthiness, Abbott quarreled with doctrine that seemed unreasonable to a self-confident young man. He referred to himself in the third person when he recalled how received dogma offended the skeptical temper, sense of justice, and strong feelings of one used to judging by his own standard:

This boy, growing to youth and from youth to young manhood, cannot bring himself to believe anything merely because he is told that he must believe it. . . . But the more he studies, the more mysterious this theology becomes. It does not fit in with his ideas of righteousness that one person should be punished for another person's sins. It does not appeal to his affections, this portraiture of a God who can be satisfied only by inflicting penalty on those who have done wrong.[18]

Abbott's difficulties were precisely those of a boy reared in a nurturing church in a democratic culture, whose conviction of his sinfulness and need of a savior was problematically small. He did quell his doubts and enter a church, though less, he saw later, on account of his "imperfect confession of faith"

of these individuals came of age after 1835, however, their passage to adulthood occurred during a period when Hudson's data suggest that the rate of growth of the religious community slowed or even stalled. Moreover, the parents of these Victorians were far more committed to church activity than the national average, since sixty-four of seventy-five of the Victorians received childhood training in some denomination. Although I have little information on the number of conversions among the Victorians' parents and my subsequent discussion of the parents' piety concludes that their religious convictions were mixed with spiritual difficulties of their own, the parents did try hard to bring their children into the Christian community and, compared with their efforts, the spiritual harvest was meager. Overall, the number of Victorian conversions must be interpreted in both quantitative and qualitative contexts: available estimates of the proportion of conversions at other times, the religious training to which they were exposed, long-term trends in the frequency and intensity of revivals, and the patterns of their personal religious disaffection. For a very different argument that religious interest has grown in America since the seventeenth century, see Butler, *Awash in a Sea of Faith: Christianizing the American People* (1990).

[18] *What Christianity Means to Me: A Spiritual Autobiography* (1921), p. 3. Nowhere in Abbott's experience was there a counterpart to the stage of humiliation in the Puritan conversion process, as explained by Edmund S. Morgan in *Visible Saints: The History of a Puritan Idea* (Ithaca, N.Y.: Cornell University Press, 1963), p. 68. A century later, Jonathan Edwards did quarrel with inherited doctrine when he resisted the arbitrariness of limited atonement, although in the end he acquiesced with a resignation once again foreign to Abbott's experience. See his "Personal Narrative" (1739), in *Jonathan Edwards,* ed. Clarence H. Faust and Thomas H. Johnson, rev. ed. (New York: Hill and Wang, 1962), p. 58.

than because "his father and his uncle were members of the church and he was believed to be a young man without bad habits."[19] Only when he discovered Henry Ward Beecher's immanent, loving God, understood best without the encumbrance of theology, did Abbott achieve religious equilibrium. Among the Victorians, however, there were more often impediments to easy conversion similar to Abbott's, including self-confidence, inquisitiveness, and restlessness, than resolutions as definitive as his.

Instead of a single upheaval, this generation commonly lived through repeated periods of reexamination and redirection. In the past, people knew that occasional doubt and spiritual languor were the inevitable consequences of flawed human nature. But the Victorians' questioning was different because it forced basic changes in values and institutional loyalty. Instability was nourished by the intense intellectual activity of a literate and dynamic society. As young men, Moncure Conway in Virginia and John Wesley North in upstate New York were both distanced from orthodoxy by their concurrent involvement with ideas and reform. Conway's Methodist upbringing culminated in his conversion during a revival in 1848, and he became a preacher. Yet he read broadly in European and American literature (Goethe, Sand, Hawthorne, Emerson, and others), to the point that Emerson's transcendentalism, mixed with Conway's disquiet with slavery, made him leave Virginia for Harvard Divinity School in 1851. He became a Unitarian minister and an abolitionist. John Wesley North was seventeen years older than Conway (he was born in 1815 and Conway in 1832), but his progress was nearly identical. He, too, was a Methodist preacher, brought up in the denomination and converted at age thirteen. His involvement with antislavery in the 1840s set off religious questioning that led, by the 1850s, to a belief in Unitarianism and to experimentation with spiritualism.[20]

Conversion did not settle religious issues for Conway and North. Rather, both men were impelled by their moral seriousness to seek out sources of social change that, in turn, provoked them to further reflection. Neither man lost interest in religion altogether, but each moved from a traditional evangelical faith to a position that was experimental and eclectic. Precisely

---

[19] *What Christianity Means to Me*, pp. 4–5.

[20] Conway, *Autobiography*, 1: chs. 7–14; Stonehouse, *John Wesley North and the Reform Frontier* (1965), pp. 4–5, 7–10, 65, 79. On Conway, see also Peter F. Walker, *Moral Choices: Memory, Desire, and Imagination in Nineteenth-Century American Abolition* (Baton Rouge: Louisiana State University Press, 1978), chs. 3–4. On the role of doubt in traditional Puritanism, see Morgan, *Visible Saints*, pp. 70–3. The Victorians were not the first generation to experience major transformations in religious feelings, views, and commitments. Consider, e.g., the odyssey of Orestes Brownson (1803–76) from Presbyterianism to skepticism to Unitarianism to transcendentalism and finally to Catholicism, as I explain in *Transcendentalism as a Social Movement, 1830–1850* (1981), pp. 44–9, 210–12. In the next generation, however, such personal revolutions seemed more common and, with increasing frequency, took individuals beyond the bounds of Christianity altogether. Consider the transcendentalist leanings and spiritualism of Conway and North respectively.

because Moncure Conway and John Wesley North came of age in an expansive temporal society, conversion did not signify the end of spiritual uncertainty but the beginning of an open-ended process of self-discovery.

In addition to the vital activity of midcentury culture, the death of loved ones or anxiety about one's own mortality opened renewed religious concern, especially among those who as young people did not settle spiritual issues. Death raises ultimate questions in any society. But this most profound evidence of the inability of human beings to master nature must have been unusually disturbing in a culture advancing technologically, yet losing religious sensibility by imperceptible degrees.[21]

Three men who failed in their youth to secure proper conversions – Zebulon Vance, William Dean Howells, and Frederick Law Olmsted – exemplify the renewed turmoil of Victorians confronted with death. In North Carolina, Zebulon Vance experienced no conversion despite his Christian education. Nor did the entreaties of his wife, Harriet, during nearly three decades of marriage change one thoroughly caught up in politics as a congressman and governor of his home state. Yet Harriet's death in 1878 precipitated Vance's profession of faith "to fit me for *reunion* blest with thee," as he wrote privately, and he entered a Presbyterian church.[22] The religious life of William Dean Howells was more confused than Vance's, as well as more inconclusive. William Cooper Howells, his father, made Swedenborgian principles dominate his Ohio home. But his son experienced no "vastation," a kind of conversion, and was led instead by his reading to doubt his faith and by the competing interests of his career as a rising author to ignore churchgoing. Howells was over thirty when his mother died in 1868, but her death brought back questions long submerged, now complicated by the growing challenge of science. As editor of the *Atlantic Monthly,* Howells contributed to public discussion of Darwin during the 1870s. Privately, he studied Christian Science. All of Howells's disquiet and study, however, produced no definite end in conviction or practice.[23] Unlike Vance and Howells, Frederick Law Olmsted was converted during a revival at Yale in 1846, but declined to join a church. Over time, he grew disillusioned by the dogmatism of professing Christians and the tangles of theology, until his faith slipped away. "I only think it is queer that I could ever have thought myself to have such

---

[21] The obsessive interest the Victorians took in the afterlife may have been one manifestation of their uneasiness with death. Although scholars do not entirely agree on the meaning of their fascination, the fact is generally acknowledged. See Douglas, *The Feminization of American Culture* (1977), ch. 6, and Halttunen, *Confidence Men and Painted Women: A Study of Middle-Class Culture in America, 1830–1870* (1982), ch. 5.

[22] On Vance's early religious views, see Vance to Kate Smith, Sept. 6, 1854, in *The Papers of Zebulon Baird Vance, 1843–1862,* ed. Johnston (1963), 1:22. On his conversion, see A. J. Witherspoon to Vance, Jan. 2, 1879, Zebulon Baird Vance Papers.

[23] Lynn, *William Dean Howells: An American Life* (1970), pp. 19–20, 41, 55, 82, 241–8.

ideas as I did," he wrote in 1887, "and queer that anyone else can continue to have them."[24] Nonetheless, in his years of mental decline after 1895, Olmsted was worried again by religion and consoled by reading the Bible.

Distracted by the stir of busy lives, Vance, Howells, and Olmsted slighted religion. Thoughts of death brought them back to questions of life's significance, although the consoling answers of traditional Christianity often continued to elude them.

These accounts of spiritual travail among the Victorians are found along with instances of continuous church membership, where the emotional turmoil of conversion was replaced by an apparently uncomplicated decision to join a church. Autobiographies are so often vague on how individuals came to religious majority that it is likely that church membership could be gained by meeting outward requirements, such as blameless living and professed belief, as well as by passing through a rigorous religious experience. In contrast to Lucy Larcom's exact memories in *A New England Girlhood* (1889) of her childhood Sabbath routine, she recalled only that she became a full church member at about age thirteen, even neglecting to name the denomination, which, other evidence shows, was orthodox Congregational. Although the year was 1837, a time of revivals, young people prepared thoroughly by Christian training may well have been admitted without evidence of personal awakening. This ritual of confirmation seems to have been sufficiently routinized, moreover, to coincide with the acquisition of other symbols of adult status. Larcom said that her sisters lengthened her dresses and put up her hair at about the same time.[25]

Biographies contain accounts of religious transition that concur with Larcom's memory of undramatic yet sustained church loyalty. As an old man in Chicago in the 1870s, John Wentworth went to services twice each Sunday and professed faith in sin and damnation. But he left no record of a single conversion, only of progress from orthodox Congregational roots in New Hampshire, through Baptist schools, to regular Protestant church attendance in Chicago as an adult.[26] Similarly, Jay Cooke was one of the most pious of these Victorians, conducting family prayer, teaching Sunday school, and supporting benevolence. Yet despite his Methodist upbringing, there is no evidence of conversion, simply of regular churchgoing after he left Ohio for Philadelphia to begin his career.[27]

Perhaps habit without too much reflection was an effective safeguard for faith in a culture open to religious uncertainty. At least as many of these Victorians maintained postures of civil righteousness as lived up to conver-

---

[24] Olmsted to Charles Loring Brace, Mar. 15, quoted in Roper, *FLO*, p. 401. On Olmsted's changing religious attitudes, see Roper, pp. 42–3, 59, 470–1.

[25] Larcom, *New England Girlhood*, pp. 205, 209–10, 166.

[26] Fehrenbacher, *Chicago Giant: A Biography of "Long John" Wentworth* (1957), pp. 6–8, 38, 228.

[27] Larson, *Cooke*, pp. 46, 57.

sion's promise of firm piety. Yet faith unprotected by a private transforming experience may have been especially liable to the slow muting of religious sensibility. Since the turn of the nineteenth century, Unitarians had been suspected of spiritual weakness by their conservative contemporaries, and despite instances of their resilient piety, the experience of two prominent Unitarian ministers seems to bear out orthodox misgivings.

As middle-aged men, Thomas Wentworth Higginson and Octavius Brooks Frothingham lost hold of some crucial dimension of religious insight that made each unobtrusively turn from a clerical to a secular career. Higginson served successively in conservative and reform-oriented Unitarian congregations in Salem and Worcester, Massachusetts, during the 1840s and 1850s. Yet when he resigned to work for antislavery in 1857, he effectively left the ministry, because he devoted himself to literature and to such reforms as women's rights in the postwar years.[28] The extent of Higginson's alienation from his profession and even from religion itself can be seen in his account of his experience as a Civil War officer of black troops, *Army Life in a Black Regiment*, published in 1870 and based on journals he kept during the war. Never mentioning his own clerical background, Higginson alternately praised and debunked the regiment's chaplain. He admired the preacher's will as fighting parson, but underlined the man's marginal status by disparaging his effort to instruct the troops, judging that "the alphabet must always be a very incidental business in a camp."[29] Higginson was fascinated, moreover, by the freed slaves' piety, devoting pages of his journal to their spirituals. He effectively dismissed the blacks' religion, however, as one that "cultivates the feminine virtues first, − makes them patient, meek, resigned."[30] Throughout his narrative, Higginson observed the interaction of black and white religion from the perspective of a decidedly secular persona, whose most prized book, he observed, was the "Morning Report" on the regiment's condition, by no means the Bible.[31] Higginson's development was thus marked by a waning of religious concern. It was a loss he never confronted directly, but the process left an undertone of hostility, manifested in remarks disparaging religion, toward values that betrayed expectations.

Octavius Brooks Frothingham was Higginson's friend at Harvard Divinity School in the 1840s. He stayed in the ministry longer than Higginson, finally serving a radical New York congregation from 1859 until 1879 when he resigned at age fifty-seven. Nor he did turn, like Higginson, from a spiritual to a strenuous life. Yet his ability to engage religious truth in an immediate way lost ground nonetheless to historical understanding. A determined polemicist, Frothingham repeatedly defended religion from such

[28] Edelstein, *Strange Enthusiasm: A Life of Thomas Wentworth Higginson* (1968), p. 205.
[29] Higginson, *Army Life in a Black Regiment* (1870), pp. 231–2, 25.
[30] Ibid., pp. 53–4.
[31] Diary, Dec. 21, 1862, quoted in ibid., p. 33.

challenges as biblical criticism and evolution during the first years of his ministry in New York. But in the 1870s, he turned increasingly from fighting religion's present battles to reporting past faith. Frothingham's biography of Theodore Parker in 1874 was his first historical work, followed in 1876 by *Transcendentalism in New England.* After his retirement, he turned out an accelerating series of biographies and memoirs, including lives of George Ripley and William Henry Channing, as well as *Boston Unitarianism* (1890) and *Recollections and Impressions* (1891). Frothingham's farewell sermon in 1879 had provoked comment that he betrayed idealism for utilitarianism and evolution. If his critics were right that his spiritual vision was obscured, he seemed to seek vicarious clarity in the assurance of past men. Decline of vital insight into inherited truths was as gradual in Frothingham's life as in Higginson's, though perhaps no less tortured for the insidious quality of the change.[32]

At a time of mounting public contention among intellectuals over the doctrinal implications of such new issues as evolution, it is noteworthy that the Victorians' private quarrels with religion were so often half-conscious, equivocal, and inconclusive. Even the most educated of the middle classes rarely came to terms with tradition simply by logic, but more often in a mood that admitted ambivalence, contradictions, and evasion. Yet there were cases of sharp criticism of Christianity, and these postures of rebelliousness characterized the final pattern of the Victorians' departure from their religious inheritance. Most dramatically, Robert Ingersoll, by vocation a lawyer from Peoria, Illinois, turned his stinging wit on Christianity as he lectured across the country. An orthodox man who believed in hell, Ingersoll told listeners who came to hear his antireligious gospel, was one who "thought he would be happier in heaven if he could just lean over and see certain people that he disliked broiled."[33] More commonly, flashes of anger against religion surfaced in the private words and actions of people who did not contend openly with Christianity as a rule. Although Mary Chesnut of South Carolina harbored a reserve of personal piety, she savored cutting observations on contemporary practice. Of a drunken evangelist, she wrote in her journal: "The devil himself could not have quoted Scripture more fluently."[34] Lewis Henry Morgan, the ethnographer, and William Tecumseh

[32] Caruthers, *Octavius Brooks Frothingham: Gentle Radical* (1977), pp. 184–5, and passim. Some of Frothingham's apologetics written during the 1860s include "Renan's Life of Jesus," *Christian Examiner* (1863), and "The Order of Saint Paul the Apostle; and the New Catholic Church," *Christian Examiner* (1865).

[33] "The Liberty of Man, Woman, and Child" (1877), in *Complete Lectures of Col. R. G. Ingersoll* (Chicago: J. Regan, n. d.), p. 64. The text of this version of Ingersoll's speech differs from the text of the Dresden edition cited in the Bibliography. The phrase quoted here does not appear in the Dresden edition, perhaps because its editor, Ingersoll's son-in-law C. P. Farrell, considered it too sarcastic.

[34] Mar. 18, 1861, *Mary Chesnut's Civil War,* ed. Woodward (1981), p. 29. Although this version of Chesnut's diary was revised by her during the two decades after the war, I quote from this text rather than the more recently issued original because I think the style improved and the substantive meaning

Sherman were friendly toward religion ordinarily – Morgan was a church-going Presbyterian and Sherman tolerated his wife's active Catholicism. Yet Morgan disinherited his nephew for becoming a clergyman, and Sherman did the same to his son. Perhaps the young men were punished for pursuing an effeminate profession, perhaps for taking religion, a tool of limited usefulness in the older men's eyes, too seriously. Either way, Morgan and Sherman behaved as if the choice of a clerical vocation posed a personal insult and family shame. Beneath their superficial accommodation to Christian habits lay a reserve of distaste for real piety.[35]

These four instances of resistance to Christian beliefs and mores, ranging from playful sarcasm to public crusading, all centered in deep disappointment that religion somehow betrayed its promises and in a desire to push it away, either gently through humor or harshly through legal exorcism. Probably the hurt that religion imposed would have been defined differently by each one of the four, yet they had their anger in common. Looking beyond individual cases, Victorian women as a group approached religion with a measure of rebelliousness more consistently than did men. Whereas the motives of men such as Morgan and Sherman are difficult to fathom, the quarrel of women with religion grew from clearer social roots.

On the whole, Victorian women, like men, left warm recollections of childhood piety, and they passed through stages of quiet disengagement from tradition as adults.[36] Some personal histories suggest, however, that women explored established religious ideas more self-consciously and critically than did men. Long restricted by Christian values and most recently by the pious phrasing of antebellum domestic ideals, women who sought intellectual and emotional space were obliged to contend with religion deliberately. Elizabeth Cady Stanton understood the need to challenge Christianity when, late in her life, she undertook an ambitious biblical exegesis, *The Woman's Bible,* published in 1895. Through commentary on Scripture, Stanton aimed to use "pure reason" to free women from "sentimental feelings" about their "divinely ordained sphere."[37] Far more privately but with similar

---

largely unchanged. For the 1860s text, see *Mary Chesnut: The Unpublished Civil War Diaries,* ed. Woodward and Muhlenfeld (1984). Because *Chesnut's Civil War* consists solely of Chesnut's diary, I do not specify the nature of the citation (i.e., diary) in subsequent notes.

[35] Resek, *Lewis Henry Morgan: American Scholar* (1960), p. 52; Merrill, *William Tecumseh Sherman* (1971), pp. 370–2, 407.

[36] Women who composed memoirs cited in this chapter that include reminiscences of strong religious training include Lucy Larcom, Virginia Clay, and Jeanne Carr. I suggest later in the chapter that Clay and Carr developed points of view as adults in which religion was displaced by secular interests. The only woman of the fourteen women studied who experienced conversion was Rebecca Felton of Georgia, who joined her parents' church after a revival at the female academy she attended. See Talmadge, *Rebecca Latimer Felton: Nine Stormy Decades* (1960), p. 9. Although she defended Christianity against science after the Civil War, she became increasingly engrossed in politics, eventually becoming the first woman to serve in the U.S. Senate. When she wrote her memoirs, it was politics, not religion, that provided the frame of reference through which she viewed her life. See her *My Memoirs of Georgia Politics* (1911).

[37] *The Woman's Bible* (1895), pp. 11, 7. Although Stanton did not publish *The Woman's Bible* until

determination to establish her freedom, Emily Dickinson reviewed Christian images in her poems between the early 1860s and her death in 1886. Her work examined Christian rituals, beliefs, and texts in an apparent effort to determine their relation to her own pressing spiritual questions: "Some keep the Sabbath going to Church – / I keep it, staying at Home" (1860); "How brittle are the Piers / On which our faith doth tread –" (1878); "The Bible is an antique Volume – / Written by faded Men" (1882).[38] Neither Stanton nor Dickinson finally resolved her views of Christianity. Stanton hovered in *The Woman's Bible* between liberal religion and skeptical rationalism. Dickinson oscillated between the evangelical doctrines of her childhood and a radical religious subjectivism that resembled the ideas soon to be articulated by William James. Still, these Victorian women were moved by a subversive impulse to take intellectual possession of their religious heritage that was absent among contemporary men.[39]

Neither binding conversion, repeated crisis, effective nurture, slow erosion of faith, nor active rebellion clearly dominated the Victorian middle classes as the prototypical religious experience, perhaps because they lived at a crucial moment in the fragmentation of the evangelical tradition, a possibility that conforms to historians' sense of when the Second Great Awakening finally closed.[40] Nonetheless, this discussion of patterns of personal development can be concluded by identifying common elements in the Victorians' religious outlook and by comparing their sensibility with that of their parents.

No matter how the Victorians reached religious majority, nearly all felt their spiritual intensity ease over time. As intriguing as this evanescence of piety, almost no one was equipped to explain his or her experience. They

1895, the book was a product of her long-standing concern about the stance of traditional Christianity toward women. See Banner, *Elizabeth Cady Stanton: A Radical for Woman's Rights* (1980), pp. 155–65.

[38] *Final Harvest: Emily Dickinson's Poems,* ed. Johnson (1961), pp. 66, 286, 297. On Dickinson's religious views, see also Ben Kimpel, *Emily Dickinson as Philosopher* (New York: Edwin Mellen, 1981), ch. 9.

[39] Although both Stanton and Dickinson were pressured toward conversion at the girls' boarding schools they attended, neither experienced saving grace. Their failure must have conditioned their persistent questions about the significance of Christian symbols. See Banner, *Stanton,* pp. 13–14, and Cleanth Brooks, R. W. B. Lewis, and Robert Penn Warren, eds., *American Literature: The Makers and the Making* (New York: St. Martin's Press, 1973), 2:1231–3. Helpful recent discussions of the relationship of gender and religion include Atkinson et al., eds., *Immaculate and Powerful: The Female in Sacred Image and Social Reality* (1985), esp. the "Introduction" by Margaret R. Miles, pp. 1–13, and Bynum et al., eds., *Gender and Religion: On the Complexity of Symbols* (1986), esp. "Introduction: The Complexity of Symbols," by Caroline Bynum, pp. 2–16.

[40] That is not to say conversion-oriented religion disappeared in the midcentury decades, simply that revivals were less able to lend coherence to American culture. For an account of the rise of modernist and fundamentalist alternatives from a single evangelical tradition, see Marsden, *Fundamentalism and American Culture,* pp. 11–39. For a more individualized view of the variety of religious choices that emerged from and transformed evangelicalism, see Marie Caskey's study of Lyman Beecher and his children, *Chariot of Fire: Religion and the Beecher Family* (New Haven: Yale University Press, 1978). Two instances that compel recognition of the continued presence, if not dominance, of revivalism are the largely urban awakening of 1857 and 1858 and the conversions in the Civil War armies. See, respectively, Miller, *Life of the Mind in America,* pp. 88–95, and Shattuck, *Shield and Hiding Place,* chs. 4–5.

were too close to religion as an unquestioned part of life to see faith objectively as a component of biography or sociology. Consequently, many lived with dissonant and unresolved impulses.

By no means all Victorians slid completely from faith to impiety. Some moved simply toward liberalism, managing to retain spiritual rigor as dogmatism declined. At age twenty-two George Atkinson of Vermont resolved in a letter to his uncle, Josiah Little, to "clean my own skirts of your blood" if Little resisted conversion. A decade later in 1855, however, when Atkinson had become an Oregon minister, he was sufficiently charitable to oppose a required confession of faith for students entering Pacific University, because "our whole spirit now is free thought" under the Bible's guidance. In practice, too, Atkinson kept his integrity while admitting diversity. He rode a Congregational circuit of 6,000 miles in one year in the 1870s, yet worked with Presbyterians, Methodists, and Episcopalians to advance temperance. Only once in his letters did he face the issue of how religious certainty could be reconciled with toleration, when he explained carefully, as much to himself as to his correspondent, why he could not in good conscience help to dedicate a Unitarian meetinghouse.[41] Here was one man who conceded intellectual rigor comfortably, feeling little apparent compulsion to comprehend his own willingness to relax standards.

Others slipped into unconventional views with as little deliberation or self-consciousness. In California in the 1880s, Jeanne Carr fondly recalled the pious habits of her Vermont childhood. Still, she now thought that organizations besides churches, such as the Grange movement, could further Christian ends better than established religion because precedent constrained them less.[42] Similarly, through successive careers as a civil servant, journalist, and minister on the West Coast, John Damon mixed Protestant orthodoxy with Freemasonry. He preached sin and Christ's mediation, yet accepted reason's knowledge of divine laws as well. His letters showed no sign that he sensed the friction between the two systems.[43]

The loyalties of James Garfield and George Templeton Strong were not similarly divided, but both suffered spiritual ennui. "I find I am living an objective life with almost no introspection," Garfield wrote in his journal in 1857 when he was a teacher in Ohio: "What will be its outcome I cannot tell, but I fear I am losing spirituality of soul."[44] Perhaps worse than indifference, Garfield stayed close enough to religion to feel repeated distress.

---

[41] Atkinson to Josiah Little, Dec. 31, 1841, Atkinson to Josiah and Sophronia Little, Mar. 6, 1855, Atkinson to Josiah Little Hale, Mar. 23–24, 1874, Atkinson to Josiah Little Hale, Mar. 28, 1868, George Henry Atkinson Papers.

[42] "My Own Story," ms. ca. 1886, "Christmas," ms. speech to a Grange group ca. Dec., 1875, Jeanne Carr Papers.

[43] L. Stowell to John Damon, Sept. 5, 1854, Damon to Mrs. Huag, May 8, 1856, M. W. Taylor to Damon, Nov. 4, 1865, Albert Pike to Damon, Mar. 5, 1882, John Fox Damon papers.

[44] Dec. 9, *Diary of Garfield,* ed. Brown and Williams, 1:308.

Figure 2. George Templeton Strong (1820–75). New York City attorney, civic leader, and treasurer of the Sanitary Commission during the Civil War. Daguerreotype, ca. 1857. Courtesy of The New-York Historical Society, N.Y.C.

"I grow more and more weary of the forms and ceremonies of religion," he reflected a decade later, after attending Episcopal services on shipboard on his way home from Europe.[45] Strong, a New York lawyer, was stirred deeply by the Oxford movement in the 1840s. But he soon became so caught up in community commitments that journal notes on church politics replaced comment on spiritual issues. "I know that I'm very 'respectable' and 'estimable,' like many a Pharisee before me," he confessed in his journal in 1854, castigating himself with the thought that "the heart knoweth its own *rottenness.*"[46] Much like Garfield, Strong continued to attended religious services with some frequency, though without the depth of private piety that once had invested ritual with value.

For Carr and Damon, Christianity no longer commanded their exclusive allegiance. For Garfield and Strong, Christian practice clashed with hidden spiritual languor. None of the four enjoyed a spontaneous relation to tradition, as they reflected on Christianity's shortcomings, borrowed elsewhere

[45] Nov. 3, 1867, ibid., 1:438.
[46] Dec. 31, *The Diary of George Templeton Strong,* ed. Nevins and Thomas (1952), 2:205. Italics that appear in this and subsequent quotations are found in the original texts.

to supplement its teachings, and finally brooded on their indifference. Only Garfield and Strong had the self-awareness to be disturbed by their drift from traditional commitments, and their consciousness made them exceptional among the Victorians overall. Even then, their power of insight exceeded their capacity for explanation, so that they could not say why childhood truths over time mattered less.

This account of broadened interpretations and slackened emotional involvement raises the question of whether these trends simply represent the aging of a generation, because childhood certainties and attachments are often modified in adulthood. A comparison of the Victorians with their parents indicates that the older generation was not altogether pious or faithless, but they were generally less anxious about their religious condition. Religion was either well integrated into individual lives or quietly ignored.

It is tempting to contrast parents' piety with the Victorians' various skepticisms, were it not for instances of religious indifference in the older generation that force a subtler conclusion. To be sure, there were many cases where conviction declined from the Victorians' parents' generation to their own. James William Beekman, a civic leader in New York City, rued his inability to match the faith of his father. Although Beekman's filiopiety may raise doubts about the reality of his declension, the son's activity in, the interest of Christian schooling, Sabbath observance, and temperance did lack the inwardness of his father's journal, devoted to religious reflection, that he kept for more than three decades.[47] In South Carolina, neither James Sanders Guignard nor John Gabriel Guignard, two brothers among these Victorians, equaled the conviction of their forebears. Their grandfather kept careful records of the Bible readings he completed and the camp meetings he attended, and their father's generation maintained family precedents of church work and personal charity. John Gabriel was nearly forty when he was confirmed in church membership, however, and James Sanders was almost seventy when he was baptized.[48] Similarly, Nathaniel Langdon Frothingham's thirty-year ministry at Boston's First Church (1820–50) may be contrasted with the flight to historicism of his son, Octavius. The younger Frothingham's *Boston Unitarianism* paid homage to his father's steady piety and faithful service.[49]

Yet a clear-cut picture of decline is complicated by parents who were distanced from religion themselves. The male kin of Franklin Benjamin Sanborn saw no need to go to church. More common, some couples who

---

[47] White, *The Beekmans of New York in Politics and Commerce, 1647–1887* (1965), pp. 554–5, 570, 579–86, 614, 627.

[48] Childs, ed., *Planters and Business Men: The Guignard Family of South Carolina, 1795–1930* (1957), pp. 19, 37–8, 120–1, 132.

[49] See Octavius Brooks Frothingham's biography of his father, *Boston Unitarianism, 1820–1850: A Study of the Life and Work of Nathaniel Langdon Frothingham* (1890).

raised children in Christian homes and attended churches long remained unconverted. The parents of Lucy Larcom made no profession of faith until all of their children were born, when the whole family of ten was baptized. The father of Jabez Curry in Alabama was a churchgoer, but felt no saving grace until age fifty-three. His son followed him into the Baptist church. John Olmsted supported Hartford's First Congregational Church financially, but never came as close as his son to conversion.[50]

Members of the Victorian generation were not simply bound less than their parents by religion, though on the whole this was true, but bothered more by religious issues and feelings. Even parents who were not moved personally by faith had few doubts that religion as a matter of institutional structure and metaphysical definition was a permanent part of their world. Adults who converted late in life did not withhold their assent to test the availability of grace, but neither did they imagine that God would not be ready at any time to meet their consent.[51] Among their children, the steady churchgoers may have felt similar security, but those who were more reflective dimly sensed the increasing marginality of religion in the modern world. Brought up in a religious culture, where family, church, and school reinforced Christian lessons, they read their diminished personal fervor as one sign of a profound transformation. Yet whether the change was cultural or metaphysical – if social conditions deprived them of spiritual assurance or if their parents' certainties were simply misguided – they were unprepared to say. More surprising, few were distraught either by this spiritual upset or by their inability to master it intellectually. Closer scrutiny of American Victorian religion from the viewpoints of ideas and behavior helps to explain why the faith of this generation was so susceptible to challenge.

CHARITABLE SPIRITS AND STRUCTURED
INSTITUTIONS

The Victorians perceived their religious task as how best to organize a community composed of diverse, and often troubled, beliefs. As an activity of the mind, they asked that religion be untheological in order to facilitate toleration and to clear the way for secular progress. As a matter of practice, they developed church bureaucracies on the one hand and private rituals on the other, at the same time that public worship, thinned to accommodate

[50] Larcom, *New England Girlhood*, p. 56; Rice, *J. L. M. Curry: Southerner, Statesman, and Educator* (1949), pp. 20–1; Roper, *FLO*, pp. 3–4, 42. See n. 17 for discussion of available estimates comparing the frequency of church membership at points throughout the antebellum period and for how the Victorians and their parents fit national trends.

[51] In other words, the Victorians' parents were less troubled than were their children by what James Turner defines as "unbelief": "the continuing absence of a conviction that any such superhuman power exists" (*Without God, Without Creed*, p. xv).

minimal consensus, satisfied individuals less. Yet as values were relaxed to allow diversity and as habits were streamlined to suit modern routines, the result was neither an engaging nor an efficient religion. Rather, liberality laced with timidity ill sustained the conviction of people beset already by doubt and ennui. Dogmatism and superstition were inevitable minor notes in a faith that was neither intellectually critical nor community controlled. An effective modern church can cope with fragmentation by making itself a place for dialogue among people with questions about their spiritual heritage. But the Victorians could not see how to make a religious community based on dynamic exchange and so settled for an institutional core to which individuals could scarcely adhere.

Loyalty to simple religious truths is an attitude most often associated with fundamentalism's biblical literalism, and critics judge doctrinal minimalism an unthinking defense against the perplexities of theology and ethics raised by science and by urban industrial society. Yet the Victorians both declined to reason about religion and embraced a tolerant liberalism, and this pairing was not accidental.[52] As a young man, Lyman Abbott turned with relief from "theological debates" and "scholastic definitions" to "the experience of fellowship with the God revealed in Jesus Christ," he recalled in 1921 in his autobiography, *What Christianity Means to Me.* He realized proudly that "his own father, who might easily have made for himself a great reputation in science or in philosophy," had chosen a similar path toward intellectual clarity rather than depth when he devoted "himself to writing books for children that children could understand."[53] Beyond freeing faith from useless complexity, Abbott saw that downplaying doctrine could serve a Christian community that was sufficiently educated and thoughtful to contain serious disagreement. Thus he made the experiential "Life of Christ" the theme for his first Bible class in his first church in Terre Haute, Indiana, in 1860. Because "men and women of every variety of religious opinions" chose to attend, he had to find a neutral common ground.[54]

Laypeople less dedicated in principle to Christian harmony nonetheless viewed speculation as an expendable impediment as well. Zebulon Vance struck out at religious reflection with a suitor's impatience in an 1880 letter to Florence Martin, soon to be his second wife: "Quit reading metaphysics

---

[52] George Marsden contests the impression that fundamentalism simply represented a dying life-style and shows that it was an intelligible faith, in *Fundamentalism and American Culture*, esp. p. 4. See also Sandeen, *The Roots of Fundamentalism: British and American Millenarianism, 1800–1930* (1970). Although the religious liberalism of the Victorians was similarly constructed around positive tenets, it is still possible to argue that a certain depth of intelligence was lost, as does Daniel Calhoun when he explains that the disappearance of a traditional intellectual community gave rise to comparatively superficial habits of comprehension by calculation and personal example in his fascinating book, *Intelligence of a People*.

[53] *What Christianity Means to Me*, pp. 9–10, 7. His father was Jacob Abbott.

[54] Ibid., pp. 14–15.

— as a general thing they are unprofitable — I know they are a confusing & impracticable, rather unpractical study."[55] Vance's conversion to Presbyterianism two years before, following his first wife's death, had not increased his intellectual interest in religion. Indeed, still preeminently a practical man, Vance probably hoped to turn the sights of his fiancée, a Catholic, from the ultimate things that divided them to thoughts of more immediate sources of bliss. If so, Vance, like Abbott, insisted that religion's social utility take precedence over a search for intellectual precision that seemed not only fruitless but bound to stir up personal differences.

The Victorians could not thus dismiss reasoning on religious subjects without exposing faith to challenges by secular values, and the intellectual weakness of institutions and individuals propelled each other in a circular manner. The fact that individuals thought independently conditioned the reserve toward public theology of such leaders as Abbott, anxious to include diversity under a loose conceptual umbrella. But as doctrine was watered down to match slender accord, churches were less able to support intelligent discussion. Members increasingly isolated from one another moved toward idiosyncratic religious views and eventually toward secular languages.

Private papers occasionally contained comments on science, for example, yet these reflections scarcely seemed linked to community dialogue. George Templeton Strong sat down in early 1860 to read Darwin's "much discussed" *Origin of Species,* and a month later returned to the subject in his journal, judging it "a shallow book," inattentive to God's purposes in designing the natural world.[56] These two entries exhausted his patience for the rest of the decade with an idea of profound consequence. Even so, at least part of the fault lay with an Episcopal community that failed to support individual questioning by engaging in sustained discussion more focused than the welter of book notices in the popular press. Strong was more put off by the fact that the Episcopal church was "afraid to speak" out on secession than by its disinterest in evolution, but both instances betrayed an equivocal temper that made Strong increasingly content to stay home from church on Sundays and read, sadly dismissing "my dreams [for religion] of twenty years ago" and, more than he realized, losing touch with a forum for intellectual exchange.[57]

[55] Vance to Florence Martin, Mar. 11, Vance Papers.

[56] Feb. 18, Mar. 6, *Diary of Strong,* ed. Nevins and Thomas, 3:10–11, 13.

[57] Oct. 2, 1862, July 5, 1863, in ibid., 3:263, 329. Ineffective public discussion grew not only from the reluctance of organized religious bodies (denominations and congregations) to confront evolution directly, but from the diverse and scattered nature of publications on Darwin, making the individual's dilemma in part the result of the unsifted quantity of information available in a modern culture. Consistent with this analysis, recent scholars generally see debate over Darwin as part of broader intellectual trends. Owen Chadwick argues that Darwin figured in discussion of the relative authority of religion and science, in *Secularization of the European Mind,* p. 170, and Bruce Kuklick suggests that Darwin helped legitimate the view of progress made persuasive already by Hegelianism, in *Churchmen and Philosophers,* p. 223. On

Similarly, in Topeka, Kansas, a decade later, Cyrus Holliday, an entrepreneur, took issue with the certainties of science in a letter to his daughter, who was studying astronomy, when he questioned the notion that the moon was uninhabited: "But could not the Almighty create a being, an intelligent being, to live in the Moon without air, just as easily as to create man to live on earth with air?"[58] What is notable is the idiosyncratic quality of Holliday's logic. The idea of airless moon men is less silly than quirky, the product of a mind puzzling out issues alone. Holliday was a regular churchgoer, but the isolation of this comment on science in a large collection of correspondence provokes suspicion of the poor quality of ongoing dialogue on science between his church and its members.

Ann Douglas argues persuasively that intellectual clarity in American Protestantism was obscured by sentiment at least a generation before 1850, as ministers and women writers transformed religion for a largely female readership and churchgoing public.[59] Lyman Abbott's pride at following his father's example supports Douglas's chronology. Yet the evidence examined here indicates that at least after midcentury, the drift from theology grew as much from men's fear that problematic ideas, subject to varying interpretations, would weaken the religious community and, by provoking contention, would inhibit society's progress. Ironically, the anti-intellectual temper of Victorian religion probably sapped its resilience more than open contention might have done. Without vigorous debate, habits learned in childhood supported adult faith only modestly. After 1850, moreover, new secular modes of thought were sufficiently well defined to challenge religion seriously.

The combination of institutional timidity and the average person's slim solitary defenses made religion liable to displacement by more persuasive intellectual tools. The pre-Darwinian belief in the compatibility of natural science and faith permitted a scientific outlook to insinuate itself in place of faltering modes of thought that probed supernatural truths. George Templeton Strong "yearn[ed] to possess" an expensive microscope with no sense of betrayal of religion, justified his purchase with the thought that he gained "insight into the marvels of God," and felt that this way of encountering nature was safe even for young people, since he had a microscopist entertain twenty children in 1856 at a "*matinée optique.*"[60] Strong did not sense the danger that the children might savor nature and science's instruments without also perceiving the elusive hand of God.

the American reception of Darwin, see also Kuklick, *The Rise of American Philosophy: Cambridge, Massachusetts, 1860–1930* (1977), pp. 21–6.

[58] Holliday to Lillie Holliday, July 23, 1874, Cyrus Kurtz Holliday Papers.

[59] Douglas, *Feminization of American Culture.*

[60] May 13, 1854, note, n.d., Apr. 19, 1856, *Diary of Strong,* ed. Nevins and Thomas, 2:174, 175, 267. On the relation of science and religion before Darwin, see Bozeman, *Protestants in an Age of Science: The Baconian Ideal and Antebellum Religious Thought* (1977).

A scientific approach proved less compelling to American Victorians than did social science, however, because of the greater usefulness of social analysis to a generation keenly interested in the opportunities of the human world. The preprofessional social science that intrigued the Victorians was characterized by concern with facts gathered by firsthand observers, carefully and, if possible, quantitatively measured, that led to conclusions judged by utilitarian standards.[61] The usual form of presentation was a first-person nonfictional narrative, which, despite its informality, aimed to present a convincing argument in the interest of a practical result. Quite typically, Frederick Law Olmsted's accounts of his travels in the South in the 1850s offered facts and observations by which to judge slavery's efficiency, so that, in contrast to earlier abolitionists, he damned the institution by its inutility as much as by its immorality. In *Army Life in a Black Regiment* (1870), Thomas Wentworth Higginson championed black rights as the just reward for a race capable of fighting rather than as a benevolent gift. His personal observation of black troops was the source of authority for his argument. Lewis Henry Morgan's *The League of the Ho-De-No-Sau-Nee or Iroquois* (1851) grew from information he collected on New York reservations. Though he presented his findings from a third-person viewpoint, his aims were not strictly scholarly. Beyond preserving knowledge of vanishing customs, Morgan sought to improve Indian policy. The existence of formal works using secular methods to explain society and prescribe change does not mean that all Victorians interpreted their experience in these terms. Still, the wide readership of some of these books indicates that a social-scientific perspective made sense to enough people to compete seriously with a religious frame of reference.[62]

Although the Victorians strayed intellectually from inherited religion, they still held onto the Bible. Yet Scripture was less a rule of life for this generation than an emotional anchor in difficulty, so that the temper in which the Bible was used was consistent with the general deemphasis of intellectual faith. Even in the South, where the comparative traditionalism of southern culture meant that Christian mores informed daily activity and that religious imagery interlaced prose, the use of biblical allusions and the habit of Bible reading struck increasingly dissonant notes in worldy lives.[63] The authoritative tone of Wade Hampton's occasional statements

---

[61] Although Turner emphasizes the disruptive influence of science on religion, he also acknowledges the role of "science-like" assumptions in providing alternative modes of analysis, in *Without God, Without Creed*, p. 194. On the rising importance of empirical and especially quantitative ways of thinking, see Cohen, *A Calculating People: The Spread of Numeracy in Early America* (1982), esp. 205–26.

[62] Olmsted, *The Cotton Kingdom: A Traveller's Observations on Cotton and Slavery in the American Slave States* (1861), ed. Schlesinger, intro. Powell (1984); Higginson, *Army Life in a Black Regiment;* Morgan, *The League of the Ho-De-No-Sau-Nee or Iroquois* (1851), ed. Lloyd (1922).

[63] This conclusion is in accord with the findings of Michael Barton, who discovered through content

about God's designs is surprising because he left no record of regular religious activity. But a closer look suggests that Hampton was able to plumb depths of traditional faith by means of feelings tied to simple certainties. "God will not forsake you," he wrote to his sister after their father's death in 1858, "for you have all trusted to him and He will now be a Father to you," a thought that hovered between resonant truth and truism precisely because of its sincere yet unexpected intrusion in the extensive secular correspondence of one of South Carolina's leading planters.[64] In the Civil War journal of Mary Chesnut, the daily profusion of comments on society and politics revealed her sensibility's strongly secular tone. When she fled to North Carolina to escape Sherman's army, however, she turned to "the Lamentations of Jeremiah, the Penetential Psalms of David, the denunciations of Isaiah, and above all the patient wail of Job. Job is my comforter now."[65] Just so, Virginia Clay's outlook was defined by social concerns until her husband, a Confederate legislator, was imprisoned in Fortress Monroe. With no sense of disjunction, she swung from temporal to spiritual resources when she advised him to read his Bible for inner strength.[66]

The writings of northerners were less often punctuated with scriptural references. But Yankees, too, stood on a margin in time where religious and secular languages shifted as occasion demanded. John William DeForest grew up in a Connecticut family sufficiently pious to produce one son who became a missionary. DeForest made his mark on American letters, however, by the clear vision and crisp prose of his Civil War pieces, straightforward accounts of his experience as a Union officer and Freedman's Bureau agent, as well as compelling battle scenes of his novel, *Miss Ravenel's Conversion from Secession to Loyalty* (1867). His secular terms of interpretation made these works akin to early social science, and DeForest has won acclaim as a pioneer of literary realism. Yet his empirical inclinations were unsteady enough to allow private Bible reading and translations of Scripture in the 1870s, when the war's end took away the literary materials that brought out his talent and he grew depressed at his foundering career.[67] The Bible was no more

analysis that southern soldiers more often used moralistic language in Civil War letters and journals than did northerners, in *Goodmen,* ch. 2.

[64] Hampton to Mary Fisher Hampton, Mar. 14, in Cauthen, ed., *Family Letters of the Three Wade Hamptons, 1782–1901* (1953), p. 57.

[65] Feb. 26, 1865, *Chesnut's Civil War,* ed. Woodward, p. 733.

[66] Wiley, *Confederate Women,* p. 73. Perhaps nineteenth-century intellectuals' attitudes toward the Bible were influenced by formal biblical criticism, but these middle-class Victorians left little evidence of an awareness of the problems that modern exegesis posed for the Christian scriptures. Weisenburger was similarly persuaded that the average person disregarded biblical criticism, in *Ordeal of Faith,* p. 85. On biblical criticism, see Jerry Wayne Brown, *The Rise of Biblical Criticism in America, 1800–1870* (Middletown, Conn.: Wesleyan University Press, 1969).

[67] Light, *John William DeForest* (1965), p. 108. See also DeForest, *A Volunteer's Adventures: A Union*

an undisputed source of values for DeForest than for his southern contemporaries. Still, reading Scripture must have called up comforting memories that revived feelings of childhood security.

Much like the attitudes of later fundamentalists, the Victorians' reluctance to reason about faith and their attachment to Scripture were responses to threats to tradition and part of an impulse to protect faith. The Victorians hoped to preserve private belief and religious community by demanding little of religion intellectually. Toleration both helped to motivate and profited by this disinterest in precise definition. Accommodation of diverging viewpoints was not simply a function of intellectual weakness, however, but a separate aspect of religious culture with its own set of guidelines.

Toleration was a positive principle to the Victorians that built on the heritage of the previous generation. William Dean Howells recalled in 1890 that his father, who ordered his family's life by Swedenborgian views, taught the equality of Catholics and Protestants. James Garfield was raised among the Disciples of Christ, who as a group opposed sectarianism in the interest of biblical simplicity. He was so committed to achieving broad sympathies that he chose to attend Williams College precisely because New England was unlike Ohio, his home state, and he hoped to see truth from a new perspective.[68] To be sure, there was dogmatic rigidity in the parents' generation as well. Howells wrote that most of his childhood neighbors disdained Catholics.[69] The point is that religious tolerance was not a faltering attitude in the midcentury decades, and its establishment may have facilitated its subtle recruitment for illiberal social uses.

Thus at times, religious toleration helped to bind communities at the expense of enemies defined by traits other than doctrine. In the postwar decades, Zebulon Vance repeatedly gave an address in North Carolina called "The Scattered Nation" to protest the "unreasonable prejudice" in "our tolerant land" against Jews, discrimination "of which I am heartily ashamed."[70] The speech might be judged a simple instance of liberal religion, were it not so peculiarly situated in the life of a defeated southern governor committed to the restoration of home rule and the perpetuation of black

---

Captain's Record of the Civil War, ed. Croushore (1946); *A Union Officer in the Reconstruction.* ed. Croushore and Potter (1948); and *Miss Ravenel's Conversion from Secession to Loyalty (1867)*, ed. Haight (1955). For an assessment of DeForest's literary realism, see Wilson, *Patriotic Gore: Studies in the Literature of the American Civil War* (1962), pp. 669–742.

[68] Howells, *A Boy's Town, Described for "Harper's Young People"* (1890), p. 112; *Diary of Garfield*, ed. Brown and Williams, 1:x, xviii–xix, and June 23, 1854, 1:248. On the emergence of toleration in the early nineteenth century, see Ahlstrom, *Religious History*, p. 393. Although toleration is rightly associated with Unitarianism (see my *Transcendentalism as a Social Movement*, pp. 12–13), these examples make the important point that a number of groups came to advocate religious diversity at the same time.

[69] *Boy's Town*, p. 112.

[70] "The Scattered Nation," in Dowd, *Life of Zebulon B. Vance* (1897), pp. 392–3.

subordination. A second reading reveals how religious inclusiveness counterbalanced social exclusiveness. Jews worked less tricky business than Yankees, who foisted the "left-handed gimlets of Jonathan."[71] Their favorable
comparison to the freedmen was unspoken, though perhaps evoked by rhetoric thus structured around contrasts. Vance was no doubt sincere in his
resistance to anti-Semitism. Nor is it probable that he deliberately manip-
ulated toleration of minority faiths to secure other useful prejudices. Nonetheless, Vance's example shows how conveniently religious liberalism could
be made to accommodate conditions of social stress by creating a sphere of
accord and by helping to legitimate exclusion on grounds besides faith.

Few Victorians had occasion to explain their belief in toleration as fully
as Vance, but many were in the habit of visiting churches of diverse creeds.
Though their reasons for going varied, this peripatetic form of religious
observance attests to their sense of the legitimacy of multiple points of view.
Some ignored denominational lines in the pursuit of excellence of presentation. Franklin Benjamin Sanborn recalled that as a young man in New
Hampshire around 1850, he attended any church with good preaching and
singing. Joseph Taylor, an Ohio lawyer and Methodist, went to a Presbyterian church in the 1860s when a favorite itinerant came to town.[72] To the
extent that criteria of style at least occasionally outweighed doctrine, these
men betrayed a detachment from religion's message. This lackadaisical approach to theology also informed the behavior of people who visited services
to satisfy curiosity, nearly reducing religion to a leisure diversion. Tourists
in Europe invariably went to Catholic churches, for example, while at home
synagogues, too, were objects of special attention.

These encounters with faiths of deep historical roots at times provoked
admiration in Protestants who were too restrained to do more than observe
the ornate rituals, but they also served to confirm their own superiority by
unfavorable contrast. Toleration blurred into intolerance precisely because
the religious context was unsettled enough to admit both liberality and
doubt. Thus James Garfield was intrigued by the exotic experience of dipping
his fingers in holy water at a "Catholic meeting house" in Ohio in 1851,
yet dismissed the liturgy delivered in Latin to German parishioners by a
priest who all the while faced the altar.[73] Similarly, George Templeton Strong
was fascinated by the hats, prayer shawls, and chanting of New York's Jews,
but judged the congregational responses to the rabbi's "monotonous solo
oculations" as discordant as the voices of "eager bidders at the sale of

---

[71] Ibid., p. 397.

[72] Sanborn, *Recollections*, 1:20; Taylor to Elizabeth A. Taylor, Aug. 9, 1868, Joseph Danner Taylor
Papers. Weisenburger also found that Victorians habitually visited different churches, in *Ordeal of Faith*,
p. 6.

[73] Apr. 13, *Diary of Garfield*, ed. Brown and Williams, 1:77.

stocks."[74] In both cases, good-natured acceptance, reinforced by honest fascination, was the dominant note, but self-justification also played a role.

Beyond seeking aesthetic satisfaction or diversion laced with serious notes, the Victorians visited churches to shop around for a new faith, a practice that indicates how nearly interchangeable varieties of Protestantism had become. Born a Quaker in Massachusetts, William Potter's long path to the Unitarian ministry was so anguished that he still wondered which sect to join after he decided to become a preacher in 1856. For much of the previous decade, however, he tried out Unitarian, Swedenborgian, and Congregationalist services, when he was not at Quaker meetings. That Potter listened seriously to each message shows that, to him, there were significant differences among them. Still, all shared equal claim in his eyes as credible choices.[75]

More often, motives unconnected with faith spurred changes in denominational affiliation, a pattern that betrayed how much religion now served social ends. Although Zebulon Vance was converted in the Presbyterian church, he later attended Baptist meetings because they were the only ones nearby. Lyman Abbott worked as an organist in an Episcopal church despite quite steady Congregational loyalties. Abram Hewitt in New York and Jay Cooke in Philadelphia left the Methodists for the Episcopal church when their rising social status spurred a taste for religious formality and a desire to worship with their peers. Children of Protestant southerners were sent to Catholic schools if they were the best at hand. A son and a daughter of Jefferson Davis boarded at Catholic academies in Montreal during their mother's postwar Canadian exile, while the sons of David Terry, a man who fought for the Confederacy, attended the junior school of St. Augustine's College in California.[76]

The Victorians were not the first Americans to tailor spiritual commitments to fit social needs. John Roebling, the engineer who designed the Brooklyn Bridge and the father of Washington Roebling, one of these Victorians, was a pantheist by conviction but bowed to propriety when he bought a pew for his family in a Presbyterian church.[77] By the time of the

---

[74] Sept. 14, 1855, Mar. 10, 1838, *Diary of Strong*, ed. Nevins and Thomas, 2:231, 1:83.

[75] Apr. 30, 1856, Dec. 12, 1847, Feb. 6 and 13, 1848, June 27, 1849, Diaries, 1853–57, 1847–48, 1849, Potter Papers. James Turner's idea that religious unbelief was a choice can also be applied to religious affiliation to emphasize not only religion's voluntarism, but the individual's degree of emotional detachment from faith. See *Without God, Without Creed*, p. 266.

[76] Tucker, *Vance*, p. 475; Brown, *Lyman Abbott, Christian Evangelist: A Study in Religious Liberalism* (1953), p. 15; Nevins, *Abram S. Hewitt, with Some Account of Peter Cooper* (1935), p. 540; Larson, *Cooke*, p. 56; on the Davis family, Wiley, *Confederate Women*, p. 123; on the Terry family, Ophelia Runnels to Cornelia Runnels Terry, May 5, [1853], and "Order of the Examination and Declamations of the Grammar School of St. Augustine's College," Benicia, California, June 6–9, 1870, David Smith Terry Papers.

[77] Steinman, *The Builders of the Bridge: The Story of John Roebling and His Son* (1946), pp. 24–5, 130, 202.

Victorians' adulthood, however, there was a casual attitude toward practices implicitly defined as incidental to faith and hence an acceptance of inter-denominational mobility. Even if testing churches was connected with vexing doubts, as was true for William Potter, the thought of changing affiliations caused little concern. A tolerant outlook was responsible for this ease of mind.

The great exception to relaxed feelings about religious differences was Protestant anti-Catholicism. Protestant Victorians' skittish hostility to Roman Catholicism did not simply violate their liberalism, however, but drew more complexly on their concern for political stability, uneasiness with Catholicism's comparative sensuousness, and need to reinforce the hazy boundaries of religious respectability by identifying at least one unacceptable choice. The activity of James Beekman in New York highlights Victorian nativism. In 1844, Beekman was a founder of the American Protestant Society, which worked, among its causes, to secure public education against the threat of parochial schooling.[78] Beyond Beekman's example, many private comments sound the traditional theme that Catholicism was antirepublican. As visitors to Rome at various times between the late 1840s and the early 1870s, William Wetmore Story dismissed Holy Week rituals as irrational "humbug," James Garfield mourned "papal symbols" that with "infinite impertinence" obscured "every emblem of [the] greatness" of republican Rome, and Lewis Henry Morgan branded the Catholic church the "apologist of unequal rights among men."[79] The combination of rising immigration in the midcentury decades and the political disruption of the sectional crisis heightened concern for the republic's durability, especially in the North, and stirred persistent anti-Catholic sentiment into a demonstrative form.[80]

Next to these straightforward dismissals, however, were responses that betrayed Catholicism's problematic appeal to a generation relinquishing the intellectual rigor of Protestant theology and creating a more purely sensible faith, not just as a residual product but as a matter of middle-class taste. If some Protestants were quick to condemn, one reason was that they felt their faith to be at considerable risk. Among instances of Catholicism's power over the Victorians, Henry Lee Higginson of Boston went to Christmas eve mass in Germany in 1852 and wrote ingenuously in his journal, "The music

---

[78] White, *Beekmans of New York*, pp. 579, 585–6.

[79] Story to James Russell Lowell, Apr. 28, 1848, quoted in Henry James, *William Wetmore Story and His Friends* (1903), 1:100; Sept. 26, 1867, *Diary of Garfield*, ed. Brown and Williams, 1:422; Diary, [1870], quoted in Resek, *Morgan*, p. 122.

[80] On nativism in this period, see Davis, "Some Themes of Counter-Subversion: An Analysis of Anti-Masonic, Anti-Catholic, and Anti-Mormon Literature," in his *From Homicide to Slavery: Studies in American Culture* (1986), pp. 137–54; Billington, *The Protestant Crusade, 1800–1860: A Study of the Origins of American Nativism* (1964); Higham, *Strangers in the Land: Patterns of American Nativism, 1860–1925* (1971), chs. 1–2; and Holt, *The Political Crisis of the 1850s* (1978), pp. 157–81.

was very fine indeed."[81] Jabez Curry of Alabama, an ordained Baptist minister, was sufficiently sophisticated, in contrast, to be torn between the seductive richness of Catholic ritual and his inherited Protestant disdain of Roman corruption. Thus some people questioned his fitness to be Grover Cleveland's ambassador to Spain in 1885 because of his uncompromising Protestantism. But once in Madrid, Curry made lengthy notes on Catholic observances, though still without bending his basic convictions.[82]

Far more radically, Isaac Hecker wandered from Methodism to transcendentalism in the 1840s, dissatisfied with the intellectual uncertainty and spiritual laxity of latter-day Protestantism, until he became a Catholic and later a priest.[83] Hecker was drawn by the structured discipline of a coherent religious tradition more than by the ritual's sensuous lure. Yet taken together, these cases underline weaknesses in Victorian Protestantism that lent a nervous acerbity to their anti-Catholicism.[84] Thin theological defenses not only obscured the line between faiths and exposed Protestants to Rome's varied attractions, but precluded an intelligent response to the threat, making Protestants all the more fearful of their autonomy and preemptive in their attacks. Though other generations as well made Catholics symbols of their own shortcomings, the sharp contrast between the Victorians' ordinary charity and their hasty dismissal of the Catholic church was an index of their sense of susceptibility, a weakness that required strong measures against a potentially persuasive intruder.

Perhaps surprising in light of their uncertain status as objects of appeal and disdain, the Victorian Catholic minority was well assimilated in the middle classes and shared prevailing tolerant attitudes. One reason for the social acceptance of Catholics may have been that symbolic resistance fulfilled the need for a scapegoat among middle-class Protestants, who, as individuals, were generally well mannered. As important, Catholics were willing to bend their religious commitments in order to live amicably with Protestants: Among lay people, Ellen Sherman was a woman of piety, but bowed to romance and the persuasive majority of Protestant bachelors in Ohio when she married William Tecumseh Sherman, a Presbyterian by birth, who as an adult was committed to no organized faith.[85] Among the Catholic clergy,

[81] Dec. 24, quoted in Perry, *Life and Letters of Henry Lee Higginson* (1921), p. 55.

[82] Rice, *Curry*, pp. 128–9.

[83] Rose, *Transcendentalism as a Social Movement*, pp. 128–9; Elliott, *The Life of Father Hecker* (1894); and Holden, *The Early Years of Isaac Thomas Hecker (1819–1844)* (1939).

[84] On the appeal of Catholicism for nineteenth-century Protestants, see Lears, *No Place of Grace*, ch. 5, and Weisenburger, *Ordeal of Faith*, ch. 11.

[85] Merrill, *Sherman*, pp. 20, 409, and Katherine Burton, *Three Generations: Maria Boyle Ewing (1801–1864), Ellen Ewing Sherman (1824–1888), Minnie Sherman Fitch (1851–1913)* (1947), esp. pp. 59, 65, 84. The Ewing–Sherman marriage is also explained by the fact that Sherman grew up as a foster child in the Ewing family. The other Catholic layman included in the sample, Pierre Beauregard of Louisiana, was far more lax than Ellen Sherman in his religious practice. Although his two successive wives were

men of the Victorian generation were prominent liberal voices in the Americanism controversy of the 1890s, where conflict centered on how much the Catholic church should accommodate national mores. Controversy turned on the precedent of Isaac Hecker after his death in 1888, because Hecker believed Catholicism was compatible with America's individualistic society and democratic government. James Cardinal Gibbons of Baltimore was young enough to be influenced by Hecker (he was born in 1834 and Hecker in 1819), and he advocated what became contested positions on the assimilation of Catholic immigrants and the acceptability of public schools. Yet despite his controversial position among Catholics, Gibbons's compromising temper earned firm respect from Protestants. Teddy Roosevelt, William Howard Taft, and Elihu Root were speakers in 1911 at the twenty-fifth anniversary of Gibbons's appointment as cardinal.[86]

Beneath the accommodating posture of Victorian Catholics, however, there was a firmer core of piety than remained among Protestants, although the small number of Catholics included in this study makes this a conclusion cautiously offered. Among the large number of personal memoirs written by the Victorians in their later years, Gibbons's *A Retrospect of Fifty Years* (1916) was the only one in which the past was not anchored by a first-person narrator, but where the reminiscence consisted instead of sermons, speeches, and other papers from past decades issued together.[87] For Protestants, both lay people and clergy, the authority of a personal voice filled a space left vacant as ideas that claimed transcendent validation grew less compelling. Although Gibbons's memoir conformed to this autobiographical genre, he declined to place himself at its center and instead focused attention on the activities of God's church. To the extent that Gibbons's suppression of self, by instinct or intent, was one sign of a difference in outlook between Victorian Catholics and Protestants, there are a number of likely reasons for Catholics' stronger extramundane focus: the conservative power of an ecclesiastical hierarchy over individuals, the marginal and hence protected situation of

Catholics, he attended church so infrequently that the priest who conducted his funeral commented on his apostasy. See Williams, *P. G. T. Beauregard: Napoleon in Grey* (1954), pp. 35, 327.

[86] Boucher and Tehan, *Prince of Democracy: James Cardinal Gibbons* (1962), pp. 27–8, 68, and chs. 11–13. On the Americanism controversy, see Hennesey, *American Catholics: A History of the Roman Catholic Community in the United States* (1981), ch. 15. In addition to Gibbons and the late Isaac Hecker, prominent Catholic clergymen who were contemporaries of these Victorians and whose views cast them as liberals in the debate of the 1890s include John Ireland (1837–1918) and Edward McGlynn (1837–1900). Other liberals were slightly younger: John Keane (1839–1918), Walter Elliott (1842–1928), and Denis O'Connell (1849–1927). The major American conservative spokesman, Bernard McQuaid, bishop of Rochester, was also a contemporary of the Victorians, because his life spanned the years 1823 to 1909. This may suggest that liberalism was not as strong a force in Catholicism as in Protestantism, as my subsequent discussion proposes. But because many of McQuaid's allies were German-born clergy and ultimately included the Vatican, it is also possible to see liberalism as the dominant viewpoint of a generation of predominantly Irish-American Catholics.

[87] Gibbons, *A Retrospect of Fifty Years* (1916). See my discussion of the Victorians' memoirs and the philosophical implications of their narrative viewpoint in Chapter 6.

Catholics in a culture inclining toward secularism, and the repeated infusions of spiritual fervor brought in by converts dissatisfied with the compromises of Protestantism.[88] Whatever the private sensibility of Catholics, however, the fact that they willingly brought their public positions in line with influences in the Protestant environment indicates an ability to set religion side by side with other priorities rather than to insist that faith decide policy unopposed.

Much as the Victorians' anti-Catholicism revealed their sensitivity to the weaknesses of their faith, their fascination with superstition and their more serious pursuit of spiritualism grew out of this generation's difficulty with traditional religion. Observations on superstition were double-edged: Irrational fears were discussed only to be dismissed with enlightened superiority, yet comments appear frequently enough to provoke suspicion that the Victorians were attracted to primitive feelings as unquestioning acts of faith of which they were increasingly less capable. Writers described superstitions as foibles of children or social subordinates, thereby distancing themselves from these credulous groups. William Dean Howells spent a chapter in his memoirs cataloging his childhood fears of gravestones, howling dogs, snakes, dying, and the end of the world.[89] His friend, Mark Twain, drew the readers of *Huckleberry Finn* into a world of children, criminals, and slaves, where adult values might be upset, by opening Huck's narrative with the hero's worry about his accidental killing of a spider.[90] Perhaps Huck's panic was silly, but he may nonetheless have been fortunate, by Twain's measure, to inhabit a world symbolically constructed where visible events were tokens of invisible things.

Whites similarly took note of the superstitions of blacks. Mary Chesnut's account of her maid, Ellen's, objection to moving on Friday because of "bad luck all round" makes one wonder if the case were as simple as reported: "Ellen succumbed — swallowed her superstitions."[91] In light of Chesnut's self-confessed "suicidal tendencies" during the same flight from Sherman's army, it is not unlikely that Chesnut, too sophisticated quite to admit a shared anxiety about Fridays, coped objectively with her feelings in her dialogue with Ellen. Thomas Wentworth Higginson struck a tourist's pose when he described his black troops' ritual "shout" — "half pow-wow, half

---

[88] Thus Catholic conservatism may have been furthered both by the distance of the Catholic community from the Protestant mainstream and by its intimate relation with Protestantism as a haven for the disaffected. On these two aspects of Victorian Catholicism, see Taves, *Household of Faith*, and the citations in n. 84. For a good comparative discussion of Protestant and Catholic Victorian religious assumptions, see McDannell, *The Christian Home in Victorian America, 1840–1900* (1986), esp. pp. 104–7. For an excellent survey of nineteenth-century American Catholicism, see Dolan, *The American Catholic Experience: A History from Colonial Times to the Present* (1985), chs. 5–12.

[89] Howells, *Boy's Town*, ch. 17.

[90] Mark Twain, *The Adventures of Huckleberry Finn* (New York: Holt, Rinehart, and Winston, 1948), p. 3.

[91] Feb. 18, 1865, *Chesnut's Civil War*, ed. Woodward, p. 719.

prayer-meeting" – where the men danced to the "drumming of the feet and clapping of the hands," all "circling like dervishes."[92] Yet the zest of Higginson's prose suggests he was not immune to the spectacle's hypnotic lure, despite disbelief in the spirits which he sensed the collective "spell" sought to evoke. Precisely because these Victorians were too rational to indulge their own fearful whims, they appropriated the spontaneity of others to answer their need for reassurance of the reality of the unseen.[93]

Victorians came closer to blunt admission of superstition by their interest in spiritualism, understood as a belief in communication with disembodied souls. Although spiritualism's popularity peaked in the 1850s, it drew a diverse following throughout the midcentury decades. In so cosmopolitan a place as New York, rappings and seances hovered on a margin between religious observance and amusement, and flourished because liberal-minded people could experiment with bizarre techniques to supplement conventional faith. George Templeton Strong's Episcopal views did not keep him from attending a spirit rapping in 1850, although he judged the moving force more likely to be magnetic or electrical energy than supernatural power. Five years later, he called spiritualism "a new Revelation, hostile to that of the Church and the Bible." Yet despite skepticism, Strong was still bemused, above all, by its acceptance by reputable people.[94] In Los Angeles, William Moore, a surveyor, pursued spiritualism in a similar mood of half-embarrassed seriousness. Using dry wit, he disparaged his efforts to evoke spirits, but continued his activities nonetheless. "I attend a spiritual circle at Burdicks and hope before long to be able to raise the devil," he wrote in his diary in 1869. Two months later, he visited "a celebrated witch and had a seance," where his "mother purported to talk with me through her." Though his choice of words dismissed the "witch," he returned two days later for another session.[95]

The case of Anna Cora Mowatt, an actress and writer, reveals the Victorians' capacity for credulity when all inhibitions were removed. Though she was raised a Presbyterian, she turned to mesmerism during an illness in the 1840s and, under hypnosis, contemplated metaphysics, talked with angels, and gained assurance of immortality by conversing with spirits. She became a Swedenborgian because of the group's belief in the proximity of the material and spiritual worlds but retained idiosyncratic views as well, such as the assistance houses lent mediums in search of former inhabitants (she visited Stratford-on-Avon to help contact Shakespeare).[96] As a young

[92] Diary, Dec. 3, 1862, quoted in Higginson, *Army Life in a Black Regiment*, p. 17.

[93] This ambivalent identification with intellectually unsophisticated people is not unlike the kinship Victorians felt with animals, as analyzed by Turner, in *Reckoning with the Beast: Animals, Pain, and Humanity in the Victorian Mind* (1980).

[94] June 16, 1850, Nov. 26, 1855, *Diary of Strong*, ed. Nevins and Thomas, 2:15–16, 245.

[95] Mar. 21, May 25, May 27, Diary, 1869, William Moore Papers.

[96] Barnes, *The Lady of Fashion: The Life and the Theatre of Anna Cora Mowatt* (1954), pp. 89–96, 278.

woman who was informally educated and an actress who was highly imaginative, Mowatt lacked the self-censoring skepticism that framed the two men's desire to believe in spiritual communion. Interpreted together, however, these instances of flirtation with spiritualism indicate this generation's desire for religious certainty otherwise masked by easygoing faith. The Victorians fell back on a few simple religious truths to circumvent the hard task of adapting traditional Christian doctrines to a changing world. But when elemental principles fell short of giving satisfaction, spiritualism offered a new route to mystical insight.[97] Built around a technique for contacting souls rather than on a set of ideas, spiritualism appealed to a generation whose members wished to restore religious feeling by stimulating imagination without exercising reason.

The Victorians' religious practice involved tensions similar to those that shaped their values. Just as ostensibly straightforward principles obscured unsatisfied longings, thriving religious bureaucracies diverted attention from privatized and disaffected spiritual expression. For individuals, either to approach religion as a business or to reserve significant practice for home meant that church fellowship focused religious life less clearly than it had in the past.

How much public worship lost ground in the Victorian generation ought not be overstated. A number of men and women, northern and southern, continued childhood habits of churchgoing.[98] As adults, however, middle-class men stepped into administrative roles that overshadowed informal involvement in church communities. The reward of prosperity and prominence, these responsibilities might have been the cause or consequence of an emotional distance from spontaneous worship. Either way, they represented a less personal style of religious participation.

The life of Charles Maclay epitomizes this trend. Maclay arrived in California in 1851 as a Methodist preacher. In 1886, he gave a large enough endowment from his personal fortune, made as an entrepreneur, to set up

---

[97] For discussion of mid-nineteenth-century spiritualism, see R. Lawrence Moore, "Spiritualism and Science: Reflections on the First Decade of Spirit Rapping," *American Quarterly* 24 (1972): 474–500; Weisenburger, *Ordeal of Faith*, pp. 287–90; and Baker, *Mary Todd Lincoln: A Biography* (1987), esp. pp. 217–22.

[98] Nineteen lay people left evidence of "regular" church attendance, if not weekly, then on a fairly steady basis throughout a good part of their lives. Those born in the 1810s include: James Beekman, Charlotte Cushman, John Wentworth, Priscilla Tyler, and Robert Tyler. Of those born in the 1820s: George Templeton Strong, Jay Cooke, William Montague Browne, Mary Chesnut, Ellen Sherman, Varina Davis, Julia Grant, Cyrus Holliday, and Samuel McCullough. Of those born in the 1830s: Oliver Otis Howard, Joseph Taylor, James Garfield, Chauncey Depew, and Rebecca Felton. The fourteen men who were ministers for at least part of their lives obviously took ecclesiastical obligations seriously as well: John Wesley North, George Atkinson, Isaac Hecker, Josiah Grinnell, Charles Maclay, Octavius Brooks Frothingham, Edward Everett Hale, Thomas Wentworth Higginson, Jabez Curry, John Damon, William Potter, Moncure Conway, James Gibbons, and Lyman Abbott. Nonetheless, because the spiritual difficulties of more than a few of these individuals are discussed in this chapter, attention to public ritual cannot be the sole measure of faith.

a theological school at the University of Southern California that was named in his honor. Yet what happened in the meantime to Maclay's private faith is puzzling. By the mid-1850s, Maclay not only did the necessary farming in addition to preaching but sold general merchandise in a wholesale and retail capacity. His daughter recalled around 1920 that ill health made Maclay quit the ministry. But since he was well enough to spend most of the 1860s in the state legislature, it is as likely that worldly interests competed seriously with Maclay's faith. Indeed, the secular focus of his legislative addresses is surprising from so recent a preacher. Maclay lobbied for Sabbath laws, for example, not to protect the sanctity of God's day, but to advance social "harmony & peace." It seems strange, too, that he lived for ten years in the southern California town of San Fernando before giving money in 1884 to build the first Protestant church.[99] All this is not to say necessarily that Maclay's generous gift to the university was a gesture to make amends for his diminished religious intensity. Rather, as benefactor and trustee of a theological school, he found a religious role appropriate to a social position that, for better or worse, demanded enough attention to secular matters to blunt his original piety.

Maclay's example suggests that the routinization of religion was advanced by the willingness of men of means to volunteer their organizational skills and wealth, making structured religious activity a function, to an extent, of middle-class mores. More modestly than Maclay, but also more typically, a number of businessmen and professionals served as trustees or vestry members of churches, including Samuel McCullough in San Francisco and, in New York, Abram Hewitt and George Templeton Strong.[100] Sociologists' analyses of denominational formation explain the growth of bureaucracy as part of the transformation of marginal sects into mainstream churches.[101] These theories take too little account, however, of unique historical influences such as the rise of the middle classes, people who not only had the money and expertise to build elaborate organizations, but who felt more comfortable in efficient churches.[102] Despite their ahistorical tenor, denominational

---

[99] On Maclay's early missionary activities, see Thomas A. Morris to Maclay, Jan. 15, 1851, and Maclay to Elizabeth B. and Thomas W. Lloyd, Aug. 28, 1855, Charles Maclay Papers. Among much business correspondence, see, e.g., George S. Rathburn to Maclay and Brothers, Jan. 8 and 22, 1856, Maclay Papers. For his position on temperance, see his "Speech to the California Assembly advocating amendment of the Sunday Law," ms., 1862, Maclay Papers. Further information is found in Josephine Lloyd Maclay Walker, "Biographical Sketch of Charles Maclay," ms. ca. 1920, Maclay Papers.

[100] Woodbridge Presbyterian Church to McCullough, Apr. 3, 1884, Samuel McCullough Papers; Nevins, *Hewitt*, p. 540; Oct. 12, 1847, *Diary of Strong*, ed. Nevins and Thomas, 1:303. Although Strong approached his appointment to the vestry in this entry as a burden, he developed a keen interest in church politics.

[101] See, e.g., Bryan Wilson, *Religious Sects: A Sociological Study* (New York: McGraw Hill, 1970). For a more complete list of thinkers (including theologians and historians) who have been concerned with the denominational cycle, see my "Social Sources of Denominationalism Reconsidered," p. 257, n. 1.

[102] Whereas Gregory Singleton has said that religious voluntary associations helped prepare the middle classes to initiate secular (and especially economic) bureaucracies, in "Protestant Voluntary Associations

models do helpfully highlight hidden flaws in outwardly prosperous religion, because they acknowledge that increasing formality constrains initial vitality and that people withdraw to begin new sects to recover stirring spiritual experience. In Victorian America, it was true that well-run institutions flourished side by side with individualized practice, one sign that public worship fell short of giving private satisfaction in just such a way.

For obvious reasons, private religious observance took a number of forms, yet several patterns emerge. Bible reading was one solitary activity to supplement or replace church attendance, valued for the ability of scriptural language to allay distress. Some Victorians, moreover, felt closer to God in nature than in church. Henry Lee Higginson apparently thought that Harvard College could handle his practical pantheism in 1907, when he told students that he preferred spending Sunday mornings outside.[103] James Garfield was more troubled by nature's lure, though no less affected. Crossing the Atlantic in 1867, he admitted the seduction of the physical setting in his diary, "especially here today, where the religion of nature is proclaimed in such sublimity as sea and sky have been declaring them [divine truths] to me, [making] the surplice and ritual seem so poor and paltry."[104] To spend quiet moments in nature as a means to spiritual insight was a thought pioneered by the transcendentalists as early as the 1830s, and their works were read avidly by a heterogeneous group of Victorians in search of private uplift. That young New Englanders found Emerson inspiring is no surprise, but it is striking that Mary Chesnut wrote in 1861, "Tried to rise above the agonies of everyday life – read Emerson."[105] Chesnut's interest in Emerson did not dislodge her habit of church attendance, but William Herndon's veneration of Theodore Parker was a self-sufficient faith. "You are my ideal," he wrote to Parker from Illinois in 1854, "strong, direct, energetic & char-

and the Shaping of Victorian America," my argument makes the opposite point that secular skills influenced religion. Part of our difference grows from my focus on a later period, when business habits were sufficiently well established to affect other areas of culture. I do not contest the importance of churches and other voluntary associations as settings where men were schooled in organizational techniques, because the relationship between religion and business in the Victorian generation was thoroughly reciprocal. For the full citation of Singleton's essay, see n. 1. One religious development probably facilitated by bureaucracy was the expansion of foreign missions at the turn of the century, a trend analyzed by Hutchison, in *Errand to the World: American Protestant Thought and Foreign Missions* (1987), ch. 4. A program initiated in this period by church leaders, missions could not only be conducted with little ongoing involvement by parishioners but with the expectation that foreign success would fan revivals at home, as Hutchison notes, p. 8. Although Hutchison does not focus on the relation of missions to the vitality of American churches, this line of thinking is not inconsistent with his argument.

[103] Perry, *Higginson*, p. 393.

[104] Nov. 3, 1867, *Diary of Garfield*, ed. Brown and Williams, 1:438. Among the literature on romantic attitudes toward nature, two sources that help place American Victorian religious feelings in perspective are Ralph Waldo Emerson, "Nature" (1836), in *The Collected Works of Ralph Waldo Emerson*, ed. Robert E. Spiller and Alfred R. Ferguson (Cambridge, Mass.: Harvard University Press, 1971), 1:7–45, and Ahlstrom, "The Romantic Religious Revolution and the Dilemmas of Religious History," esp. 158–63.

[105] Ca. June 10, *Chesnut's Civil War*, ed. Woodward, p. 56.

itable," and he confessed later to Parker's wife that her husband was "about the only man living who can hold me steady."[106]

At times, such private communion changed an individual's life. Reading Emerson helped Moncure Conway to focus his discontent with Virginia Methodism and lead him to radical Unitarianism. Yet on the whole, personal religious exploration was stillborn in the sense that it affected individual and collective action relatively little. This is an important finding in light of the notion of a denominational cycle. Whereas recurrent formation of sects presupposes a flexible institutional milieu, where like-minded people join easily in worship, the static coexistence of private and public expression signals a permanent alienation that belongs to modernity and has intensified with time.[107] Perhaps there is a point where mainstream religion is sufficiently bureaucratized to deter all but the most determined of the discontented from attempting to compete in an organized manner. In addition, to judge by Emerson's popularity, individualism was a strong and independent social force that may have made private ritual preferable to common worship. To say that peaceful moments in nature possessed an interchangeable value with traditional ritual, finally, was close to admitting that religion was sought as much for its psychological benefits as its transcendent message.[108] Why such individuals did not seek a public religious alternative to unsatisfying worship is answered by how consoling secular habits had become.

The tension in religious institutions between bureaucratic activism and private expression contributed to the comparative scarcity of voluntary associations inspired by religious goals. Benevolent efforts may have been better equipped for efficiency, and some of a community's leading men and women may have welcomed the opportunity to run more elaborate organizations. Others, however, may have felt themselves edged out of satisfying roles in social bodies based on division of labor and chains of command.

During the most intense years of the Second Great Awakening prior to 1840, spiritual fervor generated organizations collateral to churches in im-

---

[106] Herndon to Theodore Parker, May 13, 1854, Herndon to Lydia Parker, Mar. 30, 1857, in Donald, *Herndon,* pp. 55, 56. Mary Kupiec Cayton usefully reminds us that the transcendentalists could also be interpreted by their American audiences as prophets of a more worldly, entrepreneurial individualism, in "The Making of an American Prophet: Emerson, His Audiences, and the Rise of the Culture Industry in Nineteenth-Century America," *American Historical Review* 92 (1987): 597–620. The variety of readings of the transcendentalists' message must to some extent have been a function of the shifting balance of religious and secular attitudes among their public.

[107] Robert N. Bellah and his coauthors have recently analyzed individualism in contemporary American religious practice, in *Habits of the Heart: Individualism and Commitment in American Life* (New York: Harper and Row, 1985), ch. 9.

[108] William James, only slightly younger than these Victorians since he was born in 1842, in fact revolutionized religious thinking by defining the value of religious attitudes by their psychological and ethical consequences, in *The Varieties of Religious Experience: A Study in Human Nature* (1902; reprint, New York: Macmillan, 1961).

pressive numbers, including Bible societies, maternal associations, and, more distantly, antislavery societies.[109] Although the Victorians grew up in this setting, their involvement in such groups as adults was neither extensive nor sustained. Temperance was the most popular cause, but the reform claimed its most loyal advocates among older members of this generation. John Wesley North, George Atkinson, and Josiah Grinnell, born respectively in 1815, 1819, and 1821, made temperance part of the basic social structure of the communities they helped pioneer in Minnesota, Oregon, and Iowa in the 1850s.[110] For others slightly younger, however, temperance became an appropriate principle for social subordinates or the reason for an occasional convention, while no one born after 1830 gave temperance serious attention.[111] Other quasi-religious associations that these Victorians sponsored represented an odd mix of causes. Oliver Otis Howard, a fervent Methodist and Union general, ran the Freedman's Bureau, an experiment in government-sponsored benevolence. William Potter helped to found the Free Religious Association, a body offering a collective identity to radical thinkers.[112] On the whole, however, the Victorians were more inclined to engage in spontaneous religious occasions than to join an organization. Spiritualist seances brought together individuals with no necessary common ground for a brief encounter of limited goals. Similarly, hymn singing was popular among soldiers in both armies as a way for men of disparate beliefs to share religious feeling.[113]

This shift from participation in voluntary associations defined by long-term goals to gatherings that aimed at an immediate effect was a function of a religious environment where formal organizations absorbed ad hoc cam-

[109] See Ahlstrom, *Religious History of the American People*, pp. 422–8; Walters, *American Reformers;* and Ryan, *Cradle of the Middle Class,* ch. 3.

[110] Stonehouse, *North,* p. 47; Atkinson to Mary Hale, Apr. 30, 1858, Atkinson Papers; Payne, *Josiah Bushnell Grinnell* (1938), p. 41.

[111] See, e.g., the thoughts of Charles Maclay (b. 1821) on the necessity of temperance for social order, in his [Address Given at a Meeting of the Dashaways, a Temperance Organization], ms. ca. 1860, Maclay Papers. The wife of Joseph Danner Taylor (Elizabeth, b. 1828) attended a temperance convention in Cincinnati in 1874, and her participation highlights the activities that led to the founding of the Women's Christian Temperance Union (WCTU), an organization Christian in name and principle, but so autonomous of specific churches or denominations that the movement occupied a hazy ground between the religious and the secular. See Elizabeth A. Taylor to Joseph Taylor, Apr. 24, [1874], Taylor Papers. On women and temperance more generally, see Epstein, *The Politics of Domesticity: Women, Evangelism, and Temperance in Nineteenth-Century America* (1981). The social prestige of this group of Victorians may help account for their increasing lack of interest in temperance as a cause advocated by the less well-to-do. There was an aloof skepticism, for example, in the comments of the railroad entrepreneur, Cyrus Holliday (b. 1826), on the "great temperance movement" in 1874, when he wrote to his daughter that "whether they will revolutionize the world, or the country, even, upon this great evil, is very doubtful" (Holliday to Lillie Holliday, Apr. 1, 1874, Holliday Papers).

[112] McFeely, *Yankee Stepfather: General O. O. Howard and the Freedmen* (1968); Persons, *Free Religion: An American Faith* (1947), esp. ch. 3.

[113] On the northern army, see Diary, Dec. 11, 1862, quoted in Higginson, *Army Life in a Black Regiment,* p. 22, and on the southern, see George Pickett to LaSalle Pickett, ca. Apr. 2, 1865, in *Soldier of the South: General Pickett's War Letters to His Wife,* ed. Inman (1928), pp. 128–9.

paigns and where, in part as a result, individual commitments were reduced in enthusiasm and depth. As benevolence became tightly structured, as it was in the case of the Freedman's Bureau, personal effort mattered less and hence was less often contributed. The voluntary activities that survived, such as hymn singing, offered a simple emotional reward in an enjoyable form. Interpreted together, these trends reveal a growing rift between religion as business and leisure.

At the same time that religious voluntary associations declined in the Victorian generation, rituals that mediated moments of personal passage worked increasingly to connect individuals with tradition. Most consistently, people confronted with death, who were otherwise of uncertain faith, consented to the assistance of religious ceremonies with set forms of behavior to carry them through. Edwin Godkin, the editor of the *Nation,* was consumed by doubt when his daughter died in 1873, worrying that she was not "in the hands of a heavenly father." Although he complained that not even Unitarianism had cured him of his "profound weariness of doctrines," he still asked a Unitarian minister to conduct her funeral.[114] Few men were less likely subjects of deathbed conversions, moreover, than Ulysses Grant and William Tecumseh Sherman. Yet before their respective deaths in 1885 and 1891, each accepted the rites of his family's faith, a Methodist baptism for Grant and extreme unction for Sherman.[115] To note the distance between private views and public ritual is not to impugn the sincerity of these gestures, but to underline the genuine need of these families for imposed procedures at times when ordinary routine dissolved. This is one function of ritual in all cultures, but the Victorian practice was distinguished by the growing incongruity between a religious response in stress and everyday secularism and by the prominence of individual choice in determining when religion should be used.[116]

Being a minister must have been taxing in a religious community at once structured and fragmented, one that required a person to maneuver between wealthy sponsors and judgmental parishioners. Members of the clergy who found fulfillment in their vocation were those who by force of personality or circumstance could ensure enough discretion in their calling to make it an extension of personal principle. George Atkinson looked older than his fifty-one years, he wrote from Oregon in 1870 to an eastern correspondent, because of the grueling demands on a frontier minister responsible for all aspects of Christian culture. Yet "I get weary in the work not of it," he

[114] Godkin to Charles Eliot Norton, Feb. 6, 1866, Godkin to Henry W. Bellows, Apr. 2, [1873], in *The Gilded Age Letters of E. L. Godkin,* ed. Armstrong (1974), pp. 73, 199.

[115] McFeely, *Grant: A Biography* (1981), p. 503; Merrill, *Sherman,* p. 409.

[116] Among the substantial anthropological literature on ritual in traditional cultures, see, e.g., the essays in Victor W. Turner, *The Ritual Process: Structure and Anti-Structure* (Chicago: Aldine Publishing Company, 1969). On the prominence of choice in nineteenth-century American religion, see Turner, *Without God, Without Creed,* p. 266.

concluded, perhaps because his comparatively free hand in a new country gave him a sense of control and accomplishment.[117]

Among the majority of men in this group who at one time were ministers, in contrast, there were feelings of constraint. Daniel Coit Gilman, a pioneer of graduate education as president of Johns Hopkins University after 1875, cited possible restriction of his freedom of speech as a reason for the delay of his ordination until 1860, eight years after his graduation from Yale.[118] Repeatedly, too, the Victorians implicitly judged the ministry insufficiently manly. Thomas Wentworth Higginson's thrill at the challenge of soldiering and low estimate of his regiment's chaplain is a prime example. Other men, such as Charles Maclay in California and Josiah Grinnell in Iowa, drifted from the ministry toward secular careers in business and politics, effectively, if not formally, giving up preaching.[119] Entrepreneurship and public service were consistent with expectations of masculine independence, not so much because of their worldliness, but because of the opportunity they offered for self-definition at a time of economic expansion and political crisis. A clerical routine of attending committees and providing weekly inspiration to disparate listeners compared poorly if autonomy was a man's goal. William Potter, one person who stayed in the ministry, looked forward to a vacation in 1863 "to take me away from this necessity of every week scraping the bottom of a dry well to draw up a few spoonfuls of muddy water." His weariness of speaking to listeners no more responsive than "stoneheads" suggests why others left the profession.[120]

What the Victorian religious community lacked most fundamentally was fellowship. Certainly denominational differences were sufficiently entrenched by the first decades of the nineteenth century to forbid imagining a past religious consensus. Nevertheless, the drama of redemption, usually conceived as centering in individual conversion, anchored the religious sensibility of most of the Victorians' parents, even if they did not consider themselves personally among the saved. Questions about life's purposes answered diversely by individual Victorians exploded this common intellectual possession. To cope with fragmentation, members of this generation tried to form church communities based on the social principles of toleration and efficient administration. But they could not easily compensate for the erosion of shared faith. This was the religious situation of the mid-nineteenth-century middle classes at the time of the Civil War.

---

[117] Atkinson to Mary Hale, Jan. 3, Atkinson Papers.

[118] Flexner, *Daniel Coit Gilman: Creator of the American Type of University* (1946), ch. 1.

[119] Although Grinnell began his career as a Presbyterian minister and helped establish Grinnell, Iowa, in 1854 as a sort of utopian community dedicated to such reforms as temperance and antislavery as well as to civic prosperity, he became more involved in commercial farming, railroad development, and politics over the years. See Payne, *Grinnell*.

[120] Potter to George Bartlett, July 1, Potter Papers.

CRISES IN FAITH AND NATIONHOOD

Scholars have often documented the role of religion in the Civil War.[121] Efforts to evangelize the armies, revivals among the troops, and the use of Christian language by public figures to explain the conflict's purpose in God's providential design have all been seen as part of a culture that shaped the way Americans understood their national crisis. It is true, as these interpretations imply, that Christianity served as an essential value system during the Civil War. Yet if the evidence on religion and war is set within the broader temporal context of American Victorianism, wartime piety appears more as a revival of customs and ideas increasingly challenged in peacetime society than an unambiguous sign of Americans' faith. American Victorian religion was marked by serious tensions and vulnerabilities. In that setting, three conclusions may be offered about religious expressions during the war: that the war restored wavering piety, though only for a time; that it simultaneously deepened the Victorians' secular interests; and that it exposed how thoroughly a sacred perspective competed with viewpoints bounded by the natural and human worlds.

Few of these Victorians gave thought to the war's connections with religion as the fighting began. Many letters and journals focused on the endless mundane plans and calculations involved in transforming a peaceful nation into openly hostile sections. Ulysses Grant and William Tecumseh Sherman, for example, turned their attention in the spring of 1861 to estimates of how long the war would last. The conflict would be short, Grant reasoned in a letter to his father on May 6, because of the South's military weakness.[122] Sherman, on the other hand, predicted "a long war, – very long," when he wrote to his brother-in-law a month later. War's "real character" was far more horrible than Americans could foresee as they embraced its "first glittering bait."[123] People ordinarily more concerned with religion than these future generals still made only passing mention of issues of spirituality and morals. Despite his private doubts about his soul's vitality, James Garfield was the principal of a church-affiliated school and a lay minister in the Disciples of Christ when he joined the Union army in 1861. Even so, his description of a Methodist prayer meeting in his camp near Columbus, Ohio, was exceptional among his early wartime correspondence.[124]

On reflection, this evidence of inattention to matters of faith during the

[121] Key discussions of religion in the war include Moorhead, *American Apocalypse;* Shattuck, *Shield and Hiding Place,* esp. chs. 1–2; Paludan, *People's Contest,* ch. 14; and Hobson, *Tell about the South: The Southern Rage to Explain* (1983), pt. 2, ch. 1.

[122] Grant to Jesse Grant, in *The Papers of Ulysses S. Grant,* ed. Simon (1969), 2:21–2.

[123] Sherman to Thomas Ewing, Jr., June 3 and May 23, in *Home Letters of General Sherman,* ed. Howe (1909), pp. 198, 197.

[124] Garfield to Lucretia Garfield, Apr. 28, in *The Wild Life of the Army: Civil War Letters of James A. Garfield,* ed. Williams (1964), pp. 10–11.

war's opening months is not surprising. The consuming practical tasks involved in going to war must have deflected thoughts from spiritual things. More deeply, pressing ambitions among the Victorians for personal distinction, stirring adventure, and political victory – motives explored in this book's later chapters – similarly edged religion aside. While the Victorians slighted Christianity's spiritual message, however, their facility at functioning within denominational networks served them well. Throughout Garfield's military service, he received practical aid and hospitality from fellow Disciples of Christ. During campaigns in Kentucky and Alabama and on duty in Washington, D.C., Garfield was welcomed by Disciples as a man of standing in the denomination.[125] These social contacts did not allay Garfield's private spiritual discontent. But the continuity of institutional ties from civilian to army life that the Disciples of Christ provided must have offset the stresses of his military experience. On a more practical level, the organizational expertise that the Victorians gained on church committees and in wider benevolence helped to underwrite bureaucratic support needed during the war for unprecedented masses of men. George Templeton Strong's participation as an active layman in New York's Episcopal churches since the late 1840s, for example, equipped him to become treasurer of the Sanitary Commission during the war. His efforts for the commission coincided in time with his complaints about unsatisfying Sunday worship. Still, Strong's feelings of disquiet and reserve did not diminish the importance of his institutional background for his charitable work in the Civil War.[126]

This view of religion's circumscribed role in the war's early phases clashes with conclusions that have been drawn by scholars concerned with public history. Although there is some dispute over the comparative religious orientations of the Christian and Sanitary Commissions in the North, historians agree that both interdenominational agencies intended to supplement practical assistance to soldiers with a religious message, at least the moral lessons of the Sanitary Commission if not the evangelical doctrine of the Christian Commission.[127] With a similar intent to proselytize, denominations in the

---

[125] Garfield to Lucretia Garfield, Dec. 20, 1861, Feb. 23 and July 5, 1862, Garfield to Harry Rhodes, Dec. 7, 1862, in *Wild Life of the Army*, ed. Williams, pp. 52, 72, 119, 189.

[126] *Diary of Strong*, ed. Nevins and Thomas, vols. 2 and 3.

[127] On the Christian Commission and Sanitary Commission, see Fredrickson, *The Inner Civil War: Northern Intellectuals and the Crisis of the Union* (1965), ch. 7; Moorhead, *American Apocalypse*, pp. 66–7; Shattuck, *Shield and Hiding Place*, p. 24; and Paludan, *People's Contest*, pp. 351–4. Scholarly debate over the religious differences between the agencies follows these lines of argument. Fredrickson focuses on the Sanitary Commission's pride in its scientific organization of aid, to the point that he implies that its members were antireligious. Moorhead argues that despite open contention between the groups, agents in fact assisted one another in the field. Moreover, he acknowledges the implicit moralism of the Sanitary Commission's goals of personal discipline and social order by calling its objectives "less explicitly religious" than those of the Christian Commission, p. 66. This scholarly discussion is an index of the subtlety of the process of secularization. The question is not whether the Victorians moved away from

South sent missionaries, Bibles, and tracts to the armies.[128] From the perspective of culture, James Moorhead has discussed the apocalyptic expectations that framed the war intellectually in northern addresses and sermons.[129] Can these interpretations be reconciled with private lives that suggest Christianity's more limited role? One possible explanation is that religious leaders aware of midcentury Protestantism's liabilities saw the war as an opportunity – perhaps the last chance – to inspire a revival. This argument takes account of the discontinuity between strenuous public religious efforts and widespread private silence on spiritual questions as the war began. Sincere and anguished religious reflection increased, however, as the fighting wore on.

Public demonstrations of piety and the use of Christian concepts became more pronounced in the course of the Civil War. There were revivals in the Union army in 1862 and awakenings among Confederate troops in 1863 and 1864.[130] Leaders of both sections moved closer to traditional religious views. Among the southern Victorians studied, John Bell Hood, a Confederate general, was baptized while he served at the front in 1864. Varina Davis, the wife of the president, began attending church with her husband after he became an Episcopal communicant in 1862. Her friend, Mary Chesnut, quipped in 1864, "Somebody counted fourteen generals in church and suggested that less piety and more drilling of commands would suit the times better."[131] For better or worse, worship played an expanding role in mediating statesmanship and combat.

Northerners witnessed no more arresting a revival of Christian terms of understanding than in the words of their leader, Abraham Lincoln. A man older than the Victorians (Lincoln was born in 1809), but perhaps akin to them in his ordinary inclination to skepticism rather than faith, Lincoln left behind the political language of his first inaugural address to deliver a moving

Christian goals, but with what temper. I tend to agree with Moorhead that the Sanitary Commission was an expression of a bureaucratized kind of religion that reflected its members' equivocal view of traditional faith, a more insidious and powerful mode of departure from Christian standards than vocal opposition because masked by verbal deference to established beliefs.

[128] On evangelical efforts in the southern army, see Shattuck, *Shield and Hiding Place*, ch. 2.

[129] Moorhead, *American Apocalypse*.

[130] On the revivals in the northern and southern armies, see Shattuck, *Shield and Hiding Place*, chs. 4–5. Contemporary estimates cited by Shattuck suggest that 5 to 10 percent of northern soldiers experienced conversion (p. 92). Since Michael Barton found in his content analysis of soldiers' writings that the language that appeared most frequently fell within categories of "moralism," "progress," and "religion" (in that order), more soldiers than the relatively small number who made professions of faith may have had their religious interest stirred by the combination of combat experience and proselytizing initiatives. See *Goodmen*, p. 33. Still, evidence of piety is counterbalanced by many accounts of loose morals, involving drinking, gambling, and swearing. See Wiley, *Common Soldier in the Civil War*, 1: ch. 3, and 2: ch. 10. Though somewhat contrary to the pattern of religious interest I document here, Gerald Linderman's argument should also be kept in mind: that religious concern slackened among Union soldiers as hardship and suffering increased. See *Embattled Courage*, pp. 252–6.

[131] Mar. 12, 1864, *Chesnut's Civil War*, ed. Woodward, p. 585. On Hood and Davis, see, respectively, Dyer, *The Gallant Hood* (1950), p. 234, and Wiley, *Confederate Women*, pp. 102–3.

jeremiad when he took office again in 1865. In his second inaugural, Lincoln pictured the war as an expression of God's retribution for the South's commitment to and the North's toleration of slavery:

If we shall suppose that American Slavery is one of those offenses which, in the providence of God, must needs come, but which, having continued through His appointed time, He now wills to remove, and that He gives to both North and South, this terrible war, as the woe due to those by whom the offense came, shall we discern therein any departure from those divine attributes which the believers in a Living God always ascribe to Him? Fondly do we hope − fervently do we pray − that this mighty scourge of war may speedily pass away. Yet, if God wills that it continue, until all the wealth piled by the bondsman's two hundred and fifty years of unrequited toil shall be sunk, and until every drop of blood drawn with the lash, shall be paid by another drawn with the sword, as was said three thousand years ago, so still it must be said "the judgments of the Lord, are true and righteous altogether."[132]

Against this image of divine judgment, Lincoln called upon Americans to act "with malice toward none; with charity for all." His tolerant benignity distinguished his position from that of the Puritans, who would have missed no opportunity to single out and punish sin. Yet even with this nineteenth-century amendment to the jeremiad's logic, it must have been clear to Lincoln's contemporaries that he had searched the nation's religious past for an idea adequate to explain the suffering he saw.

Private statements of northern Victorians mirrored Lincoln's adaptation of inherited Christian language. Whereas George Templeton Strong began the war with busy attentiveness to the Sanitary Commission's affairs, in 1863 he referred to the struggle in his journal as "a religious war."[133] To justify the conflict's tremendous human cost, Strong needed to look beyond temporal reasons for combat to a rationale that clarified its sacred ends. In a more troubled state of mind, James Garfield probed repeatedly in his letters for God's will behind the war. "I try to see God's hand through this darkness and believe that the issue will redound to His glory," he wrote in 1862 to Mark Hopkins, the president of Williams College. To his wife, Garfield said the same year: "I am every day asking myself what this nation has done which is so much more wicked than the deeds of all others that the scourge of God should fall so heavily and not be lifted."[134] These men's anguish indicates that even without aggressive evangelical efforts, the emotional

---

[132] "Second Inaugural Address" (Mar. 4, 1865), in *The Collected Works of Abraham Lincoln*, ed. Roy P. Basler (New Brunswick, N.J.: Rutgers University Press, 1953), 8:332–3. For the text of the "First Inaugural Address," see ibid., 4:249–71. See also Paludan's discussion of the change in Lincoln's perspective, in *People's Contest*, pp. 369–73.

[133] Sept. 11, *Diary of Strong*, ed. Nevins and Thomas, 3:356–7.

[134] Garfield to Hopkins, June 9, 1862; Garfield to Lucretia Garfield, Dec. 19, 1862, in *Wild Life of the Army*, ed. Williams, pp. 109, 200.

hardships and intellectual perplexities that the war brought on probably would have deepened Americans' religious concern.

The wartime spiritual renewal thus brought back the evangelical demonstrations of antebellum revivalism and the language of Puritan jeremiads. But precisely because these religious styles seem incongruous in a Victorian setting based on ecclesiastical efficiency, toleration, and individualized faith, questions about the ability of this resurgence of piety to persist necessarily arise. In fact, fervor evoked during the war stood on weak foundations. Christian agencies in the field necessarily served soldiers as clients rather than potential coequals, because converts could be offered no sphere for participation in which to register their spiritual majority by turning their faith into evangelical activity in turn. For much the same reason, religious meetings were characterized by constantly changing membership. In consequence, men relied, either spontaneously or at the clergy's initiative, on simple Christian messages known to all, often conveyed in favorite hymns. So thoroughly were theological differences homogenized that Catholics in small posts were expected to worship along with Protestants under Protestant chaplains. In 1861, Ulysses Grant asked Lincoln to appoint a Catholic chaplain-at-large for the Union army to compensate Catholic soldiers, at least symbolically, for their slighted spiritual needs. But Lincoln never did so, and Protestantism remained the unofficial creed of northern troops, as much because of the deemphasis of distinctions in Christian belief as because of long-standing anti-Catholicism.[135] As diverse denominational doctrines were pared down to a common fund of provocative symbols, intellectual flexibility also declined. Oliver Otis Howard, for example, set out to make the Freedman's Bureau an agency of Christian benevolence. But as William McFeely has argued, Howard could not master the task of applying religion effectively in an environment troubled by social disruption and political contention, and his generous feelings achieved a limited effect.[136] Wartime circumstances were not hospitable to restoring intellectual sophistication to Victorian religion, and without a core of discriminating thoughtfulness, Christianity's efficacy fell short of its advocates' hopes.

Overall, Civil War religion strangely married traditional ideas of God's justice and human submission to the most problematic traits of contemporary

---

[135] Grant to Abraham Lincoln, Dec. 18, 1861, in *Papers of Grant*, ed. Simon (1970), 3:301–2. Grant's request to Lincoln was a response to a dispute between a Union regiment that contained a Protestant majority and the Catholic chaplain who was assigned to serve it. When the chaplain resigned under pressure that ostensibly originated among the Protestant enlisted men, Grant, along with John McClernand, proposed the creation of a post of chaplain-at-large to address the issue of Catholic interests. Although the religious implications of the incident are complex, it seems clear that neither Grant, who was pushed to act, nor Lincoln, who ignored the request, took the religious issue as seriously as did the soldiers immediately affected. The "Victorian" religious views of these leaders, in this case their relative indifference to points of doctrine, do not seem to have been shared by their less educated and less prosperous countrymen. For Simon's discussion of the incident, see ibid., pp. 302–4.

[136] McFeely, *Yankee Stepfather*, esp. chs. 5–6.

practice – aggressive bureaucracies, loosely bonded congregations, and sim-plified doctrine. James Moorhead has written that the millennial significance that northerners attached to the war raised hopes that spiritual excitement would continue after the fighting was over. Yet fervor waned instead, and Christians oscillated between "disillusionment and frantic activism" that signaled "a nervous effort at self-reassurance."[137] Although Moorhead does not stress the insecure religious basis of wartime piety as one cause of its rapid decline, he identifies a second reason for faith's circumscribed power, that war-making "heightened secular preoccupations potentially subversive of spiritual values."[138]

An undertaking as massive as the prosecution of war diverted attention from questions of faith at the same time that the consequences of violence recalled religion for consolation. Not simply at the outset but throughout the conflict, war required men on both sides to concentrate on the pragmatic problems of maintaining efficient armies, backed up by strong manufacturing and agricultural support. From an individual perspective, the importance of practical skills shifted the criteria for judging a person from his or her inner worth to outward allegiances and activities. Although sectional tensions heightened religious intolerance because of worry for the republic's security, a countervailing inclination to put religious creeds aside for the sake of political and military alliances strengthened a kind of liberalism based on the insignificance of doctrine next to secular commitments. Whereas George Templeton Strong condemned Unitarianism as a young man as "a religion at once convenient, compressible, and fashionable," by 1863 he and his wife socialized with Henry Bellows, a Unitarian minister and a fellow member of the Sanitary Commission. Indeed, one event that these Episcopal and Unitarian couples attended together was a political speech by Henry Ward Beecher, a Congregationalist, judged by Strong a "capital address."[139] Thus religious toleration was a visible outcome of wartime cooperation. But the more troubling message for the Christian community was that beliefs could be set aside for secular interests.

A more complex instance of the way encounters between diverse creeds were absorbed by common war-related objectives involves James Garfield and his superior officer, General William Rosecrans. A "Jesuit of the highest style of Roman piety" in Garfield's eyes, Rosecrans was "the intensest re-ligionist I ever saw."[140] Both to test Garfield's mettle and quickly to establish a relationship of depth with his new chief of staff, Rosecrans engaged Garfield

[137] *American Apocalypse*, pp. 217, 243, 240.

[138] Ibid., p. 224.

[139] Jan. 26, 1840, Nov. 21, 1863, *Diary of Strong*, ed. Nevins and Thomas, 1:126, 3:372. Wei-senburger also notes that the war promoted interdenominational friendships, in *Ordeal of Faith*, p. 11.

[140] Garfield to Lucretia Garfield, Jan. 26 and Feb. 13, 1863, in *Wild Life of the Army*, ed. Williams, pp. 226, 233.

Figure 3. James A. Garfield (1831–81). A native of Ohio, Garfield was a teacher and lay minister in the Disciples of Christ before the war. His military service (1861–63) helped to further his political career as a congressman and later as president. Here Garfield was photographed as a brigadier general in the Union army. Library of Congress.

in late-night discussions of faith. "I sat up with the General last night till 4 o'clock talking constantly and incessantly for hours on religion," Garfield wrote home in early 1863: "If we did not sleep till ten or twelve in the morning I should be worn out."[141] Like a spiritual retreat from everyday routines, camp life allowed some space for a focused exchanged of religious views that could lead to a genuine appreciation of diversity. Although Garfield dismissed Rosecrans's rosary soon after he arrived as "a dirty looking string of friars beads," he came eventually to praise Rosecrans for his "spirit

[141] Garfield to Lucretia Garfield, Feb. 13, 1863, in ibid., p. 233.

of muscular religion."[142] Yet even with the prominence of religion in this military relationship, Garfield finally measured Rosecrans on his loyalty to the Union. "I think I have seen the interior of General Rosecrans' nature as fully as I ever did that of any man I ever knew," he wrote to Congressman Salmon Chase, "and am glad to tell you that I believe in him, that he is sound to the bone on the great questions of the war and the way it should be conducted."[143] The war enriched Garfield's understanding of Catholicism through his encounter with a passionate and articulate Catholic. But the primary business of combat in the end cast spirituality within a framework of worldly objectives.

Garfield's experience with Rosecrans typified the way religious concerns balanced precariously in the midst of competing secular issues during the Civil War. This coexistence of sacred and profane perspectives not only signified that the Victorians lived at a crucial moment of transition in time, but revealed how much they expected languages restricted to the discussion of human affairs to assume the task of defining life's purposes. What was most unprecedented in Garfield's evaluation of Rosecrans was the way his judgment finally centered on the general's political acceptability on "the great questions of the war" and reduced Rosecrans' piety to a peripheral role. Yet in the process, questions pertaining to military strategy, patriotism, and nationhood gained an intellectual and emotional weight reserved for ideas that establish ultimate values. The Civil War did not initiate this redirection of Americans' attention from religion to politics and, more specifically, from Christianity to republicanism as the key public medium for the exploration of their common goals as a people. But the sectional crisis both revealed the depth of Americans' involvement in civil issues and enhanced the authority of political institutions as tools for defining national objectives. The transformation did not occur on an abstract level. As churches less effectively sustained public dialogue, the Victorians turned to partisan contests, government initiatives, and ideologically charged debate as a forum appropriate to their mundane ambitions. No cause since the founding of the republic so thoroughly demonstrated the power of politics to arbitrate basic cultural decisions as did the Civil War. Whether the Victorians found themselves on the winning or losing side, the war heightened their awareness of the keen competition political activity and symbols offered religion.[144]

The Victorians' embrace of the Civil War as a forum for political debate of deep philosophical resonance was one expression of their broader roman-

---

[142] Garfield to Lucretia Garfield, Jan. 26, 1863, Garfield to Salmon P. Chase, Feb. 15, 1863, in ibid., pp. 226, 235. Rosecrans had converted from Episcopalianism to Catholicism in the winter of 1845–46 while teaching at West Point. See Sylvester Rosecrans to William Rosecrans, Jan. [ca.26] 1846, William Starke Rosecrans Papers, Box 65, UCLA Special Collections, University of California, Los Angeles.

[143] Garfield to Chase, Feb. 15, 1863, in ibid., p. 235.

[144] For a more extensive discussion of the relation of Victorian religion and politics, see Chapter 5.

ticism. Time and again, this generation asked worldly activities, and the languages used to describe them, to answer their profound need for a clear sense of their own value. Certainly the Civil War promised to restore the inner quickening that came with commitment to elevated goals. But the Victorians were as alive to the promises of everyday life as they were eager for the possible inner rewards offered by participation in extraordinary events. Among the many secular efforts to which they turned, careers were one pursuit from which they demanded a return in satisfaction equal to that once supplied by religious faith.

∽☞

2

Work

Why should we be in such desperate haste to succeed, and in such desperate
enterprises?

Henry David Thoreau, 1854

Careers in Victorian America absorbed much of the task of self-definition
that past generations expected religion to perform. At the same time that
muted piety provoked questions about where now to find a sense of purpose,
the Protestant ethic remained strong enough to direct the Victorians to see
the economy as a product of personal will, consisting of malleable relations
that might be used to forge one's identity. Tempting prospects for the middle
classes for money-making, social mobility, and material gratification reinforced the Victorians' impression that earning a living might be a source
of fulfillment. Yet middle-class labor contained problems along with its
promises. Extravagant ambitions stirred by economic opportunities were
worrisome to people still committed in principle to an inherited ethic of
steady labor for modest gain. As troublesome as contradictions between
beliefs and desires, outward circumstances resisted the Victorians' determination to fashion meaning from work. Caught between the constraints of
tradition, represented by successful and intrusive fathers, and an unnerving
sense of how narrow modern specialized work might be, young Victorians
choosing careers experienced several forms of personal crisis. Precisely because
work bore new emotional burdens, settling on vocations took on the traits
of individual religious upheavals.[1]

---

[1] The best assessment of the subjective dimensions of nineteenth-century middle-class labor is Bledstein, *The Culture of Professionalism: The Middle Class and the Development of Higher Education in America*
(1976), esp. ch. 5. For the classic statement of the Protestant ethic and an explanation of the Victorians'
personalized view of society, see, respectively, Max Weber, *The Protestant Ethic and the Spirit of Capitalism,*
trans. Talcott Parsons (New York: Scribner's, 1958), esp. ch. 5, and Daniel Walker Howe, "Victorian
Culture in America," in Howe, ed., *Victorian America* (1976), esp. pp. 22–5. Perhaps one reason the
Victorians continued to see economic relations as human products well into the nineteenth century was
the importance of family capital to individual advancement. See, e.g., Johnson, *A Shopkeeper's Millennium:*

These were the subjective imperatives that impelled the Victorians to seek direction in labor. But it is also essential to note the technological and social conditions that helped to set the terms of their struggle. In the course of lives that spanned much of the nineteenth century, the Victorians in this study saw a rudimentary industrial technology based on water power and wooden construction succeeded by an economy that depended on coal for fuel and on iron and later steel for building material. Similarly, urban workshops relying on handicraft skills and rural factories scattered among farming communities were superseded by industrial plants in cities that were linked to the countryside in a reciprocal exchange of raw materials and finished goods by a dense network of railroads.[2] Middle-class Victorians were not always involved directly in these tremendous changes in industry and commerce. But most of them profited by the growing range of choices that the transformation created, as new opportunities appeared on the fringe of productive activity in, for example, politics, education, and the arts. The social prominence of the people analyzed here permitted them to experience this economic transition with the hope that ambitions would be realized and, particularly, with the expectation that the satisfactions of a career might fill inner spaces left vacant by receding faith. In that sense, their drive to make labor serve intangible longings was the privilege of prosperous classes. But precisely because of the insistent demands they made on work, they were sensitive, too, to such pressures of modern careers as the routine required for maximum output. In sum, the Victorians encountered the ongoing in-

---

Society and Revivals in Rochester, New York, 1815–1837 (1978), pp. 21–8, and Wyatt-Brown, *Southern Honor: Ethics and Behavior in the Old South* (1982), esp. ch. 7. Recent studies of the development of bureaucracies in the Civil War period include Hall, *The Organization of American Culture, 1700–1900: Private Institutions, Elites, and the Origins of America* (1982), esp. pt. 3; Aron, *Ladies and Gentlemen of the Civil Service: Middle-Class Workers in Victorian America* (1987), esp. pt. 2; and, in the context of southern plantations, Oakes, *The Ruling Race: A History of American Slaveholders* (1982), ch. 6. George M. Fredrickson argues that the war experience enhanced northern intellectuals' appreciation of social organization, in *The Inner Civil War: Northern Intellectuals and the Crisis of the Union* (1965), esp. chs. 7, 13. Other key works on northern attitudes toward labor during the midcentury period include Foner, *Free Soil, Free Labor, Free Men: The Ideology of the Republican Party before the Civil War* (1970), esp. chs. 1–2, and Rogers, *The Work Ethic in Industrial America, 1850–1920* (1978), esp. ch. 1.

[2] Among many excellent works on the transformation in the production and distribution of material goods during the nineteenth century and the social implications of that change, see Clark, *The Roots of Rural Capitalism: Western Massachusetts, 1780–1860* (1990); Hahn, *The Roots of Southern Populism: Yeoman Farmers and the Transformation of the Georgia Upcountry, 1850–1890* (1983); Hahn and Prude, eds., *The Countryside in the Age of Capitalist Transformation: Essays in the Social History of Rural America* (1985); Wilentz, *Chants Democratic: New York City and the Rise of the American Working Class, 1788–1850* (1984); Stansell, *City of Women: Sex and Class in New York, 1789–1860* (1986); Pease and Pease, *The Web of Progress: Private Values and Public Style in Boston and Charleston, 1828–1843* (1985); Mumford, *The Brown Decades: A Study of the Arts in America, 1865–1895* (1955), esp. ch. 2; Livesay, *Andrew Carnegie and the Rise of Big Business* (1975); and Soltow, *Men and Wealth in the United States, 1850–1870* (1975). To set American economic developments in international perspective, see the comprehensive works of Hobsbawm, *The Age of Revolution, 1789–1848* (1962); *The Age of Capital, 1848–1875* (1975); and *The Age of Empire, 1875–1914* (1987).

dustrial revolution from a perspective conditioned by their social status, and it is in light of their outward situation that an account of their determination to make careers yield inner rewards may best be seen.[3]

This chapter examines American Victorians' thinking and behavior with respect to work. While their religious crisis provides the broad framework in which to interpret their career decisions, a second context for their strategies for labor was economic in nature and consisted of inherited values and family resources. In both their ideas and experience, the Victorians faced contradictions created by the demands they made on the legacies they received from the past. Intellectually, they wanted to hold onto the Protestant ethic, yet they were as forcibly pulled by desires for boundless wealth, lavish goods, and consuming tasks. Socially, they used family wealth in a setting of expanding options to build distinguished careers, but they expected so great a personal return from their vocations that they chafed at parental pressures.

The Civil War was seized for its perceived power to solve these dilemmas. Here was the chance to devote oneself wholeheartedly to work for high-minded goals, free from mundane complexities. In everyday life, the Victorians contended with self-centered interests, materialism, and routinization in the course of their search to find satisfaction in labor. In wartime society, in contrast, private glory promised to be consistent with the public good, and all effort seemed to be redeemed by association with ennobling ideals such as liberty and union. Perhaps it is not surprising that work pursued during the Civil War fulfilled the Victorians' far-reaching expectations only in part. More problematically, expanding mass production and bureaucratic organization after the war increasingly restricted a man's ability to make his career a tool for exploring commitments. Against this background of narrowing practical options, however, memories of worthy tasks performed during the Civil War became an imaginative focus for the Victorians that fostered emotional resolution.

Two decisions of emphasis affect this discussion, a concentration on men and an attention to regional differences. Although the Victorian women in this study were unusually affluent and accomplished, much of their work ultimately remained family-centered, unpaid, and repetitive by virtue of rendering service rather than progressive in the sense of forwarding personal and public advancement. Labor thus domestically grounded allowed less space for manipulation to achieve individual gratification than did men's public careers. In effect excluded from probing a vocation's rewards, as much by their self-restraint as by broad social controls, Victorian women, like their mothers and their grandmothers, continued to seek self-definition through their homes and kin, and it is in a later chapter on Victorian families

---

[3] For a discussion of the way in which these individuals may be considered part of the middle classes, see the Introduction.

that a more extensive discussion of women's work may be found.[4] More pragmatically, too, I have limited gender questions in the interest of probing sectional differences. Victorians living in the North, South, East, and West shared a basic outlook, but in no two places was the role that work played in people's self-conceptions exactly the same. This is especially clear in the way Victorians thought about labor.

A WAR OF COMMITMENTS

American Victorians held three traditional beliefs about work: labor forged bonds of obligation guaranteed by personal honor, public usefulness validated private effort, and steady application assured social order. Overall, they thought community standards should mediate individual efforts, and they saw moderation as the prescribed mood. As Victorian men entered the marketplace, however, their practice ran counter to conviction too often for inner comfort, as they increasingly allowed self-interest to eclipse social duty. More seriously, a nascent sense that immodest ambition and feverish work might be acceptable contested the older ethic's hegemony. The changing role of religion in the Victorians' lives informed this conflict between old and new commitments. Whereas the Protestant view of labor as a public service and private discipline shaped inherited convictions, it was religion's diminished power to meet inward needs that fueled the Victorians' drive to squeeze from their livelihoods all possible gratifications.[5]

Expanding markets in mid-nineteenth-century America meant that an individual's work was increasingly performed without reference to known consumers. Yet the Victorians' understanding of their efforts stood in tension with emerging conditions, because they saw the products of their labor as personal contributions to communities. Entrepreneurs offered their services in a spirit of trust that may be explained by Bertram Wyatt-Brown's concept of honor as a bond of obligation in traditional societies between an individual

[4] Key studies of women's private and public activities that span the Civil War period include Ginzberg, *Women and the Work of Benevolence: Morality, Politics, and Class in the Nineteenth-Century United States* (1990); Hewitt, *Women's Activism and Social Change: Rochester, New York, 1822–1872* (1984); and Epstein, *The Politics of Domesticity: Women, Evangelism, and Temperance in Nineteenth-Century America* (1981).

[5] Recent work on economic values helps to clarify communal elements in the American tradition, obscured by the individualistic emphasis of Weber's interpretation of Protestantism and the readings he inspired. As colonial Protestants built on older folk traditions, they strongly voiced a corporate ethic that reinforced communal habits, as explained by Edmund S. Morgan in *The Puritan Dilemma: The Story of John Winthrop* (Boston: Little, Brown, 1958), esp. p. xii. Recent studies that recognize the persistence of economic communalism in nineteenth-century America include Clark, *Roots of Rural Capitalism*, esp. pt. 4; Wyatt-Brown, *Southern Honor*, chs. 2–4; Hahn, *Roots of Southern Populism*, ch. 2; Hahn and Prude, eds., *Countryside in the Age of Capitalist Transformation*, esp. pp. 3–21; and Faragher, *Sugar Creek: Life on the Illinois Prairie* (1986), pt. 4. Other historians, however, emphasize the rise of an economic liberalism that existed in tension with traditional attitudes. This viewpoint has been argued strongly by Oakes, in *Slavery and Freedom: An Interpretation of the Old South* (1990).

and the group.[6] Victorian investment bankers, for example, were sufficiently modern to seek profits without producing a useful commodity. But they felt a private duty to their customers nonetheless. As manager of a San Francisco bank in the 1850s, William Tecumseh Sherman covered losses of more than $100,000 of friends whose money he had invested, because, according to one biographer, he felt morally responsible. In Philadelphia, Jay Cooke paid debts of the firm of which he was a partner from his own pocket before he left the business after the Panic of 1857. Southerners, too, believed that ethics should regulate economic relations. John Gabriel Guignard of South Carolina intimated that human consideration ought to mediate market forces when he criticized his cotton brokers in 1866 as *"exacting"* creditors, un-principled for charging "interest through out our bloody war."[7] Although economic practice most likely diverged frequently from an ideal of personal obligation, the Victorians remained faithful intellectually to communal values.

Closely tied to the notion that work was an exchange between honest men was the idea that labor must be socially useful. Even when the Victorians disagreed about how entrepreneurship affected utility, most believed that public benefit was the measure of value. John Gabriel Guignard was offended that his brokers' personal gain was at odds with the common good. Frederick Law Olmsted, in contrast, was convinced that commercial wealth in the North justified itself by funding social improvements, particularly roads, houses, and schools. In his polemical travel narratives published collectively as *The Cotton Kingdom* in 1861, Olmsted indicted slaveholders for misdi-recting most profits to private use in the single-minded acquisition of slaves.[8] Just as these men judged business by its contribution to collective well-being, others weighed their own careers in the same terms. William Moore worked as a surveyor in Los Angeles with daunting application, but imposed such rigorous standards of social usefulness that self-satisfaction was rare. "After ten years of work," he wrote in his diary during an irrigation project in 1869, "I have succeeded in getting something begun which I think will be of use to the people of Los Angeles."[9] Oliver Otis Howard of Maine, who came from a family of staunch evangelical Whigs committed to temperance and abolition, had a hard time convincing himself that his West Point training and duties as a professional soldier served society. As a young soldier,

[6] For Wyatt-Brown's definition of honor, see *Southern Honor,* esp. pp. xvi, 45–7.

[7] Guignard to Adams and Frost, Oct. 8, 1866, in Childs, ed., *Planters and Business Men: The Guignard Family of South Carolina, 1795–1930,* (1957), p. 112. The italics found in this and subsequent quotations appear in the original texts. On Sherman and Cooke, see Merrill, *William Tecumseh Sherman* (1971), p. 119, and Larson, *Jay Cooke: Private Banker* (1936), p. 85.

[8] For Olmsted's approval of northern civic culture and a characteristic critique of the poverty of southern public life, see *The Cotton Kingdom: A Traveller's Observations on Cotton and Slavery in the American Slave States* (1861), ed. Schlesinger, intro. Powell (1984), pp. 21–2, 422–5.

[9] Jan. 29, Diary, 1869, William Moore Papers.

he wrote nervous, self-justifying letters to his mother on the virtue of army life, arguing that philosophical nonresistance served only the reformer's soul while combat benefited the nation. Eventually, Howard moved to resolve his problem of conscience by applying a military-type administration to public service as head the Freedman's Bureau.[10]

The idea that steady labor secured social discipline was the point of the Protestant ethic most often cited by the Victorians. Here the nature of the common good was clarified by extolling regularity and order. Yet the Victorians' practice stood at variance with the original meaning of the religious injunction to labor. Whereas diligence in one's calling was a personal moral commitment in classic Protestantism, Victorians who prescribed regular tasks for their social subordinates at times found it difficult to engage in routine effort themselves. John William DeForest spent nearly a decade casting about for a career. Yet on a trip to Syria in 1846 to visit his brother's mission, he found fault with the natives' laziness, with no visible sense of hypocrisy. Writing home on the "curious spectacle" of the construction for Ramadan of ritual swings, DeForest observed "how much harder these indolent Moslems worked in amusing themselves than they could have been forced to do in manual labor."[11] Before and after the Civil War, northern Victorians planning the future of freed slaves favored arrangements that forced blacks to work. Frederick Law Olmsted recommended apprenticeships, while Oliver Otis Howard lent the authority of the Freedman's Bureau to the use of contracts. Similarly, when William Tecumseh Sherman contemplated the rebellious potential of former Confederate troops in 1865, he made explicit the belief that labor sustained public order, arguing that southern soldiers must return quickly to " 'positions of industry' " lest they form "numberless bands of desperadoes [who] care not for danger and its consequences."[12] So intent was Sherman on the task of reconstruction that he may have missed the irony that his career in the peacetime army was hardly disciplined, but

---

[10] McFeely, *Yankee Stepfather: General O. O. Howard and the Freedmen* (1968), esp. p. 34.

[11] DeForest to Andrew DeForest, Oct. 5, John William DeForest Papers.

[12] Sherman to Ulysses Grant, Apr. 25, quoted in Sherman, *Memoirs of General William T. Sherman by Himself* (1875), 2:362. On Olmsted's recommendation that freed slaves work in "farm-hospitals" supervised by overseers and Howard's use of contracts in the Freedman's Bureau, see *Cotton Kingdom*, p. 566, and McFeely, *Yankee Stepfather*, ch. 8. So strongly did both men feel about industry as the groundwork of social stability that these views displaced their commitments to free labor expressed elsewhere. That independent labor was the only real source of wealth was a leading idea of Olmsted's *Cotton Kingdom*, while Howard saw earning a livelihood as a key component of black liberty, as he wrote in the *Autobiography of Oliver Otis Howard* (1907), 2:225. Although Howard tried to resolve his ideas by seeing contracts as a discipline for independence, both he and Olmsted swung between an older view of work as a component of communal well-being and an emerging perspective on work as a basis of self when they contemplated a social minority. To understand efforts to impose work on subordinates as part of a conflict between value systems should lend subtlety to interpretations of relations between unequals that emphasize motives of social control. For a critical exploration of that much-used concept, see Lawrence Frederick Kohl, "The Concept of Social Control and the History of Jacksonian America," *Journal of the Early Republic* 5 (1985): 21–34.

was disrupted by commodity and real estate speculations, as well as his interlude as a banker, all aimed at wealth exceeding the merely "good maintenance" of an officer at which he continuously chafed.[13]

Southern Victorians acted sufficiently often on this set of assumptions that made labor a duty essential to community order to signal the existence of a core of economic principles that transcended regional bounds. When John Gabriel Guignard specified in a contract with his freedmen in 1865 that he would supply food in return for labor, he spoke not only from the necessity of limited resources but from a tradition of reciprocity in which work underwrote personal bonds.[14] Yet southern Victorians were less inclined than northerners either to make labor's virtue an explicit value or to worry about their own usefulness. Most did not slight discussion of labor because they adhered to a contrary ethic of leisure. A biographer of Jabez Curry of Alabama, a man who was a planter, lawyer, politician, minister, and educator during a long working life, wrote that he found his subject's industry appalling, noting with awe Curry's ability to write in any circumstance either at home or abroad.[15] Rather, southerners' difficulty lay in extolling the benefits of labor in a context where working bore multiple meanings. In the North, the rhetoric of the Protestant ethic conveyed an image of mutual exchange in a community of men equal by virtue of their freedom. But the same language in the South mixed a kindred view of white society with problematic reminders that work involved dependency as well. If the work ethic was thus marred by ambiguity for southerners, it is also possible that as members of more traditional communities, where identity depended as much on peer opinion as on private conviction of inner worth, they had less need for a self-validating notion of service.[16] Despite these sectional differences in the transformation of labor into ideology, however, southern Victorians were not exempt from the stress that modern expectations imposed on inherited ideals.

American Victorians hungered for money, goods, and occupation with an insatiable longing at odds with the measured tone of traditional mores. Whereas fitness of means and ends was the watchword when communal well-being prescribed individual choices, this generation pursued careers in a mood of excess that obscured growing uncertainty about goals by immersion in the process of labor. An intensely acquisitive temper was the Victorians'

---

[13] Sherman to Ellen Sherman, early 1850s, quoted in Merrill, *Sherman*, p. 84.

[14] Contract dated Aug. 1, in Childs, ed., *Planters and Business Men*, pp. 106–8.

[15] Rice, *J. L. M. Curry: Southerner, Statesman, and Educator* (1949), p. 169.

[16] On social sources of self-esteem in the South, see Wyatt-Brown, *Southern Honor*, esp. pp. 45–7. The clearest recent argument for southern industriousness is Oakes, *Ruling Race*, esp. ch. 3. Whereas I suggest that there was more difference between the sections in the expression of work values than in behavior and its underlying premises, C. Vann Woodward has made a contrary case for the actual devaluation of labor among white southerners, in "The Southern Ethic in a Puritan World" in his *American Counterpoint: Slavery and Racism in the North–South Dialogue* (1971), pp. 13–46.

most common modern trait, and though men have sought riches as long as there has been a prospect of wealth, the ambitions of the Victorians were shaped by a romantic spirit that lent a fairy-tale quality to visions of financial gain. As coal-powered technology revolutionized production in the midcentury decades and entrepreneurs funded new firms by the sale of securities, fancies of sudden plenty acquired without effort became real enough possibilities to fire the Victorians' desires. "Oh, for $100,000 – well invested," swooned George Templeton Strong, the New York lawyer, in his journal in 1851: "A skilful operation resulting in an enormous profit with no risk has all the charm for me now of poetry or romance."[17] Andrew Carnegie was so extraordinarily adept as an entrepreneur that he realized rewards of which others merely dreamed. Yet he shared his peers' mood of nearly incredulous enthusiasm when he greeted his first successful speculation in 1856, he recalled in his autobiography, in the language of fantasy: " 'Eureka,' I cried, 'Here's the goose that lays the golden eggs.' "[18] The discovery of gold in California reinforced the Victorians' impression that they lived within sight of magical vistas. Samuel McCullough, a carpenter from New Jersey who wrote home from Sacramento to his future wife that he had known "enough drudgery in this world" to look sharply for the main chance, predicted that he would soon have "enough [money] to enable us to live anywhere without labor."[19]

The Victorians perceived the clash between their aspirations and the work ethic. Some men castigated themselves for their ambitions. William Tecumseh Sherman thrashed uncomfortably throughout his career between industriousness based on civic responsibility and wide-eyed speculations to support ample tastes. "I suppose I am justly punished for giving up my [army] commission for which I was well qualified," he wrote when he failed as a banker in the 1850s. But in the 1870s, he disappointed himself once again by borrowing money, "a thing I hoped *never* to do."[20] It was much more common, however, for Victorian men to work to effect a reconciliation in rhetoric and in fact between their ambitions and values, a strategy that

---

[17] Sept. 5, *The Diary of George Templeton Strong*, ed. Nevins and Thomas (1952), 2:67. On changes in technology and capitalization, respectively, see Mumford, *Brown Decades,* p. 62, and Livesay, *Carnegie,* esp. pp. 30–1.

[18] Quoted in Livesay, *Carnegie,* p. 46.

[19] McCullough to Caroline [Pumyea?], Jan. 31, 1858, Samuel McCullough Papers. Although it is difficult to measure the acquisitive aspirations of one period against another, it is possible to say that Mark Twain and Charles Dudley Warner recognized the outlandish quality of Victorian expectations in their fable, *The Gilded Age: A Tale of Today* (1873; reprint, New York: New American Library, 1969).

[20] Sherman to John Sherman, ca. 1857, quoted in Merrill, *Sherman,* p. 58; Sherman to unidentified correspondent, quoted in ibid., p. 357. Whereas I stress the way middle-class aspirations challenged the work ethic, Daniel Rogers documents how emerging industrial conditions made old values increasingly irrelevant during the same period, as well as how the middle classes even then clung to traditional rhetoric. See Rogers, *Work Ethic,* esp. chs. 1, 5. The underlying message of both arguments is the relentless quality of socioeconomic change, on one level welcomed by the middle classes, that ideas were ultimately made to serve.

attests to their desire to grasp new opportunities without abandoning old truths. John Kinkade, a native of Ohio, tried to convince himself of the justice of making "a fortune" by arguing in a letter to his brother in 1850 that he and his fellow Californians did so in a traditional spirit, adhering to an "industrous & equinomical" regimen that required "[laying] aside their satins & [taking] hold of the pick & shovel in good faith."[21] Andrew Carnegie forged an agreement on a grand scale between his belief in work's social utility and his quest for wealth when he deliberately diverted capital in the 1860s and 1870s from financial speculations to the manufacture of valuable commodities, iron and steel. Although the technological advance that he sponsored benefited a society divided by race, class, and ethnicity so unevenly that the imperfect match between his practice and communal values is painfully clear, Carnegie's motive to build private profits while promoting the common good epitomized the dual focus of Victorian culture.[22]

The Victorians' aspirations assumed grand proportions not only in response to their economy's real possibilities, but in the face of questions of identity less clearly settled by traditional sources of meaning, most critically religion, than in the past. The intensity of their need for financial reward as a tool for self-validation can be measured in three ways: the pervasiveness of material goals, personal despondency at failure, and the use of luxury for self-display.

Virtually none of these Victorian men disdained money-making, a sign not only of the strength of their acquisitive longings, but of their inclination to use entrepreneurship to test their worth. Most dramatically, even communitarians in the utopian tradition relaxed the antipathy earlier reformers felt between ideals and worldly business by now seeking profits along with intangible goals. Josiah Grinnell, born in Vermont, helped to found an Iowa community in 1854 to promote temperance, abolition, and education. At the same time, he kept one-quarter of the town's land for his private development. Cyrus Holliday moved from Pennsylvania to Kansas the same year to secure Free Soil interests, acting as an agent of the New England Emigrant Aid Company for a time. He also brought $20,000 for personal investment. John Wesley North, a peripatetic promoter of blended reform and profit-seeking schemes, cited northern "duty" to assist reconstruction when he set up an iron foundry and community in Tennessee after the war. Even so, he was no less moved by the conviction that "a fortune can be made at it."[23]

---

[21] Kinkade to James Kinkade, Mar. 21, 1850, John Thompson Kinkade Papers. Variant spellings that appear in this and subsequent quotations appear in the original texts.

[22] Livesay, *Carnegie,* pp. 71–5. Carnegie's extensive philanthropy similarly grew from his civic commitments. See ibid., pp. 127–8.

[23] North to Ann North, Jan. 8, Mar. 7, 1866, John Wesley North Papers. On Grinnell, see Payne,

With success so crucial to self-esteem, failure triggered personal crises. North was more a dreamer than businessman, and when successive ventures in Minnesota and California as well as Tennessee foundered from a shortage of practical skill, he suffered recurrent emotional breakdowns. John Kinkade's vision of riches in California dimmed more gradually. Still, the sad resignation that accompanied his growing sense of his life's far-diminished significance without wealth is no less poignant for its understatement. He had tried to move on in search of gold, Kinkade wrote to his brother in 1866. But nothing suited, and "so I am yet in my old location and an old dreary one it is [;] but for the whistle of the steam cars on the Pacific Railroad we might as well be in Africa so far as life[,] energy[,] and money-making is concerned."[24]

The Victorians' indulgence in extravagant shows of luxury may be added to these trends to establish a connection between selfhood and wealth. Beyond the simple fact that comfortable means invites spending, Victorians transformed their assets into possessions in ways symbolic of desired identities. Jay Cooke flourished his prosperity with an impresario's flair. He bought a new suit for his first trip home from Philadelphia to Ohio in 1838 and added tokens of success to match his growing financial acumen. Fluted pillars, frescoed ceilings, marble floors, and a massive safe decorated his office after the war, and he constructed a fifty-room mansion for more than a million dollars. Among this group, Cooke was an uncommonly religious man, who conducted family prayers, taught Sunday school, and supervised numerous charities. Yet all of his pious gestures must have fallen short of a sufficient statement of his self-conception, because in effect he asked to be known not only for his faith but for his power to gratify lavish desires. Indeed, Cooke's dependency on these material signs can be weighed by their practical harm to his career. Investments in palatial buildings tied up capital and brought

Josiah Bushnell Grinnell (1938), ch. 5. On Holliday, see Holliday to Mary Holliday, Dec. 24, 1854, and [Fred G. Gurley?], "The Man with the White Hat," in *Cyrus K. Holliday: Dedication of the Cyrus K. Holliday Plaque, Santa Fe Station, Topeka, Kansas, April 3, 1949*, Cyrus Kurtz Holliday Papers. Communitarians perhaps always stand in uneasy relation to society, seeking a role as harbingers of progress while also firmly convinced of their status as a chosen body of people at odds with a sinful world, as Arthur Bestor explains in *Backwoods Utopias: The Sectarian Origins and the Owenite Phase of Communitarian Socialism in America, 1663–1829*, 2d rev. ed. (Philadelphia: University of Pennsylvania Press, 1970), pp. 3–4. Among earlier communities, even those sufficiently attentive to their practical impact to admit private profit evolved complex arrangements for profit taking to avoid compromising a tone of high-mindedness and mutuality. See, e.g., my discussion of Brook Farm and American Fourierism in the 1840s, in *Transcendentalism as a Social Movement, 1830–1850* (1981), pp. 130–61. The Victorian communities made far less effort to distance themselves from conventional capitalism by organizational devices. For an overview of other communities predating the midcentury period, see Kern, *An Ordered Love: Sex Roles and Sexuality in Victorian Utopias – The Shakers, the Mormons, and the Oneida Community* (1981).

[24] Kinkade to James Kinkade, July 26, Kinkade Papers. On North, see Stonehouse, *John Wesley North and the Reform Frontier* (1965), pp. 11, 118.

adverse publicity that could not have cushioned his business collapse in 1873. Cooke made himself someone worth watching at what he must have judged a valuable risk.[25]

Not only did the Victorians bring new urgency of purpose to acquisition, but they indulged an impulse to immerse themselves in labor, as if to mute hard questions of life's goals in industry's consuming routine. With faithful application so central to the Protestant ethic, the members of this generation slipped toward compulsion to work without the struggles of conscience that call attention to their material ambitions. Nonetheless, a close look at the mood in which they labored indicates, first, the relentless temper that informed their search for careers and, second, the unyielding drive with which they pursued them.

For Henry Lee Higginson of Boston, the traditional imperative to find the calling most suitable to his talents mediated his unconventional quest for work that would provide personal direction in the most profound sense. Vacillating throughout the 1850s between prospective careers in music and business, Higginson understood his dilemma in classic terms: music, the less practical choice, enabled him to "improv[e] my own powers, which is every man's duty," far more than did commerce, a calling "not satisfying to the inner man."[26] Yet as Higginson turned over the issues repeatedly in letters and journals, he unwittingly revealed that his occupational choice was so tortured because weighed down by the task of supplying his life's purpose. "Being in a counting-room and reading is of no use – *learn one thing* and then you can go on without effort – else life is damned nonsense," he wrote in 1857, and he continued to seek resolution to this critical issue of identity throughout the war and beyond.[27] William Potter, the son of a Quaker farmer, was similarly tormented by his career decision, and his reliance on mystical language in his journal to describe the "mysterious *drawings* within me" toward the ministry signaled the emotional burden he asked his vocation to carry. Indeed, settling on a profession was so like taking possession of a charmed object capable of untangling difficulties that the issue of what occupation Potter would choose overshadowed the problem of what doctrine he would believe. Three weeks after he expressed his inclination

[25] Larson, *Cooke*, pp. 20, 180–1, 195, 201, 408–9. The Victorians were not the first generation to use tokens of wealth to etch a visible identity, a point implicitly made by the historical breadth of Thorstein Veblen's classic argument on conspicuous consumption, *The Theory of the Leisure Class: An Economic Study of Institutions* (1899; reprint, New York: New American Library, 1953), ch. 4. Still, as a quickly changing and prosperous culture, mid-nineteenth-century America provided unusual opportunities for the manipulation of tangible symbols to depict newly won social status. Historians who comment on the Victorians' taste for masking include Harris, *Humbug: The Art of P. T. Barnum*, esp. ch. 8, and Halttunen, *Confidence Men and Painted Women: A Study of Middle-Class Culture in America, 1830–1870* (1982), esp. ch. 6.

[26] Higginson to George Higginson, Sept., 1857, quoted in Perry, *Life and Letters of Henry Lee Higginson* (1921), p. 108.

[27] Diary, Mar. 7, 1857, quoted in ibid., p. 98.

to pursue a religious vocation, Potter posed these rhetorical questions in his private record: "But what am I to preach? With what sect? What creed?"[28] Potter acted on the untraditional hope that if he gained assurance in vocational purpose, spiritual uncertainties would abate in turn.

Whether or not labor answered deeper dilemmas, American Victorians understood the therapeutic effect of engrossing tasks. Time and again, biographers of the Victorians acknowledge their subjects' awesome production of only moderately valuable works, as if some crucial spark of creativity were either dimmed by incessant labor or were so modest from the start that compulsive application helped divert attention from their imperfect grasp of basic truths. Edward Everett Hale, a Unitarian minister, reformer, magazine editor, and writer of fiction and history, in one decade (1886–96) turned out ninety signed articles in monthly journals, 200 in newspapers, as well as several books. But, according to Jean Holloway, he also accepted the limitations of intellectual temper that made him a popularizer. The energy and output of the liberal Congregationlist leader, Lyman Abbott, nearly matched Hale's. Between 1865 and 1870 alone, Abbott produced a book on Jesus, a biblical commentary, an edition of sermons, and a devotional manual, and acted as a contributing editor to *Harper's Magazine*. A private library that eventually contained 6,000 volumes supported his efforts. Even so, Ira Brown concludes that Abbott cannot be judged a probing scholar. Perry Westbrook evaluates the essays that compose most of the twenty-three volumes of works of John Burroughs, a writer inspired by Whitman and Emerson, as "mediocre."[29]

Perhaps these Victorians sensed their limited depth. If so, they must have reaped sufficient reward from their work to motivate their persistent effort, not simply profits and prestige, but inner benefit as well. In fact, they relied on the psychic stability of a work schedule in which something was always produced, no matter what quality. William Dean Howells could not altogether avert the nervous breakdowns to which he was prone, but he helped to secure his self-control and self-esteem by his habitual production of 1,000 to 1,500 words every morning. Men such as Edward Everett Hale, who missed working so much on vacation that he acquired a country house where he could write, must have been oppressed by sensations of aimlessness on

[28] Apr. 6 and 30, 1856, Diary, 1853–57, William James Potter Papers. Despite the importance of choosing a calling in traditional Protestantism, there was far less actual choice of vocation in the patriarchal, precommerical society of colonial America than there was in the Victorian period. One of the problems faced by the nineteenth-century generation was simply the range of choice, a difficulty discussed more fully later in the chapter. On the Puritan notion of a calling, see Edmund S. Morgan, *The Puritan Family: Religion and Domestic Relations in Seventeenth-Century New England*, rev. ed. (New York: Harper and Row, 1966), pp. 68–75. Burton Bledstein notes the intense emotional need that informed the middle-class search for careers, in *Culture of Professionalism*, p. 196.

[29] Holloway, *Edward Everett Hale: A Biography* (1956), p. 228; Brown, *Lyman Abbott, Christian Evangelist: A Study of Religious Liberalism* (1953), pp. 238, 53–5, 57; Westbrook, *John Burroughs* (1974), preface (n.p.).

Figure 4.   William Dean Howells (1837–1920). The artist, Orlando Rowland, captured Howells's industriousness in this pencil and crayon sketch of the novelist seated at his desk in 1890. National Portrait Gallery, Smithsonian Institution.

unstructured days. That Jabez Curry, a southerner, became more disciplined after the war, writing before breakfast and on trains, or, at his most relaxed, reading Shakespeare or Macaulay in stations, measures the demands he made on labor to serve as an emotional buffer against the disappointment of defeat.[30]

To an extent, southern Victorians experienced the drive for wealth and occupation in idiosyncratic terms. Although their ambitions approached the level of fantasy as did those of northerners, they coveted status as much as raw monetary gain, a consequence of their traditional habit of seeing themselves in communities. David Terry, a native of Houston, spoke in letters from California of his land "fever" and expectations of "wealth." Yet in a more measured statement he did not omit his aim for social position, vowing to stay in "this far land" until "fortune shall smile on my efforts to attain independence and station."[31] As an army officer in antebellum New Orleans, Pierre Beauregard welcomed assignments that promised a financial return. At one time, he hoped to market a device he invented to help ships navigate Mississippi mud bars. But it was over a question of rank, his failure to be

[30] Lynn, *William Dean Howells: An American Life* (1970), pp. 252, 282; Holloway, *Hale*, pp. 191–2; Rice, *Curry*, p. 169.

[31] Terry to Cornelia Runnels [Terry], June 29, 1852, Nov. 7, 1851, Apr. 16, 1852, David Smith Terry Papers.

promoted to colonel in 1856, that he became so incensed that he considered accepting a command in a mercenary army in Nicaragua.[32] After the war, it is likely that former Confederate officers seriously considered offers to lead foreign troops, such as George Pickett's invitation from the Khedive of Egypt, as much because of the attraction of displays of power as for promised rewards.[33] Others turned their understanding of symbols of prestige into advertising skills under the duress of necessity. Pickett and Wade Hampton probably no more relished selling their good names, in effect, as insurance brokers in the late 1860s than Beauregard welcomed his job of putting an honest face on the Louisiana lottery as a supervisor of drawings for many years after 1877. Nonetheless, the ability of all three men to peddle their command of images underlines the short distance between southerners' aspirations for place and northerners' dreams of cash.[34]

Indeed, there was more kinship in career aspirations between Victorian men who inhabited different sections than between men and women. Stories of Victorian women who worked feverishly at tasks beyond simple domesticity are common. Like their male peers, women of the prosperous middle classes sought new purposiveness and equilibrium in focused and demanding labor. Repeatedly, however, women contained their ambitions within a framework of selflessness, volunteerism, and family enterprise. The incessant activity of Lyman Abbott's wife, Abby, in support of her husband's career makes it seem that she desired more from life than simply running a household. Although raising the six children she bore between 1859 and 1875 must have absorbed substantial energy, during the same years she chose to second her husband's varied enterprises in equally taxing ways. While Lyman read books on religion and philosophy received by *Harper's* for comment in the "Editor's Table," Abby reviewed the novels and reported to him. She helped with research for his *Dictionary of Religious Knowledge* (1873), did all of the visiting of parishioners at the church where Lyman was minister from 1870 to 1887, and, as "Aunt Patience" of the children's page of her husband's *Christian Union* magazine, wrote 1,300 letters to young correspondents in 1882 alone. Yet despite Abby's intelligence and fortitude, she never asked to ground her selfhood in a sustained paid career for which she might receive credit as an individual. That is not to say her labor provided no personal

[32] Williams, *P.G.T. Beauregard: Napoleon in Grey* (1954), p. 42.

[33] Pickett to LaSalle Pickett, n.d., in *Soldier of the South: General Pickett's War Letters to His Wife*, ed. Inman (1928), pp. 143–4. On former southern and northern soldiers who did join the Egyptian army, see Hesseltine, *The Blue and the Gray on the Nile* (1961). The largest number of Confederate exiles went to Mexico. Most exiles settled as civilian colonists, but some secured military and government positions. See Rolle, *The Lost Cause: The Confederate Exodus to Mexico* (1965), pp. 75–7, 118–20, 131–44. Other work on southern expatriots includes Hill, *The Confederate Exodus to Latin America* (1936), and Hanna and Hanna, *Confederate Exiles in Venezuala* (1960).

[34] Pickett to LaSalle Pickett, n.d., in *Soldier of the South*, ed. Inman, pp. 152–3; Hampton to Thomas L. Preston, Mar. 29, 1873, in Cauthen, ed., *Family Letters of the Three Wade Hamptons, 1782–1901* (1953), p. 146; Williams, *Beauregard*, ch. 18.

Figure 5. Pierre Gustave Toutant Beauregard (1818–93). Confederate general and entrepreneur from Louisiana. Photograph by Alphonse J. Liébert, 1866. National Portrait Gallery, Smithsonian Institution.

reward. But it remained traditional women's work in the sense that it was implicitly defined as part of a family effort.[35]

Some Victorian women explored the possibilities that work offered for self-satisfaction more boldly than did Abby Abbott. Still, nearly all finally circumscribed their experiments within family boundaries. The three women in this group who became actresses – Charlotte Cushman, Priscilla Tyler, and Anna Mowatt – risked a degree of self-display that must have verged on impropriety in a society that still largely identified women with the private sphere. Even so, each one either cloaked or contained her ambition in domestic mores and commitments, as Cushman (who remained single)

[35] Brown, *Abbott,* pp. 53, 56, 59, 71.

publicized her piety, Mowatt professed to work solely to support her disabled husband, and Tyler left the stage after her marriage.[36]

Like these actresses, Louisa May Alcott was curious about the potential significance of labor for women and examined the theme in her odyssey about the search for self-sufficiency of her heroine, Christie Devon, entitled *Work: A Story of Experience* (1872). Issuing a "new Declaration of Independence," Christie sets out as a young woman to become self-supporting, and Alcott observed Christie's progress through jobs as a servant, actress, governess, nurse, and seamstress.[37] Yet in the end, Christie discovers that her initial goal of independence was mistaken. Through labor, "her best teacher, comforter, and friend," she has come to understand the "larger liberty God meant [women] to enjoy": duty to family, to other women, and to God.[38] Now a wife and a mother of forty years instead of a girl of twenty-one, Christie finds her calling in instructing young working women about the moral lessons of labor:

With an impulsive gesture Christie stretched her hands to the friends about her, and with one accord they laid theirs on hers, a loving league of sisters, old and young, black and white, rich and poor, each ready to do her part to hasten the coming of the happy end.

"Me too!" cried little Ruth, and spread her chubby hand above the rest: a hopeful omen, seeming to promise that the coming generation of women will not only receive but deserve their liberty, by learning that the greatest of God's gifts to us is the privilege of sharing His great work.[39]

Alcott's conclusion hovers between a radical feminine alternative to the self-seeking spirit of capitalism and a far more cautious reaffirmation of the traditional community of the family. Either way, Alcott betrayed her discomfort with making selfhood the object of labor and warned women to redirect their ambitions.

Overall, American Victorian women experienced some conflict between a traditional communal work ethic, for them cast in terms of the family, and a yearning to find labor that they could pursue fervently for their own satisfaction. They were far more careful to leash their aspirations, however, than were Victorian men. Yet even when men permitted themselves to chase their ambitions, they were curtailed not only by inherited beliefs but by social pressures presented by parents, education, and the structure of white-collar occupations.

---

[36] Stebbins, *Charlotte Cushman: Her Letters and Memories of Her Life* (1879), ch. 14; Barnes, *The Lady of Fashion: The Life and the Theatre of Anna Cora Mowatt* (1954), chs. 5–11; and Coleman, *Priscilla Cooper Tyler and the American Scene, 1816–1889* (1955), ch. 5.

[37] *Work*, in *Alternative Alcott*, ed. Showalter (1988), p. 239.

[38] Ibid., p. 339.

[39] Ibid., p. 349.

FAMILY, SCHOOLING, BUREAUCRACY, AND THE
TRIALS OF SUCCESS

American Victorian men and, more rarely, women built careers with the aid of their parents' advantages in a culture opening new opportunities for ambition. Chosen for this study as practitioners of white-collar occupations, most of these Victorians took what their fathers acquired as men of stature in provincial communities to establish names for themselves in growing cities and across the nation. Yet ostensible success was strangely paired with persistent irresolution about callings. The Victorians' pattern of achievement was complicated both by their fathers' legacies and by modern labor's restraints, as the members of this generation in effect asked work to assist them in establishing a sense of personal purpose.

Fine prospects for middle-class mobility can be shown by selected figures and representative case histories. Rags-to-riches success stories rarely occurred, because only three of these Victorians ever worked as common farmers or artisans. Most profited by their families' assets of money, education, and connections to improve on their parents' position. Fathers of the men in the study earned livings most often as agricultural employers of slave or free labor (nineteen in number), merchants (nineteen), politicians (seventeen), and attorneys (six), and they commonly engaged in several pursuits (more than one occupation for each man have been counted in the preceding totals if he pursued several activities). The fathers paved the way for children who excelled in the same fields, as well as in more intellectually oriented vocations. Thus men in the Victorian generation found work as politicians (twenty-four), entrepreneurs (twenty-two), attorneys (eighteen), ministers (fourteen), writers (thirteen), agricultural employers (seven), journalists (seven), professional soldiers (six), reformers (six), engineers (five), educators (five), and in several other professions that drew fewer individuals.[40]

To compare generations effectively, these numbers must be read in light of several cautionary words. First, most occupations changed in nature over time. Politics, for example, increasingly involved a lifelong commitment to

[40] See Appendix B for a list of individuals' occupations. I have excluded from the totals the fourteen women studied both to avoid confusing aggregates and to remain consistent with the chapter's focus on men. I have counted separately all the occupations an individual pursued, either simultaneously or successively, to show the comparative strength of employments over two generations and to avoid the misleading practice of pigeonholing men in one calling when in fact, in an era just approaching intense specialization for the middle classes, many engaged in diverse kinds of work. In an effort to achieve a broad view of the middle classes, individuals were selected for this study because they engaged in one or more white-collar occupations. It is important to note, however, that they represented the "old middle class" of independent entrepreneurs and professionals as opposed the "new middle class" of salaried white-collar employees, if one uses the distinction coined by C. Wright Mills, in *White Collar: The American Middle Classes* (New York: Oxford University Press, 1951). The most comprehensive discussion of the nineteenth-century American middle classes is Blumin, *The Emergence of the Middle Class: Social Experience in the American City, 1760–1900* (1989).

a profession in salaried public office rather than occasional service to a community performed in addition to regular labor. Second, succeeding generations might experience similar career patterns in different ways. From the perspective of Victorian men, the fact that thirty of the fifty-one fathers whose work can be identified engaged in more than one occupation, either simultaneously or successively, was an index of the freedom of an earlier economy, and there is evidence of the validity of their view. For themselves, in contrast, the high rate of mobility among careers — forty-seven of sixty-one Victorian men did more than one kind of work — was seen as much as a sign of their discontent as of the range of their choices. Third, the same career pursued in a different social setting might take on new significance. Part of the Victorians' success consisted of making their mark in wider social spheres. The contrast between twelve men who grew up in major cities and thirty-five who spent at least part of their adult lives in such urban centers as New York, Chicago, and New Orleans attests to the Victorians' understanding of how to achieve broad influence.[41] With these thoughts about interpretation in mind, it may be said overall that the Victorians effectively used family inheritance to advance their own prospects, to the point that they acquired the prerogative of acting on their dissatisfaction with one career by moving on to another.

Histories of three individuals from families in the Northeast, South, and Midwest show fairly typical patterns of human choices behind these numerical trends. Priscilla Tyler of Pennsylvania (1816–89), Jabez Curry of Alabama (1825–1903), and Lew Wallace of Indiana (1827–1905) were able to hold on securely enough to inherited advantages to provide well for their children in turn. The grandparents and parents of each bettered themselves by decisions to move. Tyler's father emigrated in 1796 from Britain to New York, where he gained a reputation as an actor and married into a prominent family. His choice of Bristol, Pennsylvania, near Philadelphia, as a suitable place to raise his children in 1819 underlines this generation's preference for the face-to-face society of small to medium-sized towns. The grandfathers of Curry and Wallace also set out from home, in both cases Pennsylvania, near the turn of the century. Curry's grandfather bought land and slaves in Georgia, while Wallace's opened a tavern in Indiana. Their sons became local leaders. William Curry was a planter, merchant, militia colonel, and Democratic state legislator in Lincoln County, Georgia, ambitious enough

---

[41] See Appendix C for a list of individuals' residences. I have counted only men for the sake of consistency in the figures. I offer this comparison for men who lived in major cities as children and adults as an index of the Victorians' increasingly urban orientation. But because I have not counted those who established residences in smaller cities such as New Haven, Connecticut, or towns becoming suburbs such as Cambridge, Massachusetts, it is fair to conclude that more were acquainted with the conditions and customs of city life than these totals might indicate. The cities I have counted are Boston, New York, Philadelphia, Baltimore, Washington, Pittsburgh, Chicago, New Orleans, San Francisco, Los Angeles, London, and Rome.

to send his son to Harvard. David Wallace, a West Point graduate and attorney, moved his family to Indianapolis in 1837, one year after the town's incorporation, when he became the Whig governor of the Indiana Territory.[42]

Their children, the Victorians, achieved regional and national reputations. Priscilla Tyler repeated her father's success by winning acclaim as an actress and marrying a son of President John Tyler of Virginia. Jabez Curry was a planter, politician, and Confederate legislator, who, as a result of the war, lost land and slaves. He gained national respect in the postwar years, however, as a minister, college professor, advocate of black and white education, and Cleveland's ambassador to Spain. Despite their support of the Confederacy, Tyler and Curry preserved sufficient means, particularly in the form of good name and education, to send their sons to college and to marry their daughters well. Their continuing success reflects the security of their social position. Lew Wallace was a West Point graduate and attorney who profited by his northern loyalty to become a Civil War general, Republican politician, and Garfield's ambassador to Turkey. But it was the publication in 1880 of *Ben-Hur,* a best-selling novel that inspired stage adaptations and a film version in 1907, that made Wallace's fortune, as well as a career for his only son as his father's business agent.[43]

To emphasize the Victorians' debt to family resources ought not obscure the role of their own skills and fortuitous circumstances in their advancement. Jesse Grant fit perfectly the civic profile of Victorian fathers, as an enterprising tanner, Mason, and Whig mayor of Georgetown, Ohio. His son, Ulysses, floundered miserably, however, until the chance to command troops in the field evoked his brilliance as a leader and strategist.[44] War was not the only source of opportunity to enhance or replace family advantage. On the contrary, there was an inviting openness to occupational choice for middle-class Victorians that supported individual achievement. Technological innovation served the ambition of men with few personal resources. Mathew Brady, remembered for his Civil War photographs, emerged so quickly from obscure origins that he was nearly illiterate. But his skilled exploitation of new photographic techniques won him fame and wealth in the decade before the war. Ely Parker, a Seneca Indian, was refused admission to the bar because of his race. Yet he advanced through a career in engineering. He graduated

[42] Coleman, *Tyler,* ch. 1–2; Rice, *Curry,* ch. 1; Morseberger and Morseberger, *Lew Wallace: Militant Romantic* (1980), ch. 1. I have not included a representative of the Far West among these biographies because my largely manuscript sources on westerners provide comparatively sketchy family information for those individuals. They seem, however, to have conformed roughly to the general pattern of building careers on family resources. Because none struck it rich through prospecting, they relied on skills they brought with them to make their way. Although two left working-class occupations in the East (a carpenter and printer), three of the seven men who settled on the West Coast were college-educated, as was the husband of Jeanne Carr. Because that proportion was far above the national average, their education indicates solid family resources.

[43] Coleman, *Tyler;* Rice, *Curry;* and Morseberger and Morseberger, *Wallace.*

[44] McFeely, *Grant: A Biography* (1981), esp. pp. 7–8, 67–8.

from Rensselaer Polytechnic Institute as a civil engineer, worked for the army, and through his acquaintance with Grant, in 1869 became commissioner of Indian affairs. Careers in the peacetime army, offering free professional training and good prospects for promotion on an expanding frontier, also aided mobility. As sons of widows, Oliver Otis Howard and William Tecumseh Sherman relied financially on West Point's tuition-free program, and the scramble among academy graduates to get into the Mexican War dramatizes the vocational benefit of territorial conflict. Finally, occupations that served growing leisure time were good risks for talented people. The public's taste for theatergoing was especially striking in light of long-standing Protestant suspicion of dramatic representation. The fact that women could make their mark as actresses is an index of the vocation's flexibility.[45]

Thus the midcentury decades were a time of professional promise for the established middle classes. But along with rising fortunes there was private turmoil about careers. Occupational crises experienced by young men varied in nature among the nation's geographic regions. But all of the Victorians' strategies to add breadth to their vocational choices appeared as answers to their sense that work brought restraints as well as opportunities, an insight particularly troubling to a generation intent on finding personal meaning in labor. The limitations were a blend of perception and reality and were self-created, in part, as well as socially imposed. Because one source of the Victorians' disquiet was the tacit comparison they made between their situation and that of their fathers, patterns of work in the previous generation must first be explored.

Victorian men revered their fathers' accomplishments and imagined that the foundation of their parents' success was the availability of diverse options. They were close to social facts. In the early decades of the century, fathers who built names for themselves from modest beginnings had the advantage of pioneers in an undeveloped economy, moving easily among enterprises comparatively unrestricted by barriers of capital or skill or, for the same reason, developing more than one business at once. In rural and small-town settings, men engaged in related occupations. Near Columbia, South Carolina, Sanders Guignard, the father of two of these Victorians, not only administered family plantations but ran a ferry and brickworks. John Wentworth's father, Paul, served the community of Sandwich, New Hampshire,

[45] Horan, *Mathew Brady: Historian with a Camera* (1955), p. xiv; Parker, *The Life of General Ely S. Parker* (1919), esp. p. 79; McFeely, *Yankee Stepfather*, p. 31; Merrill, *Sherman*, pp. 28–32; Stebbins, *Cushman;* Barnes, *Lady of Fashion;* and Coleman, *Tyler.* On the rise of technological professions, see Bledstein, *Culture of Professionalism*, pp. 193–6. On the growing social presence of the military, see Ambrose, *Duty, Honor, Country: A History of West Point* (1966), ch. 7; Cunliffe, *Soldiers and Civilians: The Martial Spirit in America, 1775–1865* (1968), esp. ch. 5; and Johannsen, *To the Halls of the Montezumas: The Mexican War in the American Imagination* (1985). On the popularity of theater, see Bode, *The Anatomy of American Popular Culture, 1840–1861* (1959), ch. 1.

Figure 6.   Mathew Brady (1823–96). Brady appeared in this daguerreotype taken around 1850 with his wife, Julia (left), and a woman tentatively identified as his sister, Mrs. Haggerty (right). Brady was easily the premier photographer of the Victorian generation. Among many subjects, Brady and his assistants took some of the most memorable photographs of the Civil War. National Portrait Gallery, Smithsonian Institution.

as a dairy farmer and merchant.[46] Cities enhanced the risk of failure as well as success, but to resourceful individuals they seemed repeatedly to offer new chances. In New York, the father of Abram Hewitt turned his skill as a cabinetmaker to furniture manufacturing, then lost his business and worked as a carpenter, mechanic, baker, and jobber or middleman, until he set up a factory to make bedsteads. Hewitt's father-in-law, Peter Cooper, best known for his invention of the engine "Tom Thumb," nearly caricatured the openness of the early urban economy by working as a mechanic, grocer, landlord, glue manufacturer, ironmaster, and inventor of machines ranging from a torpedo to a lawn mower.[47] In addition to other labor, many fathers held political office. Although the posts were often unsalaried, these civic roles contributed to the sons' impressions of their fathers' broad competence. Sanders Guignard was a state treasurer, land commissioner, and court clerk in South Carolina, and Paul Wentworth in New Hampshire was a selectman and justice of the peace.[48]

As the Victorian sons of these fathers faced their own career choices, they approached work as an activity that threatened their freedom, not as the flexible tool for endeavor they believed served men in the past. Although there were some new restrictions on the selection and performance of labor, the Victorians' anxiety about entering vocations was sufficiently incongruous in light of growing opportunities to direct attention to reasons why they could not simply grasp the chances before them. Fears of entrapment arose to a significant extent from an inner conflict between the Victorians' compulsion to etch an identity through labor, inevitably excluding possibilities, and their yearning for great accomplishment. Decision, in other words, was self-creating and self-defeating at once. They responded to the dilemma by manipulating external conditions to secure as much discretion as possible in their working lives, and their strategies varied roughly by region.

Young men in the Northeast prolonged the process of career selection, sometimes for a decade or more, preferring the anxiety of indecision to the constraints of a job. Edward Everett Hale favored the ministry when he graduated from Harvard in 1839, but he feared that parish duties would conflict with self-culture, and he was not ordained until 1846. In the meantime, he only accepted pursuits that gave him self-control without respon-

---

[46] Childs, ed., *Planters and Business Men*, pp. 38–41; Fehrenbacher, *Chicago Giant: A Biography of "Long John" Wentworth* (1957), p. 5. For a view of the opportunities for families on the frontier in the early national period, see, e.g., Johnson, *Shopkeeper's Millennium*, ch. 1, and Ryan, *Cradle of the Middle Class: The Family in Oneida County, New York, 1790–1865* (1981), ch. 1.

[47] Nevins, *Abram S. Hewitt, with Some Account of Peter Cooper* (1935), chs. 1, 4. Although Sean Wilentz shows that early national New York was not without an emerging class structure that could frustrate aspirations, the city at the turn of the century was a comparatively open environment next to the more rigidly differentiated and conflict-ridden society of later decades. See *Chants Democratic*, ch. 1.

[48] Childs, ed., *Planters and Business Men*, p. 16; Fehrenbacher, *Chicago Giant*, p. 5. See also my discussion of the transition from amateur to professional politics in Chapter 5.

sibility, declining Harvard Divinity School for self-directed study, supplying the pulpits of others when he chose, and contributing to journals.[49] Those who stayed in the Northeast usually acquiesced in the end to a single career, discovering more room for maneuver than they had originally imagined. Although Hale served as minister to one Boston church for forty-four years (1856–99), he found that he was able to write on numerous secular and religious subjects, edit a journal, and work for a variety of reforms during his tenure.

One alternative to trying to adapt established occupations to personal desires, however, was to move west to territories invested by dreams with prospects of boundless gratification. Quite typically, John Damon, a native of Waltham, Massachusetts, turned down a lackluster job as a shoestore manager in Chicago to prospect in California for gold. Though he failed to gain wealth, he profited by fewer educational requirements for professional entry when he became a journalist and later a minister, holding positions in California, Oregon, Washington, and British Columbia.[50] Like eastern society a generation before, the transmississippi West offered men of the middle classes a fairly fluid occupational structure.

Southern Victorians before the war were less wary of modern structured occupations than the tedium of agriculture. That is not to say that aspiring whites did not seek to acquire land and slaves for the sake of financial rewards and status, as scholars have noted. Still, many prosperous southerners were too cosmopolitan and too highly trained for urban occupations to rest content with agricultural production. Without breaking ties with the tradition of slave-based agriculture, they distanced themselves from rural life by taking up additional careers. Pierre Beauregard of Louisiana and George Pickett of Virginia did not relinquish their land and slaves when they entered the professional army. But they declined to manage their plantations personally. So did Jabez Curry of Alabama, who delegated care of his crops in order to concentrate on a busy life before the war as a railroad promoter, lawyer, and politician in several Alabama cities and Washington, D.C.[51]

[49] Holloway, *Hale,* chs. 3–5. On other young New Englanders who experienced similar indecision, see Light, *John William DeForest* (1965), chs. 1–2; Edelstein, *Strange Enthusiasm: A Life of Thomas Wentworth Higginson* (1968), ch. 3; Flexner, *Daniel Coit Gilman: Creator of the American Type of University* (1946), ch. 1; Roper, *FLO: A Biography of Frederick Law Olmsted* (1973), chs. 2–7; Perry, *Higginson,* chs. 2–4; and William Potter Diaries, 1847–57, Potter Papers.

[50] For Damon's offer of work, see W. R. Smith to John Damon, Sept. 18, 1854, John Fox Damon Papers. Other work left behind by migrants to California was similarly uninspiring. John Kinkade left teaching in Virginia to prospect for gold, and Charles Maclay welcomed the challenge of being a missionary after acting as a Methodist itinerant with responsibilities as a fund-raiser for a theological seminary. See, respectively, Kinkade to James Kinkade, Dec. 21, 1848, Kinkade Papers, and Maclay, ms. "Article on the Subject of Lending Aid to Dickinson Seminary at Williamsport, Pennsylvania," Mar. 28–Apr. 30, 1849, as well as Maclay to [Dr. McClintock], Mar. 13 1850, Charles Maclay Papers. Kinkade was sufficiently unsettled about his career to acquire a license in Virginia to practice law as well. Maclay expressed his frustration with the denomination's system of soliciting donations in his letter to his superior, Dr. McClintock.

[51] Williams, *Beauregard,* esp. pp. 40–1 and chs. 1–3; *Soldier of the South,* ed. Inman, pp. vi–vii;

In the Old Northwest, finally, men who were neither prosperous enough to put off work, venturesome enough to cut childhood ties, nor traditional enough to value keeping one hand in their fathers' livelihoods moved among occupations in hopes that one might open doors to tangible and intangible rewards. Thus William Tecumseh Sherman and Ulysses Grant, both natives of Ohio, skirted around the modest opportunities of the peacetime army in the 1850s by trying out other kinds of work. Always looking for the main chance, Sherman dabbled in banking, real estate, and commodity speculations. In a more troubled frame of mind, Grant sought steady occupation that he could perform modestly well by experimenting with farming and shopkeeping.[52] Neither man, however, found an occupation before the war suitable to his expectations, work that offered the feel of freedom by putting a man in touch with large social forces and, more pragmatically, also promised a substantial financial return.

All of this commentary on the Victorians' restlessness is not to slight how emotionally taxing the Victorians' unsettlement about work often was. Although much of their anguish grew from their imperfect control of impulses that kept them from making compromises that might have brought peace of mind, their difficulties were not simply self-created. Relations with their fathers, practices in higher education, and demands made by careers constituted external pressures that heightened the Victorians' impression that they were less than free to shape their vocations.

The Victorians' fathers were such an immense presence in their sons' working lives that young Victorians entering careers were nearly overpowered by their fathers' influence. Struggles for autonomy were trying, first, because in a society still traditional enough to make labor an obligation of childhood, sons often worked under their fathers' direction from their earliest years. William Cooper Howells, an Ohio printer and editor, acted on the premise that his son, also William, owed the family his labor when the elder Howells took him permanently out of school at age ten to help with successive journals. Edward Everett Hale occasionally set type after his classes at the Boston Latin School for his father, Nathan, owner and editor of the *Boston Daily Advertiser*. Edward's habit hovered between a customary duty and a hobby because his effort brought little financial gain. Even so, working for his father forged a bond strong enough to make Hale contemplate becoming a journalist during his long vocational crisis in the 1840s. Similarly, Howells

Rice, *Curry*, ch. 2. Two discussions of the tendency of southern men to engage in supplemental careers in addition to agriculture are Wyatt-Brown, *Southern Honor*, ch. 7, and Oakes, *Ruling Race*, ch. 2. Both argue that young men pursued other work to further their prospects as planters. While I do not disagree, my sources suggest more boredom with agricultural enterprise than they discovered, perhaps because the Victorians were generally younger than the southerners they studied.

[52] Merrill, *Sherman*, pp. 66–132; McFeely, *Grant*, ch. 4. Similarly, William Dean Howells, also from Ohio, worked as a printer, reporter, editor, and diplomat before he moved toward a more settled career as a journal editor and author. See Lynn, *Howells*, chs. 4,6.

never broke completely with his father's calling, serving as editor of the *Atlantic Monthly* and other magazines through much of his literary career.[53]

In addition to the power born of intimacy and subordination, fathers intervened actively in their sons' decisions. A few were authoritarian in a traditional spirit of rule. Because Washington Roebling remembered his German-born father, John, for "almost unremitting scoldings," it is not surprising that Washington submitted to John's wish that his son work with him as an engineer, eventually completing his father's most ambitious structure, the Brooklyn Bridge, after John's death. More commonly, fathers simply stated their views and let affection work on sons' consciences. William Potter was pained to reflect in 1847 that his father "wants me to be a farmer" like himself, and "I shall have to oppose his wishes to be a teacher." In 1854, respect for his father made him hesitate once again when he quit teaching to enter the ministry, since his father, a Quaker, viewed salaried preachers as "time servers."[54] Yet Potter defied the will of his father both times, one sign that modern customs of parental control through feelings increased inner trial but, in the end, did not curb young men's independence.

Neither habits of obedience nor deliberate expressions of will equaled the awesome importance for the sons of their fathers' success. Not only were young men who were bent on achievement understandably reluctant to desert callings that generously rewarded their fathers, but the respected community position of the older generation at once raised fears of not matching their accomplishments and spurred a burdensome drive to surpass them. Joseph Story of Massachusetts, appointed to the U.S. Supreme Court at age thirty-two, was a particularly eminent father whose precedent bound his son, William, until the younger Story was nearly thirty years old. William followed in his father's footsteps by becoming an attorney. But when Joseph died in 1846, William laced his decision to leave the law with comforting gestures of filiopiety. An amateur sculptor, he was asked to carve a graveside monument to his father and insisted on a trip to Europe to study possible models. For all intents and purposes, Story never came back. Although he practiced law in Boston in 1847, he soon moved his family to Italy, amid protestations of madness by his mother, and devoted the rest of his life to sculpting. He left a statue to his father in Mount Auburn Cemetery and

[53] Lynn, *Howells,* pp. 54–6, 81, 135, 152–88, 285; Hale, *A New England Boyhood* (1893), p. 83; Holloway, *Hale,* pp. 46–7. Sons traditionally worked with their fathers as children, but they now felt more strain precisely because both assumed that sons eventually would become independent. In other words, the influence of fathers was more irksome as sons expected greater autonomy. During the decades of the Victorians' childhoods, Joseph F. Kett has noted a trend toward seasonal departures of adolescent sons from home for schooling or work, which he calls "semi-autonomy," further evidence of young men's ambiguous status in a culture poised between patriarchy and individual opportunity. See *Rites of Passage: Adolescence in America, 1790 to the Present* (1977), ch. 1.

[54] Nov. 23, 1847, Dec. 3, 1854, Diaries, 1847–48, 1853–57, Potter Papers. On Roebling, see Steinman, *The Builders of the Bridge: The Story of John Roebling and His Son* (1945), pp. 44, 194.

published a biography of Joseph in 1851, small but revealing tokens of the emotional cost of his liberation from a profession appropriate neither to his own talents nor to his tastes.[55]

Other Victorians escaped their fathers' domination by substituting metaphoric parent–child bonds for real ones, as filial relationships often shaped men's careers. Seemingly disabled by strong fathers from striking out with real independence, these Victorians were able to grow professionally only through the sponsorship of fatherlike men. Three revealing instances involve John Burroughs, Lyman Abbott, and William Herndon. Burroughs's work as a writer was anchored in his nearly thirty-year friendship with Walt Whitman. He revealed his veneration of Whitman in the seventeen articles and one book he produced during the four years after Whitman's death in 1892. A decade before Burroughs wrote, "Whitman is the Savior, the Redeemer of the modern world," and "his gospel cannot have too many and too fervent preachers."[56] Lyman Abbott found similar direction in his relationship with Henry Ward Beecher. Abbott floated among pulpits and writing jobs for nearly a decade until he became managing editor of Beecher's *Christian Union* in 1869. The fact that he became editor in chief for many years after Beecher's retirement (1881–1922) and minister of Beecher's Plymouth Congregational Church in Brooklyn after the older man's death (1887–99) underlines the dramatic way Beecher inspired Abbott's career. William Herndon seemed to find his professional center through his law partnership with Abraham Lincoln between 1844 and 1861. When Lincoln died, Herndon's dependency on his long-time sponsor became sadly visible, as his obsessive quest for the true facts of Lincoln's life correlated with his inability to function alone. The value of Herndon's tribute, finally published in 1888 as *Herndon's Life of Lincoln,* cannot be judged without taking into account the loss of his law practice, years of drinking, and personal instability that accompanied the production of this monument to his mentor.[57]

Records of these men's ties with their own fathers may be used to probe the reasons why reliance on older men was so crucial to the Victorians' accomplishment. The fathers of Burroughs, Abbott, and Herndon were imposing figures who set the terms by which they would judge and be judged, and their sons found themselves wanting. The son of a strict Calvinist

---

[55] James, *William Wetmore Story and His Friends* (1903), 1:29–32. Although a son's impulse to free himself from a father's control draws on a basic human need, the struggle is exacerbated when fathers make their mark as eminent pioneers in social or political affairs. Whereas I emphasize the Victorians' fathers' social accomplishments, George B. Forgie has made a seminal argument for the tension between the revolutionary-era generation and their antebellum offspring as the touchstone of early nineteenth-century politics, in *Patricide in the House Divided: A Psychological Interpretation of Lincoln and His Age* (1979).

[56] Burroughs to Richard Bucke, Jan. 25, 1880, June 17, 1881, quoted in Westbrook, *Burroughs,* p. 38.

[57] Brown, *Abbott,* chs. 6, 10; Donald, *Herndon,* chs. 12–21.

Baptist, John Burroughs risked failure in the eyes of his father and himself when he experienced no conversion. The father of Lyman Abbott, in contrast, humbled his son through his generosity. When the younger Abbott's New York congregation forced him to resign in 1869, it was his father, a noted author, who perhaps a bit too adeptly found him editorial work, in much the same spirit that he offered his son ongoing counsel and financial aid. William Herndon must have felt humiliated by his father's oblique condemnation when, after William spoke publicly against slavery, his Democratic parent removed him from a politically liberal school. A failing grade in mathematics must have compounded his shame. On the surface, all three men broke free of their fathers. Burroughs rejected Protestant orthodoxy for an uneasy blend of transcendentalism and determinism. At a crucial point in his life, Abbott circumvented his father's will that he not go to Kansas as a Free Soiler by changing professions, from the law to the ministry, and accepting a call from an Indiana congregation where he preached reform. Herndon declared himself a Whig as soon as his father forced him home from school.[58] Yet tangled emotions remained. Burroughs, for example, struggled financially for years to keep his father's farm in the family, though he left home at age seventeen.[59] Unable to get along with his father, neither could he let him go. This ambivalent pattern of rebellion and enduring attachment suggests that the Victorians looked to fatherlike men for approval denied by their own parents, support that they needed to move finally beyond their fathers' sphere.

Children in all societies must struggle for autonomy from their parents, but the Victorians' situation contained a combination of desires and circumstances that was particularly troublesome. Muffled but intense spiritual crises and enticing economic opportunities made the Victorians particularly eager to make their mark in the world, while at the same time their fathers' stance on a margin between traditional customs of nurture and command of new sources of status tightened their hold on their sons. In modern cultures, education ideally helps individuals to acquire skills and make decisions that establish their independence. Schooling assisted the Victorians little, however, in resolving career problems. Socialization instilled goals so generally conceived that men either resisted pigeonholing in specific vocations or were

[58] Westbrook, *Burroughs*, p. 4 and ch. 5; Brown, *Abbott*, pp. 19, 22, 53, 57, and ch. 3; Donald, *Herndon*, pp. 12–14.

[59] Westbrook, *Burroughs*, p. 2. Herndon also stayed close to his father, despite conflicting emotions, by serving as his father's attorney (Donald, *Herndon*, p. 14). Abbott's divided feelings about his father appeared as late as the autobiography he wrote in 1921. On the surface, he pointed to continuity between Jacob's simply stated religion and his own views, yet he opened his recollections by picturing himself as a boy whose mother had died and "his father is hundreds of miles away," leaving Abbott to live with kin. Abbott seems to have felt both imposed upon and abandoned, perhaps, he feared, for his unworthiness. See *What Christianity Means to Me: A Spiritual Autobiography* (1921), pp. 1, 7. See further discussion of the emotional power of fathers in families in Chapter 4.

ill prepared to identify new kinds of work suitable to their inclinations. In instances already discussed, Oliver Otis Howard and Edward Everett Hale balked respectively at the military and the ministry because they thought these allowed insufficient play to benevolence and self-cultivation. The moralistic tone of the childhood nurture each received clashed with the practical demands of the army or an urban parish. Similarly, the undergraduate education at Yale of Daniel Coit Gilman so much remained an infusion of rudimentary scholarship judged necessary over many generations for New England preachers that he had trouble envisioning an appropriate career. When Gilman graduated in 1852, he was certain only that he did not want to be an iron manufacturer like his father or a minister, although he was still so unsettled vocationally in 1860 that he secured a license to preach. In the meantime, he took graduate courses at Harvard in physical and political science. But in the end, he moved informally in the direction of university administration as a librarian, fund raiser, and administrator at Yale, until he became president of the University of California in 1872 and, more memorably, of Johns Hopkins in 1875.[60] Gilman's professional dilemma was two-faced: he floundered not only because he was not trained for a specialty, but because the work at which he excelled was not an established vocation until his own long undirected abilities helped to underline the crucial role of aggressive leadership to universities. Nonetheless, even if the disruption for individuals caused by a changing occupational structure is taken into account, it is still true that young men were unable to see how to make choices among many pursuits, a fault nurtured by the fact that learning objectives in the Victorians' education poorly matched career options.

One last reason for the Victorians' perplexities was the problem of tailoring jobs for personal ends when tasks were increasingly structured to respond to intense market demand. The prestige of the law, for example, rose throughout the nineteenth century as lawyers served expanding business and government. But from the point of view of individual attorneys, legal work often epitomized depersonalized submersion in tedious means to obscure ends. As a young lawyer in New York in the 1840s, George Templeton Strong was hardly engaged by the profession's arcane concepts and language.

---

[60] Flexner, *Gilman*, ch. 1. Bledstein discusses precisely this problem of the "amorphousness" of the "old-time college," as well as the educational trials of Gilman and others who would become postbellum academic pioneers, in *Culture of Professionalism*, chs. 4–6. An uninspired educational system helps to explain the number of autodidacts among Victorians who might have afforded schooling, as well as the motives of those who declined college or professional training. Although biographers sometimes cite ill health and parental pressure as reasons that individuals missed formal instruction, in addition to deliberate choice, the fact that young men often did not struggle for schooling attests to the meager rewards they perceived. On several Victorians who were largely self-taught, see Morseberger and Morseberger, *Wallace*, pp. 17–18; Roper, *FLO*, ch. 1; and Lynn, *Howells*, pp. 48, 55, 71–2. On others who chose not to attend college or professional school, see Light, *DeForest*, p. 21; Perry, *Higginson*, pp. 24–5; Holloway, *Hale*, p. 46.

Reading the legal scholar James Kent, Strong commented that "it was a toss-up between the ex-Chancellor and the Boston transcendentalists," since Kent "writes a book as his wife would make a pudding, by taking care to mix the ingredients – eggs, butter and all – into undistinguishable homogeneity." More than a year later, he still wrote as an outsider to the profession when he confided to his diary that "I'm beginning to get a little into business habits," but "shall inevitably get myself in some botheration or other before I'm used to the novelties of a bank account and partnership duties."[61] Because Strong filled his journal until his death in 1875 with news of New York's music, theater, churches, politics, and society, it seems that the law served as his livelihood without touching a vital imagination that appropriated others' experiences for its vicarious delight.

More generally, many of the Victorian men who at one time were lawyers (eighteen in all) must have felt Strong's cool interest or even sharper distaste for their work, because they left the profession in substantial numbers, either all at once or one step at a time, for what must have appealed as more stimulating work. Lyman Abbott became a minister, William Wetmore Story took up sculpting, John Wesley North moved from New York state to Minnesota to promote reform, and John Kinkade abandoned a plan to practice law in Virginia to go to California in search of gold. Lewis Henry Morgan quit the law to study anthropology, William Herndon left practice to investigate Lincoln, and Lew Wallace spent ever more time serving as a diplomat and working on novels. Robert Ingersoll kept up a lucrative practice in railroad, corporate, and inheritance litigation, but mainly to support his riskier passions for politics and public advocacy of agnosticism.[62] In the past, attorneys commonly applied their legal skills to kindred fields such as politics, a strategy less indicative of a distaste for their calling than an acknowledgment of its uses. This trend persisted in the Victorian generation and was particularly strong among southerners, who seemed to feel less channeled by legal practice because, perhaps, business in the South imposed fewer pressures. Thus Zebulon Vance of North Carolina turned to politics in the 1850s without signs of rebellion against the law. Nor did he try to circumvent a return to private practice after the war, when he was barred from political office, by seeking a new career. Yet what was increasingly notable among Victorians of all sections were decisions to take up widely

---

[61] Sept. 25, 1840, Jan. 8, 1842, *Diary of Strong*, ed. Nevins and Thomas, 1:146, 174.

[62] Brown, *Abbott*, pp. 16–17; James, *Story*, ch. 2; Stonehouse, *North*, pp. 13–21; Biographical sketch of John Kinkade, *Guide to American Historical Manuscripts in the Huntington Library* (San Marino, Calif.: Henry E. Huntington Library and Art Gallery, 1979), p. 193; Resek, *Lewis Henry Morgan: American Scholar* (1960), p. 85; Donald, *Herndon*, pp. 246–7; Morseberger and Morseberger, *Wallace*, pp. 21–2, 42, 46–7, 51; Cramer, *Royal Bob: The Life of Robert G. Ingersoll* (1952), esp. pp. 65–6. Other Victorians who were attorneys but who did not practice consistently throughout their lives were Cyrus Holliday, Joseph Taylor, Robert Tyler, Richard Henry Dana, David Terry, Zebulon Vance, Jabez Curry, Chauncey Depew, and William Montague Browne.

different pursuits – sculpting, prospecting, preaching – as if to condemn the capacity of often profitable labor to satisfy yearning to produce something of special personal value.[63]

Impatience with detailed, repetitive work helps to explain the midcareer changes of Victorian men as well as their initial reluctance to enter callings flagged as demanding close application with no touch of romance. This understanding of the dynamics of career choices makes it possible, finally, to assess the Victorians' impression that they were more constrained in work than their parents.

If subjective forces may be said to make bonds as real in effect as objective conditions, then the Victorians coped with circumstances more adverse than their parents confronted, though in the end they may have achieved more. Opportunity made possible by family resources and economic expansion helped them to earn recognition on regional and national levels. But their advancement was obstructed by obstacles that included imposing fathers, inappropriate schooling, restrictive vocations, and, most difficult to control, their own high standards of success that precluded satisfaction and kept them searching for elusive fulfillment. Read in this light, the fact that seventy-seven percent (forty-seven of sixty-one) of the Victorian men engaged in more than one occupation in the course of their lives, while fifty-nine percent (thirty of fifty-one) of the fathers whose occupations are known did the same, may be at least as indicative of their determination to circumvent what they perceived as dead ends as of their command of broadening horizons.[64] Although the Victorians' difficulty settling on careers produced anxiety and consumed energy, it is important to keep in mind that their dilemma was created to an extent by their prosperity. It was a privilege to choose among a growing number of middle-class vocations, to ask that work satisfy subjective as well as material needs, and to act on their discontent by changing professions. These expectations about work shaped the way the Victorians responded to the Civil War.

DREAMS OF GLORY AND MEMORIES
OF ACHIEVEMENT

If the Victorians had imagined circumstances in 1861 to remedy their ambivalent commitments and frustrated sense of accomplishment, they might have envisioned the Civil War. The war promised that intense individual

---

[63] On Vance, see Tucker, *Zeb Vance: Champion of Personal Freedom* (1965), chs. 5, 27. Alfred S. Konefsky has shown how attorneys earlier in the century used their expertise to establish broader cultural power, without turning away from their profession, in "Law and Culture in Antebellum Boston," *Stanford Law Review* 40 (1988): 1119–59.

[64] See Appendix B for a listing of the Victorians' occupations.

ambition might be compatible with a common good conceived with a clarity no longer possible when contemplating growing cities and towns. High-minded goals might be sought without everyday encumbrances to yield, to the able, the satisfaction of glory in a just cause. It is perhaps less surprising that men of uncertain purpose welcomed the war's prospects of personal trial than that they felt as fulfilled as they did by an experience prosecuted, after all, at great human cost. Equally striking, although postwar economic and political conditions chipped relentlessly away at men's control of their vocations, members of this generation were able to keep alive feelings of self-worth by reference to what they made of themselves in a crisis that transcended their own discontents. Drawn to the Civil War by the expectation of real solutions to career difficulties, the Victorians more often found that their war experience provided symbolic answers to their questions about vocations.

American Victorians were eager for labor's material rewards and intangible resources to build private purpose, and the war unleashed both impulses with a force born of pent-up desire. In the North, professional soldiers such as Ulysses Grant scrambled for advantageous commissions, politicians such as James Garfield lobbied for prestigious civilian or military appointments, and entrepreneurs such as Jay Cooke, who marketed Union bonds, jockeyed for government contracts.[65] Probably many northerners mistook this insistent ambition for crass self-interest, without comprehending the deeper issues of identity that pushed the Victorians to reap all possible professional benefit from the unusual circumstances of war. William Tecumseh Sherman, for one, spoke unsparingly in a letter during the Vicksburg campaign of the "mere politicians who come to fight not for the real glory and success of the nation but for their own individual aggrandizement."[66] Yet in a way typical of Sherman's perennial division of personality between acceptable values and monumental dreams, he shared the self-centered hopes that he criticized in others. Writing home from Savannah in 1865, Sherman relished the thought that he would go down in history as "a great general." "I do think that in the several grand epochs of war, my name will have a prominent part," he wrote to his wife, Ellen, "and not least among them will be the determination I took in Atlanta to destroy that place, and march on this city, whilst Thomas, my lieutenant, should dispose of Hood."[67] Sherman might not have sought fame per se at the war's outset, but neither is it likely that a man who spent much of the 1850s in successive self-promoting schemes

---

[65] McFeely, *Grant*, pp. 74–6; *The Wild Life of the Army: Civil War Letters of James A. Garfield*, ed. Williams (1964), pp. 3–24; Larson, *Cooke*, ch. 7. Similar stories may be found in Stonehouse, *North*, pp. 124–31, and Nevins, *Hewitt*, chs. 11–12.

[66] Sherman to [Ellen Sherman ?], in *Home Letters of General Sherman*, ed. DeWolfe Howe (1909), p. 241.

[67] Sherman to Ellen Sherman, Jan. 5, 1865, in ibid., p. 325.

entered the Civil War in an altogether disinterested mood. No less than the aggressive seekers of place and recognition he condemned, Sherman thoroughly mixed patriotic motives with a personal drive to forge a career of distinction.

Southern Victorians behaved essentially the same. "Everybody who comes here wants an office," Mary Chesnut wrote in her diary in Montgomery, Alabama, in 1861.[68] At home in South Carolina she observed later that year, "Privateering mad in Charleston."[69] So stimulated was Chesnut by the war spirit of "parade, fife, and fine feathers," the "wild awakening from everyday stagnant life," that she allowed herself to draw closer to public ambitions of her own than at any other time in her life. Away from the restrictive plantation life of rural Camden, "that hot hole," Chesnut promoted the interests of her friends in Richmond: "I have worked like a beaver – or rather a mole – for my friends, and this is the first one who has thanked me – seeing shrewdly my fingers in the pie."[70] With special care, she nurtured the prospects of her husband, James, and in that context, Chesnut verged on the unfeminine admission that she could imagine selfish goals. "I wish Mr. Davis would send *me* to Paris," she wrote in August, 1861, while waiting for news of James's possible diplomatic appointment.[71] In the South as well as the North, the Victorians approached the Civil War as an extraordinary event that opened new outlets for self-advancement. Indeed, as Chesnut's case incisively suggests, aspiration seemed to intensify in the face of possibilities hitherto unanticipated. Certainly this was a privileged view of the war reserved for those who could expect leadership positions. Even so, the Victorians' optimism about their wartime prospects must also be seen in the more somber light of their anguished career crises.

Henry Lee Higginson of Boston was one man who embraced the war as if fleeing a demon of self-inflicted indecision. "I always did long for some such war, and it came in the nick of time for me," Higginson wrote in his diary in 1863, and further explained his feeling in a letter to a friend:

I, for one, have felt merely delight from the beginning of the war, that the day had come, which was to make me a soldier fighting for freedom for man, for the right and the good, for God. My whole religion (that is my whole belief and hope in everything, in life, in man, in woman, in music, in good, in the beautiful, in the real truth) rests on the questions now really before us. . . . Thank God that we were born in these days![72]

[68] Diary, Feb. 25, 1861, *Mary Chesnut's Civil War*, ed. Woodward (1981), p. 8. Future references to this work do not specify "diary" because all entries are from Chesnut's Civil War journal.

[69] June 10, 1861, ibid., p. 69.

[70] June 28, 1861, ibid., p. 83. She made reference to Camden, South Carolina, on June 27, 1861, p. 81.

[71] Aug. 12, 1861, ibid., p. 142.

[72] Higginson to A. J. Thayer, Mar. 15, 1863, quoted in Perry, *Higginson*, pp. 179–80. The diary excerpt was recorded by Higginson on Apr. 13, 1863, and may be found in ibid., pp. 183–4.

Behind this paean to idealism stood nearly a decade of irresolution about careers, as Higginson contested family pressure and the prospect of tedious labor by dickering with his father, in countless letters from Europe, about the comparative merits of music and commerce. Because he relinquished his artistic goals at last in late 1860 and sailed for home to go into business, Higginson's sense of providential rescue by a commission as a second lieutenant the following spring might indeed be seen as a stunning turn of fate. Not especially religious in youth or age, Higginson had sought an ideal worthy of devotion in music. But how could even the gratifications of beauty compare with the mythic dimensions of a vocation as "a soldier fighting for freedom for man, for the right and the good, for God?" Higginson's need for release and his ability to frame his experience in visionary terms may have been unusually strong, but this response to the war cast in sharp relief common elements of a prevalent mood.[73]

William Potter cast his war experience in less grandiose language than Higginson, but the value to Potter of military service similarly hinged on the fact that being a chaplain saved him from the nearly intolerable pressures of his civilian vocation. Over thirty years old in 1860 when he accepted his first church in New Bedford, Massachusetts, Potter was tormented by parish work. Writing soon after his installation to a close friend from Harvard Divinity School, George Bartlett, Potter reported that he suffered repeated "mortification" from his failure as a preacher and rarely slept either the night before or after he preached.[74] By July 1863, he admitted to Bartlett that "I am in no great health of mind" and longed for a vacation on his father's farm to live "over again the life of my boyhood."[75] In this despondent mood, Potter was drafted into the Union army. Perhaps a dogged commitment to the ministry, despite its torments, kept him from volunteering earlier. Once called, however, Potter appreciated his military occupation as a relief. "I accepted the Draft the more gladly as it was to take me away from this scene of conflict here," he wrote to Bartlett from New Bedford.[76] From Washington, where Potter was assigned to duty as a chaplain to Union hospitals and prisons, he reported, "I rather enjoy the work," though he admitted that he was sufficiently troubled by his conscience to hide the fact that he was a "conscript" from the men he served.[77]

---

[73] George Fredrickson documents how widespread enthusiasm for the war was at its outset, in *Inner Civil War*, ch. 5. Marcus Cunliffe and Robert Johannsen help to set the response of 1861 in a romantic tradition of war-making that was accentuated during and after the Mexican War, in, respectively, *Soldiers and Civilians*, esp. chs. 7, 11, and *To the Halls of the Montezumas*, esp. chs. 2–5. A number of the Victorian generation first fought in Mexico and approached the Civil War in a spirit conditioned by Mexican victories.

[74] Potter to George W. Bartlett, Feb. 7, 1860, Jan., [1861?], Potter Papers.

[75] Potter to Bartlett, July 1, 1863, Potter Papers.

[76] Potter to Bartlett, Sept. 11, 1863, Potter Papers.

[77] Potter to Bartlett, Oct. 14, 1863, Potter Papers.

Although southern Victorians exploited the war's professional opportunities as avidly as did northerners, they were less inclined to embrace wartime occupations as an emancipation from regular labor, such as the business routine Henry Higginson struggled to avoid or the parish duties that drove William Potter toward emotional breakdown. The slower preindustrial temper of southern entrepreneurship probably combined with white southerners' awareness that they were fighting to defend established mores, including customs of labor, to deter open expressions of discontent with peacetime careers. Thus none of the southern men in this study approached his work during the war with the nearly religious fervor of a convert who had found his calling, a spirit that pervaded the testimonies of Higginson and, to an extent, Potter. People of both sections, however, appreciated how much the Civil War reconciled individual ambition with a renewed commitment to common enterprise.

The economic ethic inherited by the Victorians measured private effort by its consistency with the public good. Yet the Victorians' experience contested this principle at seemingly every point, particularly in their self-centered ambitions, conflicts with parents, and inward-turning struggles to find rewarding work. The Civil War opened the prospect of a new accord between vigorous personal enterprise and communal well-being. Established communities across the nation were united in 1861 by patriotic feeling. New bonds based on abstract commitments took shape as well. Mary Chesnut used her diary to chronicle the formation of communities based on shared allegiances both in the larger South and in the Confederacy's governing inner circle. To an extent a true account of the way the South rallied together, Chesnut's picture of sectional unification was also colored by her ardent hope that her compatriots would discover sources of collective strength. Rhetorically, she turned southern women's display of loyalty into a demonstration of military force. On her journey from Camden to Richmond, Chesnut saw her "sister patriots" stand as a "solid phalanx," as "every woman from every window of every house we passed waved a handkerchief" that together seemed a "fluttering of white flags."[78] Once in the capital, Chesnut's extensive reporting of social relations among the new nation's leaders was infused with her wishful sense that this was a time of integration around ideals.

Yet despite decades of prewar debate about sectional identities, southern principles remained ill-defined, one source of serious internal divisions that eventually weakened the Confederacy. In one conversation Chesnut recorded in Richmond in June 1861, she included this mélange of values:

Mr. [Lucius] Lamar, who does not love slavery more than Sumner does — nor than I do, say — laughs at the compliment New England pays us. We want to separate from them — to be rid of Yankees forever at any price. And they hate us so and

---

[78] June 27, 1861, *Chesnut's Civil War*, ed. Woodward, p. 79.

would clasp us – or hook us, as Polonius has it – to their bosoms with hooks of steel. We are an unwilling bride. I think incompatibility of temper began when it was made plain to us that we get all the opprobrium of slavery and they all the money there was in it – with their tariff.[79]

If Lamar – and Chesnut – hated slavery as much as Sumner, was the Confederacy committed to slavery's defense? Or was the South, the "unwilling bride," simply fighting for its independence? Did the Confederacy seek to defend its distinctive "temper," or to redeem its pride from blame for slavery, or to keep its rightful profits gained through slave labor? Chesnut correctly saw that the Confederacy was not a traditional community bound by custom and history, but a society centered in ideology, where members understood their value by their contribution to definite objects. What she missed, however, was how murky and conflicting those principles were. The wartime community perpetuated more of the tensions of southern Victorian society than Chesnut wished.

In much the same spirit that Mary Chesnut used a military metaphor to convey community coherence, northern Victorians valued army life for the clarity of common and individual purpose afforded by military objectives and duties. Thomas Wentworth Higginson, a distant cousin of Henry, was one who found gratification in military discipline. Suspended among careers as a minister, reformer, and writer in 1861, Higginson hesitated before joining the army. In the *Atlantic Monthly* in 1862, he warned young writers not to be "misled by the excitements of the moment into overrating the charms of military life," because war "interrupts all higher avocations."[80] This perhaps heretical message stirred one reader, Emily Dickinson, to open what became a lifelong correspondence with Higginson. Yet Higginson himself soon deserted his position by entering the army as an officer of black troops. In the wartime diary that he reworked as *Army Life in a Black Regiment* (1870), Higginson reported his blended passions for the army's romance and routine. Although he relished an officer's life for its "adventure," he was equally pleased to discover in himself qualities needed for governing troops, "system, promptness, patience, tact," backed up by "the admirable machinery of the army." Once "the details of camp life" were in place, Higginson could relax and enjoy the zestful ambience created by his free black troops. But he only permitted "religious enthusiasm," for example, so long as it did not disrupt the rules.[81] Perhaps it was Higginson's uneasy sense of

---

[79] June 28, 1861, ibid., p. 84.

[80] "Letter to a Young Contributor," p. 409.

[81] *Army Life in a Black Regiment* (1870), pp. 47, 227, 255. Some historians have argued that Americans' appreciation of military efficiency led to increasing value placed on organization and expert leadership in civilian life. See, e.g., Fredrickson, *Inner Civil War*, esp. chs. 12–13, and Hall, *Organization of American Culture*, ch. 11. Although Fredrickson also acknowledges that the war was seized intellectually for its ability to generate new values, such as loyalty (ch. 9), neither writer takes full account of how mixed

the resemblance of army routines to the bureaucratized jobs the Victorians resisted in peacetime society that helped him decide to return to Newport, Rhode Island, and a writing career in 1864.[82] A generation so at sea about careers idealized the army's potential for providing fixed labor in a bounded community. But just as the Confederacy incorporated the ideological differences of the prewar South, the Union army's kinship with structured middle-class vocations put off men who, on a different level, savored their restlessness.

North and South, the Civil War invigorated labor in communities. Yet these were not traditional societies grounded in reciprocal duties to which the Victorians' inherited values alluded, but directed and disciplined settings in which an individual's task was defined more in relation to common goals than to his or her neighbors' needs. Precisely because they were modern in nature, wartime communities imported such contemporary social difficulties as ideological conflict and rigid systems.[83] These ambiguities portended growing problems in the postwar years for men intent on designing careers capable of yielding inner rewards.

Whether the Civil War enhanced or diminished a man's wealth and reputation, the conflict encouraged the development of a variety of conditions that made it more difficult for the men of the middle classes to control their labor. Circumstances in the North and South were significantly different, but the outcome was much the same. The military defeat of the South meant that the work of prominent men was forcibly denied personal significance. As planters were cut off from traditional means of production, politicians were barred from office, and soldiers lost their commands, southern Victorians entered livelihoods for which they often had neither training nor taste. When the consequences were emotionally devastating, it became clear, by implication, how crucial it was for the Victorians to have work attuned to values. George Pickett of Virginia tried to be optimistic at the war's end about moving to a "cottage home" when his plantation was destroyed and his troops were disbanded. But his embrace of bourgeois mores was too

bureaucratization was with romanticism, expressed both as expectations of personal heroism and inspired communal purpose.

[82] Edelstein, *Strange Enthusiasm,* ch. 16. Ill health also contributed to Higginson's decision.

[83] One of the distinguishing features of modern communities has been their reliance on articulated values for cohesion, making individuals' allegiance to abstractions a more important source of bonds than inherited customs. Karl Marx and Friedrich Engels pioneered recognition of the social power of ideology not long before the American Civil War, in *The Communist Manifesto* (1848; reprint, New York: International Publishers, 1948), esp. sec. 2. Twentieth-century theorists have elaborated on the crucial role of value systems, either in general, as did Karl Mannheim, in *Ideology and Utopia: An Introduction to the Sociology of Knowledge* (New York: Harcourt, Brace, 1936), or in particular, as did Hannah Arendt, in *The Origins of Totalitarianism,* rev. ed. (New York: Harcourt, Brace, Jovanovich, 1973). That the American Revolution gave ideas a crucial role in structuring the nation was one sign of its innovative force. The Civil War, coming after decades of cultural change, provided both northerners and southerners with the opportunity to redefine collective purposes in terms more relevant to current circumstances and, in so doing, to reinforce the role of ideology in society.

halfhearted to reconcile him to the tacky customs of businessmen with whom he dealt when he sold insurance. Feelings of uselessness as a man displaced from his proper calling must have hastened Pickett's death at the age of fifty in 1875.[84]

Overall, however, the way southern Victorians successfully weathered Reconstruction is more impressive than their failures. Their flexibility and resourcefulness about jobs probably grew from practiced habits of manipulating vocations to serve private needs. Jabez Curry, who settled in Virginia after the war, and William Montague Browne, who moved from Richmond to Georgia, took up work as a minister and lawyer respectively when their former careers in politics appeared closed. Neither man proved to be suited to his new livelihood, yet both were sufficiently resilient to choose another path without lasting emotional cost. Curry decided to be ordained in 1866 during his tenure as president of a small Baptist college in Richmond. A leading Baptist layman in prewar Alabama, Curry was qualified by his piety for the ministry. But his varied past enterprises in the law, railroad promotion, and agricultural reform, in addition to politics, made the sphere of a preacher seem narrow in comparison. Looking back in 1902, Curry judged himself mistaken to have chosen a clerical vocation, a conclusion confirmed by his decision in 1868 to become a professor of the humanities at nearby Richmond College.[85] Browne, a native of Ireland, edited a leading Democratic newspaper, the *Constitution,* in Washington before the war, and served as the Confederacy's assistant secretary of state. But in 1865, he was so destitute that his wife was reduced to marketing strawberries, and, in a mood of desperation, he enrolled in law school at the University of Georgia. Even Browne's straitened circumstances could not force him to continue in practice beyond a brief partnership with a law professor. In 1869, he regained some vocational stability as editor of the *Southern Farm and Home.* In 1874, he returned to his political interests as a professor of history and political science at the university.[86] For Jabez Curry and William Browne, professional blind alleys, encountered at a time of civil restriction and financial distress, must have been bitterly disappointing. Still, both were sufficiently adept at maneuvering career changes to survive one more crisis.

The careers of some southern politicians actually benefited, in the end, from their willingness to endure the deprivations of Reconstruction as a sign of their loyalty to the South's distinctive and continuing cause. From a professional standpoint, the postwar decade was exceedingly trying for Zebulon Vance, who had served as the wartime governor of North Carolina, and Wade Hampton, a U.S. senator from South Carolina in the years pre-

---

[84] Pickett to LaSalle Pickett, n.d., in *Soldier of the South,* ed. Inman, pp. 148, 152–3.
[85] Rice, *Curry,* chs. 4–5.
[86] Coulter, *William Montague Browne: Versatile Anglo-Irish American, 1823–1883* (1967), p. 128 and chs. 10–17.

ceding the war. Prohibited briefly at the war's end from practicing law, Vance was so despondent that he considered emigrating to Australia. As late as 1873, Vance declined to act as vice-president of the Southern Historical Society because "my daily business and limited means," he explained in a letter to Jubal Early, precluded interests beyond securing necessities.[87] Hampton, who declared bankruptcy in 1868, was still trying a make ends meet as a planter in 1875. Supervising production himself had so little appeal that he called himself an "overseer" in a letter to a friend. Hampton was beaten down by his day-to-day struggle to the point that he reasoned "it will make but little difference in the long run where the rest of my life is spent."[88]

The end of Reconstruction dramatically reversed the fortunes of men who had demonstrated their worth to fellow southerners by accepting vocational setbacks rather than cooperating, in principle or in fact, with the Yankees. Once southern self-rule in politics was restored, both Vance and Hampton were elected at different times as senators and governors of their states. Over the course of their lives, their careers resembled a professional roller coaster, and despite their final acclaim, they remained the defensive public spokesmen of a defeated people. That they remained reasonably self-possessed, even in the face of the vocational displacements of Reconstruction, attests to the experimental and thus resilient frame of mind in which they approached their careers.

The postwar experience of northern Victorians is less susceptible to generalization, but patterns of opportunity reveal constraints similar in effect to those in the South. Northern men broken down by the war remind us that civil conflict may occasion no less personal upheaval among the victors than among the defeated. Mathew Brady, whose photographs continue to shape Americans' perception of the Civil War, invested so much of his capital in wagons equipped to take pictures of battle that, when the prints sold poorly, he went bankrupt in the early 1870s. The victim of a slow market for Civil War memorabilia in the early postwar years, Brady lost control of his plates and could not profit by the revival of interest in the conflict that began at the end of the decade. As tragically, William Herndon lost his capacity to concentrate on work after Lincoln's death. Probably grief took a similar toll on the ambition and productivity of many men who lost friends and kin.[89]

Other northern men seemed less able than in the past to direct their careers because they shared the success of a society growing madly in triumph. Fame

---

[87] Vance to Jubal Early, Sept. 27, 1873, Zebulon Baird Vance Papers. For further information on Vance during Reconstruction, see Tucker, *Vance,* chs. 27–8.

[88] Hampton to Mrs. Thomas Preston, Apr. 27, 1875, in Cauthen, ed., *Family Letters of Wade Hamptons,* p. 151. For further information on Hampton during Reconstruction, see ibid., ch. 4.

[89] Horan, *Brady,* p. 64; Donald, *Herndon,* esp. ch. 16.

acquired on the battlefield catapulted men into demanding civilian jobs for which they had little helpful experience. Ulysses Grant, though supremely honored as president, was less able to master the political forces that besieged him than the military circumstances he once faced, and he left a record of scandal-ridden administrations over which he exercised at best partial control.[90] Even if an individual did not falter with power, the Victorians found that postwar business was conducted on so large a scale that work produced little sense of private accomplishment. Routine, impersonality, and mass production, all forbidding images in the earlier career traumas of Victorian men, now figured more prominently than ever in northern society. This was the world to which Henry Lee Higginson finally returned from his idealized quest. The year of Grant's election, Higginson became a stockbroker and prospered so grandly over the next half-century that he was able to found, support, and manage the Boston Symphony Orchestra (1881–1918), each year hiring, paying, and sometimes firing the conductor and musicians himself. Commerce may have been even less gratifying than he feared as a young man, due to a volume of trade that made him just one partner in a vigorous firm. But he found, in compensation, that wealth opened an avocation as an orchestra manager that both realized his dream to become a musician in an unexpected way and enlisted qualities of command that he so much savored in war. Looking back in 1918, Higginson wrote to a friend that of all his endeavors, he felt most qualified as a leader of men: "I enjoyed my army life, and, on the whole, did it better than anything else – that is, I was a good regimental officer, but I could not have gone above the command of a thousand men."[91] Taking charge of the orchestra, perhaps conceived as a kind of musical army, must have put Higginson in touch with a part of his past that enhanced his self-esteem.

Higginson's inclination to turn his attention to a war-related activity when everyday work fell short of satisfaction was a common response. In 1861, the Victorians embraced the Civil War as a crusade capable of infusing labor with personal and communal meaning. As the war ended, northerners who viewed their future as civilians with uncertainty chose to prolong wartime occupations. Before settling down as a stockbroker, Henry Lee Higginson spent two years trying to squeeze profits from a Georgia plantation while at the same time teaching former slaves. Acting with a typically Victorian blend of acquisitiveness, altruism, adventurousness, and fantasy, Higginson not only translated his self-image as a military redeemer into civilian terms but took on and transformed the identity of his old enemies, the planter "cavaliers," by reconciling their aristocratic demeanor with con-

[90] McFeely, *Grant,* chs. 20, 24.
[91] Higginson to Mrs. George Agassiz, July, quoted in Perry, *Higginson,* p. 507. For an overview of northern economic growth in the postwar decades, see Trachtenberg, *Incorporation of America: Culture and Society in the Gilded Age* (1982), chs. 2–3, and Livesay, *Carnegie,* chs. 6–10.

siderations of justice.[92] In another instance, Oliver Otis Howard recalled in his autobiography of 1907 that he was uneasily "pondering the subject of my future work" in 1865 when Edwin Stanton, the secretary of war, offered him a position as head of the Freedman's Bureau. Work that combined military organization with benevolence "seemed providential" to Howard, and he accepted with enthusiasm and relief.[93] Lew Wallace of Indiana, a Union general by 1865, was still not sated of war after sitting on the army commissions that tried the conspirators in Lincoln's assassination and the commander of Georgia's Andersonville prison, Henry Wirz. Wallace pursued his twin passions for republicanism and combat by serving in the Mexican army of Benito Juarez. His wife thought he went to Mexico for the glory, whereas Wallace professed the appeal of a promised salary to avert the "hideous spectre" of poverty and, in honesty, must have counted himself among the soldiers he described to a friend as soon "wearied of the monotony of home."[94] No doubt all these motives impelled Wallace in search of ways to hold onto a soldier's life.

Yet these warlike tasks too often lacked the emotional edge of real life-and-death struggles, as well as proved susceptible to the influence of ordinary economic and political forces. By 1868 Higginson gave up the drudgery of farming, Howard left his post under political fire, and Wallace quarreled with Juarez over money and came home.[95] Not surprisingly, the Victorians turned from forms of Civil War reenactment within evolving careers to the more malleable medium of language to recapture their war experience. War memoirs by many of these Victorians proliferated in the postwar decades because literary remembrance drew on their deep-seated impulse to transcend routine by touching a heroic conception of their former selves. These writers melded idealism and careers. They intended not simply to crystallize prose images at once self-justifying and didactic as if part of a cultural exercise, but to redeem their mundane working lives by projects that made reference to inspired times. It was crucial for a person such as Mary Chesnut, at home in reduced circumstances in South Carolina, to make time in the years before her death in 1886 to rework her Civil War memoirs, taking herself back through labor to a setting where her life's purpose was clear in relation to great events.[96] Neither Chesnut nor most others who wrote about their past

[92] Perry, *Higginson*, pp. 248–66. Other northerners bought plantations for similar reasons. See Powell, *New Masters: Northern Planters during the Civil War and Reconstruction* (1980).

[93] Howard, *Autobiography*, 2:208; McFeely, *Yankee Stepfather*, p. 64.

[94] Wallace to Thomas Buchanan Read, Apr. 30, 1865, quoted in Morseberger and Morseberger, *Wallace*, p. 196. For Wallace's statement about poverty, see his letter to his wife, Susan, Sept. 1, 1865, quoted in ibid., p. 198. On Wallace's military activities after the war, see ibid., chs. 13–15.

[95] Perry, *Higginson*, pp. 248–66; McFeely, *Yankee Stepfather*, ch. 14; Wallace, *Lew Wallace: An Autobiography* (1906), 1:210–13; Morseberger and Morseberger, *Wallace*, p. 308 and ch. 14.

[96] On Chesnut's process of revising her diary, see *Chesnut's Civil War*, ed. Woodward, pp. xx–xxiv. For an extended discussion of the significance of Civil War memoirs, see Chapter 6. Exemplary memoirs include DeForest, *A Volunteer's Adventures: A Union Captain's Record of the Civil War*, ed. Croushore

could have turned reminiscing into a full-time career. Nonetheless, setting down their reflections was one occupation that promised meaning and proved susceptible to their private control. The occasional relief such writing afforded must have made everyday pressures more easily endured.

Both the Victorians' career trials and the way the Civil War served, in fact and in memory, to ease social pressures were luxuries permitted by their basic prosperity. As members of established middle classes, the Victorians were in a position to ask that their work be satisfying, to manipulate job options, and to experience war with sufficient education and without such extreme hardship that it might become, in their eyes, a source of personal significance. If in the end their careers could not be freed of troublesome restraints to yield the sense of immense accomplishment they desired, they were simultaneously creating new leisure resources to cushion the shortcomings of work.

(1946), and *A Union Officer in the Reconstruction,* ed. Croushore and Potter (1948); Higginson, *Army Life in a Black Regiment* (see n. 81); Sherman, *Memoirs of General William T. Sherman* (see n. 10); Grant, *Personal Memoirs of U.S. Grant* (1885), ed. Long (1982); Wallace, *Lew Wallace*; and Hood, *Advance and Retreat: Personal Experiences in the United States and Confederate States Armies* (1880), ed. Current (1959). Thomas C. Leonard discusses the selective quality of Civil War reminiscences, as authors emphasized heroic and strategic aspects of the war at the expense of the suffering and hardship they witnessed, in *Above the Battle: War-Making in America from Appomatox to Versailles* (1978), chs. 1–2. See also Edmund Wilson's discussion of DeForest, Grant, Thomas Wentworth Higginson, and others, in *Patriotic Gore: Studies in the Literature of the American Civil War* (1962).

3

Leisure

No pain, no dressings or doses, a pleasant languor, nothing to do and no wish to do anything, a beautifully kept house and nobody but Dr. R. and myself in it, the hostess herself absent . . . to lie all day on a breezy balcony with green leaves and floating clouds, why it is Arcadia, Syrian peace, immortal leisure.

Thomas Wentworth Higginson, 1863

Of all aspects of the lives of American Victorians, leisure was least bound by prescriptive traditions and hence most open to the application of energies directed at crafting satisfying identities in a vital society. From the early decades of settlement, Protestant scruples allowed some space for amusements. But Victorian privileges of prosperity, free time, and a consumer-oriented marketplace vastly increased opportunities for pleasure, guided by few normative values once pious reserve toward self-indulgence relaxed. Yet leisure was not a simple arena of carefree expression. The Victorians were sufficiently modern to cultivate diversions deliberately, and their sensitivity to leisure's rewards made them seek stimulating and convivial activities in an insistent mood. Imagination was their key resource for enjoyment, and by deftly arranging their natural and human environments, they experimented with pleasing self-images and enriching social bonds. Against a troubling background of spiritual and vocational questions, the Victorians expanded their personal horizons through play. As important, the elective relations they forged in settings of no obvious practical utility reveal how much social contacts made deeper perplexities more easily borne.[1]

---

[1] Although scholars often assign the expansion of leisure to the post–Civil War decades, Daniel T. Rogers acknowledges that pleasure seeking gained intensity in the middle classes from the 1850s on, in *The Work Ethic in Industrial America, 1850–1920* (1978), ch. 4. For a sense of the diverse forms of enjoyment available, see Bode, *The Anatomy of American Popular Culture, 1840–1861* (1959). On middle-class leisure organizations, and particularly on the transition from voluntary associations inspired by religion to clubs devoted to secular ends, see Gilkeson, *Middle-Class Providence, 1820–1940* (1986), esp. chs. 2, 4. Some of the best recent studies of nineteenth-century American leisure have focused on the working classes. For arguments that working people successfully used free-time activities to express their distinctive class identity, see Rosenzweig, *Eight Hours for What We Will: Workers and Leisure in an American*

The exuberance of the Victorians' enjoyment is all the more arresting because the social conditions of their pleasure contained elements of routine and impersonality that might have made leisure a source of frustration rather than freedom without the influence of imagination. In the past, leisure consisted of such occasional rituals as harvest celebrations and weddings that brought together many members of a community. Among Americans less prosperous and less urban than these Victorians, diversions still largely conformed to the irregular rhythms of nature and aging. As people who engaged in white-collar careers in growing towns, the Victorians sought entertainments more steadily. A party, a play, or a walk in the park became part of a weekly schedule. Yet these pastimes risked being as limited in emotional return as they were frequent in time, not simply because they competed with work for commitment and energy, but because they commonly took place among strangers. The diverse resources of urban places, the possibility of travel, and the command of enough wealth to pay for amusements enhanced individual choice. The same circumstances made it less likely, however, that neighbors came informally together. Heightened pleasures of imagination among the Victorians helped both to repay the loss of intimate community and to create new social ties. While the spectacles of travel and the artistry of staged productions expanded individual identities, customs to aid sociability among casual acquaintances built transient communities appropriate to a society eager for the stimulation of varied company. Victorian leisure forfeited the depth of shared enjoyment possible in traditional celebration, but acquired a new breadth of possibilities through habits of weaving fictions into daily life.[2]

So crucial was leisure to Victorian society that the Civil War inevitably drew on the habits of peacetime enjoyment. With perverse yet natural deception, war lured the Victorians with accustomed prospects of travel, adventure, and spectacle. More constructively, patterns of sociability carried over into the war and helped to ease interaction among strangers through established customs of civility. The war changed the Victorians' perception

Industrial City, 1870–1920 (1983), and Peiss, *Cheap Amusements: Working Women and Leisure in Turn-of-the-Century New York* (1986). On perhaps the greatest midcentury creator of public entertainments, P. T. Barnum (1810–91), see Harris, *Humbug: The Art of P. T. Barnum* (1973).

[2] The best account of traditional amusements is Rhys Isaac's discussion of social pleasures in eighteenth-century Virginia, in *The Transformation of Virginia, 1740–1790* (1982), pp. 70–114. On attitudes toward enjoyment in the North, Edmund Morgan makes an important case for the Puritans' toleration in practice of needs generated by human nature, in "The Puritans and Sex" (1942), reprinted in Gordon, ed., *The American Family in Social–Historical Perspective* (1978), pp. 363–73. Laurel Thatcher Ulrich explains that northern women turned cooperative work such as quiltings into occasions of sociability, in *Good Wives: Image and Reality in the Lives of Women in Northern New England, 1650–1750* (1982), pp. 50–1 and ch. 3. In all regions, taverns served town dwellers as places of recreation from the seventeenth century on, as explained in Lender and Martin, *Drinking in America: A History* (1987), pp. 12–14. The best explanation of the consequences of social impersonality for culture is Halttunen, *Confidence Men and Painted Women: A Study of Middle-Class Culture in America, 1830–1870* (1982), esp. ch. 6.

of leisure in critical ways as well. Once the Victorians realized that the soul-shaking experience of war was no imagination-laced sojourn, they sensed the poverty of fancy as a source of inner satisfaction. War's pain, in other words, strangely pierced their infatuation with pleasing images and exposed leisure's shallowness. Yet the war also invited the Victorians to reestablish the legitimacy of pleasure seeking on a firmer basis. Through such Civil War commemorative activities as the Grand Army of the Republic and Confederate reunions, enjoyment was in effect redeemed by demonstration of its potential seriousness and depth. Initially devalued by the war's assertion of realism over fantasy, leisure was exorcised of suspicions of frivolousness, in the end, by its connection with the Civil War. As if they had paid a debt to high-mindedness, the Victorians seemed to feel freer than ever to indulge in whatever lighthearted diversions they willed.

This chapter divides leisure pastimes into those that allowed individuals to broaden their experience and others that encouraged social interaction.[3] The refreshment offered by nature, the excitement of travel, and the provocative zest of amusements designed for anonymous crowds enlivened individuals. Entertainments prized for their sociability no longer presumed the existence of a community, but often centered in the privacy of families. Conversely, clubs that fostered more formal relations epitomized modes of intercourse that acknowledged both the need to counter the impersonality of a growing society and the benefit of retaining some social reserve. In nearly all these pursuits, women were more visible and influential than in the Victorians' career struggles, though still less self-determining than men. The chapter concludes with an assessment of the mutual effects of Victorian leisure and the Civil War.

IMAGINATIVE ACQUISITION AND THE EXPANSION OF SELF

American Victorians were as eager for lively experience as they were for wealth. They used their resources to indulge tastes for pleasure, yet they also asked leisure to ease their sense of limitation that arose from their

---

[3] I use the concept of leisure to designate a sphere of human effort where activities aim primarily at securing pleasure. Although modern leisure must be understood as a specialized pursuit conditioned by work, it is not simply free time, but consists of enjoyments cultivated by conscious intent. For one definition that insists that elements of spontaneous play, free time, and pleasurable activities must all be acknowledged as part of leisure, see Michael A. Smith, "Leisure: A Perspective on Contemporary Society," *Leisure and Society* 1 (1978): 18–19. Sociological studies of twentieth-century America that deal theoretically with leisure are also useful. See David Riesman's analysis of the relation of play to individual personality, in *The Lonely Crowd: A Study in the Changing American Character* (New Haven: Yale University Press, 1950), esp. chs. 5, 7, 16, 17, and Sebastian De Grazia's argument that leisure must be transformed into a sphere of freedom, in *Of Time, Work, and Leisure* (1962).

inability to realize their boundless material dreams. If they could not possess all the world's tempting objects, they might still appropriate rich sensations to be interpreted by active imaginations in ways that built inner gratification. Contact with nature, chances for travel, and exposure to diverse entertainments were relished for their intangible personal rewards.

Like men and women before them, the Victorians approached nature both in a mood of religious awe and for the purpose of acquisition. Quiet moments outdoors were savored for their spiritual tranquillity. At the same time, men as different as the California forty-niners and Henry Thoreau hoped to make a living from their contact with the physical world.[4] Yet perhaps only a generation sufficiently modern to be one step removed from daily reliance on nature for metaphysical assurance and material needs could so enthusiastically turn back to the landscape for amusement. In the course of their lives, the Victorians sought nature's pleasures with increasing deliberation. As children in small towns and on farms, they engaged nature through play. William Dean Howells recalled that boys swam with the zest of savages in the Ohio River and dove off boats passing from Lake Erie through a canal.[5] Southern men remained closest as adults to a child's intimacy with untamed forces, not simply because of their section's rural landscape (Californians saw their land as potential wealth), but because of a more traditional outlook that accepted reciprocal exchanges of physical power as evidence of selfhood. Thus antebellum letters describing Wade Hampton's sojourns on his family's Mississippi plantations were filled with news of riding, driving, and hunting for bear, deer, and smaller game. Nor did the war curb his forays, since he killed 574 partridges during three years in the army before 1864.[6] Yet the

---

[4] See Chapter 1 for discussion of encounters with nature that functioned as private religious experience. When Thoreau described Walden Pond in his opening chapter of *Walden* as a "good place for business," on the other hand, he tried not only to convince his reader of his investigation's importance, but tackled his own problem of vocation, so common among the Victorians, by conceiving himself as an experimenter and observer of nature. See *Walden,* ed. Shanley, *The Writings of Henry D. Thoreau* (1971), 1:21.

[5] *A Boy's Town. Described for "Harper's" Young People* (1890), p. 31.

[6] Wade Hampton II (the father of the Victorian, WH III) to Mary Fisher Hampton, Apr. 22 and Nov. 17, 1855, Feb. 14, 1864, in Cauthen, ed., *Family Letters of the Three Wade Hamptons, 1782–1901,* (1953), pp. 39–40, 103. Among the Californians studied of both northern and southern background, appreciation of nature as a place of beauty or a testing ground of selfhood rarely edged aside a view of the land as a source of wealth (see discussion in Chapter 2 of how gold fueled dreams of riches). On one unusual occasion, William Moore, a native of Maine, retired to the sequoia forest on July 4, 1876, for "a calm quiet place" to spend an otherwise raucous holiday. See his Diary, 1876, William Moore Papers. Southerners, on the other hand, approached the natural world not only in entrepreneurial and leisured ways, but in the intimate yet confrontational temper of a more traditional society. On the importance of physical bravery to southern men, see Wyatt-Brown, *Southern Honor: Ethics and Behavior in the Old South* (1982), ch. 2. The most memorable expression of this sensibility is William Faulkner's "The Bear" (1942), discussed in relation to the way modernity eroded the tradition of the hunt by Myra Jehlen, in *Class and Character in Faulkner's South* (New York: Columbia University Press, 1976), pp. 2–14. For an excellent perspective on the broader significance of ritual and regenerative violence in early American encounters with the frontier, see Slotkin, *Regeneration through Violence: The Mythology of the American Frontier, 1600–1860* (1973).

Figure 7. Wade Hampton III (1818–1902). Photographed as commander of the Confederate cavalry at the Anderson-Cook Galleries in Richmond in late 1864. Hampton managed to present an elegant appearance, including waxed mustache, in the midst of trying military and social circumstances. South Caroliniana Library, University of South Carolina.

zeal of Hampton's plunges into nature did not preclude elements of forethought that were accentuated over time. With his home in South Carolina, Hampton used his frontier plantations before the war to entertain guests eager to hunt. By the 1890s, he traveled as far as Texas and California to fish.[7] The pursuits of a man so attuned to nature's allure thus shaded into leisure, sustained by wealth and enhanced by planning. Deliberation did not diminish their value but rather ensured that a sophisticated person fully benefited from an experience appropriately presented.

Although the amenities the Victorians brought into nature became evermore elaborate, this generation also made progressively more space for individual enjoyment uncluttered by ideology or restrictive routine. Imagination embellished leisure's pleasurable effects, at the same time that theories justifying relaxation fell into disuse. Water-cure establishments, for example, grew popular in the 1840s and were patronized by these Victorians in the

[7] Wade Hampton II to Mary Fisher Hampton, Nov. 7, 1857, Wade Hampton III to W. G. Curtis, June 12, 1896, in Cauthen, ed., *Family Letters of Wade Hamptons,* pp. 52, 160.

1850s and during the war, yet rarely thereafter. Freighted with beliefs about water's medicinal power and regulated by strict schedules for baths, diet, and walks, spas offered clients a highly focused experience. The predictable rhythm of days spent sampling nature in measured doses aimed to calm jagged nerves. As young men, John DeForest and Henry Higginson patronized spas for maladies as ill-defined as their lives' goals and perhaps profited by the stiff regimen. Pierre Beauregard was so thrown off balance in 1862 by the forced retreat of his army from Corinth, Mississippi, that he left his command without permission, a serious breach of discipline, to regain a sense of order at nearby springs.[8] Overall, water cures combined elements of religious retreats and modern therapy and sought to restore a sense of personal integration through control.

Yet if water cures demonstrated leisure's capacity to bring rest through structure, they served the Victorian's yen to explore nature's possibilities far less well. Frederick Law Olmsted left as little to chance in his design of parks as did water-cure operators in their therapies, but his artistry fostered an illusion of as many ways to appropriate a landscape as there were visitors to traverse it. Conscious of how much of leisure was subjective, Olmsted insisted that city parks supply props to aid imagination, "shade, turf, swings, cool spring-water, and a pleasing rural prospect, stretching off half a mile or more each way, unbroken by a carriage road or the slightest evidence of the vicinity of the town."[9] In spaces so large and varied as his Central Park in New York, designed in the late 1850s, individuals were at liberty to stroll and see, and although carefully constructed vistas set the terms of the users' experience, guidance came by a gentle hand. Thus Olmsted's friend, George Templeton Strong, roamed Central Park in 1862 in the intended spirit of active cooperation with the landscape's creator. Depressed at the Union's military prospects, Strong set out from the city to the park and escaped his mood once he saw "the crowds of gents and giggling girls [suggesting] peace and prosperity." "There was nothing," he wrote with

---

[8] Williams, *P.G.T. Beauregard: Napoleon in Grey* (1954), pp. 157–9. On DeForest and Higginson, see DeForest to Andrew DeForest, Oct. 20, 1851, John William DeForest Papers, and Perry, *Life and Letters of Henry Lee Higginson* (1921), p. 26. Jane B. Donegan details the doctrines of water-cure advocates, in *"Hydropathic Highway to Health": Women and Water-Cure in Antebellum America* (1986), esp. introduction and chs. 1, 9. Like water cures, self-improvement associations of earlier decades were also based on comparatively doctrinaire goals for leisure. On the insistence of the antebellum middle classes for "rational recreation," see Gilkeson, *Middle-Class Providence*, ch. 2. On the assimilation of purposes of self-cultivation by some workers under the influence of employers, see, e.g., Wilentz, *Chants Democratic: New York City and the Rise of the American Working Class, 1788–1850* (1984), p. 272.

[9] "Public Parks and the Enlargement of Towns" (1870), in *Civilizing American Cities: A Selection of Frederick Law Olmsted's Writings on City Landscapes*, ed. Sutton (1971), p. 79. While debate among historians has often centered on the supposed intent of middle-class designers to control working-class leisure through park design, landscape architects aimed to manipulate the moods of the middle-class users as well. Rosenzweig acknowledges these dual motives, in *Eight Hours*, p. 128. He ably discusses the relation of park design to social-class issues in ch. 5. On Olmsted's work on Central Park, see also Roper, *FLO: A Biography of Frederick Law Olmsted* (1973), ch. 13.

approval, "from which one could have guessed that we are in the vortex of a momentous crisis and in imminent peril of a grave national disaster."[10] Far from lessening nature's pacifying power by the interplay of designer's and patron's imaginations, Strong's pleasure was heightened by the arrangement's tacit acknowledgment of the sophisticated satisfaction required by a cultured person.

At other times, the Victorians sought strenuous trials of inner fiber by contest with natural forces to achieve a peace that consisted of self-mastery rather than the self-forgetfulness of Strong's pastoral stroll. Even so, personal testing relied for success on the deft handling of fictions of rusticity not unlike the effects Olmsted worked into parks. Edward Everett Hale perhaps endured life as a Boston minister because he applied his income and influence on a regular basis to the acquisition of rough experience. Most dramatically, in 1864 he broke his resolve to assist the Union cause at home by accepting a job at the front as a general's aide. But on either side of this taste of battle, Hale contrived wilderness challenges. As a boy, he tramped through the woods outside Boston two days a week after school, riding a train to the city limits and carrying a guidebook published by his father, who was also president of the railroad he took. Military life during the war so revived his love of outdoor exertion that he hiked near Lake Champlain soon after he left the army. Eventually, as president of the Appalachian Mountain Club, he had a peak named for him in New Hampshire in 1895.[11] That Hale worked hard to find provocative surroundings for his excursions does not impugn the sincerity of his passion for expending energy in nature, but simply calls attention to the aesthetic requisites that had to be satisfied if his outings were to produce their desired effect. In addition to hiking, the Victorians enthusiastically fished, hunted, rowed, and rode horseback in places not only scenic but comfortable.[12]

[10] Aug. 31, *The Diary of George Templeton Strong*, ed. Nevins and Thomas (1952), 3:251.

[11] On Hale's boyhood treks, see Hale, *A New England Boyhood* (1893), pp. 115–20. On his Civil War involvement and later outdoor activities, see Holloway, *Edward Everett Hale: A Biography* (1956), pp. 149, 254.

[12] Although historians often identify enthusiasm for the "strenuous life" with the progressives' rebellion against the Victorians' reputed rigidity, instances of the Victorians' participation in outdoor sports indicate continuities throughout much of the nineteenth century. Virtually all southerners recalled hunting, fishing, and horse racing as part of their childhoods, and many engaged in these activities as adults. See, e.g., Rice, *J. L. M. Curry: Southerner, Statesman, and Educator* (1949), pp. 5–6. In Springfield, Illinois, William Herndon hunted avidly throughout the antebellum decades. Jay Cooke, while living in Philadelphia, purchased land in rural Pennsylvania and Ohio during the war in order to hunt and fish. See Donald, *Lincoln's Herndon* (1949), p. 52, and Larson, *Jay Cooke: Private Banker* (1936), p. 195. When Alexander Agassiz built a house in Newport, Rhode Island, in the 1870s, he rowed and rode horseback for exercise. See *Letters and Recollections of Alexander Agassiz*, ed. Agassiz (1913), p. 152. James Cardinal Gibbons walked vigorously for exercise even after he became prelate of Baltimore in the 1880s, as explained in Boucher and Tehan, *Prince of Democracy: James Cardinal Gibbons* (1962), p. 186. For discussions of the significance of physical activity at the end of the century, see John Higham, "The Reorientation of American Culture in the 1890s," in Weiss, ed., *The Origins of Modern Consciousness* (1965), pp. 28–30; Lears, *No Place of Grace: Antimodernism and the Transformation of American Culture,*

The Victorians saw no need to exclude civilized amenities from their encounters with nature, reasoning that senses tried too much by harsh conditions ill received available pleasures. Over time, they lost patience with the therapeutic rigors of spas such as cold baths and opted to spend leisure more self-indulgently. Those who could afford vacation houses did not choose simple cabins but substantial retreats, such as the three-storied gabled mansion Zebulon Vance bought in the North Carolina mountains in the 1880s. A serious hunter, who imported dogs from England and gave time to selective breeding, Vance did not feel that lavish surroundings dulled nature's rewards.[13] Others either uninclined or unable to maintain private homes went away to boardinghouses and hotels in the mountains or by the sea. Yet they did not need to sacrifice freedom or luxury by their choice. Indeed, some resorts after the war offered more spectacular effects than the pleasures within most individuals' private means, and these settings were so varied in possible experience that visitors made of their stays what they willed. Thaddeus Lowe, a balloonist who pioneered aerial reconnaissance in the Civil War and later prospered near Philadelphia by marketing natural gas, made his entrepreneurial and technical skills serve his passion for scenic beauty when he constructed a group of resorts in the 1890s in southern California's San Gabriel mountains. Vacationers took one of two cable railroads up to several restaurants and hotels, where they dined, danced, or simply enjoyed views not unlike those Lowe once saw from his hot air balloons.[14] Much as Olmsted planned parks to help cultivated people approach nature, Lowe humanized his mountains just enough to make them relaxing without dimming their native splendor.

As nature lifted the Victorians above narrow cares to find renewal in its recurrent vitality, travel similarly offered refreshment by the stunning variety of peoples and things in the human world. In past generations, trips beyond

1880–1920 (1981), esp. pp. xiii, 107–24; Green, *Fit for America: Health, Fitness, Sport, and American Society* (1986), pp. 128–32, 219–58; and essays by Teddy Roosevelt, such as *Hunting Trips of a Ranchman: Sketches of Sport on the Northern Cattle Plains* (New York: Putnam, 1885). One aspect of progressive-era effort that was not prominent during the midcentury decades was team sports. Despite the Victorians' taste for social pleasures, physical testing remained a private assertion of self.

[13] On Vance's vacation home and dog breeding interests, respectively, see Tucker, *Zeb Vance: Champion of Personal Freedom* (1965), p. 473; Alexander Collie to Vance, Apr. 3, 1866, and Jonah [Turness?] to Vance, Sept. 1866, Zebulon Baird Vance Papers.

[14] Block, *Above the Civil War: The Story of Thaddeus Lowe, Balloonist, Inventor, Railway Builder* (1966), pp. 130–9. While some Victorians vacationed regularly in the 1850s, most acquired second homes or visited resorts after the war, not only an indication of changing tastes, but of their advancing age and attendant prosperity. In the 1870s, Edward Everett Hale and Alexander Agassiz owned houses in Rhode Island, Ely Parker built one in Connecticut, and Octavius Frothingham bought a home on the Massachusetts coast, as described in Holloway, *Hale*, p. 192; *Agassiz*, ed. Agassiz, pp. 115, 151; Parker, *The Life of General Ely S. Parker* (1919), p. 159; and Caruthers, *Octavius Brooks Frothingham: Gentle Radical* (1977), p. 205. Among the greater number who stayed in hotels, Joseph Taylor of Ohio vacationed in the Alleghenies in the 1870s, and Varina Davis spent summers on the Rhode Island coast in the 1890s. See, respectively, Elizabeth A. Taylor to William Hill, July 14, 1877, Joseph Danner Taylor Papers, and Wiley, *Confederate Women* (1975), p. 136.

those required for business or family duty were commonly taken as remedies for emotional or physical breakdowns, with an understandable emphasis on rest. During Ralph Waldo Emerson's time in Europe in 1832 and 1833, for example, after his wife's death and his resignation from the pulpit, all his sightseeing and meetings with authors did not erase a temper of genteel reserve accentuated by a concern for health.[15] The Victorians could go more places more quickly on growing networks of steamships and railroads, and, less mindful of therapeutic justifications, they asked travel to serve tastes for pleasure. Not content with the aesthetic satisfaction of viewing noted landmarks, they wanted to take home tokens of exotic cultures. They shopped either modestly, as did William Tecumseh Sherman in Paris in 1871, buying chignons and clothes for his daughters, or with the sustained application visible in the numerous porcelains and bronzes from China and Japan collected by the Boston naturalist Alexander Agassiz.[16] The Victorians pampered themselves, moreover, in ways that might be scandalous at home. Away from South Carolina in Richmond in 1861, where she "could read and write, stay at home, go out at her own sweet will," Mary Chesnut exulted at her possession of liberty, so precious to one who was otherwise the son's wife in her father-in-law's household, "sitting for hours with her fingers between the leaves of a frantically interesting book while her kin slowly dribbled nonsense by the yard."[17] To Chesnut, travel meant indulgence in otherwise forbidden sensations.

Victorian men took for granted Chesnut's cherished freedom, but they similarly exceeded the limits of domestic mores abroad. Away from Boston, where leisure nearly matched caricatures of high-mindedness and prudence, Henry Lee Higginson tried rock climbing in Europe in the 1850s and stayed out until the small morning hours at balls and cafés. Similarly, the appeal

[15] Gay Wilson Allen, *Waldo Emerson: A Biography* (New York: Viking, 1981), ch. 10. Traveling for health was not simply the prerogative of the well-to-do, but took more modest forms as well. When doctors suspected around 1820 that Sarah Hale, who later became a well-known writer and editor, had contracted consumption, her husband, an attorney in Newport, New Hampshire, spent six weeks driving her through the countryside in an open-air buggy, a sojourn from which she returned cured. See Ruth E. Finley, *The Lady of Godey's* (Philadelphia: J. B. Lippincott, 1931), p. 32.

[16] Burton, *Three Generations: Maria Boyle Ewing (1801–1864), Ellen Ewing Sherman (1824–1888), Minnie Sherman Fitch (1851–1913)* (1947), pp. 193–4; Agassiz, ed. Agassiz, pp. 269–71. The comments of other Victorians support the impression that shopping had become a central event of travel, though at times as much a tiresome obligation as an exciting diversion. Susan Wallace complained in 1881 that her Atlantic crossing had been so slow that she would have to skip sights in Paris in order to shop. James Garfield similarly commented that European travel was less pleasant since "mixed up with shopping." See Susan Wallace to Henry Wallace, July 10, Lew Wallace Papers, and Oct. 14, 1867, *The Diary of James A. Garfield*, ed. Brown and Williams (1967), 1:431. As collectors of art objects in particular, the Victorians stood midway between the modest purchasers of the antebellum decades and the intensely competitive art patrons of the turn of the century. On the earlier and later phases, see Harris, *The Artist in American Society: The Formative Years, 1790–1860* (1966), pp. 103–4, and Samuels, *Bernard Berenson: The Making of a Connoisseur* (1979).

[17] Diary, Aug., *Mary Chesnut's Civil War*, ed. Woodward (1981), p. 181. Further references to this text will not specify "diary" because the entire volume consists of Chesnut's journal.

Figure 8. Lew Wallace (1827–1905). Indiana attorney, soldier in the Mexican War and the Civil War, Republican, and author of *Ben-Hur* (1880). Photographed in uniform, ca. 1862, by Charles DeForest Fredericks. Gift of Mrs. F. B. Wilde, National Portrait Gallery, Smithsonian Institution.

of Rome as a place to live for William Wetmore Story must not only have been its superior ambience for a sculptor's work, but the city's hospitality to a range of diversions that nearly tipped life's balance from labor to leisure. As Story played billiards and cards, rode donkeys and strolled, attended concerts and plays, and picnicked and shopped during many years in Italy, he turned the privileged spaciousness of travel into the norm of an expatriate's days.[18]

[18] On Higginson, see his recollections of 1918 and his diary, Dec. 6, 1852, quoted in Perry, *Higginson*, pp. 48, 55. On Story, see James, *William Wetmore Story and His Friends* (1903), 1:132, 245, 249, 273. Intriguingly, the same year James issued his memoir of Story, he also published his own tale of the scandalous possibilities for pleasure of life abroad, Strether's scrutiny of the relations of Chad Newsome and Madame de Vionnet, in *The Ambassadors* (1903; reprint, New York: Signet, 1960), esp. chs. 30–1.

So seduced were the Victorians by travel that Story was not alone in peppering ordinary obligations to work and kin with the excitement of new places. Men relieved their uneasiness in middle-class occupations by seizing work opportunities that involved going abroad. Among those who left the United States to do research or to act as diplomats, Lew Wallace most persistently found ways to make his vocation more palatable by foreign experience. Resigned for years to the practice of law for his livelihood, Wallace was enamored of exotic cultures and, in fact and in fantasy, nourished his passion. "You know Mexico is Lew's *darling,*" wrote his wife, Susan, in 1865 when, after serving in the Mexican and Civil Wars, he returned to Mexico as a partisan of Benito Juarez.[19] Wallace kept Mexico alive in imagination, too, by working on and off on his novel about the Aztecs, *A Fair God,* from the mid-1840s until its publication in 1873. His reputation as an authority on Mexico opened new vistas. In 1878, Wallace was named New Mexico's territorial governor, and though he savored the desert's stark beauty, Susan, who aspired to a more civilized post, did not: "One day we saw no living thing but the mail boy on a sort of cart, not a horse, sheep, cow, scarcely a bird — not a house."[20] Thus in 1880, when James Garfield read Wallace's new book about the ancient Mideast, *Ben-Hur,* and offered to send the author as ambassador to the Ottoman Empire, the Wallaces accepted. Susan lacked Lew's romantic capacity to see any landscape's transcendent appeal, but she had a knack for exploiting the foreign materials she deemed worthy, publishing four books on Mediterranean culture as a result of living abroad.[21] Together, the Wallaces epitomized the Victorians' success at so thoroughly cultivating leisure that it paid enough to replace more drudging careers.[22]

One danger of so closely allying labor and leisure, however, was that the

---

[19] Susan Wallace to Delia Wallace, Mar. 10, Wallace Papers. The italics that appear in this and subsequent quotations are found in the original texts.

[20] Susan Wallace to Joanne Elston, May 23, 1879, Wallace Papers.

[21] On the Wallaces' work and travel, see Morseberger and Morseberger, *Lew Wallace: Militant Romantic* (1980), esp. chs. 17, 21.

[22] Among Victorians who combined research and travel, Lewis Henry Morgan, the anthropologist, spent time in the West studying Native Americans, and Alexander Agassiz visited Latin America, the Caribbean, and the Pacific in the course of his work as a marine zoologist. Among men of letters who sought diplomatic posts, William Dean Howells and Jabez Curry represented the United States in Venice and Madrid respectively. See Resek, *Lewis Henry Morgan: American Scholar* (1960), pp. 75–7, 86–90; *Agassiz,* ed. Agassiz, esp. chs. 6, 11, 13; Lynn, *William Dean Howells: An American Life* (1970), ch. 6; and Rice, *Curry,* ch. 8. It was not unprecedented for men of romantic inclinations to seek work abroad, especially if foreign settings might supply literary materials. Washington Irving and Nathaniel Hawthorne were emissaries to Spain and Liverpool respectively. Among the Victorians, however, the urge to travel was at once less easily controlled and more readily indulged. So deeply was Morgan stimulated by his frontier life spent studying Indians that when both of his daughters died of scarlet fever in 1862 while he was away, he guiltily blamed his wanderlust and foreswore field work for the rest of his career. Nonetheless, so essential was travel to his well-being that Morgan, his wife, and son spent fourteen months in Europe in 1870 and 1871 as part of an effort to assuage his continuing grief (Resek, *Morgan,* p. 120).

pursuit of enjoyment might become work. Perhaps there was a bit too much industry in all cases where the Victorians amused themselves energetically, betraying a far from frivolous need to answer sensations of aimlessness. But the cure's burdens could be worse than the affliction. The two-year round-the-world tour of Ulysses and Julia Grant, a couple who, in the words of William McFeely, in 1877 "had nowhere to go and nothing to do," must have assumed aspects of a grueling job, as they tried to see everything and to meet everyone of consequence on their travels.[23] Although discovery was in moderation a welcome task, foreign sights must have grown wearing in excess. Too much travel ill disguised a draining physical rootlessness as well. The Grants were only one of a number of couples who for years at a time had no real home. For Ulysses to run in 1880 for a third term as president, they set up housekeeping in Galena, Illinois, where they lived briefly before the war. But to call Galena home was so much a political fiction that their move to New York as soon as his prospects faded was simply one more relocation in a nearly perpetual odyssey, sometimes in search of labor and sometimes leisure, fitting the protagonist's name.[24] To such people as the Grants, travel was less a welcome break from everyday discipline and a chance to grow through novel experience than a troubling, and tiring, reminder of questions that relentlessly pursued them about their life's goals.

In addition to seeking stimulation in nature and travel, the Victorians demonstrated a talent for uncovering strange sights close to home that served to awaken, excite, and gratify longings to broaden identities. Although entrepreneurs contrived some of these spectacles in an effort to draw audiences, the success of commercial designs depended on the public's preexisting curiosity. James Garfield tapped Ohio's surprisingly varied opportunities in 1851. During one term when he worked as a teacher, he toured a prison and a Shaker community, heard a Catholic mass and a female Methodist preacher, and admired the newly macadamized National Road, which he judged "a splendid affair."[25] New York City offered far more amusements than Ohio, but its inhabitants' offbeat use of the city's resources is more revealing of the Victorian sensibility than the simple frequency of provocative events. As if part of a secret life, George Templeton Strong sought out horrors, oddities, and bizarre effects in his spare time, in addition to entertainments such as concerts and plays more fitting a respectable lawyer. New technology rarely failed to provide Strong with a chance to witness or ponder a fire, explosion, collision, or sinking. "Stagnated at home in the evening till half-past ten," he wrote in his diary in 1857, "when an alarm

---

[23] *Grant: A Biography* (1981), p. 453; ch. 26 documents the Grants' tour.

[24] McFeely, *Grant*, pp. 482–8. See Chapter 4, on Victorian families, for further discussion of this generation's peripatetic habits and, in particular, their penchant for living in hotels.

[25] Feb. 27, Jan. 12, Apr. 13, May 18, May 25, *Diary of Garfield*, ed. Brown and Williams, 1:72, 69, 77, 82, 83.

of fire started me out and I chased the conflagration up Lexington beyond the bounds of civilization into desert places where Irish shanties began to prevail."[26] A taste for the occult similarly engaged him. Embarrassed even in the privacy of his journal at the credulity his interest invited, Strong habitually opened then belittled and closed subjects that fascinated him. A professor, he reported in 1855, was lecturing on "ghosts and their revelations!!! Had half a mind to go and hear him but too busy and rather distrustful of the whole subject beside."[27] In 1860, he was lured on two successive nights to P. T. Barnum's show, where he pondered the "What-is-it" and concluded, in a tone as impatient of his incorrigible fascination as of Barnum's hoax, that "it" was an "idiotic dwarf nigger."[28] Nor did the same rhetorical sleight of hand that deflated his "silly experiments with hashish" keep him from testing his mind's possibilities with drugs more than once.[29] Strong took larger and larger doses until he achieved a "phantasmagoria of living and moving forms."[30]

Needless to say, Garfield's stimulants were tame next to Strong's. But both enlisted unusual occurrences to expand daily horizons with an insistence that casts light on the Victorians' compulsion to squeeze such outrageous experience from leisure that they were assured of their own vitality. The fact that entrepreneurs marketed oversized and riveting effects was both a response and a spur to the Victorians' extravagant tastes. P. T. Barnum, for example, transformed classical music from a sedate diversion to a sensory assault when he presented a "musical congress" of 1,500 performers in 1855. The printmakers Nathaniel Currier and James Ives produced mild lithographs of domestic life and sporting scenes along with mementos of human disasters, including the sinking of the steamship *Lexington* in 1840 and the Chicago fire of 1871.[31] As religious enthusiasm receded and dreams of greatness fell short of fruition, the Victorians placed extraordinary demands on sensory excitement to fill the inner spaces of their minds.

Probably few Victorian producers or consumers of the grandiose and the tragic fully realized how solitary a strategy for self-construction observing

[26] July 16, 1857, *Diary of Strong*, ed. Nevins and Thomas, 2:349.
[27] Nov. 23, ibid., 2:244.
[28] Mar. 2, 3, ibid., 3:12.
[29] Sept. 1, 1855, ibid., 2:290.
[30] Sept. 1, 1855, ibid., 2:291.
[31] See reproductions of prints in Crouse, *Mr. Currier and Mr. Ives: A Note on Their Lives and Times* (1930). George Templeton Strong reported Barnum's extravaganza in his diary, June 18, 1855, *Diary of Strong*, ed. Nevins and Thomas, 2:176–7. Commenting on the direction Barnum's showmanship took in the latter part of his career, Neil Harris writes that he aimed more at "passive spectatorship" than his earlier focus on "problem solving and competition between showman and audience" (*Humbug*, p. 244). This view conveys the overbearing quality of some Victorian diversions that ultimately challenged, rather than fueled, individual autonomy. Consider, too, other art forms that assumed more demonstrative styles as both a stimulant to and an expression of a romantic mentality. The ornamentation of Gothic architecture increasingly replaced the functional simplicity of Greek revival designs after 1850, for example, as explained by Bode, *Anatomy of Popular Culture*, ch. 3.

novelties was. As Garfield and Strong reached out to new phenomena, they demonstrated this generation's freedom to select among experiences unknown in societies that were less socially diverse, technologically adept, and commercially oriented. But the process of viewing spectacles produced by people with whom the observer was unacquainted was also an impersonal one. An individual might acquire vivid impressions, but dialogue with actors of no importance to oneself could not give knowledge the kind of significance gained when ideas were the object of community consensus. In addition, it was not accidental that most of the amusements that drew Garfield and Strong catered to crowds, large or small, but by definition composed mainly of strangers. Precisely as Herman Melville showed by surrounding his "Confidence Man" with shifting, aimless audiences in his novel, *The Confidence-Man*, in 1857, a world without sincerity could easily provide endlessly varied excitement to patrons as shadowy as the facades on stage, without touching a deeper uncertainty that joined all in the same dilemma.[32]

Modern readers will not be surprised at this early form of the mass media's obsession with presenting consumers, at least as eager for stimulation as the Victorians, with provocative images. But the disturbing excesses of Victorian culture and our own ought not devalue the wide opportunities of Americans at both times to choose from a range of pleasures and to tailor them to private ends. When individual Victorians felt that they stood at the center of natural and human worlds to be appropriated through play, assisted by imagination, they should not be charged with cultural myopia without conceding that their situations in time and society did allow privileged access to resources of impressive scope. Even so, they were sensitive to the limitations of individual interaction with impersonal forces. As the Victorians lost the assurance of sharing in cosmic purposes as conceived by traditional religion, the rich inner experience made possible by the romantic imagination lent them diversion, but not direction. Perhaps sociability was just as incapable of replacing deep security, but the predominance of social forms of

---

[32] *The Confidence-Man: His Masquerade* (1857), ed. Hennig Cohen (New York: Holt, Rinehart and Winston, 1964). Although Karen Halttunen argues convincingly that after 1850 Americans increasingly accepted a culture composed of gestures that seemed to belie the fleeting possibility of "sincere" communication, David Riesman's classic, *The Lonely Crowd*, highlights the persistent problem of autonomy in a society consisting of "other-directed" personalities. Without reducing Riesman's complex view (and overstating the advantage of the "inner-directed" person), Riesman underlines the difficulty of achieving self-determination if a person identifies with the crowd. See Halttunen, *Confidence Men and Painted Women*, esp. ch. 6, and Riesman, *Lonely Crowd*, pp. 295–306 and pt. 3. Another aspect of the Victorians' dilemma was captured by Karl Marx, when he wrote of the impersonality of a society not so much composed of strangers as dominated by commodities. George Templeton Strong's curious spectacles, for example, were products of the market. See Karl Marx, *Capital: A Critique of Political Economy*, ed. Friedrich Engels (New York: Modern Library, 1906), p. 83 and pt. 1, sec. 4. Contemporary historians who comment on the challenge that the commercialization of leisure posed to Americans' self-determination echo Marx's concern. See, e.g., Gilkeson, *Middle-Class Providence*, pp. 224–5 and ch. 6, and Peiss, *Cheap Amusements*, esp. chs. 5–6.

leisure among the Victorians attests to the solace they must have found in interpersonal bonds.

SOCIAL CONSTRUCTION THROUGH PLAY

Despite all the Victorians' individual efforts to engage their culture's wealth of possible sensations, they chose most often to spend leisure in company. Part of their motive was the emotional reward of human contact pursued in the free space of unstructured time. Less obvious, they used leisure as an experimental sphere in which to test elective relations, as other areas of social discourse grew too complex for easy exchange. Religion, work, and politics became increasingly bureaucratic in the midcentury decades. Family life, as the next chapter shows, involved feelings at times so tangled that satisfying communication was not simply obtained. The Victorians evolved customs and institutions for enjoyment as well, but they left little sign that they felt these developments betrayed their aim of enhancing sociability and became sources of constraint instead. In comparison with other activities, Victorian leisure remained an open field for social expression.

How deliberately the Victorians turned commonplace activities into communal entertainments may be seen in their treatment of reading and writing. In past generations and less educated circles, limited literacy required reading aloud. Sharing texts orally was more a part of life's business, as a means of religious or political communication, for example, than one of its pleasures. But the mid-nineteenth-century middle classes were sufficiently adept at handling language to use words to heighten enjoyment, and they read to each other to build bonds of sentiment by savoring literature together. Parents and children in the family of William Tecumseh Sherman in the 1850s habitually read aloud in the evenings. More formally, at an "at home" in Rome in 1849, William Wetmore Story offered his guests his own reading of *The Bigelow Papers* by Oliver Wendell Holmes, trying to recreate among ex-patriots intimacies associated with their native land.[33] Both occasions confirmed the value of interpersonal ties based on feelings that might be considered frivolous in a more traditional society committed to mutual duties. Both, too, acknowledged the importance of recruiting literacy for leisure as a tool of social construction.

Children, who are adept in all cultures at enlisting everyday activities in the service of fantasy, similarly used writing in Victorian homes to draw household members into imagined communities. With the help of brothers and sisters, Priscilla Tyler edited a family newspaper, *Paul Pry*, as a girl in

---

[33] On the Shermans, see Burton, *Three Generations*, p. 121; on the Storys, Story to James Russell Lowell, Mar. 21, quoted in James, *Story*, 1:170.

New York in the 1830s. Lucy Larcom compiled *The Diving Bell* in the 1840s for her family and boarders in Lowell, Massachusetts.[34] As adults, women were less able than men to move into public activities. But there could be practical advantages to staying in touch with leisure habits rooted in childhood. Elizabeth Cady Stanton and Susan B. Anthony tapped their facility at cooperative composition to inspire the larger community of women. Stanton recalled the two friends' joint writing efforts, most often undertaken in Stanton's home during the early years of the women's movement after 1848: "In writing we did better work together than either could alone. While she is slow and analytical in composition, I am rapid and synthetic. I am the better writer, she the better critic. She supplied the facts and statistics, I the philosophy and rhetoric, and together we have made arguments that have stood unshaken by the storms of thirty long years."[35] The explosive results for feminism of what two women put together in spare time hard won from domesticity underlines the potential social consequences of leisure.

Just as reading and writing in company laced mutual feelings with shared intelligence, parlor games enhanced sociability through fictions more elaborately constructed. A few of these Victorians grew up with proscriptions against plays judged as frivolous, distracting, and housed in theaters frequented by prostitutes. By the midcentury decades, however, private theatricals were a favorite amusement.[36] Amateur drama that was once seen as a pastime for children later drew enthusiastic adults. In the 1820s, the father of Anna Cora Mowatt built a stage to serve his children's penchant for producing plays, which, because there were fourteen offspring, rarely lacked an adequate cast. By the 1850s, parents invaded the children's preserve. When Alexander Agassiz arrived as a Swiss émigré in Cambridge, Massachusetts, in 1849, he found local society amused by dramas staged in homes for audiences of friends. In the same way, Confederate statesmen and their wives put on full-length plays for their mutual enjoyment during the war,

---

[34] Coleman, *Priscilla Cooper Tyler and the American Scene, 1816–1889* (1955), p. 46; Larcom, *A New England Girlhood: Outlined from Memory* (1889), pp. 170–4. On the traditional custom of reading aloud, David Hall notes that hearing, reciting, and memorizing language at home was also a common way to learn to read, in "Introduction: The Uses of Literacy in New England, 1600–1850," in Joyce et al., eds., *Printing and Society in Early America* (1983), pp. 23–6.

[35] Reminiscences from Elizabeth Cady Stanton et al., eds., *The History of Woman Suffrage* (Rochester: Charles Mann, 1881), 1:458, 459, quoted in Rossi, ed., *The Feminist Papers: From Adams to Beauvoir* (1973), pp. 380, 379.

[36] One of the surprisingly few Victorians who grew up with proscriptions against the theater was Lyman Abbott, as discussed by Brown in *Lyman Abbott, Christian Evangelist: A Study in Religious Liberalism* (1953), p. 16. One of the objections to the theater was that prostitutes used the balconies as places to solicit customers. See Claudia D. Johnson, "That Guilty Third Tier: Prostitution in Nineteenth-Century American Theaters," in Howe, ed., *Victorian America* (1976), pp. 11–20. Thus the acceptability of parlor theatricals was based in part on their private location. Nonetheless, by the 1850s theaters themselves were sufficiently reformed to make going out to plays a popular middle-class entertainment. See Bode, *Anatomy of Popular Culture*, ch. 1.

as well as passed time in Richmond drawing rooms with impromptu acting games such as charades.[37]

Karen Halttunen argues that the rage for private theatricals signified an embrace of symbolic gestures by rising middle classes committed previously to sincere communication, now comfortable with ritual.[38] An essential insight, Halttunen's remarks about amateur acting may best be seen in relation to other Victorian pleasures that scintillated by embroidering fantasies through the ordinary. Because Victorian leisure gained value in general by its ability to stir imagination, the formal role playing involved in producing well-known dramas put fellow actors in touch with each other in particularly intricate ways.

Private theatricals were also appealing because they were entertainments enjoyed at home. Rhys Isaac and other historians have documented a movement in America away from easy community relations and toward family privacy dating from the late eighteenth century.[39] Localities no longer consisted mainly of neighbors and kin because of the increasing size of towns and mobility of population, and thus a dichotomy opened up between a public sphere perceived as consisting of strangers and a person's intimate circle. When the Victorians sought relaxation in leisure instead of excitement, they needed the protected milieu of the family in which to unwind. Abram Hewitt, a New York iron manufacturer and Democratic politician, never vacationed until he broke down from overwork during the Civil War and still rarely took time off thereafter. But he took the rest he allowed himself exclusively at his country house in New Jersey, watching, if not engaging in, the walking, riding, driving, fishing, hunting, tennis, and croquet he provided his children and guests.[40]

Indeed, the Victorians relied on young people and company to ease both public pressures and the strenuous dynamics of family relations and thus, overall, to set a lighthearted mood. Priscilla Tyler, who bore nine children between 1840 and 1857, turned her skill as a former actress to creating special moments out of children's birthdays and relatives' visits. With characteristic flair, she hosted a costume party for one daughter's birthday in 1843. A decade later, she made her sister's stay in the Tylers' home outside

[37] On Mowatt and Agassiz, respectively, see Barnes, *The Lady of Fashion: The Life and the Theatre of Anna Cora Mowatt* (1954), pp. 5–6, and *Agassiz*, ed. Agassiz, p. 18. On Confederate theatricals, see Wiley, *Confederate Women*, p. 55, and Dyer, *The Gallant Hood* (1950), p. 213.

[38] Halttunen, *Confidence Men and Painted Women*, ch. 6.

[39] Isaac, *Transformation of Virginia*, pp. 302–5. The growing dichotomy between private and public spheres did not preclude interaction between them, either in leisure, as I propose later, or in preparing family members for careers, as Mary Ryan argues in *Cradle of the Middle Class: The Family in Oneida Country, New York, 1790–1865* (1981), esp. ch. 4. For further discussion of the Victorian family in society, see Chapter 4.

[40] Nevins, *Abram S. Hewitt, with Some Account of Peter Cooper* (1935), pp. 135, 530.

Philadelphia deliberately festive by orchestrating sightseeing, shopping, dancing, and treats such as ice cream to eat.[41] Similarly, Victorians in the midst of war solaced themselves with the joy of children and cordiality of friends. Christmas of 1863 would have afforded little celebration to George Templeton Strong had he not been able to perceive its magic through his children's eyes, as they "were admitted to the beatific vision of their presents and made the middle parlor a bedlam for an hour."[42] In 1864, Wade Hampton helped himself face the prospect of defeat by imagining his daughter's thrill to receive a doll for which he assiduously shopped in spare moments away from duty at the Virginia front.[43] Mary Chesnut's diary documents the insistent mutual visiting of southern leaders in Richmond that perhaps served to make temporary lodgings seem more like homes in a holiday spirit than the lately recruited quarters of a shaky republic.[44]

A paradox about the Victorians' reliance on family circles as places for warm interaction may be drawn from these instances. Just as homes without children or guests were less able to stir pleasant feelings, thoughts or simulations of domesticity's soothing features, such as Hampton's doll hunting and Richmond's calling, evoked a leisurely mood in lieu of actual families. Indeed, kin were nearly as valuable in imagination as in fact, particularly if families fell short of storybook expectations of happiness. This helps explain why Victorians whose home life was especially disrupted spent their leisure memorializing their families. For unknown reasons, John Wentworth of Chicago and his wife, Roxanna, lived apart for most of their twenty-six-year marriage. Though she bore five children, they never kept house independently, and she spent most of her time at her father's home in Troy, New York. Perhaps her husband's lifelong passion for genealogy, eventuating in a two-volume *Wentworth Genealogy* published in 1871, gratified his leisure in a more orderly and thorough way than could their unconventional living arrangement.[45] Lew Wallace's family was not only unusually peripatetic, but the only one among these Victorians in which husband and wife left evidence of an explicit agreement to produce a single child. With the family pared down to just Lew, Susan, and Henry, and with Lew often away from Indiana in Washington, Mexico, and elsewhere, it is noteworthy that family history became the Wallaces' common hobby. Susan assembled eight hefty volumes

---

[41] Coleman, *Tyler*, pp. 100, 124–7. See Chapter 4 on the Victorians' reliance on children for consolation and, more generally, on the significance of home and family.

[42] Dec. 25, *Diary of Strong*, ed. Nevins and Thomas, 3:385.

[43] Wade Hampton to Mary Fisher Hampton, Jan. 5, in Cauthen, ed., *Family Letters of Wade Hamptons*, p. 101.

[44] For a sample of Confederate social life during the early days in Richmond, see *Chesnut's Civil War*, ed. Woodward, ch. 5. Woodward calls the temper of relations during the time that leaders mainly inhabited the Spotswood and Arlington hotels, before at least some moved to private residences, that of an "extended house party" (p. xl). See also Muhlenfeld, *Mary Boykin Chesnut: A Biography* (1981), ch. 5.

[45] Fehrenbacher, *Chicago Giant: A Biography of "Long John" Wentworth* (1957), pp. 55, 229.

of clippings to document her husband's successes, and Henry compiled one last volume after his father's death.[46] In similar circumstances, Ellen Sherman, often separated from her husband by demands made on a professional soldier, collected family mementos in a japanned tin box for nearly forty years. After her death, William filled his time by making a scrapbook of condolence letters.[47] In all three cases, the Victorians used treasured objects to construct a spirit of family harmony that may have better served affections than their uneven domestic realities. Thoughts of loved ones enriched idle time, while the activities of leisure – collecting, handling, and aesthetically arranging precious things – deepened family bonds.

So powerfully were the Victorians attracted to an image of family intimacy that they tried hard not only to enjoy leisure at home, but to model elective friendships on what they envisioned as resonant family bonds. One way they engaged acquaintances in tight circles of feeling was to conduct much entertaining in private. Some city residents patronized restaurants, and boardinghouse dwellers dined casually with fellow lodgers. But the Victorians' preference was to share meals with friends at home.[48] Sociability in so modest a town as Cambridge, Ohio, consisted of teas and suppers, which, as Joseph Taylor, a lawyer and banker, reported to his absent wife, opened their house to a steady stream of neighbors.[49] Robert Ingersoll, an epicure as well as an agnostic who argued that religious orthodoxy was a result of coarse food, hosted dinners in Peoria and later in Washington that encouraged relaxed interaction by means of elegant repasts. His considerable weight, oscillating between 200 and 280 pounds, was an index of the prosperity that furnished a lavish table, but also of his fondness for good company. The fact that biographers of a number of these Victorians make a point of how heavy their subjects became indicates that Ingersoll was not alone in his tastes. Jabez Curry and John Wentworth, for example, each gained nearly 100 pounds during his middle age.[50] Thus the Victorians expressed their desire for

---

[46] The scrapbooks are in the Wallace Papers. On Feb. 17, 1853, Wallace wrote to his brother, William, that if their first child was a boy, they had agreed to have only one. The couple stood by the terms of their agreement. The letter is in the Wallace Papers.

[47] Burton, *Three Generations*, p. 274.

[48] Even in New York, George Templeton Strong ate in restaurants as desirable as Delmonico's most often when his wife was away. See, e.g., June 21 and Sept. 14, 1855, *Diary of Strong*, ed. Nevins and Thomas, 2:227, 231. No doubt his servants would have cooked him a meal, but it was the disruption of his family that impelled him to dine out. On boardinghouses, see Chapter 4.

[49] Taylor to Elizabeth A. Taylor, July 17, 1867, Aug. 9, 1868, Taylor Papers.

[50] Rice, *Curry*, p. 10; Fehrenbacher, *Chicago Giant*, pp. 142, 231. On Ingersoll, see Cramer, *Royal Bob: The Life of Robert G. Ingersoll* (1952), pp. 64–5, 182, 185. Other historians who comment on the Victorians' weight include Glenn Tucker, who says that Zebulon Vance ate so enormously that he weighed 230 pounds before he was forty, and William McFeely, who observes that Julia Grant outweighed her husband at 175 pounds to his 165 in 1878. See Tucker, *Vance*, pp. 474, 159, and McFeely, *Grant*, p. 25. More than reflecting our twentieth-century obsession with weight, these comments highlight the Victorians' indulgences. Although it seems ironic that the members of this generation pursued outdoor exercise and adventure as zestfully as they did rich food and company, the contradiction is resolved in

friendliness by eating together, and the weight of many individuals signaled their enthusiasm for society as well as for food.

William Dean Howells, another substantial man who went out nearly every night, came to see that at some critical point enthusiastic entertaining undercut both actual domesticity and friendly intimacy. If guests came and went too often, homes were no longer familial but grew depersonalized instead. Thus Howells's wife, Elinor, begged off from the flood of invitations when her children rebelled at her absences, while Howells registered his sense that he cheated himself of peace of mind when he denounced his habitual running as an "uncontrollable way of living."[51] Yet Howells persisted in socializing, a decision suggesting how much the Victorians eventually bracketed homelike sincerity in one corner of leisure, though not without conceding the ideal of family intimacy without sensations of self-betrayal.

Friendships sustained by correspondence blended elements of openness and reserve and thus occupied a middle ground between private and public leisure. Intimacy on selected themes was possible precisely because circumstances precluded extended relations. Communication across sectional and gender lines, complicated by geographic distance, thrived on disclosure made safe by the unlikelihood of close acquaintance and subsequent disappointment, as well as on the element of fantasy in bonds so private that they found expression only on paper.

Two sets of postwar correspondence, between William Montague Browne of Georgia and Samuel Barlow of New York and between Jabez Curry of Richmond and Robert Winthrop of Boston, grew from the need on both sides to convey each one's sectional viewpoint to a respectful audience in an otherwise hostile milieu. The exchanges provided a protected space in which the writers shared feelings and thoughts on subjects of deep concern. Browne and Barlow had been friends in the 1850s, brought together by Democratic politics and an interest in rare books and autographs. They did favors for one another once again during Reconstruction, as Barlow lent Browne money and Browne sent fresh peaches for thanks. Intimacy was not restored, but the gestures of mutual trust that the men exchanged were still significant as symbols bringing emotional reassurance.[52] Curry and Winthrop, on the other hand, became acquainted in the 1880s through correspondence concerning their common work for southern education. Though they never met, they gradually amended discussion of business by sharing opinions on women's rights, immigration, and race. Yet even as their friendship flourished in writing, they must have sensed that their relationship's single dimension

part by the thought that the sports they favored were not the most vigorous. They preferred hunting, for example, to team competition.

[51] Quoted in Lynn, *Howells,* p. 252.

[52] Coulter, *William Montague Browne: Versatile Anglo-Irish American, 1823–1883* (1967), pp. 31–3, 58–64, 143–4, 149–51.

gave it a privileged quality that might easily have been violated had the men been in constant contact.[53] Neither friendship, in sum, was valuable for its everyday durability, but both allowed the participants a private sphere for the expression of essential sentiments.

Long-term correspondence between men and women, most often with each one married to someone else, similarly provided focused interaction removed from pedestrian lives. In an era when intellectual compatibility was not a principal requisite of marriage, extramarital communication could be strikingly cerebral, as if those involved were titilated by the nearly illicit tenor of serious discussion. Neither Pierre Beauregard nor Zebulon Vance was particularly interested in ideas. But Beauregard wrote for years to Augusta Evans, an Alabama novelist, while Vance communicated with Cornelia Spencer, a self-styled intellectual and widow in Chapel Hill, North Carolina, who first sought him out in 1866. Vance and Spencer continued their dialogue through much of Vance's marriage, widowerhood, and remarriage in 1880.[54] The postwar friendship of Ely Parker in New York City and Harriet Converse of the upstate town of Elmira centered on her interest in Indian lore. Parker habitually addressed her by her Seneca name, Gayaneshaoh, and signed with his tribal title, Donehowaga.[55] Their sharing of esoteric knowledge epitomized the way all these relationships insinuated themselves in the interstices of commonplace lives by offering a kind of sociability unimpeded by the complex feelings of real intimacy. In lieu of evidence of extramarital affairs among these Victorians, such rarefied friendships approximated modernity's clandestine sexual liaisons in the sense that they promised simple gratification to sensibilities aroused by imagination.[56] If the Victorians had more restrained physical expectations than we, they were no less attracted to the romance of free communion and no less successful at creating privileged space.

Friendships forged across geographic and social distances indicate how much Victorian leisure offered more choice than in the past of who would

---

[53] Rice, *Curry*, pp. 157–8, 163–4. Next to the substantial literature on women's friendships, much less has been said of relations between men. But these, too, thrived on greater leisure to explore sentiment between peers in a society significantly divided by beliefs in gender differences. Men, moreover, must have welcomed intimacy in private life that was restricted in the competitive public sphere. The best analysis of women's friendships remains Carroll Smith-Rosenberg, "The Female World of Love and Ritual: Relations between Women in Nineteenth-Century America," in her *Disorderly Conduct: Visions of Gender in Victorian America* (1985), pp. 53–73. Steven M. Stowe has argued for the importance of correspondence in creating interpersonal bonds, in *Intimacy and Power in the Old South: Ritual in the Lives of the Planters* (1987). esp. pp. 2–4. I do not disagree, but contend as well that the selective, crafted quality of feeling generated by writing created a specialized kind of friendship.

[54] On Beauregard, see Williams, *Beauregard,* p. 160. The Spencer–Vance correspondence began with her letter to Vance, May 4, 1866, Vance Papers. Other letters to Vance are also located in the Vance Papers, while the North Carolina State Archives houses a collection of Cornelia Phillips Spencer Papers as well.

[55] Parker, *Parker,* p. 164 and ch. 15.

[56] See discussion of the sexual inclinations of these Victorians in Chapter 4.

be cultivated. There was also more discretion in what kind of relationships would be made. Some acquaintances, not treated as intimates, were instead ushered into a realm of formal manners that removed them from a crowd's anonymity without admitting them to full confidence. Not only did the Victorians see the impossibility of self-disclosure in all the encounters of a growing, mobile society, but they understood that restricted expression answered key social needs as well.

It may seem puzzling that the Victorians' enthusiasm for leisure coexisted with strict guidelines for interaction that directed sociability by tacit rules. Yet as was true for friendships by mail, this generation realized that smooth relations among individuals of differing opinions and backgrounds depended on selective discourse. Receptions, dinners, and, most important, clubs were social settings in which concern for good manners was especially strong. Gatherings of large numbers of guests were especially common in cities, where a person was apt to have many passing acquaintances. By the late 1850s, George Templeton Strong was a man of sufficient stature in New York to initiate a weekly "at home" for about fifty people. "Ellie works hard to entertain her guests," Strong wrote of his wife, "and does it with tact, ease, and great success," a comment revealing the existence of unspoken measures of adequacy for managing crowds invited for light conversation and refreshments.[57] Even while praising his wife's social skill, Strong remained ambivalent about the superficiality of large-scale entertaining. Writing in his diary in 1859, he half-rebelled at the insincerity of the similar custom of New Year's Day calling, a "usage that requires everybody to receive everybody else with the shew of kindness and cordiality." Yet he turned around to say that "one day in the year does no harm."[58] Thus fighting off his distaste of the artificiality of high society's manners, Strong conceded that mere perceptions of mutual friendliness had value and, in conjunction with his remarks about Ellie, that social gestures had to be nurtured by a hostess's guiding hand.[59]

Public occasions of either elaborate or more modest pretensions, such as dinners, often imposed barriers to communication between the sexes. Yet these restrictive conventions, seen more positively, focused conversation. While manners dictating public interaction between men and women con-

[57] May 15, 1857, *Diary of Strong*, ed. Nevins and Thomas, 2:336.

[58] Jan. 3, 1859, ibid., 2:430. Variant spellings that appear in this and subsequent quotations are found in the original texts.

[59] There has been much provocative literature on the evolution and function of manners as social tools in Europe and America. See Elias, *The Civilizing Process: The History of Manners,* trans. Jephcott (1939); Persons, *The Decline of American Gentility* (1973); Lyn Lofland, *A World of Strangers: Order and Action in Urban Public Space* (New York: Basic Books, 1973); Leonore Davidoff, *The Best Circles: Social Etiquette and the Season* (London: Croom Helm, 1973); Halttunen, *Confidence Men and Painted Women.* Stow Persons makes the important point that many nineteenth-century Americans, especially those less well-to-do than these Victorians, were ambivalent about rules they sensed might be no more than elite affectations out of place in a democracy. See *Decline of American Gentility,* esp. chs. 2, 3.

tained numerous tacit prohibitions, they also guaranteed open dialogue within single-sex groups. At a dinner in 1860, the ladies left the table none too soon for George Templeton Strong, who engaged the men in "good healthy talk on the value of unconditioned loyalty."[60] On the other side, Mary Chesnut was so cheered in Richmond during the war by the "feminine gossip" of "our party of matrons" that, when she later reworked her journal in the 1870s and 1880s, she transformed women's conversation into a dramatic setting where she placed scattered remarks she heard.[61] By thus making discrete comments part of semifictional exchange, Chesnut implicitly asserted the value of all-women's discussions as scenes of intellectual revelation. In sum, there was a certain utility in manners that enforced distance between the sexes. For a generation convinced of gender differences, proprieties observed in mixed company worked less to inhibit conversation than to instruct participants in how to speak publicly with members of the opposite sex.[62] In addition, public restrictions secured private freedom for gatherings composed exclusively of men or women, because the message hidden in the assumption of decisive gender differences was the existence of strong natural bonds among members of each sex. One consequence of this view was the proliferation of all-male clubs.

Voluntary associations devoted to benevolent goals were displaced increasingly in the midcentury decades by secular clubs that without embarrassment aimed simply at pleasant society. That is not to say that high-minded organizations disappeared altogether, because the Victorians took an interest in lyceums, library associations, historical societies, and Civil War commemoration, even as religious commitments waned. Yet when societies for sociable dining appeared alongside civic projects, it was one sign of the rising legitimacy of leisure unencumbered by serious goals.[63] Most popular in

---

[60] Feb. 11, *Diary of Strong,* ed. Nevins and Thomas, 3:296.

[61] Aug. 29, 1861, *Chesnut's Civil War,* ed. Woodward, p. 171. One of the principal changes Chesnut made in her journal when she reworked it in the postwar decades was to cast her recollections in dialogue in specific social settings. Such conversations may or may not have taken place as later described, but her choice of a situation as a dramatic device attests to its importance to her. If her original and revised entries are compared for Aug. 27–29, 1861, conversation among a group of women as they apparently did handwork appears only in the later text. See *Mary Chesnut: The Unpublished Civil War Diaries,* ed. Woodward and Muhlenfeld (1984), pp. 141–6 (original text), and *Chesnut's Civil War,* ed. Woodward, pp. 168–73 (revised text).

[62] Rosalind Rosenberg shows that ideas about gender differences remained intact throughout the nineteenth century, in *Beyond Separate Spheres: Intellectual Roots of Modern Feminism* (1982). Although to a great extent gender relations in practice remained restrained as well, recent work indicates some areas of more relaxed interaction. Cindy Sondik Aron demonstrates that men and women in the new middle class of clerical workers mixed quite freely in offices, in *Ladies and Gentlemen of the Civil Service: Middle-Class Workers in Victorian America* (1987), ch. 7. Kathy Peiss suggests that dance halls and amusement parks afforded new opportunities for public intimacy to the working classes especially, in *Cheap Amusement,* chs. 4, 5. Nonetheless, both writers refer to later decades and less well-to-do groups than studied here.

[63] Gilkeson records that the first men's club in Providence was formed in 1856, but designates 1865 to 1914 as the "golden age" of clubs that served sporting and other interests as well as socializing and dining, in *Middle-Class Providence,* ch. 4. For the most inclusive list of clubs in major cities between

northeastern cities, dining clubs invited men of diverse social roots to participate in relations of controlled intimacy. With admission based more on accomplishment than lineage, sons of old Boston families shared meals catered in restaurants with upwardly mobile men such as William Dean Howells, editor of the *Atlantic Monthly,* and William Potter, who came in from his Unitarian parish in New Bedford in the early 1860s specifically to dine in company.[64] Clubs served at once to define social space, distinguishing men of consequence, and, more subjectively, to provide a sphere for friendly conversation in an otherwise bustling society. Although George Templeton Strong liked feeling "nobby and exclusive" when he was elected in 1860 to the New York Club, his membership's long-run personal benefit depended less on acquired status than on the opportunity to interact with his peers in public on terms about as easy as acquaintances in his society were allowed.[65]

The Victorians thus used the comparative freedom of leisure to craft social relations that satisfied in various ways. They instinctively understood that reserve could be as valuable as familial closeness, if restraint of some impulses permitted more amicable communication on selected themes. Not all of the Victorians participated equally in diverse kinds of leisure, however. Women and southerners inclined toward personal forms of interaction at the expense of entertainments outside households that involved strangers.

As the task of defining private purpose passed gradually within the Victorians' lifetime from religion to leisure, as one key secular pursuit among several, perceptions of women's value similarly shifted from their piety to their manners. The prominence of women in this discussion of leisure as skilled hostesses, ready company, and astute observers of customs is evidence of their willingness to exercise social graces. As high society began to entertain on grander scales, women gained a new visibility derived from staging events. In a culture that increasingly took its bearing from its pleasures, women's influence could thus be considerable. Yet there were limits to their prerogatives. On the whole, Victorian women were still not ready to make a case for crossing an invisible line between private and public occasions. In contrast to the prominence of women in gatherings in homes, only one of the women studied, Jeanne Carr in California, was associated with a women's club around 1880, an organization with purposes of benevolence and self-culture still more seriously conceived than the often bluntly sociable gatherings of men.[66] Nor did middle-class women strive as aggressively for the

1830 and 1890, see Persons, *Decline of American Gentility,* pp. 103–9. Although Persons identifies clubs as centers of gentry culture, he acknowledges that rising men in a democracy often acquired genteel symbols, and Gilkeson confirms that clubs drew a wide sample of the middle classes.

[64] Perry, *Higginson,* pp. 400–3; Lynn, *Howells,* p. 195; Potter to George W. Bartlett, Mar. 4, 1861, William Potter Papers.

[65] Aug. 16, *Diary of Strong,* ed. Nevins and Thomas, 3:39.

[66] Carr was elected an honorary member of the Los Angeles Woman's Club founded by Caroline Severance in 1878. The club disbanded in 1881. See Mrs. Burton M. Williamson, *Clubs and Societies in*

individual stimulation afforded by cities. They left no record of mingling with crowds in search of spectacles such as that found in the diaries of James Garfield and George Templeton Strong. American Victorian women exercised more social power than did their mothers, as both sexes invested greater energy and expected profounder return from encounters that wove bonds among strangers. Nonetheless, they took care to be neither too conspicuous, frivolous, nor independent. That leisure was so tentatively women's terrain underlines their persistent social marginality.

Southerners, like women, chose informal sociability more often than they explored options for structured clubs and mass gatherings. While the leisure of Victorian women was channeled by concern for propriety, however, the pastimes of southern Victorians involved groups of friends simply because of their stronger identification with traditional communities. Even with this difference, customs governing private mores were being transformed in both cases to meet new conditions. Much as women's work as hostesses changed in function as the company who came more often included acquaintances than neighbors and kin, so the significance of southern amicability shifted as impersonality grew. In established communities, visiting reinforced settled bonds of obligation. But presenting oneself to households in a new town served aspirations for social mobility, companionship, and romance. When Zebulon Vance left home in Asheville, North Carolina, in 1851 to study in Chapel Hill, he could barely restrain his impulse to call on local families containing young women, so strong was the push of loneliness and the pull of fresh pretty faces. "I have set myself bounds, as to how often I shall go visiting," he wrote with studious resolve, "and I am determined not to exceed them on any pretence whatever."[67] Because historians have shown that antebellum southerners were more mobile than once supposed, such adaptations of communal mores must have predated Confederate society's hasty formation in Richmond, where the intense visiting, dining, and partying of southern leaders crystallized the tendency to apply traditional customs to the task of constructing rather than preserving interpersonal ties.[68]

Los Angeles in 1892 (Los Angeles: Elmer R. King, 1892). I am grateful to Karen Blair for this information. On the comparatively moralistic goals of women's clubs, see Blair, *The Clubwoman as Feminist: True Womanhood Redefined, 1868–1914* (1980), esp. ch. 2. Although Elizabeth Cady Stanton, one of these Victorians, was one of the most aggressive women of her time, it is intriguing that she did not campaign as insistently for women's right to leisure as for political participation and work opportunity. Perhaps she and other suffragists arranged their priorities as they perceived the need for reform, yet it is also likely that their secondary concern with pleasure for women was one index of an underlying social conservatism.

[67] Vance to Martha Weaver, Sept. 24, in *The Papers of Zebulon Baird Vance, 1843–1862*, ed. Johnston (1963), 1:10.

[68] On southerners' restlessness, see Oakes, *The Ruling Race: A History of American Slaveholders* (1982), ch. 3. Steven Stowe is less interested in transitional aspects of southern culture, but argues helpfully for the kinship of personal and social meanings in southerners' more traditional outlook. See *Intimacy and Power in the Old South*, esp. p. xviii.

In sum, southern leisure took sufficient account of social displacement to be akin to northern bonding strategies. Yet a comparatively homey quality remained. It is hard to imagine northern leaders, accustomed by the 1860s to receptions and clubs, pulling taffy or playing charades with fellow heads of state as did their Confederate counterparts.[69] Closer at least in feeling to memories of simple community pleasures, southerners seemed nearly to resist formal relations in the spirit of rebels dedicated to preserving their culture's perceived uniqueness.

Moved by the persuasive tug of custom and the complementary pull of choice, women and southerners dominated the same corner of leisure devoted to private socializing. Yet Victorian pastimes overall were impressively diverse, and included family-centered entertaining, privileged intimacies, formal society, and exclusive clubs. The decisive importance of leisure in Victorian society was the most basic reason for the intimate connections between habits of enjoyment and the Civil War.

THE RECIPROCAL DEBTS OF PLEASURE AND WAR

American Victorians did not go to war because of their aspirations for excitement, but neither were habits of peacetime leisure irrelevant to the way they experienced civil conflict. War promised adventure on a scale bound to excite people eager for release from routines and cares. Skill at forging elective bonds lent army life some of the comfortable texture of civilian pastimes, while outside the military, clubs confirmed their legitimacy by aiding war efforts. Beyond these mutual influences of pleasure seeking and war, combat raised basic issues about leisure's meaning. The terrible realism of war made the Victorians wonder if imagination could ever provide solutions to questions of purpose or if leisure could only provide diversion. When they made Civil War commemoration a focus of communal celebration in the postwar decades, they answered, in effect, that enjoyment might be justified by connection with serious goals. In the end, the Civil War helped American Victorians to legitimize leisure and thus to secure enjoyment in culture more firmly than ever.

In 1861, Americans on both sides felt dismay at the dissolution of the Union. But the war also lured them by the deceptively familiar prospects of outdoor life, travel, and human drama. John William DeForest, the

---

[69] On these pastimes, see Dyer, *Hood,* p. 213. Lincoln's White House, in fact, favored large receptions and diplomatic dinners. Not only was this style of entertaining a reflection of northern acceptance of social formality, but, on the one hand, a necessity in an established state that had to host official foreign guests and, on the other hand, a function of Mary Todd Lincoln's private ambition to match the elegance of the wealthy and powerful, as if in rebellion against her provincial southern birth in Lexington, Kentucky. See Baker, *Mary Todd Lincoln: A Biography* (1987), ch. 7.

Connecticut writer who would pioneer realistic war reporting in fiction in his novel, *Miss Ravenel's Conversion from Secession to Loyalty,* in 1867, wrote home to his wife in 1862 using language borrowed from conventional travel narratives. Perhaps he sensed the irony of adapting genteel prose to depict the "uninterrupted succession of lovely pictures" he saw from the deck of his transport ship on the Mississippi in Louisiana. But he went on to luxuriate in the blended visual and literary richness of the "windings of the mighty river, the endless cyprus forests in the background, the vast fields of cane and corn, the abundant magnolias and orange groves and bananas, the plantation houses showing white through dark-green foliage."[70] DeForest came to understand that there was sadly more to war than pretty images. Yet when he revised his war letters for publication, he left this sensuous prose as a testament to his first, if naive, encounter with military life.

Thomas Wentworth Higginson, more impetuously caught up than DeForest in the thrill of physical challenge, seemed less aware of the potential tragedy hidden in the similarity of mock and real contests. Literary conventions associated with heroic quests fully informed Higginson's descriptions of combat. Glorying in his war memoirs of 1870 in the "free and adventurous life of partisan warfare," Higginson wove stories of prowess tested in natural surroundings that were more provocative of extraordinary feats than foreboding of harm.[71] In so doing, he drew directly on themes and vocabulary he used in his recent articles in the *Atlantic Monthly.* In "The Maroons of Surinam," published in 1860, Higginson described the adventures of an expedition in the 1770s to subdue escaped slaves, a story centered in romantic elements of stunning South American scenery, the maroons' "wild freedom," and the doomed love of the Dutch commander for "his beautiful quadroon wife and his only son."[72] With a tamer subject but the same message, the need for release from civilized pressures, Higginson advocated "bodily enjoyment" to restore "the zest of savage life" in an article entitled "Gymnastics" in 1861.[73] When the war came, combat became the fortuitous showplace for toughness otherwise confined to the neighborhood gym. Thus, as the wartime writings of DeForest and Higginson show, established Victorian passions for natural beauty, exotic scenes, and physical awakening colored perceptions of war and rendered the conflict in familiar terms.

Sometimes romantic expectations poised the Victorians for swift disillusionment. The crowd who came out from Washington in August 1861 to watch the fighting at Bull Run seemed to expect the outsized effects of

---

[70] DeForest to Harriet DeForest, May 2, 1862, in his *A Volunteer's Adventures: A Union Captain's Record of the Civil War,* ed. Croushore (1946), p. 17.

[71] *Army Life in a Black Regiment* (1870), p. 167. Representative tales of his adventures may be found in chs. 6 and 7.

[72] "The Maroons of Surinam," pp. 557, 556.

[73] "Gymnastics," p. 285.

Victorian theater rather than the uncompromising sternness of battle. William Potter, who had preached in Washington that day, was much moved by the northern defeat, and he went back to Massachusetts convinced, as he told a friend, that "a great & bloody judgment awaits us."[74] What is more difficult to fathom is that even the brutal realism acquired by experience, however humbling, failed to eclipse the fascination of combat. When DeForest put down his recollections of violence, sickness, and suffering in *Miss Ravenel's Conversion,* he hovered near these moments of intense experience like a fly around a flame. He could neither close his ears to the amputee who "uttered an inarticulate jabber of broken screams," nor his eyes to the sight of the man still sitting upright after a bullet "traversed the neck, and cut the spinal column where it joins the brain," nor contain his wonder at the "thin and yellow ghosts in ragged uniforms [who] go calmly to their duties without murmuring, without a desertion."[75] It is possible to argue cynically, and in part accurately, that these privileged Victorians maintained a protective distance from hardship sufficient to allow appreciation of the war as a series of stirring scenes. DeForest was a Union officer after all. Yet it is equally true that war's sad face jolted observers and put them in touch with deep sentiments far better than leisure's simulated adventures. Perhaps this generation had expected amusements to supply a remedy for aimlessness more profound than entertainment could ever provide. When war injected life-and-death stakes into sojourns that felt superficially like peacetime excursions, the value gained by realism helped to offset the pain of suffering and grief.[76]

The eagerness with which individuals and organizations ordinarily devoted to leisure sought roles in the Civil War grew similarly from a powerful desire for direction. Charlotte Cushman and William Wetmore Story, longtime expatriates who savored Europe for its openness to pleasure and artistry, worked for the Union not because war was romantic but because it was consequential. Cushman left Rome during the winter of 1862 to undertake an acting tour to benefit the Sanitary Commission. She appeared in plays in Philadelphia, Boston, New York, Washington, and Baltimore before returning to Italy.[77] Story, a close friend of Charles Sumner, was repeatedly confronted in their correspondence with Sumner's conviction of the war's unparalleled importance. There is "a delight here which you have not," Sumner wrote from Washington in 1860: "It is the standing up for truth

---

[74] Potter to George W. Bartlett, Aug. 20, Potter Papers. On the cultural significance of Bull Run, see Cunliffe, *Soldiers and Civilians: The Martial Spirit in America, 1775–1865* (1968), ch. 1.

[75] *Miss Ravenel's Conversion from Secession to Loyalty* (1867), ed. Haight (1955), pp. xiv, xv, 335.

[76] Writing of a slightly later period around the turn of the twentieth century, Jackson Lears has also commented on the search for authenticity of the prosperous middle classes. In contrast to the emphasis in my analysis on the shortcomings of imagination, however, Lears stresses the alienating force of the capitalist marketplace. See *No Place of Grace,* esp. pp. 300–12.

[77] Stebbins, *Charlotte Cushman: Her Letters and Memories of Her Life* (1879), pp. 185–7.

and liberty."[78] "This will be a free country," Sumner trumpeted with equal idealism in 1864: "Be its sculptor. . . . You are the artist for this immortal achievement."[79] Story professed that any disruption of his Roman routine went "terribly against my grain."[80] Thus he must have been touched deeply by Sumner's logic in order to contribute to the northern cause by writing a series of letters to the *London Daily News,* making a case for England's neutrality in the American conflict.[81] Neither Cushman nor Story was long deflected from a life of comparative leisure by the demands of the Civil War. Cushman wrote to a friend from an English spa in the summer of 1865 that the social pace she had resumed in Rome wore her out. Although Story accepted commissions to sculpt busts of American public figures for display at home, he continued to live abroad.[82] Yet it is no less true that Cushman and Story had been impelled by civil struggle to wonder poignantly, even if briefly, about the relative merits of enjoyment and duty.

At home in America, leisure organizations turned in the same spirit from pleasurable to political ends. Clubs in the North composed of educated men sought to exert political pressure. George Templeton Strong went to the Century Club in 1863 "for the sole purpose of showing a cold shoulder to two or three of its habitués who seceshionize [and to manifest] to them my desire we may be better strangers."[83] It was a short step to the formation the same year of the Union League Club, with the partisan goals Strong described in his diary:

We may thus associate into an organism some eight hundred or one thousand influential New Yorkians who desire to sustain government against Southern re-bellion and Northern sectionalism, and strengthen Northern loyalty to the nation, and stimulate property-holders and educated men to assert their right to a vote in the conduct of public affairs, national, state, and municipal, and do a little something toward suppressing the filthy horde of professed politicians that is now living on us and draining our national life by parasitical suction.[84]

Accompanied by early intimations of the mugwump impulse to clean up politics, the Union League Club's appearance is significant from the per-spective of leisure as an instance of how readily clubs, organizations conceived to provide amusement, embraced weighty aims. Much as individual Vic-

---

[78] Sumner to Story, Jan. 27, in James, *Story,* 2:48.

[79] Sumner to Story, Jan. 1, in ibid., 2:158.

[80] Story to Charles Eliot Norton, May 3, 1862, in ibid., 2:72. In this letter, Story referred specifically to his disinclination to travel. I interpret his remark broadly as a sign of his attachment to his habitual activities in Rome.

[81] The letters appeared in the *Daily News* from Dec. 26 through Dec. 28, 1861. See ibid., 2:102–3.

[82] Cushman to Fanny Seward, summer 1865, quoted in Stebbins, *Cushman,* p. 197; James, *Story,* 2:167.

[83] Feb. 9, *Diary of Strong,* ed. Nevins and Thomas, 3:296.

[84] Mar. 20, ibid., 3:307.

torians gravitated toward the war's realism for a kind of emotional ballast, clubs betrayed their need of a goal beyond entertainment to give members the inner resonance they expected leisure to provide. American Victorians were modern in their willingness to indulge themselves in amusements of so many kinds, but they were not satisfied with simple enjoyment and yearned to make their efforts of consequence.

War's philosophical value was of less immediate use to men under strain, however, than their capacity to find solace in company. This was a society where people knew how to use leisure to form relationships suited to diverse situations, and soldiers as well as civilians came together for emotional reinforcement through established social strategies. Their facility was particularly crucial in the army, where free time quickly became oppressive. Army routines themselves were initially exciting, but long stretches in camp between battles soon portended little except the prospect of boredom. "Drill is no longer an amusement as at first," wrote DeForest's character, Colonel Colburne, in *Miss Ravenel's Conversion,* "but an inexpressibly wearisome monotony."[85] Colburne's remark drew directly on DeForest's own impression during his encampment near New Orleans in 1862 that military experience outside combat "is a healthy, monotonous, stupid life, and makes one long to go somewhere, even at the risk of being shot."[86] Soldiers who understood that leisure was a crafted product of human will soon learned to fill idle hours with familiar pastimes. In both the Union and Confederate armies, they sang, played cards, competed in sports, and celebrated holidays.[87] They achieved not only diversion, but valuable, though temporary, interpersonal bonds.

In the context of this leisured sociability, class differences were particularly visible, making it important to pinpoint the role of the Victorian middle classes, most often serving officers, in campwide amusements. In the close quarters of the army where men of diverse backgrounds came together, the Victorians were cast in positions of observers and disciplinarians of enlisted men. Rather than find rest easily in warm relationships, they took their leisure by watching the pleasure of others. As a colonel of black troops, Thomas Wentworth Higginson thrilled at the unexpected spectacle of his men's religious practices, noting in his journal that "these quaint religious songs" were "a source of relaxation" as well as "a stimulus to courage and a tie to heaven."[88] Higginson's enjoyment consisted of listening to them.

[85] *Miss Ravenel's Conversion,* p. 341.

[86] DeForest to Harriet DeForest, Mar. 15, in *Volunteer's Adventures,* ed. Croushore, p.7.

[87] Wiley, *The Life of Billy Yank: The Common Soldier of the Union* (1951) and *The Life of Johnny Reb: The Common Soldier of the Confederacy* (1943), reprinted in *The Common Soldier in the Civil War* (n.d.), 1: ch. 7, 2: ch. 9.

[88] *Army Life in a Black Regiment,* p. 221.

The distance between the Victorians and their troops widened when the soldiers' diversions clashed with both military discipline and middle-class mores. John William DeForest, for example, estimated that one-fifth of his men were drunk all the time when they were camped in Louisiana, and it was his job to serve on a military court "condemning poor devils to forfeiture of pay, to ball and chain, etc."[89] The religious passions of Higginson's troops and the unrestrained drinking of DeForest's subordinates perhaps made the Victorians reflect on the comparatively rarefied and demure character of their own leisure. Contact with wild pleasures did not significantly change the Victorians' tastes, however, and when they had the chance to forge wartime friendships among themselves, these resembled their peacetime relationships.

North and South, the Victorians instinctively understood that their private well-being and practical success depended on a supportive network of interpersonal ties. As much as possible, they tried to perpetuate civilian bonds in new situations. Ulysses Grant chose friends from his most recent home in Galena, Illinois, to serve on his military staff. They provided, in William McFeely's graphic words, "that utterly essential comradeship in the small cluster of tents in Grant's army headquarters."[90] James Garfield, also in the Union army in the West, built a set of intricately textured relationships, both in his correspondence and in fact, that must have made him feel more settled in strange surroundings. Rather than address all of his letters to individual acquaintances and kin, Garfield sent news to a community of "Dear Friends at Home," who would then circulate his communications.[91] He worked to draw them close by offering "a touch of camp life."[92] In addition, Garfield reported his steady stream of encounters with Ohio neighbors and former students, meetings that he seemed to savor as reminders of home. He was drawn toward new relationships at the same time. With a feverish haste induced by war, General William Rosecrans sought to know Garfield in 1863 by having his subordinate share his quarters and listen to the Catholic general's tumultuous religious views.[93] In a similarly insistent mood, Confederate leaders gathered for camaraderie and sometimes intrigue in Richmond boardinghouses. The extraordinary record of this society contained in Mary Chesnut's diary suggests the inextricable links between the

[89] DeForest to Harriet DeForest, June 29, 1862, in *Volunteer's Adventures*, p. 29.

[90] *Grant*, p. 88 and ch. 7.

[91] Garfield actually sent the letter with this salutation to his friend J. Harrison (Harry) Rhodes, Aug. 19, 1861, in *The Wild Life of the Army: Civil War Letters of James A. Garfield*, ed. Williams (1964), pp. 25–7. Garfield wrote another letter to the group on Aug. 31, 1861, in ibid., pp. 34–5.

[92] Garfield to Lucretia Garfield, Oct. 8, 1861, in ibid., p. 39. In this case, Garfield hoped to involve his friends in his military life through their proposed visit to his encampment near Columbus, Ohio. But the extensive prose reporting of his letters certainly also aimed to give them a taste of his experience.

[93] For an example of Garfield's meetings with friends, see Garfield to Harry Rhodes, Oct. 5, 1862, in *Wild Life of the Army*, ed. Williams, p. 152. On his relationship with Rosecrans, see my discussion in Chapter 1.

Confederate war effort and the social ties that the South's leading men and women evolved in leisure.[94]

Yet beyond the war's demonstration of the emotional uses of Victorian sociability, the conflict revealed the fragility of these bonds as well. Although the Victorians were adept at exchanging confidences of sufficient number and depth to erect a framework of interdependence, the feelings evoked risked being evanescent and superficial, particularly in comparison with the complex relationships that their parents and grandparents developed in more stable communities in the past. As if at the tempestuous end of a whirlwind romance, Garfield and Rosecrans stood on hostile sides of a question of strategy within months of their intense initial acquaintance, an issue so serious that it cost Rosecrans his command.[95] Not only was their loyalty to each other ephemeral, but it is fair to wonder if all their discussion ever enabled them to know each other well. More troubling, courtesies so consciously applied, disengaged from traditional bonds, could be abridged with an unnerving ease that allowed civility to exist side by side with brutality. Ulysses Grant, for one, could swing between gestures of respect for his Confederate opponents and tactics verging on cruelty. When a son was born to the wife of George Pickett, the Confederate general, in July 1864, Pickett's troops lit a bonfire to honor the child. But "I did not know till this morning," Pickett wrote to his wife, "that dear old Ingalls, at Grant's suggestion, had kindled a light on their side of the lines, too, and I was overcome with emotion when I learned of it."[96] A courtesy offered with sincere kindness but without intimation of thorough accord, Grant's order epitomized the Victorians' ability to modulate social exchange to meet varied conditions. But how thin a veneer of manners – and feeling – cloaked Grant's simultaneous resolve to demoralize the South. The same summer that Grant saluted Pickett, he gave strict orders to hang deserters, take hostage kin of rebel guerrillas, and destroy civilian enemy property, policies viewed even by Abraham Lincoln as questionably harsh.[97] To an extent, the Victorians' skilled manipulation of social symbols made combat more tolerable by locating the conflict within a civilized culture. Even so, the intimate juxta-

---

[94] *Chesnut's Civil War*, ed. Woodward. Sociability in wartime Richmond also built on acquaintances made among southern politicians in Washington, D.C., in the prewar years. On the social ambience of antebellum Washington, see Green, *Washington: Village and Capital, 1800–1878* (1962), pp. 148–51, 155, 226–9.

[95] For an account of their conflict, see *Wild Life of the Army*, ed. Williams, pp. 217–21.

[96] Pickett to LaSalle Pickett, in *Soldier of the South: General Pickett's War Letters to His Wife*, ed. Inman (1928), p. 111.

[97] On Grant's tactics, see McFeely, *Grant*, pp. 182–3. Controversy also surrounded Sherman's deliberate pillaging and burning during the Atlanta campaign and, after the war, the inhumane treatment of Union prisoners at Andersonville, Georgia. All of these instances suggest the ability of modern people at once to abrogate ethics and to be disturbed by their disregard of standards they value. On Sherman and the northern war crimes trial of the ranking officer at Andersonville, see, respectively, Merrill, *William Tecumseh Sherman* (1971), pp. 286–7, and Morseberger and Morseberger, *Wallace*, ch. 14.

position of expressions of generosity and hardheartedness must have made at least some Americans reflect on the range of possible feelings hidden within gentility.

Thus leisure during the Civil War followed peacetime patterns. Yet wartime pastimes revealed the significance of everyday habits with unusual clarity precisely because this was a time of crisis. Looking at the war, astute observers of culture might have better understood the Victorians' infatuation with romantic adventure, as well as their problematic desire to find real philosophical answers in flights of imagination. They might have seen the Victorians' facility at social construction, as well as the sometimes limited depth of feeling behind fine manners. Although the Victorians themselves could not have phrased their contradictory impulses so bluntly, their actions suggest that they were sensitive to these dilemmas. Yet awareness did not lead them to seek to reform their leisure in any fundamental way. Rather, the Victorians enlisted the Civil War in a subtle campaign to legitimate pleasure.

From the end of the Civil War until at least World War I, Americans of the North and South engaged enthusiastically in activities commemorating their national crisis. Veterans' clubs, reunions, and historical societies were not simply leisure organizations. They served as settings for patriotic rituals, vehicles for political pressure, and places to act out ambivalent feelings about progress, inviting their members to honor the past within their protected space while at the same time advancing change outside.[98] Among these varied roles, one goal of commemoration was to provide conviviality and

[98] The religious, political, and social functions of Civil War commemoration have been analyzed by Wilson, *Baptized in Blood: The Religion of the Lost Cause, 1865–1920* (1980); Dearing, *Veterans in Politics: The Story of the G.A.R.* (1952); and Foster, *Ghosts of the Confederacy: Defeat, the Lost Cause, and the Emergence of the New South, 1865–1913* (1987). Many historians have noted Americans' uneven interest in Civil War celebration. Although waves of enthusiasm existed, I stress the fairly continuous underlying concern for the Civil War throughout the period, particularly if the private lives of individuals are considered along with public commemoration. After an initial wave of publications and memorial activities in the late 1860s, attention slowed until the 1880s, when a rise in the number of memoirs issued and commemorative organizations formed began that lasted until the turn of the century. Perhaps Americans for a time grew tired of thinking about the war, as they have of most wars that inevitably bring great stress. Mathew Brady, for example, went bankrupt in 1871 because he could not sell the photographs of battle in which he had heavily invested. See Horan, *Mathew Brady: Historian with a Camera* (1955), p. 83. Gaines Foster argues, on the other hand, that the 1880s initiated rapid social change and consequent disruption that generated a need to reaffirm ideals epitomized by combat, in *Ghosts of the Confederacy*, esp. pt. 2. Foster's sense that the revival drew in a new constituency of men who had fought as junior officers and enlisted men, presumably younger than these Victorians, is especially useful (p. 109). Similarly, Mary Dearing notes the lull in interest in the 1870s in the largely northern organization, the Grand Army of the Republic, and points to a broader social base in the 1880s with the formation of auxiliaries for loyal women and sons of veterans, in *Veterans in Politics*, chs. 6–8. Overall, the Victorians rode the waves of war nostalgia, initiating the movements of the 1860s, sharing leadership after 1880, and becoming symbols of heroism. But privately, many nurtured war memories more constantly, as they worked quietly on memoirs or spoke at local gatherings even during the less fervent 1870s. John Hood and William Tecumseh Sherman worked during that decade on writings about the war, and Zebulon Vance lectured frequently in North Carolina on war-related topics. See Dyer, *Hood*, pp. 317, 319; *Memoirs of General William T. Sherman by Himself* (1875); and Tucker, *Vance*, ch. 27.

diversion, and it is in the context of leisure that the significance of retrospective celebration may be analyzed here. The Victorians in this study warmly participated in social gatherings recalling the Civil War. In 1896, Wade Hampton and Varina Davis, now a widow, were among a mass of southerners who spent three days at a Confederate reunion in Richmond, one of many such celebrations in the postwar years. In 1911, Henry Lee Higginson joined onetime enlisted men for the fiftieth reunion of the Second Massachusetts Infantry on the site of their first encampment. He was also a member of a Civil War officers' club composed of fellow Bostonians for more than forty years. In New York, Ely Parker was one of many former soldiers who belonged to a local lodge of the Grand Army of the Republic. Among their activities, they collected Civil War memorabilia, soliciting the widow of Ulysses Grant for one of the general's personal possessions after his death in 1885. In Alabama, Virginia Clay was an honorary lifetime president of the United Daughters of the Confederacy. Finally, former Confederate soldiers and politicians formed the Southern Historical Society in 1869 and began a number of state historical societies in subsequent years.[99]

All of these organizations offered sociability built around a calming, past-centered focus that must have supplied welcome occasional relief in an ever more bustling society. Combining elements of antebellum camp meetings and Fourth of July celebrations along with established patterns of leisure such as public entertainments and clubs, Civil War commemoration appealed to the Victorians and their children because it lent pleasure moral depth. To say that this pairing of reflection and enjoyment helped to legitimize leisure does not mean that the Victorians set out deliberately to cast their modes of relaxation in ideologically acceptable terms. But in a culture just moving away from Protestant imperatives to be high-minded and productive, people probably felt better about themselves by spending some of their free time in pursuits that merged pageantry, good company, and an outdoor excursion with thoughts of undeniable importance. Nor did war commem-

---

[99] On Davis and Hampton, see Wiley, *Confederate Women*, p. 136, and Hampton to W. G. Curtis, June 12, 1896, in Cauthen, ed., *Family Letters of Wade Hamptons*, p. 160. On Higginson and Parker, see Perry, *Higginson*, pp. 404–5; Parker, *Parker*, p. 177; and Parker to [Frederick D. Grant?], Aug. 17, [18]85, Ely S. Parker Papers. On Clay, see Wiley, *Confederate Women*, p. 77. With respect to rising historical interest in the South, the Southern Historical Society was formed in 1869 by Jubal Early and others, as discussed in Foster, *Ghosts of the Confederacy*, esp. p. 50. Other men, such as Zebulon Vance who was one founder of the Historical Society of North Carolina in the mid-1870s, were involved in historical preservation efforts in individual states. See, e.g., Zebulon Vance to Jubal Early, Sept. 27, 1873, Vance Papers. It is important to note that postwar historical interest built on antebellum initiatives. On the formation of the historical societies in Illinois and Minnesota during the 1840s and 1850s, the Mount Vernon restoration in the 1850s, and the rise of historical interests in New England literature, see, respectively, Donald, *Herndon*, p. 50; Faragher, *Sugar Creek: Life on the Illinois Prairie* (1986), ch. 20; Stonehouse, *North*, p. 35; and Forgie, *Patricide in the House Divided: A Psychological Interpretation of Lincoln and His Age* (1979), pp. 169–76; and Buell, *New England Literary Culture: From Revolution through Renaissance* (1986), pt. 3.

oration have to preclude other pastimes in order to serve the Victorians' self-esteem. Throughout their adulthoods, the Victorians participated without interruption in the variety of pleasures this chapter has described. Civil War remembrance worked as a license that resolved some of their ambivalence about play, but it neither originated nor closed off the wider field of leisure.

Two more specific conclusions may also be offered about the impact of Civil War remembrance on Victorian leisure. First, commemoration often took the form of mass celebrations, whether these were called reunions or encampments, and like earlier Victorian spectacles, these events cast participants in the role of consumers of standardized experiences in fairly impersonal settings. Their popularity did not eclipse more private and intimate pastimes such as hunting or home entertaining. Nonetheless, as a favored diversion of a mass society, these extended dramas, orchestrated by a core group of organizers and subsuming large numbers of observers, advanced a certain kind of leisure that has grown more common in the twentieth century and takes such forms as sporting events, street festivals, and rock concerts.[100] Second, because Civil War celebration was a national pastime, its popularity in the South meant that southern Victorians superimposed modern, bureaucratized leisure quite abruptly on more traditional diversions. Precisely because the South's connection with its past was violently jeopardized by military defeat and the imposed changes of Reconstruction, southerners adopted strategies serviceable in a society in flux to keep in touch with their history. Moving away from the informal entertaining of their customary leisure, they organized public societies and reunions that drew strangers together to advance abstract purposes. Perhaps some understood the irony that the idealized traditionalism of the "Lost Cause" was guarded in the postwar South by modern social means.

Overall, the Civil War impelled the Victorians to explore the intricacies of leisure and provided them with a way to come closer to making their peace with pleasure seeking. Yet well before the war, it was the Victorians' insistence that free-time pursuits serve individual and social demands of the most urgent kind – for stimulation, inspiration, and communication – that gave leisure such prominence in their lives. Among the lessons learned, the most enduring was the capacity of imagination to construct settings hospitable to individual growth and social exchange. Much as they discovered during the war that diversions often lacked an elemental human realism

---

[100] It is possible that the evolution of one kind of mass leisure celebration influenced others. Specifically, although middle-class efforts to control working-class leisure had antebellum precedents, it is possible that efforts to organize "safe and sane" Fourth of July festivals around 1900 for the benefit of immigrants owed a debt to skills acquired in staging middle-class patriotic celebrations commemorating the Civil War. Mary Dearing discusses efforts of the Grand Army of the Republic to secure patriotic education in the 1890s, although without specifically linking the campaign to a concern with social order, in *Veterans in Politics*, chs. 11–12. On the "safe and sane" movement, see Rosenzweig, *Eight Hours*, ch. 6.

necessary for inner satisfaction, however, they also sensed that this richly textured sociability could not give their feelings full play. As a result, the Victorians turned to their families to find the emotional resonance they wished to draw from personal relationships.

4

Family

I take my pen on this quadrennial anniversary [of our wedding] with mingled feelings of sadness and happiness. *Sad,* as I review the past, that it should have been so strangely, painfully, trying to us, who groped about in the darkness and grief trying to find the path of duty and peace, and being so often pierced with thorns. . . . But I am also happy in the reflection that we were both seeking the path of duty and honor and that we each bore in silence many griefs, and each drank bravely and uncomplainingly many a bitter cup. Happy that in those days we were each borne up by the trust that the other was of true noble soul, and however great the errors might be there was still integrity of heart. Happy, above all, that this patient waiting and mutual forebearance has at last begun to bear the fruits of peace and love and that the buds of this hope give promise of a harvest of calm joyful peace as we go down the lengthening shadows of life.

James Garfield to Lucretia Garfield, 1862

American Victorians were impelled by broad impulses to define life's meaning, but they created a world of specialized relations, where, at the same time that work served personal ambition and leisure facilitated sociable exchange, families became scenes for the interplay of deep feelings essential to the formation of identities. As self-discovery relied less in the midcentury decades on transcendent communion, who an individual might be was determined increasingly by family dynamics. Precisely because networks of kin so crucially channeled emotion, homes were not the peaceable enclaves in a bustling society pictured in domestic ideals. Rather, explorations of feeling brought intense pleasures mixed with taxing intimacies and struggles for domination. These domestic exchanges conformed to prevailing gender inequalities. Because families shared social tasks with the larger culture, power at home more mirrored than inverted the prerogatives of a society that gave preeminence to men. Rhetoric offered women mastery in domestic affairs, and Victorian wives made themselves felt more effectively than did previous generations. But men still used their families with greater assurance to probe feelings, whereas women moved with a reserve symptomatic of their tenuous status. In the end, Victorian families offered their members inner rewards, far less, however, because they were comfortable havens than because they spoke through tensions borne of clashing wills to a generation's most compelling desires.

To grasp fully why the Victorians' dramas of sentiment evolved as they did, it is important to see families in a broad social context. Victorian families were more autonomous of surrounding communities and less cohesive with respect to their individual members than were circles of kin in the past. They no longer clearly served local societies through bonds of obligation and ritual, such as family prayers intended to support public order. As towns and cities were marked by impersonality and transience, families evolved a protective privacy. Yet public and private spheres continued to influence one another in crucial ways. Expanding markets and changing technology, for example, affected household economies. In addition, the social space between homes and society was traversed with growing freedom by individual family members, as each one pursued Victorian culture's opportunities and pleasures. Nonetheless, the same centrifugal force that lured individuals from kin seemed also to impel families away from communities. In consequence, the emotional enrichment sought so insistently by families newly aware of their power as separate social bodies was contested at every turn by their members' personal prerogatives. [1]

The Victorians' preoccupation with family strongly shaped the kind of civil war they fought. Rather than leave their families at home, military and civilian leaders on both sides sought to surround themselves with kin, hoping to receive the kind of emotional sustenance they habitually valued. From

[1] Among the substantial literature on nineteenth-century American families, works on several themes are particularly relevant. Studies that stress trends toward family privacy include Isaac, *The Transformation of Virginia, 1740–1790* (1982), pp. 302–5; Greven, *The Protestant Temperament: Patterns of Child-Rearing, Religious Experience, and the Self in Early America* (1977), pp. 25–7, 152–5, 266–8; and, to place American developments in long-term and transatlantic perspective, Ariès, *Centuries of Childhood: A Social History of Family Life*, trans. Baldick (1962). Works that examine the functional interaction between homes and society are Ryan, *Cradle of the Middle Class: The Family in Oneida County, New York, 1790–1865* (1981), esp. ch. 4; Mintz, *A Prison of Expectations: The Family in Victorian Culture* (1983), esp. p. 5; and Cowan, *More Work for Mother: The Ironies of Household Technology from the Open Hearth to the Microwave* (1983), esp. ch. 1. Perhaps the best study documenting the trend toward individualism in families, although in a later period, is Lynd and Lynd, *Middletown: A Study in Modern American Culture* (1929), esp. pp. 118–22, 132–7. Early studies of the "cult of domesticity" most strongly suggested that homes were in fact "woman's sphere" as portrayed in domestic ideology, although scholars often judged harshly the implicit restrictions on women. Nancy Cott refined that argument when she wrote that early nineteenth-century homes were one place in early industrial society where traditional relations were maintained, in *The Bonds of Womanhood: "Woman's Sphere" in New England, 1780–1835* (1977), esp. pp. 5–9, 199. But Cott was also aware of significant adjustments even then occurring in domestic space, as was Daniel Scott Smith, whose idea that women's status first changed within the family has been influential. See his development of the concept of "domestic feminism," in "Family Limitation, Sexual Control, and Domestic Feminism in Victorian America," in Hartman and Banner, eds., *Clio's Consciousness Raised: New Perspectives on the History of Women* (1974), pp. 119–36. For a recent discussion of the complex dynamics of gender relations in Victorian America, see Smith-Rosenberg, *Disorderly Conduct: Visions of Gender in Victorian America* (1985).

the perspective of their wives and children, these domestic relations transported to scenes of battle and government cast the character of family roles in sharp relief, revealing the potential and limits of each member's options, without initiating basic changes in the balance of domestic power. Nor were relationships in families that stayed home transformed by the conflict in fundamental ways. Looking beyond specific aspects of family structure, however, the Civil War did affect the mood in which the Victorians approached ties of kin. In the midst of heightened and, particularly in the South, persistent public uncertainties, the Victorians turned to their families for solace more decisively than ever. On a symbolic level, Civil War commemoration honoring the self-sacrifice of the fathers and mothers resolved some of the tensions that tested Victorian families and reaffirmed the family's importance in culture.[2]

This chapter begins by examining relationships within Victorian families, first between husbands and wives and then between parents and children. The principal theme is the way the Victorians' search for emotional engagement was mediated by an attachment to individuality that injected alternative notes of assertiveness and reserve into interpersonal ties. The chapter's third section places Victorian families on a historical continuum. Mid-nineteenth-century middle-class families were in the process of changing from centers of social order, with tangible economic, political, and social functions, to a set of relationships defined by feeling. One aspect of the change was the erosion of fathers' authority, as families grew more egalitarian and parents tried to command by persuasion instead of obedience. Throughout the chapter, the traditional system of family deference is designated by the term "patriarchy," while the emerging customs based on reciprocal sentiments is called "paternalism."[3] The Victorians did not initiate all of the family patterns analyzed here. They inherited some of their attitudes from their parents and perhaps from their grandparents. Nonetheless, the Victorians' spiritual perplexities combined with their curiosity about society's resources to make them test relentlessly what families could give, thereby accenting domesticity's subjective dimension. It was in that frame of mind that they entered the Civil War. Discussion of the connections between the war and Victorian families concludes the chapter.

[2] Recent discussions of patriarchy include Wyatt-Brown, *Southern Honor: Ethics and Behavior in the Old South* (1982), esp. ch. 3, and Ryan, *Cradle of the Middle Class,* esp. pp. 31–43. Although Eugene D. Genovese uses the term "paternalism" to designate a more traditional social system than this study does, his development of the concept remains seminal. See esp. *Roll, Jordan, Roll: The World the Slaves Made* (1972).

[3] Most recent discussions of families in relation to the Civil War focus on women's roles and on the South. See Rable, *Civil Wars: Women and the Crisis of Southern Nationalism* (1989), and Faust, "Altars of Sacrifice: Confederate Women and the Narratives of War." On the North, see Ginzberg, *Women and the Work of Benevolence: Morality, Politics, and Class in the Nineteenth-Century United States* (1990), ch. 5; Paludan, *"A People's Contest": The Union and the Civil War, 1861–1865* (1988), pp. 156–60, 186, 327–31; and Massey, *Bonnet Brigades* (1966).

HUSBANDS AND WIVES

Victorian families began with marriages that grew from the romantic dreams and private decisions of young people, freer than in the past of family pressure and eager for a feast of emotion that, to a striking extent, they found. Yet the prospect of wide prerogatives also inspired caution in the expression of feeling, while deep-seated restlessness in other ways strained marital bonds. Marriages often achieved the warm sentiments of love matches, but they were subject, too, to crosscurrents that grew from the choices open to husbands and wives.

Victorian courtships began with a combination of musing and planning that underlines how much young people insisted on autonomy from their parents to make marriage a source of private fulfillment. Dreams of married bliss ranged from simple images of pleasure to anguished cries of frustration at gratifications deferred. "Why do not some pretty women come[?]," John Kinkade wrote home from California in 1852, "they would not have any difficulty securing husbands." Soon women were "very numerous," and Kinkade married within months.[4] George Templeton Strong, more circumspect than Kinkade in his fantasies, wrote enviously in his journal in 1845 of his cousin's propitious marriage and vowed to "[try] on myself the medicine that's dissipated all his causes of complaining and fairly made a different person of him."[5] For William Potter, sweet anticipations turned painful when high ideals were unmatched by actual feeling. "Thirty-three years, & I know nothing of [love] by experience, only by theory," he wrote in anguish to a friend in 1863: "Yet I believe most generously in love, in marriage, in no marriage without love. None knows how I have longed & prayed for this completion of my being."[6] As if to escape the torment of tempting prospects, Potter soon chose a wife.

---

[4] John Kinkade to James Kinkade, Mar. 20, 1852, Mar. 6, and May 20, 1853, John Thompson Kinkade Papers.

[5] July 10, 1845, *The Diary of George Templeton Strong,* ed. Nevins and Thomas (1952), 1:264.

[6] Potter to George W. Bartlett, Apr. 15, 1863, William Potter Papers. There is no evidence among these Victorians that parents had more than an occasional and limited advisory role in the choice of marriage partners. Although there has been considerable debate about the timing of the transition from marriage choice controlled by parents to selection by the couple themselves, this group was quite autonomous of parents compared with prior generations. They did not manipulate parents by premarital pregnancies, as did many young Americans in the late colonial and early national periods. See Robert A. Gross, *The Minutemen and Their World* (New York: Hill and Wang, 1976), p. 100, and Ulrich, *A Midwife's Tale: The Life of Martha Ballard, Based on Her Diary, 1785–1812* (1990), pp. 147–60. Even parental advice was less evident at midcentury than Bertram Wyatt-Brown found in the antebellum South, in *Southern Honor,* p. 207. For an assessment of the transition to independent mate selection in one locality over two centuries, 1635–1880, see Daniel Scott Smith, "Parental Power and Marriage Patterns: An Analysis of Historical Trends in Hingham, Massachusetts," in Gordon, ed., *The American Family in Social-Historical Perspective* (1978), pp. 87–100. For more general discussions of courtship, see Rothman, *Hands and Hearts: A History of Courtship in America* (1984), esp. ch. 1, and Lystra, *Searching the Heart: Women, Men and Romantic Love in Nineteenth-Century America* (1989).

Courtships could be protracted, however, by the expectation that husbands would be financially independent at marriage. David Terry in California assured his fiancée of his prospects as part of the courtship ritual. "I have a law practice & enjoy the confidence of the public," he assured Cornelia Runnels in 1851, "& although I am not gathering gold as fast as I could wish yet I am by my own labour independant and see before me the [certainty?] of acquiring wealth though it must be the work of years."[7] If Victorian men did not command sufficient means, they were not inclined to ask for their parents' help, perhaps because they wished to exclude their fathers' influence, so visible in the sons' career choices, from their marriage decisions. Rather, they changed or at least adjusted their livelihoods in order to facilitate taking a wife. Contemplating marriage, John Wesley North gave up antislavery lecturing to study law. Alexander Agassiz left his job as an engineer with the Coast Survey in California when he found that it paid too little to set up housekeeping comfortably. Thomas Wentworth Higginson agreed to a four-year engagement in order to finish Harvard Divinity School and settle in his first church before he wed.[8] In practice, the economic independence of couples was often eroded over time by the complications of extended families, particularly by the intrusions of wives' fathers. Nonetheless, an ideal of domestic privacy, made possible by a husband's career, shaped the way Victorian marriages were made.

Marriages once contracted released ecstatic feelings of joy at belonging to a community capable of contesting wearying solitude. "I now know the new birth," William Potter wrote in a letter soon after his marriage, "which neither religion nor theology has been able to make me comprehend heretofore. That miserable burden of self-consciousness, which has oppressed me so long has fallen off."[9] George Templeton Strong reveled in his journal during his engagement in "perfect, entire happiness," blending the rhetoric and cadences of religious ritual and sensuous release: "Happiness that teaches one gratitude to God and faith in him. . . . Happiness that I can dwell upon and luxuriate in freely and unrestrained, because it includes the anticipation of a life no longer cold and selfish and objectless and indolent, but henceforth to be built on joyful self-denial and hearty labor for a worthy end."[10] Perhaps Potter and Strong likened love's poignancy to spiritual vitality simply to emphasize their feeling's power. Yet both so nearly said that they needed passion for a woman to bring religious truth to life that human sentiment seemed to edge aside troubled faith. Neither, moreover, found as much relief

---

[7] Terry to Cornelia Runnels [Terry], Nov. 7, 1851, David Smith Terry Papers. Variant spelling and punctuation that appear in this and other quotations are found in the original texts.

[8] Stonehouse, *John Wesley North and the Reform Frontier* (1965), p. 11; *Letters and Recollections of Alexander Agassiz*, ed. Agassiz (1913), pp. 25–7; Edelstein, *Strange Enthusiasm: A Life of Thomas Wentworth Higginson* (1968), pp. 48, 79.

[9] Potter to George W. Bartlett, Oct. 14, 1863, Potter Papers.

[10] Apr. 9, 1848, *Diary of Strong*, ed. Nevins and Thomas, 1:315.

from isolation in communion with God as was promised by a wife. Thus marriage acquired a task of providing meaning that would be difficult to execute well.

Whether love answered deep questions became less pressing, however, as experience enriched shared emotion. Cataclysmic feeling might dissipate in time, but in its place mutual reliance and regard commonly strengthened. David Terry left Texas for California a slighted suitor. But when Cornelia Runnels again changed her mind, he renewed his offer of marriage, though with understandable reserve: "I will not say that my love for you is the same devoted feeling I once entertained but you still possess a hold upon my affections no other could ever obtain."[11] They married in 1852, and any defensiveness provoked by Cornelia's fickle behavior dissipated in growing bonds of sentiment. When Cornelia visited her home in Texas in 1860, Terry wrote playfully that he missed the children *"almost* as much as Mama."[12] By 1867, the trials of war changed the tone of a man who chose to fight on the Confederate side, but his message to his wife was the same: "You have been to me for many years the greatest boone it is possible for the almighty to bestow on a mortal."[13]

Women, too, gave voice to sustained affection, though notes of ambivalence sound more often in the writings of women than men. Harriet Vance was one wife of unvarying constancy. She and Zebulon exchanged 121 love letters in the two years before their wedding in Asheville, North Carolina, in 1853. Later separations revived a sentimental correspondence. "My beloved Husband," Harriet began in 1859 when Zebulon was serving in Congress, "how we miss you, is impossible to express – Our sweet home seems gloomy indeed, and but for the cheerful voices and bright faces of our charming boys would be almost beyond endurance."[14] A pious woman, Harriet expressed her love in part by patiently urging her husband's conversion, not simply for his private well-being, but to complete their conjugal community. No wonder that as she approached her death in 1878 she dwelled more on the need for enduring spiritual bonds. Thus Harriet put a postscript on a son's letter to his father: "May you enter upon your new year in the fear of God & improve to His glory & your souls eternal good."[15]

To cite the reflections of Elizabeth Cady Stanton next to the words of Harriet Vance highlights both the second thoughts of Victorian women about domestic rewards and marriage's still tenacious pull. Many of the women studied stood back from the demonstrative sentimentality of men, as they sensed their vulnerability implicit in the inequality hidden in effusive

---

[11] Terry to Cornelia Runnels [Terry], Nov. 7, 1851, Terry Papers.
[12] Mar. 9, 1860, Terry Papers.
[13] Oct. 11, 1867, Terry Papers.
[14] Harriet Vance to Zebulon Vance, Dec. 1, 1859, Zebulon Baird Vance Papers.
[15] Postscript, David Vance to Zebulon Vance, Apr. 19, 1874, Vance Papers.

Figure 9. Elizabeth Cady Stanton (1815–1902). Though a strenuous advocate of women's rights, Stanton's decorous appearance reflected her willingness to bow to some social conventions, particularly in her private life. Despite her reservations about contemporary Christianity, she even chose to wear a cross for this photograph by Napoleon Sarony, ca. 1870. National Portrait Gallery, Smithsonian Institution.

emotion. Stanton understood their caution better than most, as well as the persistent seductiveness of marriage. Looking back in her memoirs of 1898, Stanton wrote with empathy of her marriage crisis in 1840, when she broke her engagement for fear of "changing a girlhood of freedom and enjoyment for I knew not what."[16] Over the years, she became increasingly convinced that marriage meant disability for women, a fact she conveyed in her reminiscences by commenting that she chose a lawyer for a husband, a profession inevitably identified with "odious statute law and infamous decisions."[17] Yet

[16] Stanton, *Eighty Years and More: Reminiscences, 1815–1897* (1898), p. 71. Emotional turmoil connected with the prospect of marriage was not uncommon for women. See Cott, *Bonds of Womanhood*, p. 80.
[17] *Eighty Years and More*, p. 50. Her husband was Henry Stanton.

even Stanton took for granted that family life was normative for women, not simply as custom but as a forum for emotional exchange. When she "entered the charmed circle at last," she married on Friday, deemed by many an unlucky day. Still, "we lived together, without more than the usual matrimonial friction, for nearly a half a century, had seven children, all but one of whom are still living, and have been well sheltered, clothed, and fed, enjoying sound minds in sound bodies, [so that] no one need be afraid of going through the marriage ceremony on Friday for fear of bad luck."[18] Stanton's marriage was no more a fairy-tale romance than, as a young woman, she feared. But it repaid her by a dense network of feelings, some rewarding and some strained, despite her intellectual reserve.[19]

With so much invested in marriage, death provoked intense bereavement in surviving partners. Men, whose attitudes were less divided than women's, fell more seriously prey to anguish. Expressions of loss appeared in the letters of ambitious professionals. Edwin Godkin was so unnerved by his wife's death in 1875 that he gave up responsibility for editing the *Nation* for one year to Wendell Garrison, his associate. He wrote to Garrison: "You may guess I am not in very hearty condition when I say that the one pleasant thought that has come to me in the last three weeks is that of a speedy end to my troubles."[20] Alexander Agassiz, a museum director at Harvard and marine zoologist, was confronted with the death of his wife only eight days after his father's passing in 1873. He paused to describe his grief in a letter to Thomas Huxley: "Few young men have reached my age and have attained, as it were, all their ambition might desire, and yet the one thing which I crave for, and which I care to keep me interested in what is going on, is

---

[18] Ibid., pp. 70–1.

[19] For a good discussion of Stanton's mixed feelings about her marriage, see Banner, *Elizabeth Cady Stanton: A Radical for Woman's Rights* (1980), pp. 18–22, 32–8. Although Stanton was better equipped than most women to see beyond her second thoughts to the social questions they raised, her feelings were not unique. Only two other women among the large group I survey, either as primary subjects or as wives of men studied, supported suffrage publicly, Virginia Clay and Rebecca Felton. Yet, on the other side, only Varina Davis was sufficiently outspoken in her conservatism to oppose suffrage openly. Moreover, there were many signs of the struggles of women to come to terms with their discontent in the context of families, the only sphere where most ever coped with issues of gender. Anna Cora Mowatt left her second husband. Ann North refused after the early 1870s to participate in her husband's successive communal experiments and lived apart from him in rented rooms. Mary Chesnut allowed herself to speak disparagingly about her father-in-law in her journal to a notable extent. She wrote on Dec. 6, 1861: "His métier is to be an autocrat, a prince of slaveholders. . . . His forefathers paid their money for them [slaves]. They are his by that right divine, he thinks." See *Mary Chesnut's Civil War*, ed. Woodward (1981), p. 255. On the other women mentioned, see Wiley, *Confederate Women* (1975), p. 77, 137 (on Clay and Davis); Talmadge, *Rebecca Latimer Felton: Nine Stormy Decades* (1960), p. 103; Barnes, *The Lady of Fashion: The Life and the Theatre of Anna Cora Mowatt* (1954), pp. 364, 378; and Stonehouse, *North*, p. 238. Further discussion in this chapter of women's emotional reserve as a form of resistance focuses on widowhood, spinsterhood, and bonds between mothers and daughters.

[20] Godkin to Wendell P. Garrison, May 5, 1875, in *The Gilded Age Letters of E. L. Godkin*, ed. Armstrong (1974), pp. 217–18. See also Godkin to Garrison, [May 1, 1875], in ibid., p. 217.

wanting. How gladly I would exchange all that I have for what I have lost."[21] Even more poignant was the experience of Zebulon Vance. Not an especially literary man, Vance poured his loneliness into a poem of nearly one hundred lines he composed after Harriet's death. Filled with graphic details depicting habits of grief, such as his reluctance to return home and his hours spent alone in their room, Vance's "Lament" ended with his resolve to become a converted Christian to live a *"life that once was thine."*[22] Thus Vance was moved less by an impulse for personal salvation than a need to retrace his wife's steps when he entered Raleigh's Second Presbyterian Church as a professing member several weeks later.[23] Almost perversely, death completed the Vances' marriage bond by giving it the religious foundation Harriet had urged for twenty-five years.

The urgency with which widowers especially remarried attests further to the satisfactions of marriage, though significantly, widows took new husbands less often. Second marriages for men with young children were in part a necessity, yet most formed new families with an enthusiasm generated by mating's appeal. The sincerity of Vance's grief and religious conversion in late 1878 after Harriet's death seems incontestable. But by the spring of 1880, he had a new wife after a courtship strikingly romantic for a fifty-year-old man. In a characteristic letter to "my blessed love" from "your big boy," Vance declared: "How fortunate I am, that I can love my sweetheart with my whole heart, and defer to her intellect and *repose* in her judgment at the same time."[24] So fervent was his passion that Vance ignored the scruples of his born-again Protestant faith by tolerating his wife's Catholicism. Men who did not remarry, in contrast, slipped into lonely lives. Alexander Agassiz buried himself in his work. John DeForest halfheartedly nursed his literary career while living in the 1890s in the second-rate New Haven hotel. William Montague Browne, though active in the Athens, Georgia, community during the decade between his wife's death and his own in 1883, indulged his hypochondria to an extent that brought comment from friends.[25]

Victorian widows were less apt to remarry than were widowers. In an age

[21] Agassiz to Huxley, [1873], in *Agassiz,* ed. Agassiz, p. 124.

[22] "A Lament," Dec. 6, 1878, Vance Papers. Italics in this and subsequent quotations are found in the original text.

[23] Vance's conversion is described in A. J. Witherspoon to Vance, Jan. 2, 1879, Vance Papers. Heightened sentimentality in connection with death in this period has been discussed by Douglas, *The Feminization of American Culture* (1977), ch. 6, and Halttunen, *Confidence Men and Painted Women: A Study of Middle-Class Culture in America, 1830–1870* (1982), ch. 5. Douglas argues that women and clergymen drew attention by sentimentalism to one social process they controlled. Halttunen sees demonstrative mourning as a badge of social status.

[24] Vance to Florence Martin, Apr. 4, [1880], Vance Papers.

[25] *Agassiz,* ed. Agassiz; Light, *John William DeForest* (1965), p. 168; Coulter, *William Montague Browne: Versatile Anglo-Irish American, 1823–1883* (1967), p. 256.

when men initiated marriage proposals, it is true that older men often preferred younger women and simply did not ask for widows' hands. But since these widows had the advantages of prominence and means to offset the liability of age, it is equally likely that the women chose to steer away from further marital entanglements. More specifically, a desire for personal independence combined with the gratification of children to contest the appeal of married life. Armed with the respectability of women once married and a knowledge of autonomy's value gained in male-controlled, though perhaps loving, relationships, widows used their freedom to pursue their own interests. Varina Davis traveled in a New York circle of southern expatriates in the 1890s while trying to make her mark as a writer. Virginia Clay wrote articles, worked for suffrage, and served as president of the United Daughters of the Confederacy during a long widowhood of twenty-three years. Of the two second marriages by widows, one ended in separation when Anna Cora Mowatt, accustomed as an actress to exercising her will, left the newspaper editor she married on the grounds that he expected more obedience than she was willing to give.[26]

These women might not have welcomed liberty from husbands so readily had they not commanded the loyalty of their children, offsetting the loss of married companionship. Indeed, the only widows who remarried at all were childless. Widows with grown children moved in with them. Priscilla Tyler kept house first with her sister and then her daughter after her husband's death. Varina Davis lived with her daughters. These were cost-saving expedients in part, but arrangements, too, that drew on elemental bonds between mothers and daughters.[27] Widows no less than widowers sought family bonds, but the cost in self-determination of marriage for wives led widows to forgo adult relationships if the alternative offered freedom and sentiment at once.

The disquiet of bachelors and spinsters confirms in negative terms the Victorians' reliance on marriage, although the same crosscurrents, a desire for independence and emotional involvement with children, moved unmarried people to think twice about making commitments. Notes of unsettlement sound in the lives of single Victorians. William Moore of Los Angeles

[26] On Davis and Clay, see Wiley, *Confederate Women*, pp. 137, 77. For Mowatt, see Barnes, *Lady of Fashion*, pp. 364–6, 378. The one successful remarriage by a widow was contracted by Virginia Clay. She was widowed in 1882, married a judge in 1887, lost her second husband in 1892, and remained single until her death in 1915 (Wiley, *Confederate Women*, pp. 77–8).

[27] Priscilla Tyler had limited financial resources after her husband's death. She seems to have chosen to share housekeeping expenses with female kin rather than to seek economic security with a second husband. See Coleman, *Priscilla Cooper Tyler and the American Scene, 1816–1889* (1955), pp. 171–5. On Davis, whose finances were less straitened, see Wiley, *Confederate Women*, pp. 136–7. To appreciate the freedom of middle-class Victorian widows to determine their future, compare their options to those of earlier widows described in Alexander Keyssar, "Widowhood in Eighteenth-century Massachusetts: A Problem in the History of the Family," *Perspectives in American History* 8 (1974): 83–119, and Premo, *Winter Friends: Women Growing Old in the New Republic, 1785–1835* (1990), pp. 29–38.

was self-conscious of the lonely aimlessless of his life outside work during a long bachelorhood before marrying at age forty-six: "I loaf about all day," he wrote in his journal on a typical Sunday in 1869, and he later added half-humorously: "I believe I shall have to get religion or get married or do something curious."[28] Charlotte Cushman, a Boston-born actress who never married, devalued her professional accomplishments by comparison with a domestic role. *"No artist work* is so high, so noble, so grand, so enduring, so important for all time," she told a correspondent, "as the making of *character* in a child."[29] She arranged her life to approach family intimacy. One loyal servant attended her many years, and she surrounded herself with pets, including a dog who liked carriage rides and took milk in his tea. She adopted a nephew and called herself "mother" in letters to his wife.[30] Note, however, that Cushman drafted dependents into her circle rather than an adult to stand in place of a spouse. Just as widows reached out to family solutions that combined autonomy and sentiment, spinsters savored control of their circumstances, less so the prospect of loneliness. Among the small number of these Victorians who stayed single (seven in all), women were slightly more inclined to skirt entangling bonds, since four did not marry.[31] But both sexes showed some reluctance to seek married closeness, and their choice raises a further question, whether there were unspoken limits to the emotional engagement Victorians could comfortably share.

Although American Victorians relished marriage for the way its dynamics nourished personal feeling, they also worried that conjugal bonds might grow so strong that the bounds of individualities were obscured. Indeed, fears for privacy probably arose from the intensity of their longing for community, as well as from a simultaneous commitment to self. This attachment to antinomies led to strategies for interpersonal ties that both enhanced and controlled intimacy. Victorian attitudes toward sexuality and age differences between husbands and wives involved this ambivalence about conjugal space.

Next to the almost universal appeal of marital sentiment, thoughts of physical passion evoked from men extreme reactions of enthusiasm, revulsion, and silence. This array of responses reveals the Victorians' uneasiness with sexuality, not simply because of its raw physical passion, but

---

[28] May 9, 1869, Jan. 2, 1870, Diaries, 1869, 1870, William Moore Papers.

[29] Stebbins, *Charlotte Cushman: Her Letters and Memories of Her Life* (1879), p. 172.

[30] Ibid., pp. 37, 121–9, 161–2, 192.

[31] The following individuals were bachelors or spinsters (each one's principal place of residence is in parentheses): Charlotte Cushman (Massachusetts and Europe), Lucy Larcom (Massachusetts), Emily Dickinson (Massachusetts), Louisa May Alcott (Massachusetts), Henry David Thoreau (Massachusetts), Isaac Hecker (New York), James Gibbons (Maryland). That two of the men, Hecker and Gibbons, were Roman Catholic priests and thus celibate on principle reduces the number who chose not to marry simply because they preferred being single, reinforcing the point that the Victorians favored family intimacy. The fact that all but Gibbons were northerners, and were indeed concentrated in Massachusetts, suggests that southerners' more traditional regard for lineage and lack of appreciation of individualism made forming families in the South as much an obligation as an option.

on account of its potential for unstructured openness. Robert Ingersoll, the vocal advocate of religious skepticism, championed passion within marriage with the sharp edge of an iconoclast's discontent. Ingersoll was a sensuous man, fond of amenities, and so there is little reason to doubt the depth of enjoyment behind hundreds of letters to his wife detailing sensual pleasure. But his enjoyment was sharpened by a rebel's thrill at calling such marriage "the holiest institution among men."[32] Strident defense of sexuality did not necessarily signal easy acceptance, in other words, any more than did more common expressions of distaste. William Dean Howells, for example, was so horrified as an adolescent by the seduction of a seamstress who worked for his family that he refused to associate with her. Thomas Wentworth Higginson, in middle age, voiced revulsion at the sensuousness of freed slave women.[33] The majority of Victorian men, however, left no record of their feelings about passion. Even if many had no reason to set down their thoughts, this was a telling omission for otherwise graphic diarists, suggesting reluctance to probe physical drives.[34] In all, this mix of attitudes was grounded in discomfort with eroticism that drew on passion's antipathy to self-control. Victorian men enthusiastically courted marriage's appealing variety of sentiments but stood back from more risky engagement.

Victorian women perceived sexual issues differently but with the same effect of curtailing sensuality in marriage. At the rare times that wives spoke of passion, they assumed sexual drives were exclusively men's. Perhaps there was wistful longing in Mary Chesnut's exposure in her journal of planters' lusts, but her conscious belief was that only men were impelled by desires that imposed infidelity's hypocrisy on their wives. Thus she

[32] "The Liberty of Man, Woman and Child," in *The Works of Robert G. Ingersoll*, [ed. Farrell] (1909), 1:357. On Ingersoll's letters, see Cramer, *Royal Bob: The Life of Robert G. Ingersoll* (1952), p. 61. For a sample of his public advocacy of physical love, consider this excerpt from his poem "Declaration of the Free": "We love no phantoms of the skies, but living flesh, / With passion's soft and soulful eyes, Lips warm and fresh, / And cheeks with health's red flag unfurled, / The breathing angels of this world" (*Works*, 4:418).

[33] Lynn, *William Dean Howells: An American Life* (1970), pp. 57–8; Edelstein, *Strange Enthusiasm*, p. 257.

[34] Men who produced substantial diaries include George Templeton Strong, *Diary of Strong*, ed. Nevins and Thomas, 4 vols. (1835–75); James Garfield, *The Diary of James A. Garfield*, ed. Brown and Williams, 4 vols. (1848–81) (1967); William Potter, Diaries, 1847–57, Potter Papers; and William Moore, Diaries, 1869–91, Moore Papers. Although these diarists recorded their romantic interests, none mentioned sexuality directly. The generally accepted view of Victorian sexual repression has been contested by Gay, in *The Bourgeois Experience: Victoria to Freud*, vol. 1, *The Education of the Senses* (1984), and vol. 2, *The Tender Passion* (1986). Yet even Gay acknowledges that control tempered passion, when he says Victorians accepted physical pleasure within marriage only. His argument is important because it highlights the dynamic of indulgence and restraint in Victorian culture. G. J. Barker-Benfield documents men's anxieties about sexuality, in *The Horrors of the Half-Known Life: Male Attitudes toward Women and Sexuality in Nineteenth-Century America* (1976), esp. pt. 3. See also Steven Marcus's classic study of the fascination with sexuality that coexisted with official repression, *The Other Victorians: A Study of Sexuality and Pornography in Mid-Nineteenth-Century England* (1964), esp. ch. 7.

castigated men, not excluding her husband's father, who posed as "the best husband and father and member of the church" and yet gratified hidden passions in "a hideous black harem."[35] Women also averted thoughts of their sexual impulses by approaching any discussion of physical sensation through the respectable theme of childbearing. Pregnancy alone might have spurred communication, yet Victorian wives seemed to use changes brought on by gestation to open channels of franker exchange. Mary Holliday in Pennsylvania circled around the subject of how her expanding figure affected her husband's regard when she wrote during her first pregnancy to her husband, away in Kansas, "I do not want you to see *one* who has changed so much in her personal appearance lest you doubt *it* being the one you left *behind* – and take fright and be off to the western wilds again."[36] Whereas Holliday worked to evoke reassurance, Elizabeth Potter, too shy to share with her husband her suspicion of pregnancy, confided in her mother:

Now, Mother I want to talk *privately*. How soon shall I know for *certain?* Do you really think it all means *baby?* When will he begin to let me know that he *is there?* Everything is just as still as a mouse. I sometimes have a slight nausea or a little dizzy turn – but that is about all that looks suspicious – except of course the non-appearance of a certain periodical event. Do you feel certain that you are to be a *Grandmother?* That's what I want to know. Burn this sheet.[37]

The blend of circumspection and desire to talk about their bodies evident in the correspondence of these women indicates just how tangled their feelings about their femininity were. Women's writings suggest not only that erotic impulses played small part in their marriages, but that wives voluntarily curtailed their desires. Precisely how they felt they protected themselves and their relationships by containing sensual pleasure is unclear. But, like their husbands, wives acted as if married sentiment was most secure when they avoided deep passion.

Wide differences in age between husbands and wives worked similarly to accentuate comfortable bonds not unlike those between fathers and daughters, while averting the more egalitarian, less predictable relations of partners of about the same age. Some of the reasons older men took young wives grew from the mores of Victorian courtship. A suitor waited until he could support a wife. At age forty-six, William Moore wrote in his diary: "I have attained to a position where I can make a living and have the respect of my fellow citizens. In a few days I shall probably take a wife."[38] In tune with how much Victorian love thrived on romantic fancies, moreover, young women

---

[35] Aug. 27, 1861, *Chesnut's Civil War,* ed. Woodward, p. 168; see also pp. 29–31, 71–2, 276.
[36] Mary Holliday to Cyrus Holliday, Dec. 29, [1854], Cyrus Kurtz Holliday Papers.
[37] Potter to Lydia Babcock, Feb. 23, 1864, Potter Papers.
[38] Dec. 31, 1873, Diary, 1873, Moore Papers.

offered the charm of a pretty face, and for widowers, a fresh start. Thomas Wentworth Higginson wasted little time finding a second wife when his first wife, Mary, died in 1877, after a thirty-year marriage that remained childless by her choice. He was fifty-six when he took his new bride, also named Mary, who, in her mid-thirties, bore him the child he desired.[39] Yet the fact that Victorian men so often married young women, including girls in their teens, suggests motives at work beyond the circumstances of court-ship. James Mowatt of New York City was thirty, for example, when he eloped with Anna Cora Ogden, then fifteen. John Wesley North was a widower of thirty-three when he married seventeen-year-old Ann Loomis in upstate New York. Southern men most consistently took young wives. Mary Chesnut, Virginia Clay, and Varina Davis all married men who were between eight and eighteen years older than themselves when they were still under twenty.[40]

This pattern of age drew on the appealing security of having definite, if distant, relations between husband and wife. Faced with a workplace that made men wonder about their self-determining power, husbands clung at home so tenaciously to a patriarchal role that they sought dominion by choosing to act as a parent. For women dimly critical of men's superior rights yet uninclined to contest them, it was safer to prolong the familiar subordination of childhood than to harbor submerged discontent. Thus a number of husbands and wives acted nearly like fathers and daughters. James Mowatt spent the early years of his marriage directing his wife's education. Jabez Curry and his second wife, Mary, respectively forty and twenty-one when they married, lived with her parents in Richmond after the wedding for over two years, perhaps a sign of a tacit agreement by all parties on Mary's minor status.[41] Such age relations spurred feeling, moreover, by accenting the romance of having a young wife, while controlling sexuality that seemed out of place in a paternal setting. The fact that four of the seven couples mentioned in this context were childless may be a sign of limited sexual contact. In sum, marriages between men and women of unequal age invited strong attachment, but excluded the troubling give-and-take of part-ners more evenly matched.[42]

---

[39] Edelstein, *Strange Enthusiasm*, pp. 332–7.

[40] Barnes, *Lady of Fashion*, p. 28; Stonehouse, *North*, p. 18; *Chesnut's Civil War*, ed. Woodward, p. xxxiv; Wiley, *Confederate Women*, pp. 42, 85.

[41] Barnes, *Lady of Fashion*, p. 19; Rice, *J.L.M. Curry: Southerner, Statesman, and Educator* (1949), p. 69.

[42] The marriages without children included those of the Mowatts, Chesnuts, Clays, and Currys. A slightly different tone in northern and southern marriages involving age differences should be noted. Whereas northerners, farther removed from patriarchal assumptions, turned back toward gender hierarchy in a defensive mood, southerners made such matches more as part of an undisturbed tradition. Bertram Wyatt-Brown, who found that antebellum southern women generally married at younger ages than their northern counterparts, reasonably argues that this custom grew from the persistence of patriarchy, in *Southern Honor*, pp. 203–5. Still, sectional differences were mainly a matter of degree. As Mary Ryan

Figure 10.   Varina Howell Davis (1826–1906). Varina Howell married Jefferson Davis in 1845, when she was eighteen years old and Davis, a widower, was thirty-six. This watercolor on ivory miniature was painted by John Wood Dodge in 1849. Gift of Varina Webb Stewart, National Portrait Gallery, Smithsonian Institution.

Just as relationships were challenged from within by the Victorians' determination to limit emotional involvement, disruptive elements in the wider culture made sustaining marriage more difficult. Although this generation wished to turn to domestic rewards from wearying uncertainties, self-made dilemmas pursued them. The complex questions of identity that Victorian men posed in their careers made it nearly inevitable that the families they promised to support were instead subject to the demands they made on their work. None of the four men mentioned earlier for their efforts to establish themselves financially before marrying could contain a restlessness that strained family peace. John Wesley North, though trained as a lawyer, was too enamored of successive utopian schemes in Minnesota, Tennessee, and California to be a steady provider. His wife, Ann, and their children went home to her father during the family's hard times. Thomas Wentworth Higginson lost his church on account of his antislavery advocacy and crusaded

shows, family hierarchies in the North remained intact at the turn of the nineteenth century, and if northern men and women were more sensitive to threats to social cohesion, they did not have far to go in order to recover traditional mores. For Ryan's view, see *Cradle of the Middle Class*, ch. 1.

as a reformer and soldier through much of his marriage. Alexander Agassiz speculated in Michigan copper mines to supplement what he earned as a scientist and relished the challenges of harsh weather and technological puzzles during long on-site visits. David Terry left his family in California to fight for the Confederacy and fled to Mexico without them to raise cotton after the war.[43] Families headed by husbands more anxious for stirring experience than financial security were thus vulnerable, both practically and emotionally, to the insistent aspirations of Victorian men.

Geographic differences in the childhood homes of Victorian husbands and wives, inviting diverging tastes and commitments, similarly taxed Victorian marriages. Many of these men still found wives in their home communities or even wed cousins. But in a society that offered single women new prerogatives of travel and social exposure, many other men chose women with backgrounds unlike their own.[44] The romance of Priscilla Cooper of New York and Robert Tyler of Williamsburg was unusual because of her acting career, but bonds forged during young women's visits to relatives or friends grew from the same freedom of mobility for women. Thus Elinor Mead of Brattleboro, Vermont, met William Dean Howells in 1860 when she was introduced to society in Columbus, Ohio, by Fanny Hays, her hostess and friend.[45] Matches made across cultural distances drew on the unfamiliar's special appeal. Lew Wallace of Indianapolis was fascinated by Susan Elston on his visit to Crawfordsville, Indiana, in 1848, and her charm was not wholly uncalculated. Away at a Poughkeepsie, New York, boarding school just months before, Susan wrote to her sister that she missed her native

---

[43] Stonehouse, *North,* pp. 42, 199; Edelstein, *Strange Enthusiasm,* pp. 93–4; *Agassiz,* ed. Agassiz, ch. 4; Terry to Cornelia Runnels Terry, Oct. 11, 1867, Terry Papers.

[44] Among these Victorians, children of prominent families in well-established communities were most inclined to find a spouse close to home. In Boston, Octavius Brooks Frothingham, William Wetmore Story, and Thomas Wentworth Higginson wed local women. In New York, James Beekman, George Templeton Strong, and Abram Hewitt did the same. See Caruthers, *Octavius Brooks Frothingham: Gentle Radical* (1977), p. 25; James, *William Wetmore Story and His Friends* (1903), 1:39; Edelstein, *Strange Enthusiasm,* p. 39; White, *The Beekmans of New York in Politics and Commerce, 1647–1887* (1965), p. 343; *Diary of Strong,* ed. Nevins and Thomas, 1: esp. 315, and Nevins, *Abram S. Hewitt, with Some Account of Peter Cooper* (1935), p. 147. Sometimes, however, geographic mobility enhanced the appeal of a familiar face. Thus Oliver Otis Howard married a woman from his home town of Leeds, Maine, after an eight-year courtship, during which he attended college and moved among army posts. Samuel McCullough opposed the wishes of his fiancée's father in order to bring his future wife from their home in New Jersey to join him in California. See McFeely, *Yankee Stepfather: General O. O. Howard and the Freedmen* (1968), p. 29, and McCullough to Caroline [Pumyea?], Aug. 16, 1859, Samuel McCullough Papers. Victorians who married their cousins included Thomas Wentworth Higginson, Lewis Henry Morgan, and Lyman Abbott. See Edelstein, *Strange Enthusiasm,* p. 39; Resek, *Lewis Henry Morgan: American Scholar* (1960), pp. 48–9; and Brown, *Lyman Abbott, Christian Evangelist: A Study in Religious Liberalism* (1953), p. 18.

[45] Coleman, *Tyler,* p. 66; Lynn, *Howells,* pp. 102–3. Academies were another setting in which young men and women of different places of origin could meet and interact with some freedom. James Garfield, e.g., met Lucretia Randolph at Hiram Seminary in the early 1850s, and he chronicled their courtship in his *Diary of Garfield,* ed. Brown and Williams, 1: esp. 271–336. William Potter also left a record of informal friendships with women at the normal school he attended in Bridgewater, Mass., in the late 1840s. See his Diary, 1847–48, Potter Papers.

West, but hoped to *"astonish the natives"* with skill acquired by lessons on the guitar.[46] Because men who chose wives from outside their hometowns often married upward socially as well, they must have been drawn, too, by the aura of superior station and manners. Howells, for example, was the son of a ne'er-do-well printer and editor, whereas Elinor Mead was the daughter of a leading citizen of Brattleboro, founder of the town's first bank. Mathew Brady rose from obscure origins in upstate New York to wed a Maryland planter's daughter. Ely Parker did not marry another Native American, but at age thirty-nine planned to wed a white woman, Minny Sackett. He was apparently so unnerved by the prospect of a social as well as conjugal leap that he failed to show up at the wedding. His great-nephew and first biographer reported that Parker was drugged, but more likely he quailed at the trial of a large public ceremony. Several days later, the couple was privately married.[47] Thus geographic mobility, the appeal of the exotic, and the romance of superior status combined to bring together young men and women of dissimilar social backgrounds.

These were not couples willing to sacrifice private feeling to the thought that marriage between people of different habits and values might require unusual toleration. Perhaps Elinor Howells's invalidism and Ely Parker's long-term friendship with a woman besides his wife attest to the difficulty of crossing social barriers. But other couples gracefully compromised. Priscilla and Robert Tyler represented poles of sectional loyalty that they reconciled more than once. First Robert, born in Virginia, agreed to move north to Pennsylvania, then Priscilla left the North for Alabama at the start of the Civil War. Yet at heart she remained a northerner and spent her summers as a widow in New York.[48] Although the Tylers' marriage bore the mark of a persistent individualism that placed unlike personalities in tandem, their ability to maneuver together through great social trials was the work of strong marital sentiment.

Indeed, mutual affection is the key to understanding Victorian marriages. To engage each other emotionally was the main reason the Victorians wed, and they often did so successfully because of their insistence on self-

[46] Susan Elston [Wallace] to Joanne Elston, Aug. 12, 1848, Lew Wallace Papers. On the Wallace's courtship, see Morseberger and Morseberger, *Lew Wallace: Militant Romantic* (1980), p. 39.

[47] Horan, *Mathew Brady: Historian with a Camera* (1955), p. 13; Parker, *The Life of General Ely S. Parker* (1919), p. 145. Other stories indicate that a group of Senecas may have gotten Parker drunk to prevent him from marrying a white woman or that he simply went on a binge, as was reportedly his habit. See Armstrong, *Warrior in Two Camps: Ely S. Parker, Union General and Seneca Chief* (1978), pp. 132–3.

[48] Coleman, *Tyler*. Scholars generally agree that nineteenth-century invalidism represented a social as well as physical disorder, although precisely what kinds of stress brought on disability is less clear. For a provocative discussion of the roots of invalidism in conflicting expectations for women, see Carroll Smith-Rosenberg, "The Hysterical Woman: Sex Roles and Role Conflict in Nineteenth-Century America," in *Disorderly Conduct*, pp. 197–216. For an analysis of extramarital friendships, including Parker's, see my discussion in Chapter 3.

determination in choosing partners they enjoyed. Yet their fears and struggles arose from the same autonomy. The Victorians seemed to control passion rigidly because they felt that responsibility for guiding their relationships fell so squarely on themselves. When elements of restlessness and choice disrupted family harmony, members of this generation perhaps recognized their own desires' consequences. Even more problematically, the freedom of men and women to make marriages may have seemed to the Victorians one sign of a metaphysical autonomy that many sensed dimly stood behind faltering faith. Feeling awesomely alone in a world where the familiar images of God the Father and Christ the Son were less compelling than in the past, young Victorians set off in a mood blending trepidation and exhilaration to find intense, and reassuring, family sentiment. In the process, they discovered the irony that marriages contracted by men and women who aimed to act autonomously would soon be complicated by ties of feeling that bound parents and children.

PARENTS AND CHILDREN

American Victorians welcomed children for the rich sentiment they brought to families, simpler and more innocent than even the sincerest adult feeling and hence capable of being returned without reserve. But children grew up, and relations among fathers, mothers, sons, and daughters became complex, as all involved reached through family ties to tempting emotional rewards. Just as the durability of marriages was tested by the Victorians' unsettling inclinations, moreover, so families confronted tastes for mobility, sociability, and privacy, perhaps inconsistent among themselves, but together capable of making families adjust expectations of what domesticity should be.

The correspondence of Victorian couples is filled with exchanges on children, as parents worried about their health, planned their education, and doted on their accomplishments in ways indicative of the bonds children brought to their families. Harriet Vance loved her husband the more for his fatherly instincts. "You have no idea how delighted I am to read your warm hearted and affectionate letters," she wrote in 1854, "in which you talk so much of our dear blessed little boy!"[49] Writing again in 1860, she told Zebulon that their two boys slept in a bed and crib on each side of her, a habit that reveals the intensity of her mothering as well, perhaps, as the way devotion to her sons blended with love of their father.[50] With children so crucial to a family's sense of well-being, it was inevitable that parents would be desolate at their loss. John Kinkade's terse prose could not obscure

---

[49] Harriet Vance to Zebulon Vance, Nov. 27, Vance Papers
[50] Harriet Vance to Zebulon Vance, Feb. 4, Vance Papers.

his grief when he told his brother of the death by diphtheria of three of his five children. "I may be allowed as a parent to say they were among God's most interesting creatures," he wrote from California in 1863: "They were as all our Children beloved by all who knew them."[51] Although Kinkade had talked for a decade of moving home to Ohio from California, these deaths gave his family tragic roots in the West: "Our dear children lye in the Church Yard here and I expect when our pilgrimage ends we will rest near them."[52] Wade Hampton was more visibly distraught by his son's death of malaria in 1879, though his son was no longer a child. "Life seems closed for me," he wrote after several months to his sister-in-law, "and I have nothing but duty to live for."[53]

Beyond the sentiment children brought to their families, adults relied on children emotionally to offset personal hardship, whether real or perceived. David Terry had lost three sons in their infancy, two in adulthood, and his wife by 1886, and he turned with a longing mixed with pathos to Nealie, the daughter of his surviving son. He wrote from Stockton, California, to Clint, Nealie's father: "I want much to see Nealie. I have not been so long without seeing her for over a year and I am anxious to see how she likes the ranch and how the strawberries get on, though I suppose it is too wet for her to attend them."[54] Thomas and Maria Ewing felt similarly bereft when they gave up their daughter in marriage to William Tecumseh Sherman in 1850. In compensation, they asked to raise Minnie, the Shermans' first child. Minnie spent so much of her childhood with her grandparents that she felt them to be her parents, and they called her "daughter" in turn.[55] In a world increasingly subject to tangible and intangible dislocations, children anchored adults by their soothing unconsciousness of life's dilemmas.

Yet as children grew old enough to participate in relationships more actively, family members created networks of feeling differentiated in expression and significance. Fathers and daughters drew together in mutual reliance, as did mothers and sons. Conflict of fathers and sons centered on issues of independence and betrayed affection. Mothers and daughters, sensitive to

[51] John Kinkade to James Kinkade, June 25, 1863, Kinkade Papers.

[52] John Kinkade to James Kinkade, Mar. 13, 1864, Kinkade Papers. Child mortality remained common among this prosperous segment of the middle classes. The biographies and documents that supply the core of my information refer to children's deaths too erratically to calculate mortality precisely, but it is clear that families in all regions experienced losses, at times of devastating proportions. In Troy, New York, four of five of the children of John and Marie Wentworth died in childhood. In Cass County, Georgia, William and Rebecca Felton also lost four of five children. The sources indicate that epidemic diseases such as measles, malaria, diphtheria, and scarlet fever were often responsible for children's deaths. On the Wentworths and Feltons, see Fehrenbacher, *Chicago Giant: A Biography of "Long John" Wentworth* (1957), p. 55, and Talmadge, *Felton*, pp. 15, 22, 24, 26.

[53] Wade Hampton to Mrs. Thomas Preston, Mar. 20, 1880, in Cauthen, ed., *Family Letters of the Three Wade Hamptons, 1782–1901*, (1953), p. 156.

[54] David Terry to Clint Terry, Jan. 23, 1886, Terry Papers.

[55] Burton, *Three Generations: Maria Boyle Ewing (1801–1864), Ellen Ewing Sherman (1824–1888), Minnie Sherman Fitch (1851–1913)* (1947), pp. 89–90, 132.

women's vulnerability, kept their feelings from view. Both northern and southern families conformed to these patterns for the most part, but women exerted less influence in southern society. Ties that crossed gender lines between fathers and daughters and between mothers and sons were less prominent in the South's more traditional patriarchy because women were marginal to the self-image of kin networks conceived as lineages traced through men. Northern families, in contrast, were more sentimental in the sense that women became touchstones for exchanges of feeling between the sexes. Women still did not shape the family as actively as did men, but they stirred emotions that gave northern domesticity a distinct inner fervor. Attention to the geography of cases discussed in the following paragraphs may suggest the subtle sectionalism in American Victorian families.[56]

One of the most prominent relationships in mid-nineteenth-century middle-class families was the mutual reliance of fathers and daughters. As daughters grew up, fathers made them companions. Young women, in turn, found it hard to break free of the same affectional ties. Cyrus Holliday made his daughter, Lillie, his main correspondent when she toured Europe in the 1870s with her mother and brother, while he pursued business in Topeka. His early letters aimed to direct her education, but Holliday soon began to chat with Lillie as an equal, reporting civic improvements and *"dis*-improvements," such as fires, at home.[57] In contrast, letters to Mary, his wife, concerned practical matters, and few were addressed to his son. Holliday's feelings for Mary were no less generous as Lillie moved into a role that once belonged to her mother. All "praise" for the benefit of the trip to the children, Holliday wrote graciously to Mary in 1875, "is due entirely to you."[58] Nonetheless, the importance of Lillie's companionship to her father became increasingly clear. In a similar instance, William Tecumseh Sherman escorted Minnie, his daughter, to social events after the war, in part to spare his wife, Ellen, a duty not to her taste, but also to enjoy Minnie's company.

---

[56] Many historians have discussed the comparative importance and nature of families in nineteenth-century northern and southern society. Among those who argue that the South was more family-oriented, C. Vann Woodward states that southerners gave more attention to the home and personal feelings than did northerners, in "The Southern Ethic in a Puritan World" in his *American Counterpoint: Slavery and Racism in the North–South Dialogue* (1971), pp. 13–46. Michael Barton reaffirms this conclusion, in *Goodmen: The Character of Civil War Soldiers* (1981), esp. p. 77. Other scholars who have interpreted southerners' attachment to family, in values as well as in fact, as a consequence of the region's traditionalism include Bertram Wyatt-Brown, *Southern Honor,* and Eugene D. Genovese, *Roll, Jordan, Roll.* Some recent analyses warn observers not to romanticize southern families, however, by demonstrating the complexity of southern family relationships, particularly Fox-Genovese, *Within the Plantation Household: Black and White Women of the Old South* (1988). In addition, historians' growing awareness of the indulgence of feeling in the Victorian North forces reconsideration of a conventional dichotomy between individualistic Yankees and familial Cavaliers. Consider Douglas, *Feminization of American Culture,* which builds on older work on popular culture such as Pattee, *The Feminine Fifties* (1940). My position on the relationship of northern and southern Victorian families has been shaped by this continuing debate.

[57] Cyrus Holliday to Lillie Holliday, Nov. 21, 1874, Holliday Papers.

[58] Cyrus Holliday to Mary Holliday, Feb. 19, 1875, Holliday Papers.

Thomas Wentworth Higginson, too, spent much time with his daughter, Margaret, in the decade before his death in 1911. He was glad she chose not to attend college so that she stayed close to him instead, in spirit as well as in fact.[59]

Daughters were just as caught up in relationships with their fathers of loyalty and love. Ellen Sherman was bound as tightly to her father, Thomas Ewing, as her daughter was to William Sherman in turn. Gratified by Ewing's religious conversion shortly before his death in 1871, Ellen honored him posthumously with a story that documented his change of heart. More dramatically, a number of young married women were unable to move out of their fathers' homes. Why Robert Ingersoll gave both his daughters the middle name "Robert" at their births in the 1860s is unclear, but the fact that Eva found after her marriage in 1889 that she could not live apart from her father conforms to a common pattern. Although Eva's husband was a railroad and banking entrepreneur of independent temper and means, he agreed to live with the Ingersolls six months a year.[60]

It is essential to note that Victorian wives inclined even more than their daughters to coresidence with fathers, making this kind of bond a phenomenon that persisted through generations. Although the Victorians asked families to help provide meaning in a more secular world, they did not altogether originate practices of domestic interaction, but adapted what they learned as children to their own ends. Thus the marriage of Roxanna to John Wentworth in 1844 barely touched Roxanna's relations with her father. The Wentworths' only residence together through more than two decades of marriage was Roxanna's childhood home in Troy, New York. When she visited John in Chicago, where he pursued careers as a politician and entrepreneur, the family stayed in hotels.[61] Harriet DeForest moved with her husband, John, through a series of houses and hotels following their marriage in 1856. None of their residences apparently felt as much like home as her father's house in Charleston, South Carolina, where she made long visits and eventually died in 1878.[62] Joseph Taylor all but implored his wife, Elizabeth, after six months of marriage in 1867 to leave her father in North Berwick, Maine, and return to Cambridge, Ohio: "Oh I am so anxious to live and board and sleep in the house of which you are empress and manager."[63] Yet through the next decade, Elizabeth spent months at a time with her father, with growing numbers of children in tow.[64]

---

[59] Burton, *Three Generations*, p. 188; Edelstein, *Strange Enthusiasm*, p. 393.

[60] Cramer, *Royal Bob*, pp. 61, 253. It should also be noted that Eva was named after her mother as well, who was also "Eva." On Ellen Sherman's account of her father, see Burton, *Three Generations*, p. 193.

[61] Fehrenbacher, *Chicago Giant*, p. 55.

[62] Light, *DeForest*, pp. 39–42, 103, 108.

[63] Joseph Taylor to Elizabeth Taylor, July 9, 1867, Joseph Danner Taylor Papers.

[64] See Joseph Taylor to Elizabeth Taylor, Oct. 3, 1876. Among famous precedents for this kind of

This companionship was the way fathers and daughters made a patriarchal culture in the midst of transition serve their individual needs. Fathers found neither society nor their own families altogether easy to control and so welcomed this cozy remnant of patriarchy, though power over daughters now came less from authority than from paternal love. In a society where increasing choices for women also imposed more ambiguity and ambivalence upon them, intimacy with fathers must have served as a refuge from confusion. Yet it is significant that these women, despite their inclination to seek a haven from stress, were not unusually retiring. Eva Ingersoll was an activist on behalf of suffrage, child welfare, world peace, and antivivisection. Elizabeth Taylor attended a temperance convention in Cincinnati in 1874, leaving her children home with their father.[65] Perhaps daughters gained a healthy self-assurance from association with strong fathers that supported their risky assertions of independence. This was a society, after all, where fathers could provide more than mothers by way of example and guidance to women inclined to step beyond a traditional role. Still, there was an emotional timidity to the daughters' strategy, as they crept toward autonomy without relinquishing childhood certainties. Nor was restraint all self-imposed. When daughters struck out for real freedom, fathers did not hide their displeasure. Cyrus Holliday was surprised and distressed when Lillie rebelled at his plan that she train to be a teacher just in case of financial need. "You speak in your letter as though I was *compelling* you to be educated especially for the profession of a teacher," he wrote in a tone of apology, though he continued to press his argument in favor of teaching.[66] For the most part, fathers and daughters observed tacit rules in a setting that excluded divisive issues. Fathers and sons, in contrast, found reason to quarrel more often.

Struggles fired by the Victorians' fathers' powerful influence and their sons' desire for independence have been discussed in the context of careers. Yet when Victorian men became parents themselves, they duplicated their fathers' intrusive temper. As if nurturing their sons' boldness, Victorian fathers encouraged aggressive achievement that they associated with masculinity. Awareness of gender stood behind Wade Hampton's directives for

father–daughter bond was the case of Lyman and Catharine Beecher. As Kathryn Sklar explains, Catharine struggled with mixed success to win independence of her father, but also gained strength from their close relation that stood behind her achievements in the fields of religion, education, and domestic theory. See *Catharine Beecher: A Study in American Domesticity* (1973), esp. chs. 1–3. That Catharine was born in 1800, making her older than the women studied here, underlines continuities in gender relations that influenced the choices the Victorians made. Catherine Clinton has observed close relations between fathers and daughters in the early antebellum South, although her brief discussion suggests that such bonds were not as strong as my research indicates they later were in the North. See *The Plantation Mistress: Women's World in the Old South* (1982), p. 44. For another suggestive discussion of fathers and daughters in the context of girls' education, see Rable, *Civil Wars*, pp. 18–19.

[65] Cramer, *Royal Bob*, p. 63; Joseph Taylor to Elizabeth Taylor, Apr. 24, [1874?], Taylor Papers.

[66] Cyrus Holliday to Lillie Holliday, Nov. 27, 1874, Holliday Papers.

training his son, McDuffie. "I shall expect to hear the baby talking quite well when I get back; don't make a girl of him," he told his sister in 1859. Two years later he gave a second order, followed by a promise: "Tell McDuffie that he must be a man and that I will bring him a gun."[67] Yet fathers did not wish sons to use this force of character to contradict the parent's will. They acted erratically, in moods ranging from compulsion to panic, when sons turned the independence intimated in the ideal of masculine strength into license to lead their own lives. Jabez Curry, a thoughtful and cosmopolitan man who came of age in the antebellum South, could not quite grasp the priorities of his son, Manly, a St. Paul entrepreneur after the war. Curry did not bluntly contest his son's decisions but poured out letters almost daily in the 1880s urging Manly to marry, to take religion seriously, and to study literature and history.[68] William Tecumseh Sherman reacted more explosively when his son, Tom, decided to become a priest. Sherman had long accepted his wife's serious practice of Catholicism, but he argued that Tom's choice betrayed family duty. He refused to attend Tom's ordination, told him to stop writing, and cut him out of his will.[69]

Victorian fathers thus inherited a key contradiction in the nineteenth-century masculine ethos: sons' success must at once be self-made and conform to parents' expectations in order to please ambitious fathers. Yet conflict with sons was provoked even more by the strength of fathers' affection. Victorian fathers lost patience with sons less for disobedience, as they did in the more authoritarian families of the previous century and even of the last generation, than for betrayed loyalty, since they wanted very much to be loved as much as they gave love themselves.[70] Tussles with sons were therefore strangely akin to close relations with daughters, because both were rooted in the tight bonds of families seeking intense sentiment. Both relationships, moreover, show fathers exerting an emotional presence in the family. To an extent, fathers' frequent use of letters as a channel of influence was itself evidence of sporadic day-to-day family involvement, due to the absence either of themselves or their children. But sentiments expressed in writing conform sufficiently closely to other evidence of fatherly behavior, such as coresidence with married daughters, to confirm the emotional power of fathers at home.

This is surprising in light of what scholars have said of the woman-centered

[67] Wade Hampton to Mary Fisher Hampton, Oct. 28, 1859, Sept. 4, 1861, in Cauthen, ed., *Family Letters of Wade Hamptons*, pp. 67, 77.

[68] Rice, *Curry*, pp. 137–9. Although it might seem that the success ethic, including parental pressure, was more pronounced in the entrepreneurial North, one of the best recent discussions of fathers' manipulation of sons deals with the South. See Oakes, *The Ruling Race: A History of American Slaveholders* (1982), ch. 3.

[69] Merrill, *William Tecumseh Sherman* (1971), pp. 367–72.

[70] For an excellent discussion of the mores that governed traditional patriarchal households, see Ryan, *Cradle of the Middle Class*, pp. 31–43.

tone, in theory and practice, of nineteenth-century families.[71] But these Victorian mothers did not set the mood of family life as decisively as did their husbands. Two practical circumstances curtailed their influence. Wives of prominent men who lived outside major towns continued to do taxing labor. George Atkinson, a minister in Oregon, told a New York cousin in the 1850s that high prices forced his wife to keep house without help, yet he also wrote that he had "a study to which I may retire daily for improvement and meditation."[72] No doubt Atkinson's wife's ill health came in part from hard work, and these conditions together must have restricted what she could emotionally give. In addition, although wives outlived husbands more often than husbands survived wives, men became widowers at younger ages than women became widows. Women enjoyed longevity if they survived middle age, but changes in their childbearing years put them at considerable risk. Thus mothers were less often able than fathers to see their children become adults.[73]

That housework, pregnancies, and child care restricted women's domestic influence was certainly not without precedent. Biographers note the shadowy presence in the historical record and passive role in the family of some mothers of the Victorians. William McFeely writes of the laconic, almost withdrawn temper of Hannah Grant, who never visited her famous son, Ulysses, at the

---

[71] Scholars who pioneered studies of the prescriptive literature of domesticity most often assumed that the nineteenth-century family was in fact, as in rhetoric, a mother-centered institution. See, e.g., Barbara Welter, "The Cult of True Womanhood, 1820–1860," *American Quarterly* 18 (1966): 151–74. Since then, historians have thoughtfully probed precisely how women exercised power in the family. Nancy Cott, e.g., argues that domestic values challenged the patriarchal ideal, though not necessarily the reality, in *Bonds of Womanhood*, pp. 86–7. Daniel Scott Smith writes that women gained a role in family decision making, in "Family Limitation, Sexual Control, and Domestic Feminism in Victorian America," in Hartman and Banner, eds., *Clio's Consciousness*, pp. 119–36. Jean H. Baker emphasizes that the frequent absences from home of ambitious husbands gave their wives more latitude in household management in the late antebellum decades, although bearing domestic burdens alone could also be draining, physically and emotionally, for women. See *Mary Todd Lincoln: A Biography* (1987), esp. pp. 108–9, 113, 120, 122.

[72] Atkinson to Josiah Hale, Oct. 20, 1851, George Henry Atkinson Papers. For Atkinson's description of his wife's difficulties, see Atkinson to Hale, Aug. 8, 1851.

[73] The proportion of the women surveyed who survived their husbands (seven of nine, or 77.8 percent) was considerably higher than men who survived their wives (fourteen of twenty-four known cases, or 58.3 percent). But men became widowers at younger ages than women became widows. The data that follow pertain only to widows and widowers who survived their spouses by more than five years. Of the fourteen women included as principal members of the sample, seven survived their husbands (four were single). The age at which each was widowed is designated in parentheses: Anna Cora Mowatt (thirty-two), Virginia Clay (fifty-seven and sixty-seven), Julia Grant (fifty-nine), Priscilla Tyler (sixty-one), Varina Davis (sixty-three), Elizabeth Cady Stanton (seventy-two), Rebecca Felton (seventy-four). In contrast, at least a dozen men became widowers in middle age (prior to age sixty): John Wesley North (ca. thirty), Wade Hampton (thirty-four and fifty-six), Alexander Agassiz (thirty-eight), Jabez Curry (forty), William Herndon (forty-three), Edwin Godkin (forty-four), Zebulon Vance (forty-eight), William Montague Browne (fifty), John William DeForest (fifty-two), Pierre Beauregard (fifty-four), Thomas Wentworth Higginson (fifty-four), John Wentworth (fifty-five). Because only three of the men studied were bachelors, the large number of unknown cases is due to the lack of information on this point supplied by autobiographies or collections of letters and papers.

White House. Henrietta Larson finds the mother of Jay Cooke less stern than the father, but also "less definite."[74] Mothers in the Victorian generation are easier to grasp, because women were more literate, had more leisure, and bore fewer children. But some left an impression as hazy as did their mothers and for much the same reasons. It is not surprising that there is little record of the accomplishments of William Herndon's second wife, Anna, who was younger than her husband by eighteen years, inherited six children, and bore three of her own.[75] The everyday care of her household must have absorbed most of her energy before she could begin to contemplate the emotional needs of either her family or herself.

Yet when mothers did express themselves, they did so more openly in relations with sons than with daughters. The records left by these Victorians suggest the strong maternal emotions that at varying stages of the sons' lives invested these family bonds. Cornelia Terry's letters in the 1860s to her boys away at school in California have not survived, but the quality of her feelings may be judged by the fact that she made inquiries concerning lodging to stay near them and by the message of her son, David, "I feel very lonesome without you."[76] Susan Wallace used the occasion of her son's engagement to reaffirm her maternal role. In a long letter to Henry, then twenty-nine, she praised the devotion of Maggie, his future bride, but patronized Henry's fiancée in turn for being so young as to seem childish. *"Do not be critical"* when things go wrong in the household, Susan advised, and remember that "through all changes I am unchangeably your best friend, and devoted Mother."[77] This intense involvement of mothers with sons had precedents in the Victorians' parents' generation. In Massachusetts in the 1830s, Louisa Higginson took seriously her obligation to give her children moral instruction, and so tenaciously bound Thomas by the insistence of her mothering that as a young man, he assumed a posture of rebelliousness as a strategy to break free. Well into the 1850s, William Dean Howells could neither leave his mother nor endure the tedium of Jefferson, Ohio. A man in his twenties, he moved indecisively in and out of his childhood home.[78] Thus over many decades, both adult Victorian men and their sons experienced, and to an extent savored, the effusive devotion of mothers.

In his biography of Howells, Kenneth Lynn offers a clue to understanding the mutual dependency of mothers and sons when he says that Mary Howells lived vicariously through William.[79] Just as daughters' association with

---

[74] McFeely, *Grant: A Biography* (1981), pp. 8–9; Larson, *Jay Cooke: Private Banker* (1936), p. 9.

[75] Donald, *Lincoln's Herndon* (1948), pp. 151–3, 285.

[76] David Terry, [Jr.] to Cornelia Terry, June 11, 1867, Terry Papers. I. C. Simmons wrote in reply to Cornelia Terry's request for information on housing for herself near the boys' school on Aug. 26, 1867, Terry Papers.

[77] Susan Wallace to Henry Wallace, June 15, 1882, Wallace Papers.

[78] Edelstein, *Strange Enthusiasm*, pp. 11, 21, 32–3; Lynn, *Howells*, pp. 60–1, 78–80; 104–5.

[79] Lynn, *Howells*, p. 31.

fathers helped girls to extend themselves beyond conventional roles, mothers' reliance on sons attests to the way social restrictions on women made them appropriate the freedom available to men by close association with the only men they could hope to control. Sons, on the other hand, must have relied on mothers for a sense of secure family roots, because relations with fathers were so often shaded with tension. Both responses demonstrate how much the Victorians relied on family interaction to nurture a sense of self. In a world that presented obstacles to both women and men, families promised fulfillment, with the ironic result that domesticity elicited emotional maneuvering as complex as strategies to secure satisfaction in society at large.

Bonds between Victorian mothers and daughters are less easy to document than any other family relationship. Perhaps girls occasioned less correspondence because they stayed closer to home. Looking beyond letters, however, the scarcity of other kinds of writings that might have demonstrated feelings between women in families suggests an inarticulate quality to their interaction. Although Ellen Sherman wrote a memorial sketch of her father, Thomas Wentworth Higginson did the same for his mother, and William Wetmore Story honored his father by sculpting a monument, no daughter commemorated a mother in a similar way.[80] Daughters accustomed to judging by standards of male success may not have clearly seen their mothers' accomplishments. Yet it is at least as likely that mothers and daughters kept feelings private that were no less valued for their concealment. Elizabeth Potter wrote in confidence to her mother about her suspected pregnancy. Widows who declined to remarry moved in with their daughters without comment. This absence of emotional demonstration must have been conditioned by circumscribed options for women. Like members of other subordinate groups, women were moved by an impulse to protect relations perceived as vulnerable by keeping them comparatively invisible. Yet as historians have said of workers and slaves – people with positions analogous to middle-class women, though also far less advantaged from the perspective of freedom as well as prosperity – guarded expression should not be mistaken for emotional emptiness.[81] Victorian women seemed to rely on each other for unquestioning acceptance in the midst of demanding families.

This analysis of feelings between Victorian parents and children indicates that lines of emotional influence grew less from domestic literature that centered on mothers than in conformity with social circumstances that favored the power of fathers. Not only did fathers feel free to ask families to serve their needs, but all household members acted on the tacit assumption that families, no less than society at large, were based on the preeminence of men. Yet it was the incipient erosion of men's prerogatives that gave fathers'

---

[80] Burton, *Three Generations*, p. 193; Edelstein, *Strange Enthusiasm*, p. 17; James, *Story*, 1:23.

[81] Classic analyses of the veiled culture of subordinate groups are E. P. Thompson, *The Making of the English Working Class* (New York: Random House, 1963), and Genovese, *Roll, Jordan, Roll*.

claims to favor a defensive edge. On the one hand, men sought dominion in families to replace the sense of control that seemed in a tumultuous culture increasingly to elude their reach. On the other hand, women's quiet strategies to draw on the power of fathers and sons, either for vicarious strength or satisfaction, constituted a modest challenge from within families to the authority of men. Southern families do not lend counterevidence to these observations. The bonds of feeling between Harriet DeForest and her father, Wade Hampton and his son, and Jabez Curry and his young second wife all show families eager to tap their potential for producing inner rewards. Neither, however, did southerners leave as rich a record of emotional striving, especially crossing gender lines, as did northerners. Perhaps southern men were just that much more assured of their social position and women that much less determined to assert themselves through ties with male kin to give southern patriarchy a more settled tone.

To an extent, the Victorians supported their wish to explore family feeling by structuring domestic life to enhance their ability to do so. Scholars have documented the fact that American women over the course of the nineteenth century bore fewer children and better educated each one in order to gain family status and promote individual achievement. But historians have not emphasized that the same social outcome of controlled fertility, focused homes filled with responsive people, served the cultivation of sentiment. Available evidence indicates that the Victorians sought this goal by trying to avoid both large families and childlessness. Although a number of these Victorians grew up in homes with many brothers and sisters, they created large families less frequently themselves. Thomas Wentworth Higginson, Anna Cora Mowatt, and Lucy Larcom had fourteen, thirteen, and ten siblings respectively, for example. In the next generation, John Bell Hood fathered the most children, a total of eleven in a single decade after the war, by the unusual chance of having three sets of twins.[82] Childlessness, on the other hand, was experienced as an affliction. Couples who failed to have children adopted them to fill an emotional gap. Mathew Brady, the photographer, and his wife, Julia, treated Julia's nephew as a son throughout their lives. Anna Mowatt, the actress, and her husband, James, took legal and parental responsibility for three poverty-stricken orphans.[83] Closer to the Victorians'

---

[82] Edelstein, *Strange Enthusiasm*, p. 8; Barnes, *Lady of Fashion*, p. 3; Larcom, *A New England Girlhood: Outlined from Memory* (1889), p. 56; Dyer, *The Gallant Hood* (1950), p. 318. Only in the case of the family of nativity of Thomas Wentworth Higginson were these large numbers of children produced by successive wives. For one version of the argument on fertility control that stresses the economic benefits for families of bearing fewer children, see Richard A. Easterlin, "The Economics and Sociology of Fertility: A Synthesis," in Tilly, ed., *Historical Studies of Changing Fertility* (1978), pp. 57–133. Mary Ryan emphasizes the investment in nurturing that middle-class families made in limited numbers of children, in *Cradle of the Middle Class*, pp. 155–79.

[83] Horan, *Mathew Brady: Historian with a Camera* (1955), p. 13; Barnes, *Lady of Fashion*, pp. 114–18. Single adults also adopted children, either virtually or legally. See the previous discussion of Charlotte Cushman. Another variation on the pattern of acquiring children to fill emotional needs was the effectual

domestic ideal, small families consisting of only one or two children seem to have been the choice of at least seven couples, because they were unconstrained by such factors as age or economic hardship and might have borne more. One couple, Lew and Susan Wallace, left evidence that the outcome was discussed. Just before the birth of his only son in 1853, Lew wrote to his brother: "I insisted that there should be two [children]; she insisted on one. . . . I consented to *one,* in consideration of a solemn promise on her part that one should be a *boy.*"[84] Susan assiduously nurtured Henry, writing holiday poems, keeping family scrapbooks, and dispensing advice once he was grown. If she was characteristic of mothers of small families, a decision to restrict the number of one's children permitted the luxury of showering attention on those few.

Fathers no less than mothers took an interest in their children's upbringing. In so doing, they acted not only from moral obligation and concern for their children's future promise, but from deep affection for which, on some level, they may have hoped to secure a return in feeling from offspring exposed to influences designed to touch the recesses of character. Parents studied advice literature to improve their effectiveness as nurturers. Elizabeth Cady Stanton recalled that her reading "centered on hygiene," whereas William Potter turned to John Ware's *Home Life.*[85] Fathers were also thoughtful about the environment in which children grew up. When Edwin Godkin considered accepting a Harvard professorship, his children's development was one motive in his plan. Living in Cambridge, he told Charles Eliot Norton, would provide a proper atmosphere for the children, "whom I can hardly bear to see growing up in New York."[86] George Atkinson in Oregon was attentive to the role of play in learning. George, Jr., "employs himself with his little wood saw or hammer & nails & whistle & kites & balls," the

---

adoption of boys by fathers whose only surviving children were daughters. Octavius Brooks Frothingham and John Wentworth were each the father of an only child, in both cases girls. Each man took a nephew under his wing, casting him in the role of a son. See Fehrenbacher, *Chicago Giant,* p. 209, and Caruthers, *Frothingham,* p. 221. Although men's relationships with boys were filled with more tensions than bonds with girls, men must not have felt fulfilled unless they sponsored male progeny.

[84] Lew Wallace to William Wallace, Feb. 17, 1853, Wallace Papers. In addition to the Wallaces, the families of the following men were limited to one or two children (the number of children is designated in parentheses): Henry Lee Higginson (one), Octavius Brooks Frothingham (one), John William DeForest (one), Washington Roebling (one), Robert Ingersoll (two), Josiah Grinnell (two). The list includes only couples who had no obvious reason for not producing more children. Thomas Wentworth Higginson, e.g., was nearly sixty when his first and only surviving child was born. Probably his age helped dissuade the couple from having more children (Edelstein, *Strange Enthusiasm,* pp. 334–7). The wife of George Pickett bore one son during the war. The personal disruption of Reconstruction, apparently hastening Pickett's death at age fifty in 1875, most likely deterred the couple from having more children. See George Pickett to LaSalle Pickett, letters no. 33, 42–6, in *Soldier of the South: General Pickett's War Letters to His Wife,* ed. Inman (1928), pp. 109–10, 138–57.

[85] Stanton, *Eighty Years,* pp. 120–1; Potter to George Bartlett, Mar. 18, 1866, Potter Papers.

[86] Godkin to Charles Eliot Norton, July 28, 1870, in *Letters of Godkin,* ed. Armstrong, p. 149.

father wrote to his cousins in the East, while "Annie has her dolls & paper & scissors & needle & thread & sticks & blocks & tea sets," and both have miniature Noah's arks.[87] Most parents took steps to provide formal learning by finding good schools, but a few educated their children themselves. Robert Ingersoll, the dedicated religious skeptic, taught his daughters at home to shield them from the Christian views of both public and private schools.[88] Finally, travel supplemented schooling for the more affluent, and Cyrus Holliday's expectations were typical when he urged his daughter in Europe to look to her "*mental* and *moral* improvement."[89] This catalog of efforts underlines how much parents centered families in the children's well-being. It is not surprising that young people reared in this way were capable of the sustained emotional engagement of Victorian family life.

Yet families were also buffeted by forces of dislocation to which feelings had to adjust. As one expression of Victorian individualism, family members separated temporarily for increasing numbers of reasons that all viewed as legitimate, and their absences strained domestic integrity. In the past, pioneers and politicians had left their families behind for extended periods, but they did so with greater ease in the midcentury decades. Cyrus Holliday's decision in 1854 to settle his pregnant wife with her parents in Pennsylvania while he went out to Kansas was facilitated by improved mail communication that allowed couples to maintain distant residences without losing touch.[90] Similarly, faster travel made it reasonable for Abram Hewitt to live in Washington hotels during his twelve years in Congress (1874–86), while his wife and children stayed near her father in New York.[91] Neither of these families' decisions was unprecedented. Even so, bureaucracy and technology

---

[87] Atkinson to Josiah and Sophronia Little, Mar. 10, 1854, Atkinson Papers.

[88] Cramer, *Royal Bob*, pp. 62–3.

[89] Cyrus Holliday to Lillie Holliday, Sept. 15, 1872, Holliday Papers.

[90] In fact, probably most families in earlier decades migrated together, as did people less prosperous than these Victorians. Studies that show the prevalence of family migration include Johnson, *A Shopkeeper's Millennium: Society and Revivals in Rochester, New York, 1815–1837* (1978), ch. 1; Ryan, *Cradle of the Middle Class*, ch. 1; and Faragher, *Women and Men on the Overland Trail* (1979). James Oakes emphasizes individual entrepreneurship on the southern frontier that separated extended families. Yet nuclear families still commonly moved together. See *Ruling Race*, ch. 3. The fact that in society at large, single young men and, at times, women increasingly left their families in the nineteenth century to become urban in-migrants or foreign immigrants, in both cases boarding with strangers, represented another step in the direction of individualism. See, e.g, John Modell and Tamara K. Hareven, "Urbanization and the Malleable Household: An Examination of Boarding and Lodging in American Families," in Gordon, ed., *American Family*, pp. 51–68. Yet the contrast between that pattern and the middle-class Victorian practice of male pioneering is instructive, because the latter arose from an apparent attentiveness to female delicacy among people who could afford to do without a wife's labor and to keep two residences. Other men who pioneered alone before sending for their wives were John Wesley North (in Nevada and Tennessee), John Wentworth (Illinois), William Tecumseh Sherman (Louisiana, California, Kansas), and David Terry (Mexico). See Stonehouse, *North*, pp. 149, 178; Fehrenbacher, *Chicago Giant*, p. 55; Merrill, *Sherman*, pp. 89–98, 127–9; David Terry to Cornelia Terry, Oct. 11, 1867, Terry Papers.

[91] Nevins, *Hewitt*, p. 402.

that fostered an impression of family connection between an absent member and the folks at home seemed to work as a license permitting fathers to go away in good conscience.

Families also approved reasons for separation that were comparatively new. In an era of determined career ambition for men, promised advantages to a husband's work warranted his sustained absences. Robert Tyler saw his wife and young children in Bristol, Pennsylvania, only twice a week when he lived in Philadelphia in the 1840s to launch himself as a lawyer.[92] John William DeForest moved after the war from New Haven to New York, without his wife and son, to pursue his literary prospects.[93] In addition, leisure and benevolence licensed women's absences, a striking development in a culture where people felt more comfortable when assured that women were anchoring the family. Lillie Holliday's more than two-year sojourn in Europe in the 1870s might be seen as advancing the family interest by the acquisition of culture, but her trip still precluded everyday intimacy with her father. Ellen Strong's decision to nurse Union soldiers in 1862 frayed her husband's nerves, as he translated his own sensations of loneliness into worries about her health, poured daily into his journal. Their marriage may have benefited in the end from Ellen's resolve to aid the Union because of her husband's heightened esteem for her "enterprise, pluck, discretion, and force of character."[94] But the separation itself, though judged for a worthy end, consumed Strong's peace of mind.

The Victorians' longing for family cohesion was sufficiently tenacious to contest separation, however, so that they adjusted to individual ambitions in unusual ways. Rather than let restless temperaments disrupt domestic peace, families themselves became peripatetic, at times in the extreme. The case of William Dean Howells is dramatic. From the time of his marriage in 1862 until his death in 1920, Howells and his family tried almost every conceivable kind of domicile in Europe and the American Northeast. They lived in apartments, boardinghouses, and hotels. They bought houses, built houses, and engaged a summer house. According to Kenneth Lynn, Howells's biographer, they moved to gain status, regain health, and indulge an interest in architecture.[95] Howells's fiction reflected his attention to the interplay of human inclination and changing locale. *Suburban Sketches* (1871) and *The Wedding Journey* (1871) began his career. *The Rise of Silas Lapham* (1885) was set against a social background of Boston's changing neighborhoods. *A Hazard of New Fortunes* (1890) opened memorably as the March family tried to agree on New York housing to suit everyone's tastes. Perhaps much as

---

[92] Coleman, *Tyler*, p. 113.

[93] Light, *DeForest*, p. 101.

[94] July 11, 1862, *Diary of Strong*, ed. Nevins and Thomas, 3:239. Ellen left the family on May 5 and returned on July 11.

[95] Lynn, *Howells*, p. 136.

this fictional family contained discrete personalities all expecting a voice, the Howells family honored its members' diverse impulses to the point of chronic mobility. Yet even thus tested by the stress of near rootlessness, family sentiment adapted to circumstances far different from ideals of stability and seclusion.

Akin to their taste for mobility, the Victorians relished the sociability of boardinghouses and hotels. Childless couples in particular welcomed the friendly bustle of public abodes. At least ten of the husbands and wives in this study spent part or all of their marriages in rented rooms where they did not keep house themselves. Jay Cooke in Philadelphia and Henry Lee Higginson in Boston each boarded with his wife until their children were born, then they moved into houses. Neither Mathew Brady and his wife nor William Montague Browne and his ever had children. Both spent much of their marriages in hotels. Virginia Clay, whose only child was stillborn, eschewed the Alabama plantation where her husband settled after the war for a boardinghouse and later apartment in Huntsville. John Wentworth, who inhabited Chicago hotels, was in effect childless, since his wife and one daughter who survived infancy lived in Troy, New York, with his father-in-law.[96] A need to economize or a wife's ill health sometimes contributed to a choice against housekeeping. But wives without children were articulate, too, about the oppression of solitary homes. Southern women, such as Virginia Clay, Lizzie Browne, and Mary Chesnut, for whom a house often meant a place far from friends in the country, voiced their preference for boarding most bluntly. Thus Chesnut tartly dismissed "the social desert of Sahara of Camden," the site of her husband's family plantation, and blithely peppered her journal with memos of whom she saw in the drawing room and with whom she conversed at meals in her wartime Richmond hotel.[97]

The taste for hotel living curiously critiqued and affirmed conventional domesticity, loosened and repaired family bonds. Whereas nineteenth-century families generally sought privacy as a condition of emotional exchange, the popularity of hotels signals a sense by midcentury of the friction possible in self-contained families and the advantages of public connections. In practice, hotel dwelling may have eased stifling bonds by permitting family members to function on their own more freely in a broader social sphere. While life in the public eye circumscribed intimacy, it equally diffused frustration. Yet Victorian boarding also revealed a profound commitment to a specific kind of family, one with children. Whether child-

---

[96] Larson, *Cooke*, p. 56; Perry, *Higginson*, p. 275; Horan, *Brady*, p. 13; Coulter, *Browne*, pp. 87, 225–6; Wiley, *Confederate Women*, pp. 74–7; Fehrenbacher, *Chicago Giant*, pp. 55, 144, 155. Ruth Cowan alludes to boardinghouse living as a transient fancy of the middle classes, in *More Work for Mother*, p. 108.

[97] Jan. 1, 1862, *Chesnut's Civil War*, ed. Woodward, p. 273. For a characteristic entry during her stays in Richmond, see July 16, 1861, in ibid., p. 100. On Clay and Browne, respectively, see Wiley, *Confederate Women*, pp. 74–7, and Coulter, *Browne*, p. 88.

lessness was a stage of life or an enduring condition, adults on their own seem to have preferred hotels not simply because keeping house was less necessary, but to avert feelings of emptiness generated by a home without children. Mary Chesnut, inexplicably barren, revealed her sense of her own inadequacy when she lied for Lizzie Browne. "I told those women that she was childless now, but that she had lost three children," she wrote in her journal in 1861: "Women have such a contempt for a childless wife."[98] Nor was Chesnut's sensitivity self-induced, because especially in the South, couples without children sometimes lived for years with the husband's parents, as did Chesnut herself, as if a family were not quite a family without offspring.[99] In short, this was a culture where domestic privacy was almost a privilege of fertility. No wonder childless couples who were in a position to choose opted for residences with stimulating diversions and without self-incriminating reminders of their failure to create the kind of family their behavior nonetheless ironically endorsed.

Much as boarding betrayed limits to family privacy in favor of sociability, personal seclusion within families signaled mild intolerance of the emotional demands of close kin. Individuals in prior generations also maintained personal space, through diary keeping for example. But Victorians took new kinds of liberties that said much about their notion of family. Most uniquely, fathers constructed buildings near family homes for use as private retreats. As aging men in the 1890s, John Burroughs and Lew Wallace built these glorified studies, as work space in part, because both were writers working at home, but as physical statements of personal identity as well. Burroughs put up a hut a mile from home to escape a nagging wife and to entertain friends. Wallace's room was so filled with military memorabilia and art objects collected on travels that his study easily became a museum after his death.[100] This way of claiming private space as adults stands in contrast to arrangements made during the Victorians' childhoods. In several decades following 1820, young people rather than fathers lived in separate quarters, when families divided at all. The father of Priscilla Cooper Tyler put up a

---

[98] Mar. 18, 1861, *Chesnut's Civil War*, ed. Woodward, p. 28.

[99] Perhaps the prevalence of this custom in the South was related to the importance of producing heirs in a more strongly patriarchal society. Like Chesnut, Virginia Clay, who was also childless, lived with her in-laws for a decade after her marriage (Wiley, *Confederate Women*, p. 42). Priscilla Tyler lived nearby her husband's parents in Williamsburg in the early years of her marriage and then moved in with them at the White House. Although she bore several children during these years, her residence with her husband's parents nonetheless conformed to southern expectations of filial duty. In the North, couples who lived with parents tended to stay with the wife's parents and resided in those households whether or not they produced their own children. This pattern depended more on affection between fathers and daughters than on custom and reinforced a strategy for capital formation that built wealth along lines of feeling from fathers through daughters to sons-in-law, as I subsequently explain.

[100] Westbrook, *John Burroughs* (1974), p. 8; Morseberger and Morseberger, *Wallace*, p. 412. On the trend toward creating more private space in household design, see Handlin, *The American Home: Architecture and Society, 1815–1915* (1979), pp. 353–5.

house for his children next door to the family's main residence in Bristol, Pennsylvania, in 1820. As a young bachelor, George Templeton Strong spent five years in the 1840s in an apartment set up in a building designed as a bathhouse behind his parents' home in New York, which he deemed "my peaceful retreat."[101]

Taken together, earlier and later examples of residential separation indicate a persistent desire for privacy, increasingly, however, a function of the individuality of men who left the family circle to spend time alone. If, as indicated by housing design, parents constituted the center of the childhood families of Tyler and Strong, mothers and children were the basic family unit by the century's end, a pattern consistent with domestic ideals. Yet this analysis of household privacy also underlines how much the marginality of fathers was voluntary and a matter of privilege, on the one hand, and how limited it was, on the other. These Victorian fathers did not so much lose touch with their families as gain the right to determine how they would interact. If men did withdraw defensively from homes that felt less securely their own, they adeptly turned their liability into a new lever of power. In addition, family life was hardly less prized by husbands than wives. Men such as Wallace and Burroughs satisfied their need for privacy in close proximity to home.

In the end, challenges to families by individual ambitions, sociable inclinations, and secluded self-expression disrupted circles of kin surprisingly little. So attached were the Victorians to family that each countervailing impulse contained ambivalent notes: families followed their mobile members, couples with children forswore public residence, and men asserted their taste for privacy within steps of home. Yet trials brought on by the Victorians' restlessness did teach families to be flexible in their habits and self-understanding. Families worked hard to achieve an ideal of stable coresidence of parents and children as the condition for the construction of emotional bonds. When necessary, however, they adjusted to absences, movement, and their members' scattered interests. In a culture marked deeply by uncertainty and the strivings it engendered, accommodation served families well. The kinds of families the Victorians created, by volition and circumstance, differed discernibly from those of previous generations.

VICTORIAN FAMILIES IN TIME

Favored by prosperity, yet beset by questions of life's meaning, the mid-nineteenth-century middle classes cultivated family sentiment as a rich hu-

---

[101] Oct. 20, 1843, *Diary of Strong,* ed. Nevins and Thomas, 1:215. Strong lived in the apartment until Oct., 1848. On the Tyler family, see Coleman, *Tyler,* p. 12.

man resource. At the same time that the family's subjective uses grew more important, contributions that families made to communities in the past grew less visible. In the Victorian generation, four traditional attributes of families that made them serviceable to society were transformed: family pride, economic production, religious observance, and public participation. The attenuated community role of Victorian families was by no means caused altogether by their emotional demands. More correctly, social changes often in progress facilitated, and in turn were reinforced by, spiritual needs.[102]

Historically, a concern for family honor constrained individuals to anticipate how public opinion would judge kin in light of personal actions. The Victorians may have felt an allegiance to family name, but their pursuit of individual satisfaction obscured such pride in practice. Sons who overturned their fathers' wishes in their career choices and couples who married for love took for granted that personal happiness mattered more than family reputation. Yet next to these assertions of selfhood, a new kind of family loyalty emerged, marked by an insistence on coresidence as a correlate of emotional bonds. As traditional allegiance to a comparatively abstract conception of family lost force, yearning for physical proximity took its place.

The decline in the practice of putting children out to board illustrates the rising preference for day-to-day family involvement. During the Victorians' childhoods, young people were shuttled among neighbors and kin. Alexander Agassiz, living in Germany, went to board with an uncle after the death of his mother in 1848, while his sisters stayed with their aunt. His father did not send passage for the boy to join him in Boston until 1849. The girls came in 1850, after their father remarried. The father of Washington Roebling, another German émigré, left his children so often after his move to America that they were effectively brought up by grandparents.[103] European-born fathers were especially tolerant of distance from

---

[102] The Victorians did not transform traditional families into more modern ones in a single generation. Still, it is useful to set up rather abstract traditional traits against which to measure Victorian mores, with the understanding that the Victorians represented one step in gradual change. Selected works on key family characteristics may serve as background. On family honor, see Wyatt-Brown, *Southern Honor*, pt. 1. On family production in the context of nineteenth-century changes, see Cott, *Bonds of Womanhood*, ch. 1; Johnson, *Shopkeeper's Millennium*, chs. 1–2; Ryan, *Cradle of the Middle Class*, chs. 1, 4; Faragher, *Sugar Creek: Life on the Illinois Prairie* (1986), chs. 11, 19; Hahn, *The Roots of Southern Populism: Yeoman Farmers and the Transformation of the Georgia Upcountry, 1850–1890* (1983), chs. 1, 4; Hahn and Prude, eds., *The Countryside in the Age of Capitalist Transformation: Essays in the Social History of Rural America* (1985); and Clark, *The Roots of Rural Capitalism: Western Massachusetts, 1780–1860* (1990), esp. pts. 4–5. On family religion and the effect of the Second Great Awakening, see Edmund S. Morgan, *The Puritan Family: Religion and Domestic Relations in Seventeenth-Century New England*, rev. ed. (New York: Harper and Row, 1966), esp. ch. 1; Mathews, *Religion in the Old South* (1977), esp. chs. 1, 3; Johnson, *Shopkeeper's Millennium*, p. 108 and ch. 5; and Ryan, *Cradle of the Middle Class*, esp. pp. 83–104. On the trend from corporate to individualistic participation in communities, see Morgan, *Puritan Family*, ch. 1; Ryan, *Cradle of the Middle Class*, pp. 41–3; and Lynd and Lynd, *Middletown*, esp. pp. 118–22, 132–7.

[103] *Agassiz*, ed. Agassiz, pp. 9–16; Steinman, *The Builders of the Bridge: The Story of John Roebling and His Son* (1945), p. 109.

their children, but native-born parents also sent sons in particular away when families were confronted with hardship. In New Hampshire in the early 1840s, Thaddeus Lowe was bound out to a farmer at age ten because his parents were too poor to support him. In Indiana, Lew Wallace was sent at age seven to board with a neighbor after the death of his mother in 1834. Although Wallace and his brother came home briefly when their father remarried in 1837, they were sent again to a succession of boarding schools and relatives' homes during the next several years. Poverty was not a factor, because Wallace's father served as governor of Indiana during that time. In Ohio, William Tecumseh Sherman was raised by a friend of the family after his father's death in 1829. Because William was one of nine children still living at home, his mother, Mary, had no choice but to break up her family. [104]

No child of the Victorians was similarly removed from the nuclear family. The new practice was a product of the Victorians' wealth to an important extent. Prospering families now had sufficient control of their material circumstances to avert dispersion in hard times. But because economic adversity was only one of their parents' reasons for letting their children go, there must also have been a strengthened desire among the Victorians to keep families together. One correlate was the increased social distance of self-sufficient families from the larger community. Whether this separation was the cause or consequence of the identification of family with home life is difficult to say, but close ties with neighbors atrophied by disuse. Communities bound by debts of service became looser circles of acquaintance. How others viewed a family might aid self-esteem or wound feelings, but public opinion affected their practical ability to get on less seriously than before. An attitude that made families more cohesive in a physical sense reduced their relations with surrounding families from substantive helpfulness to symbolic gestures.

In economic terms, Victorian families functioned less as centers of production than as agencies of capital formation. Both roles presupposed that families advanced society's well-being at the same time that they sought their own interest. As family members were less often simple co-workers, however, economic relationships among kin were arranged to serve emotional demands as well as to further prosperity.

Changes in women's work may introduce the new prominence of sentiment in economic strategies. Although Victorian women nearly always contained their desires for accomplishment within acceptable bounds set by the pre-

---

[104] Block, *Above the Civil War: The Story of Thaddeus Lowe, Balloonist, Inventor, Railway Builder* (1966), p. 13; Morseberger and Morseberger, *Wallace*, p. 8–15; Merrill, *Sherman*, pp. 18–19. Putting children out of the family was a practice with colonial roots. There were many reasons for such decisions, including easing family finances, coping with family stress such as a parent's death, learning a trade, and ensuring their strict discipline at the hands of strangers. See, e.g., Morgan, *Puritan Family*, pp. 75–9.

dominance of their husbands' careers, many tested the possibilities for personal gratification within self-imposed limits. Southern women worked most often as women had in the past, either performing domestic labor or assisting their husbands in business. Harriet Vance in North Carolina informed her husband, away in Washington in 1859, that the hogs had been killed and salted. Lizzie Browne took strawberries and poultry to market in postbellum Georgia. When her husband became editor of *Southern Farm and Home* in 1869, she handled the column on "Domestic Receipts."[105] In northern and western homes, women's relations to work were more complex. A conviction that women ought not be consumed by domestic tasks, even under duress, distanced middle-class families from tradition. Although conditions were sufficiently primitive in Minnesota in 1850 for salt pork and cod to be staple foods, Ann North gave piano lessons and spent some time reading. Among women in California and Oregon, evidence of visiting, writing, and participating in community groups outweighs records of labor.[106] The implicit right of wives to some choice of pursuits could be stretched to advance their self-fulfillment. Women sometimes stepped in to aid husbands with too much alacrity and tenacity to cloak their ambitions under conventions' guise. Emily Roebling battled critics to retain her effective role as chief engineer of the Brooklyn Bridge, a post inherited from her husband, Washington, in the decade between his paralysis by caisson disease in 1872 and the project's completion.[107] As this series of examples shows, growing numbers of Victorian wives assumed that their work could be tailored to satisfy their inclinations.

Women's aspirations were less commonly expressed through labor, however, than were men's desires to bestow love and assert control through the dispersion of capital. Decisions concerning the use of family wealth in all historical settings provoke, and are affected by, strong mutual feelings. But in the Victorian generation, building sentiment through the manipulation of money was a goal along with making profits. Most dramatically, fathers-in-law in the North assisted their daughters' husbands financially, as much

[105] Harriet Vance to Zebulon Vance, Dec. 1, 1859, Vance Papers; Coulter, *Browne*, pp. 130–1, 199. On southern white women's labor, see Clinton, *Plantation Mistress*, ch. 2, and Fox-Genovese, *Plantation Household*, chs. 1–2.

[106] On Ann North, see Stonehouse, *North*, pp. 34–5. Certainly women on the western frontier worked hard, as did the wife of George Atkinson. But they often engaged in leisure activities that gave their identities a dimension beyond household work and revealed their command of some prerogatives in how to dispose of their time. In the Los Angeles area, William Moore bought his wife a piano in 1884 (May 24, Diary, 1884, Moore Papers). Jeanne Carr wrote extensively and gave time to local organizations, first in northern and later in southern California. Consider, e.g., her "Christmas," ms. speech to a Grange organization, [Oakland, Calif., ca. 1875], and "Address Relative to the Horticulture of California, Given at the Third Annual Exhibition of the Bay District Horticultural Society," [Sept. 30, 1873], Jeanne Carr Papers.

[107] Barnes, *Lady of Fashion*, p. 62; Steinman, *Builders of the Bridge*, ch. 19. On the assistance women traditionally lent their husbands, in business as well as domestic pursuits, see Ulrich, *Good Wives: Image and Reality in the Lives of Women in Northern New England, 1650–1750* (1982), ch. 2.

to secure their hold as patriarchs as to extend their fortunes. A gift to a son-in-law presumed the father's right to a voice in his daughter's affairs. Fathers-in-law bought western lands for John Wesley North and John Wentworth. Abram Hewitt married into the iron business of Peter Cooper's and Cooper's son when he wed Cooper's daughter. In all these cases, the fathers remained a presence in their daughters' lives. Ann North's father repeatedly sheltered his daughter when her husband's plans foundered. Roxanna Wentworth's father apparently viewed his son-in-law as an adequate channel for western investment but did not trust him enough to let his daughter live permanently with her husband or even to name Wentworth the executor of his estate. Most aggressively, Peter Cooper refused to let Abram Hewitt move the family business west in the 1860s on the grounds that he wanted to stay in New York and to have his daughter close by.[108]

This combination of beneficence and restriction was made possible by the converging inclinations of all those involved. Sons-in-law, drawn by the romance of an affluent wife, moved upward socially with her father's aid, even though paying the price of sharing a wife's affection with an exacting parent. Daughters were able to marry without relinquishing a doting father's regard, as each drew her husband through a combination of wealth and feeling toward her family's sphere. Fathers used their money to avert the erosion of power threatened by a daughter's marriage. Instead, they extended their influence by gathering sons-in-law and grandchildren into a family where material gain sweetened control. All of these feelings conformed to the aggressive paternalism of a society sensitive to encroaching limitations on men's prerogatives, yet willing and able to contest intimations of weakness. In the South, wealth passed with less visible emotional manipulation from fathers to sons. Bonds with daughters, accented by modernity's uncertainties, were sufficiently less pronounced to preclude the disruption of traditional claims of male heirs.[109] Southern families resembled northern ones

---

[108] Stonehouse, *North*, pp. 42, 199; Fehrenbacher, *Chicago Giant*, pp. 114, 208; Nevins, *Hewitt*, pp. 82–94, 147–8, 256–7.

[109] The importance of northern families as capital-forming entities has been studied in the case of antebellum Rochester by Paul Johnson, in *Shopkeeper's Millennium*, pp. 22–8. Johnson found that among the original proprietors of 1815, brothers-in-law often pooled resources. By 1837, the wealthiest men in Rochester were their sons and sons-in-law. The Victorians studied here and their parents were roughly contemporaries of these two generations. In the South, the emphasis on inheritance through male heirs in established areas such as South Carolina is reflected in the publication of the papers of successive generations, such as Cauthen, ed., *Family Letters of Wade Hamptons,* and Childs, ed., *Planters and Business Men: The Guignard Family of South Carolina. 1795–1930* (1957). Yet even on the southern frontier, there is no evidence that fathers passed wealth through daughters. During the midcentury decades, the importance of family capital was being superseded by new forms of capitalization, such as the sale of stocks and bonds. See, e.g., Livesay, *Andrew Carnegie and the Rise of Big Business* (1975), pp. 30–1. Although the Victorians' material ambitions made them receptive to such changes, sentimental bonds could work against economic progress. Thus Peter Cooper's refusal to let Abram Hewitt introduce innovations into the family's iron business contributed to the firm's obsolescence in the context of the steel industry's growth. See Nevins, *Hewitt*, pp. 256–66.

in their determination that homes serve the nurture of feeling, but it was mainly in the Victorian North that new attachments became strong enough to reorient economic decision making and to accent the subjective components of family economy.

Much as Victorian families were diverted from straightforward contributions to society's production by assertions of sentiment, private religious habits supported public observance less reliably than in the past. In traditional Protestantism, family worship mirrored public ritual in a way that acknowledged that families were key components of social order. Church and state, in turn, worked through families to enforce individual morality.[110] The Victorian did not engage in this interplay between private and public religion. Family prayers, for example, fell into disuse. Whereas family worship was common during the Victorians' childhoods, the regularity with which Jay Cooke brought family, servants, and guests together each morning for private services in the midcentury decades stands out in these records as unusual.[111] No doubt the Victorians' protracted crisis of faith blunted their enthusiasm for domestic religion. In addition, the Victorians dealt with religion primarily as individuals because the complexity of their questions favored private solutions. Precisely because George Templeton Strong gave serious thought to religious matters, his family's practice paled in comparative significance. Perhaps his wife attended church, his children Sunday school, and they all met for family prayer. But if so, their routines must have seemed so banal next to current issues and institutional politics that he did not mention their habits in his journal.[112]

Yet at the same time families less easily served a religious community as corporate units, they became more adept at adapting rituals for private use. Not surprisingly, people less sure of heaven and less integrated by daily observance into a cohesive religious culture leaned more on the sporadic intercession of men with special authority to baptize, marry, and bury. Families went out of their way to engage clergy to perform rituals. Neither Mathew Brady, John DeForest, John Wentworth, nor William Tecumseh Sherman was an adherent of the faith in which he was married, but all acceded to the wish of practicing wives that clergy preside at the weddings.[113] Because the women's involvement in churches was more sustained, these

---

[110] See, e.g., Morgan, *Puritan Family*, esp. ch. 1. On similarly permeable boundaries between the home and religious institutions in the colonial South, see Isaac, *Transformation of Virginia*, pp. 58–70.

[111] Larson, *Cooke*, p. 193.

[112] For a sense of the specific aspects of religion that interested Strong, see *Diary of Strong*, ed. Nevins and Thomas, vols. 2–4.

[113] Horan, *Brady*, p. 13; Light, *DeForest*, p. 42, Fehrenbacher, *Chicago Giant*, p. 55; Merrill, *Sherman*, pp. 80–1. Colleen McDannell makes the slightly different, though I think compatible, argument that Victorian values emphasized the importance of family worship as established modes of religious transmission, such as revivals, lost their efficacy, in *The Christian Home in Victorian America, 1840–1900* (1986). She does not evaluate the extent to which behavior conformed to prescriptions.

cases indicate that family members tended to participate as individuals in religious activities except at times of family transition. Thus family habit gave way to occasional rituals and loyal support of communal beliefs became private use of public symbols. With no assurance of intellectual accord on religion's doctrines, the Victorians, by changing the terms of discussion, kept in touch with Christianity's spiritual aura.

The fact that American families in the past acted together to support public religion was one sign of their corporate importance more generally. In a traditional patriarchy, where family heads represented dependents, the community consisted of families engaged in stable relations. Now geographic mobility, accented by the Victorians' restlessness, upset the predictability of interaction over time. On a day-to-day basis, moreover, both family integrity and social patriarchy were challenged by the independent participation of individuals in community life. Fathers joined clubs, mothers attended churches, and young people went courting with significant autonomy. Husbands made friends, wives worked for charity, and children went out to school. This license to encounter communities on one's own was a correlate of the right of individuals to make an emotional mark on, and draw support from, their families. For although the prerogative of fathers both to indulge feeling and cultivate opportunities outweighed the privileges of children and wives, the Victorians' strenuous sentimentality and eager sociability represented a more egalitarian family system than prevailed in the past. How ironic, then, that precisely the same appreciation of discrete personalities that gave families an inner fire chipped away at their social cohesion.[114]

In the Civil War era, American families of the affluent middle classes assumed postures of vibrant emotional expectancy, as their members asked one another for unprecedented returns of feeling. But precisely because internal and external family relations were so unsettled, Victorian domesticity contained the potential for both interpersonal enrichment and tension. As a time of national crisis, the Civil War brought these possibilities more clearly to light.

THE DOMESTICATION OF WAR AND THE
SENTIMENTALIZATION OF CULTURE

The Civil War inspired a generation caught between sagging faith and encroaching routinization with the chance of a heroic adventure, and the Victorians embraced combat to escape such civilian dilemmas as troubled careers. But the same extraordinary demands threatened to upset the subtle

---

[114] One of the most graphic assessments of the twentieth-century consequences of this trend toward individual participation in communities is the classic study of Lynd and Lynd, *Middletown*, esp. pp. 118–22, 132–7.

family dynamics that crucially centered the Victorians' personalities. Rather than leave their kin behind, officers in both armies who had the means to bring their families to camp did so with an initiative born of pressing emotional need. So, too, they wove reminders of domesticity into military life to simulate family sentiment. The Victorians acted out these dramas of feeling with an instinctive force, but a more reflective observer might have drawn two lessons from their actions. First, the Civil War cast the Victorians' reliance on family, as well as the varied texture of the different relationships within homes, in bold relief. Second, the war spurred the men and women of this generation to create new symbols that expressed their devotion to family. Removed from the daily complexity of family struggles, these images connecting idealized kinship bonds with Civil War themes allowed the Victorians to rededicate themselves to domesticity in a society where actual families felt the weight of numerous pressures.

As a social experience, the war could not help but strain domestic integrity and impose hardships on families that consisted of worry, grief, and, particularly in the South, material need. But within the more rarefied sphere of culture, the Victorians responded to the war's impositions with a determination to involve their families emotionally in the conflict. For army officers, this resolve usually meant arranging for kin to stay in hotels near military camps. Wives came most frequently to be near their husbands. Julia Grant, Ellen Sherman, and Eva Ingersoll, the wives of two leading Union generals and a colonel, boarded near their husbands as much as possible throughout the war. Other couples tried to work out visits, although sometimes with less success. James Garfield, who became a general, urged Lucretia on separate occasions to accompany him to Florida and to meet him in Nashville. Harriet DeForest, at home with her son in New Haven, wished to travel to Louisiana to be with her husband, John, a Union captain.[115] Extended family sought to join soldiers as well. In the Confederate army, Wade Hampton found a boardinghouse for his sister near him in Virginia just before a head wound instead sent him home. Among the families of Union troops, Ellen Sherman brought her children several times to be with their father, until, after a summer spent near Vicksburg in 1863, their oldest son, Willy, died of typhoid fever contracted in camp. Ulysses Grant had his son, Fred, stay with him for companionship during a campaign near Cairo, Illinois, in late 1861. Grant's father, Jesse, came to see his son at the same time.[116]

[115] Light, *DeForest*, p. 66. On the foregoing couples, see McFeely, *Grant*, pp. 80–1; Merrill, *Sherman*, p. 232; Cramer, *Royal Bob*, p. 59; and James Garfield to Lucretia Garfield, Oct. 19, 1862, July 23, 1863, in *The Wild Life of the Army: Civil War Letters of James A. Garfield*, ed. Williams (1964), pp. 165, 288.

[116] Ulysses Grant to Julia Grant, Oct. 6, 1861, in *The Papers of Ulysses S. Grant*, ed. Simon (1970), 3:23. On Fred's visit to Grant, see Ulysses Grant to Julia Grant, Sept. 29, 1861, in *Papers of Grant*, ed. Simon (1969), 2:327–8. On the Hampton and Sherman families, see Wade Hampton to Mary Fisher

Family groups worked with similar cohesion outside the military. When William Potter was drafted as a Union chaplain in late 1863, his new wife, Elizabeth, followed him to the camp outside Washington where he was assigned. There Elizabeth both aided her husband's efforts, accompanying William on hospital visits, and developed charitable activities of her own, including teaching her free black servant girl to read. "It is real fun to teach her," Potter wrote to her mother, "her eyes fairly dance with joy."[117] During Reconstruction, husbands and wives similarly engaged together in war-related benevolence. On the Georgia plantation that Henry Lee Higginson bought in 1865, Higginson's wife, Ida, shared her husband's conviction that our "one great reason for coming here was the work of great importance to be done for these blacks."[118] She taught black women to keep house and to read and write, until the plantation was sold at a loss in 1867. Both Elizabeth Potter and Ida Higginson were childless young women, married within months of each other in late 1863, and so it was relatively easy for them to work along with their husbands in challenging circumstances. Yet even if their stories were unusual from the perspective of their age and family situation, their experience underscores the Victorians' desire to keep families together in civilian as well as military enterprises.

Why were the Victorians so insistent that women and children follow men to scenes of struggle? The Civil War was the only American war fought on native soil at a time when good transportation was available, and these circumstances permitted the proximity of families to men actively involved in the conflict. But kin might as easily have stayed home, and thus the Victorians' choice to use their wealth to take advantage of possible mobility must have been rooted in their cultural attitudes. Most basically, the intimate participation of families in the war reveals how essential these relationships were to this generation's sense of well-being. Beyond this point of consensus, each family member found distinctive rewards in the war experience.

So important was family to Victorian husbands that they violated their own notions of propriety concerning the sexes' separate spheres in order to keep their loved ones close by. "You know in general I am opposed to having women go into the army," James Garfield wrote to his wife, probably voicing a prevalent view, "but I should be very glad to have you [in Florida] with me."[119] The benefit of Lucretia's presence to James was not simply to provide solace in a time of stress. Even more, the crisis made both James and Lucretia reflect on their family's value, thereby deepening their mutual

Hampton, May 19, 1863, in Cauthen, ed., *Family Letters of Wade Hamptons*, p. 93; and *Home Letters of General Sherman*, ed. Howe (1909), p. 274.

[117] Potter to Lydia Babcock, Mar. 16, 1864, Potter Papers.

[118] Perry, *Higginson*, p. 261. Ida Higginson did find the work in Georgia taxing, however, and spent some time at home in Boston during the two years of her husband's Georgia enterprise. See ibid., ch. 8.

[119] Garfield to Lucretia Garfield, Oct. 19, 1862, in *Wild Life of the Army*, ed. Williams, p. 165.

commitment. So many deaths occurring during family separations caused by the war made James comment pensively in a letter to a cousin, "Should Crete and [their daughter] Trot die while I am in the army, I should hope never to return."[120] Similarly, the poignant circumstance of meeting in an army camp in 1861 induced the Garfields to kneel together on "that last sacred and solemn night," as James wrote to Lucretia soon after her departure.[121] For husbands and wives, the effects of marriage and war were reciprocal. Not only did the emotional support provided by marital love sustain soldiers, but the crisis drew attention to the importance of families now seriously jeopardized by public events.

Certainly wives gained emotionally, too, from this reexamination of married affection. But the practice of following husbands to war also offered women greater liberty, though in the end on cautious terms. A survey of the records of Victorian couples indicates that the initiative for a wife's visit came at least some of the time from bold women as well as from lonesome men.[122] But precisely as Victorian women in their roles as daughters and mothers reached through their ties with fathers and sons to gain vicarious social access, wives who traveled and worked with husbands during the war relied mainly on men in order to touch broader horizons. They were able to leave home, see unusual sights, and perhaps test new identities without having to act autonomously, a step even beyond the capability of most of the advantaged middle-class women studied here. At times, the bounds of acceptable behavior to which husbands and wives agreed were blurred in the new situations the war posed. When Ellen Sherman did more than provide her husband emotional support and instead followed him in public activism by agreeing to sell war memorabilia at a Sanitary Commission fair in Chicago in 1865, William wrote from North Carolina that her behavior was "unbecoming."[123] "Still do as you please," he told Ellen, a sign of the small triumphs of self-determination that a wife of guarded ambition might win in the unsettled conditions of war. Because the Shermans once again took up discussion of the fair the following month, it is clear that Ellen had stood her ground.[124] Domestic exchanges where a wife in effect bargained for prerogatives are not insignificant. Despite the miniaturist scale of such negotiations, the disposition of family power strongly affected the Victorians' identities. But in the larger social view, wives' adventures in the Civil War were still contained within those of male kin. Their modest strikes for freedom honored home life even while exposing its limits, as they expressed

---

[120] Garfield to Phebe Clapp, Feb. 28, 1863, in ibid., p. 241.
[121] Garfield to Lucretia Garfield, Oct. 27, 1861, in ibid., p. 43.
[122] Harriet DeForest, e.g., initiated plans to join her husband, John. See Light, *DeForest*, p. 66.
[123] Sherman to Ellen Sherman, March 23, 1865, in *Home Letters of Sherman*, ed. Howe, p. 335.
[124] William Tecumseh Sherman to Ellen Sherman, Apr. 18, 1865, in ibid., p. 346.

their yen for excitement and achievement primarily in family terms and found stirring scenes in paths set out by men.[125]

Despite the visible presence of women in military camps, the Victorians' strong belief in gender differences still made them think of war-making as the work of men. These Victorians left no record that fathers and daughters, so affectionately bonded in civilian life, interacted similarly in wartime settings. Instead, the Victorians used the war to probe relationships between fathers and sons. Victorian fathers seemed to see the army as a privileged sphere where sons might learn the lessons of manhood. As soon as Ulysses Grant enlisted in the spring of 1861, he took his eleven-year-old son, Fred, to Camp Yates in Illinois for several weeks. Later that year, Grant asked Julia to send Fred back for the remainder of his campaign in Cairo, Illinois, noting that the other officers already had their sons with them.[126] Removed from the usual range of options that tempted Victorian sons to make choices independent of their fathers, relations between fathers and their boys in camp promised to be less tense and more intimate than bonds outside the military. Part of the pleasure of combat for Victorian fathers, moreover, was the chance to experience struggle along with their sons, as if half the value of war lay in this special form of male companionship. "Oh, that Willy could hear and see," William Tecumseh Sherman wrote plaintively to Ellen on his march north from Georgia in 1865. "His proud heart would swell to overflowing," Sherman concluded, his own victory diminished by the solitude of his triumph.[127] Thus in the Civil War armies, Victorian fathers saw opportunities both to express love for their sons and to exert a gentle control, a combination of circumstances sadly rare, in their view, in mid-nineteenth-century society.

At least some of the surprising power of war to enhance family relations came from the selective quality of personal encounters. Family members did not have to get along day after day, only during brief periods often devoted to visiting. Still, the Victorians were not unaware that the disruptions and even opportunities caused by war could bring out the worst in relationships as well as the best. At the same time that Ulysses Grant sought idyllic moments with Fred, he contended strenuously with his overbearing father, Jesse, a man eager not only to exploit his son's growing power but to enter vicariously into Ulysses' success. Early in the war, Jesse asked Ulysses repeatedly for favors, including military appointments, contracts, and safe

[125] Daniel Scott Smith pointed out the importance of changes in the self-determination of women that occurred within households and families in his seminal article, "Family Limitation, Sexual Control, and Domestic Feminism in Victorian America," cited in n. 1

[126] Ulysses Grant to Julia Grant, June 26 and Sept. 29, 1861, in *Papers of Grant*, ed. Simon, 2:50, 327–8. Fred stayed with his father on and off during the war. See McFeely, *Grant*, pp. 45, 81, 153–4, 195.

[127] Sherman to Ellen Sherman, Apr. 5, 1865, in *Home Letters of Sherman*, ed. Howe, p. 342.

passes to Confederate territory for his friends. Writing frequently to Jesse and at least tolerating his father's appearances in camp, Ulysses seemed involved in a strong, if tense, relationship with his parent.[128] By late 1862, the contending wills of a father and son produced explosive results. "I have not an enemy in the world who has done me so much injury as you in your efforts in my defence," Ulysses wrote to Jesse from Corinth, Mississippi: "I require no defenders and for my sake let me alone."[129] The incident did not lead to enduring alienation between them, but it did contain two lessons. First, Ulysses' relations with Jesse were to an unnerving extent the mirror image of his own with Fred. Both fathers approached their sons with high expectations for involvement in the sons' lives, a fervency that could turn easily to hurt and anger if intimacy were refused by either one. Second, the Civil War tested bonds between fathers and sons, less because the conflict threatened to sever ties than because it intensified the problems as well as pleasures of established habits of interaction.

Overall, Victorian family patterns persisted during the war, both by design and by the strength of long-standing expectations and practices. The emotional initiative of men, the circuitous aspirations of women, and the dilemma of autonomy for children were key characteristics of Victorian families, and the war highlighted their importance. The Victorians' conservative instincts are not surprising. As people who took pleasure in these intricate bonds of feeling, they had little reason to use the unsettlement of war to reform their domestic arrangements and, instead, a strong motive to draw support from families as they were. Certainly not all families were literally mobilized to scenes of battle by influential men. When husbands stayed home, domesticity, particularly in the North, continued in the usual way. When husbands either left or were engaged in the taxing demands of war-related business, the responsibilities of wives, often at an age when they were already managing small children, increased. In one case indicative of how stressful the experience of Victorian women could be, Harriet Vance in North Carolina had all of her household furnishings confiscated by Union troops during her husband's two-month imprisonment in 1865 for his role as the state's Confederate governor. A mother of four young boys, Harriet had already endured four years as the wife of a busy and often embattled politician, and the added strain of defeat made her seriously ill.[130] Even so, neither the Vances nor other Victorian couples left a record of permanent shifts of power in marriages caused by such extraordinary demands. Husbands and wives must have viewed wartime trials as temporary. When husbands

---

[128] Ulysses Grant to Mary Grant, Oct. 25, 1861, Ulysses Grant to Jesse Grant, Nov. 27 and 29, 1861, in *Papers of Grant*, ed. Simon, 3:76, 227, 238–9.

[129] Grant to Jesse Grant, in *Papers of Grant* (1977), ed. Simon, 6:62.

[130] Tucker, *Vance*, pp. 428, 430–1.

came home or, if they did not return, when new husbands were found, marital relations returned to prewar norms.

The Victorians' reliance on family affections not only influenced their personal choices during the war but affected the symbols they created, both the gestures of informal behavior and speech and more formal literature. In the Union and Confederate armies, living arrangements reminiscent of families were adopted during the war. Soldiers lived in family-sized units in winter quarters. Southerners also cooked in small groups, while northerners in more permanent camps evolved a system of division of labor by having cooking details prepare food for large messes.[131] These arrangements probably grew from the combined effect of available supplies and technology, the inclinations of ordinary soldiers to replicate homelike conditions, and officers' recognition of the value of perpetuating domestic habits as an aid to military order, except when overruled by a push for efficiency in some northern camps. Enlisted men, generally less privileged than the Victorians of this study and without the resources to board their families near encampments, not surprisingly shared their officers' fond yearning for kin and thus built reminders of home life into army routines. Their practice of giving officers familial nicknames arose, too, from an impulse to domesticate military service. The troops of William Tecumseh Sherman called him "Uncle Billy," and southerners borrowed the image of loyal slaves implicit in the paternalistic notion of the "family black and white" when they gave Robert E. Lee the nickname "Marse Robert." Troops under George Pickett called his son the "Little General," thereby acknowledging the importance of their leader's fatherhood in winning their affection and respect.[132]

Yet for all the homage to family that the combined images of living habits and language conveyed, soldiers inadvertently altered domesticity, in a way for the better. Family routines engrafted on soldiering lost much of their emotional complexity, because camps filled mainly with men enjoyed a camaraderie associated with home without the tangled feelings experienced by actual kin. Soldiers had the luxury of indulging a domestic sensibility in a peaceful way, although on a deeper level they must have missed the gratification that came at the price of real family struggles.

When works of literature similarly wove allusions to families through their portrayals of war, they revealed the Victorians' dependency on family not only as a symbol conducive to emotional rest, but as a source of meaning, providing terms to establish intellectual order. *Miss Ravenel's Conversion from*

[131] See Wiley, *The Life of Billy Yank: The Common Soldier of the Union* (1951) and *The Life of Johnny Reb: The Common Soldier of the Confederacy* (1943), reprinted in *The Common Soldier in the Civil War* (n.d.), 1:55–8, 244; 2:60–3.

[132] George Pickett to LaSalle Pickett, July 17, 18, 1864, in *Soldier of the South*, ed. Inman, pp. 109–11. Lee's nickname is noted in Pickett's letter of July 18. On Sherman, see Merrill, *Sherman*, p. 297.

Secession to Loyalty, for example, written by John William DeForest at the end of the war and published in 1867, examined the political crisis through the lens of marriage. Lillie Ravenel, the daughter of a southern-born doctor, first makes a bad match in the novel with the dashing but deceiving and unfaithful Colonel Carter, a Virginian serving in the Union army. After his death in battle, she marries Captain Colburne, an unglamorous but morally solid Yankee, clearly, in DeForest's view, a more enlightened choice on Lillie's part. The way the family imagery works in this fable about the Union's redemption is clear: through a painful though purgative struggle like that following Lillie's discovery of Carter's infidelity, an immoral "marriage" of the sections will be replaced by a righteous and beneficent one. [133]

By thus using domestic metaphors to describe political relations, DeForest was writing in an established intellectual tradition. Antebellum political discourse commonly cast the North and South as warring brothers descended from virtuous "founding fathers." Women's fiction, ranging from Sarah Hale's *Northwood* in 1827 to Harriet Beecher Stowe's *Uncle Tom's Cabin* in 1852, searched for means of sectional reconciliation through stories that reduced social differences to the manageable scale of family relationships. [134] But for DeForest to liken the republic to a family involved more intellectual risk and wishful thinking than writers in previous decades had incurred. Ever more impersonal and formally structured, mid-nineteenth-century public life was hardly familial, nor were real Victorian families credible models for the smooth resolution of conflict. DeForest's determination to use the family as a literary device probably came from the availability of romance as a literary convention, his characteristically Victorian enthusiasm for kinship, and a half-conscious inclination to craft a reassuring message about the prospect of achieving peace within taxing marriages as well as in the nation more broadly. The theme of marriage anchors *Miss Ravenel's Conversion* because its Victorian author was seriously concerned with families. Nonetheless, the book contains elements of imbalance, particularly the questionable equation of republic and family and Lillie's all-too-real marital struggle, that mark this wartime fiction as part of a complex social context.

DeForest's final picture of domestic accord was an early indication of the idealized family images that proliferated in connection with Civil War commemoration. Victorian army officers had recruited their families as visitors during the war to provide emotional reassurance. Conversely, men and women after the war asked the sanctified memory of the crisis to help preserve

<hr>

[133] *Miss Ravenel's Conversion from Secession to Loyalty* (1867), ed. Haight (1955).

[134] Hale, *Northwood: A Tale of New England* (Boston: Bowles and Dearborn, 1827); Stowe, *Uncle Tom's Cabin; or Life Among the Lowly* (Garden City. N.Y.: Doubleday, 1960). For a discussion of the sectional theme of *Northwood* and other fiction by Sarah Hale, see Taylor, *Cavalier and Yankee: The Old South and American National Character* (1957), pp. 115–41. For an excellent analysis of the imagery of fratricide, see Forgie, *Patricide in the House Divided: A Psychological Interpretation of Lincoln and His Age* (1979).

orderly relations among kin. Memorial activities contained implicit affirmations of women's respect for men and children's for parents. As numerous Ladies' Memorial Associations in towns across the South tended cemeteries and erected monuments to Confederate soldiers in the late 1860s, members effectively pledged themselves to the supportive gender role of honoring men. More elaborately, the principal veterans' organizations of the 1880s and 1890s, the Grand Army of the Republic in the North and the United Confederate Veterans in the South, inspired subsidiary associations for the wives, daughters, and sons of Civil War soldiers. Through the United Daughters of the Confederacy, the United Sons of Confederate Veterans, the Woman's Relief Corps of the Grand Army of the Republic, and many similar local groups, families at the turn of the twentieth century enacted rituals of devotion to domesticity. Built around thoughts of the heroic sacrifices of fathers and mothers during the war, the Victorians and their children paid homage to family in discrete organizations that reaffirmed the well-defined boundaries of each one's family role.[135] In sum, the Civil War set off a process of reflection about family that eventuated in demonstrations of ritualized nostalgia for an imagined paternalistic ideal conceived in terms of the war itself.

This devotion to a conception of family did not deter the far less peaceful exchange of feelings within actual families or deflect the pressures that increasingly tested their social integrity. Still, the change in mood was not simply a matter of symbols. Members of Victorian families seemed to draw closer to one another after the war because they had lived through a precarious and soul-wrenching experience. In the white South, where hardships were prolonged by Reconstruction, men turned back on their families for emotional nourishment with particular need. John Guignard of South Carolina, who lost fifty slaves, his house, and all his plantation buildings, understated his social situation in 1868 when he described his status as "reduced," because "my expectation will be fully realized if I get one bale of cotton."[136] Against his distress, Guignard's cautious joy at the birth of a son the year before gains significance as a bright event savored for the spark in himself it evoked. He wrote to his brother that "although reason tells us that these are not times for additional responsibilities nature gives us the same attachment for the Little fellow which we have for the older ones and we are proud of him."[137] More broadly, the significance of instances of emotional display among southerners already discussed – David Terry's profession of marital love, Zebulon Vance's middle-aged courtship, Wade Hampton's grief for

[135] Foster, *Ghosts of the Confederacy: Defeat, the Lost Cause, and the Emergence of the New South, 1865–1913* (1987), pp. 108, 113, 124–5.

[136] Guignard to Adams and Frost [cotton brokers], Oct. 8, 1868, in Childs, ed., *Planters and Business Men*, p. 112.

[137] John Guignard to James Guignard, Mar. 30, 1867, in ibid., p. 114.

his son – can be appreciated fully only in light of the defeat that made these men turn to the warmth of kinship with singular force.

This intensification of domestic sensibility among southern Victorian men was one factor that reduced the social distance between their families and northern ones in the postwar years. Less inwardly focused before the war, powerful southern families now lost the tangible symbols of pride in lineage that once fixed attention on their outward community standing. Southern families forcibly became more like northern ones in their embrace of affection because the conflict assaulted tradition. Northern families met them on a new middle ground, however, conditioned by sorrow and reflection. Prewar northern sentimentality was a kind of joyful feast made possible by prosperity and domestic stability. Now even among the most privileged of the victors, families who had witnessed the crisis must have eyed each other in a more thoughtful mood.

Both the enhanced strength of private feelings about kin and the invigoration of family themes in public discussion were signs of the way the Civil War reinforced a sentimental strain in Victorian culture. Had the Victorians been less curious about domestic feelings at the war's outset, family relationships would have been less important to the mood in which they fought and remembered the war. But members of this generation were intently interested in establishing bonds among kin as a means of locating themselves securely, and passionately, in a more secular world. At the same time, they sensed that they might find further solutions to their spiritual dilemma in the public world beyond families. The Victorians' enthusiasm for politics grew from this perception.

5

Politics

We are swallowed up and hurried along the rushing tides of time, and having reached a point where we can no longer steer [the Union], it now becomes us to prepare, if possible, for our safety and honor, by steering with, and not against the rushing volume. . . . I hold that issues such as these, embracing such extraordinary and fundamental changes in her national condition should be committed directly to the people, in whom all political power is vested. . . .

The people must and should rule, but we must see to it that we do our duty in warning, instructing, and advising them, as they have made us their servants for guarding their rights.

Zebulon Vance, 1860–61

To say that politics was the Victorians' chosen medium of public discourse will probably evoke little surprise. As a civic event of great consequence, the Civil War involved such issues as the respective rights of the nation and states, the implications of race for personal liberty, and the legitimate extent of government control in citizens' private affairs. It is less apparent, however, that behind these pressing political questions stood the Victorians' romanticism. Precariously balanced between the diminished authority of inherited religion and the lure of physical and social worlds at once morally indifferent and richly endowed, the Victorians' spiritual dilemma inevitably affected their public life. Religious and moral institutions so important as channels of collective self-expression to Americans in the past were now less central to the Victorians' interests. Politics offered a well-established alternative language and set of procedures to address their secular concerns. Nonetheless, as people in search of answers of the most profound kind, the Victorians did not use politics in a rational mood but in a temper of restless striving. Public participation was thoroughly informed by the Victorians' insistence that their actions have value beyond the ultimately prosaic issues of political power.

This cultural framework for Victorian political activity encouraged seemingly contrary trends toward professionalism and bureaucracy, on the one hand, and ideological fervor, on the other. Building on a civic heritage that combined an evolving partisan system with opportunities to nurture patriotic feeling, the Victorians embraced politics with a zest for its contests that gained force from their inclination to seek satisfaction more in temporal than spiritual excitement. How ironic, then, that this taste for partisanship advanced careerism among politicians and complexity in government. Widespread enthusiasm for electioneering thus set the stage for growing distance between the middle classes and a professionally run state. At the same time, the Victorians asked politics to serve, increasingly in place of religion, as a forum for ideas of sufficient depth to give them a sense of purpose. This gave public affairs an ideological cast that made their polity volatile, particularly because they enlisted their organizational expertise to resolve questions of equity.

The Civil War demonstrated the power and exposed the problems of this political culture. The conflict revealed how thoroughly the Victorians made politics a public tool capable of confronting issues of personal and collective rights central to the nation's life. Fired by ideological convictions, Victorians on both sides mobilized politics to defend their respective beliefs with practiced skill. But the war also spurred the expansion of bureaucracy without increasing its managers' abilities and underscored the utility of symbols without encouraging the intelligent exploration of principles. These were trends that in the future would limit the capacity of politics to act as a moral arena open to public discussion.

Paradoxically, the Victorians' politics finally resembled their religion, as organizational efficiency and images provocative of feeling advanced at the expense of communities of shared values. Nonetheless, politics remained the Victorians' preferred means of public discussion, not simply because government addressed the secular issues they so keenly pursued but because the political process better retained its authority in the midst of competition and compromise. Religious vitality rested ultimately on faith that proved fragile without the support of nurturing congregations. But the health of politics inhered much more in dialogue and contention than in consensus and accord. Even if flawed, political exchange provided language and rituals suitable to the commanding interests of a society eager to expand in secular spheres.[1]

---

[1] Historians acknowledge that popular interest in politics reached a peak between the 1840s and 1890s unequaled before or after, suggesting the central role of political expression in Victorian culture. Michael E. McGeer writes that the average turnout for presidential elections between 1840 and 1872 was 69 percent of eligible voters, a figure that rose to 77 percent between 1876 and 1900, as compared with about 50 percent today. See *The Decline of Popular Politics: The American North, 1865–1928* (1986), pp. 5–6. Richard L. McCormick likewise notes the enthusiasm for politics demonstrated in partisan clubs, marching companies, and parades, and proposes that increasingly strong party organization was responsible for eliciting the people's involvement, in *The Party Period and Public Policy: American Politics from the Age of Jackson to the Progressive Era* (1986), p. 163 and ch. 4. Although partisan competition

This chapter begins with an assessment of the political culture that the Victorians encountered in childhood and then examines two themes pertaining to the consequences of their actions as adults: first, the rise of political professionalism and a socially active state and, second, the reasons why individuals were determined to probe basic questions of nationhood. The role in these changes of middle-class women, who were formally disenfranchised, is specifically discussed. The chapter closes with consideration of the mutual effects of the politics of the midcentury middle classes and the Civil War. Victorian political culture clearly was not the sole cause of the Civil War. Constitutional questions, economic interests, and social institutions of long-standing importance were at least as influential in precipitating the conflict. The chapter does not directly explore such substantive points of contention between the sections as slavery and the conditions of union.[2] Rather, my purpose is to explain the Victorians' approach to public affairs as one key influence in the national crisis.

POLITICAL NURTURE

Historians recognize the Second Party system that took shape in the age of Jackson as a turning point for Americans' tolerance of and indeed interest in partisan competition. For a generation born during slightly more than two decades after 1815, this was the political environment in which they grew up. Children absorbed patriotic values and observed fathers vie for office. Young men were offered routes to participation themselves. The Victorians' coming of age in politics was not without elements of rebellion, but their reliance on civic life as a key arena of public discussion was thoroughly conditioned by their parents' culture. When their religion fell short in its message, politics presented itself as an appealing alternative.[3]

took on some distinctive features in southern society, national parties functioned similarly in the South and the North. See especially Cooper, *The South and the Politics of Slavery, 1828–1856* (1978), ch. 2, and Perman, *The Road to Redemption: Southern Politics, 1869–1879* (1984), esp. pp. 127–31. Probing reasons for the depth of political interest, Jean H. Baker suggests that politics replaced religion as the "center of many a white man's universe," in *Affairs of Party: The Political Culture of Northern Democrats in the Mid-Nineteenth Century* (1983), p. 269 and ch. 7. Drew Gilpin Faust offers a more focused but kindred argument that southern intellectuals coped with their sense of malaise by formulating proslavery arguments, in *A Sacred Circle: The Dilemma of the Intellectual in the Old South, 1840–1860* (1977), esp. chs. 3, 6.

[2] Recent syntheses of the political history of the Civil War era and of the issues that led to the conflict are Freehling, *The Road to Disunion: Secessionists at Bay, 1776–1854* (1990); McPherson, *Battle Cry of Freedom: The Civil War Era* (1988); and Foner, *Reconstruction: America's Unfinished Revolution* (1988). For an overview of historical interpretations of the Civil War, see Pressley, *Americans Interpret Their Civil War* (1954).

[3] Richard Hofstadter has called attention to the changing view of partisanship among the second generation of national leaders, such as Van Buren, in *The Idea of a Party System: The Rise of Legitimate Opposition in the United States, 1780–1840* (1969), esp. ch. 6. For a review of works on Jacksonian politics

From their earliest years, the Victorians were drawn toward political culture by images of heroes. Through both their parents' designs and the older generation's own fascination with public achievement, the Victorians were surrounded as children with models of civic virtue. Some must have pondered the significance of the famous names they were given. In Pennsylvania, John Roebling, a German immigrant, called his first son "Washington." In Georgia, William Curry chose two middle names for his boy born in 1825, "Lafayette" for the distinguished European visitor of that year and "Monroe" for the president. More provocatively, the parents of Robert Ingersoll were sufficiently inspired by the abolitionist Beriah Green to make their child's middle name "Green" in 1833.[4] No doubt the heroes of many of the Victorians growing up differed from those of their parents. But they were so thoroughly schooled in an appreciation of symbols that they still took pleasure, as adolescents and adults, in the imaginative identification with greatness involved in hero worship, and they particularly revered the accomplishments of politics. Thus Thomas Wentworth Higginson kept a bust of Daniel Webster in his room at Harvard Divinity School in the 1840s. Setting their sights more broadly, Pierre Beauregard was inspired by Napoleon, Varina Davis dressed as Madame de Staël for a prewar Washington costume ball, and the husband of Jeanne Carr, in California, modeled himself on Domingo Sarmiento, the Argentinian educator and statesman.[5]

One reason why political heroes so effectively attracted young Victorians toward civic affairs was the way these figures evoked emotion, and patriotic feelings were reinforced by habits of visiting civic shrines. The nation was old enough by the 1830s and 1840s not only to take pride in its history but to see that commemoration inspired future citizens. The construction

as of 1976, see Ronald P. Formisano, "Toward a Reorientation of Jacksonian Politics: A Review of the Literature, 1959–1975." Among more recent literature on the Second Party system, studies particularly helpful in showing Americans' attitudes toward politics include Cooper, *The South and the Politics of Slavery;* Howe, *The Political Culture of the American Whigs* (1979); Baker, *Affairs of Party;* Greenberg, *Masters and Statesmen: The Political Culture of American Slavery* (1985); and Kohl, *The Politics of Individualism: Parties and the American Character in the Jacksonian Era* (1989). On the end of the Second Party system, see Holt, *The Political Crisis of the 1850s* (1978), esp. ch. 5.

[4] Steinman, *The Builders of the Bridge: The Story of John Roebling and His Son* (1945), p. 41; Rice, J. L. M. *Curry: Southerner, Statesman, and Educator* (1949), p. 1; Cramer, *Royal Bob: The Life of Robert G. Ingersoll* (1952), p. 20. Jabez Curry apparently felt that a name so weighted with allusions was burdensome, because as a young man in the 1840s he changed "Lafayette" to "Lamar" and used his initials in adulthood to make his name "J. L. M. Curry." See Rice, *Curry*, p. 1.

[5] Edelstein, *Strange Enthusiasm: A Life of Thomas Wentworth Higginson* (1968), p. 1; Williams, *P. G. T. Beauregard: Napoleon in Grey* (1954), p. 5; Wiley, *Confederate Women* (1975), p. 93; Jeanne Smith Carr, [Biographical Notes relating to Ezra Slocum Carr], ms. ca. 1890, Jeanne Carr Papers. On deliberate attempts in the early republic to create heroes in order to reinforce republican values, see Forgie, *Patricide in the House Divided: A Psychological Interpretation of Lincoln and His Age* (1979), ch. 1. For a fascinating view of the symbolic uses of Lafayette's return to America a half-century after the Revolution, see Somkin, *Unquiet Eagle: Memory and Desire in the Idea of American Freedom, 1815–1860* (1967), ch. 4. To place hero worship in broader perspective, see Walter E. Houghton's analysis of the phenomenon among British Victorians, in *The Victorian Frame of Mind, 1830–1870* (1957), ch. 12.

of the Bunker Hill Monument was the first of many efforts to give instruction visible form. Visiting Boston at age sixteen in 1836, George Templeton Strong did not miss the still-incomplete structure, "a superb thing" in his eyes, and he enriched his sense of the past when he wandered among the graves on nearby Copp's Hill, finding "many very curious old monuments of the early settlers."[6] By far the most popular destination for sightseeing was not a historical site, however, but the U.S. Congress. People journeyed to Washington to sit in the galleries and to watch the statesmen at work. Republican duty impelled some, such as William Wetmore Story, who judged political machinations an "Augean stable," but who still made an obligatory trip to the Capitol in 1845. Others were drawn by genuine fascination. Jabez Curry missed the political excitement of his southern childhood so much when he went to Harvard Law School in the 1840s that he attended political meetings in Boston. He was eager to see Congress on his way home. Nor were women exempt from feelings of obligation or interest. Priscilla Cooper Tyler, during her years as the president's daughter-in-law, attended Congress often enough to write in her journal on legislative debate.[7]

Although many of the Victorians' early encounters with politics involved experiences provocative of feeling, enthusiasm was balanced by instruction in republican ideals. There was no political equivalent for Sunday schools, because common schools focused on basic skills rather than civics. Yet political lessons were learned. David Terry, born in Kentucky and raised in Texas, developed firm values, despite the death of both parents by the time he was two. "I was educated to believe," he told his wife in 1856, "that it is the duty of every American to support the Constitution of his country [,] to regard it as a sacred instrument – not to be violated in its least provision & if necessary to die in its defense."[8] Terry probably arrived at this conviction

---

[6] May 8, *The Diary of George Templeton Strong*, ed. Nevins and Thomas (1952), 1:19.

[7] William Story to Joseph Story, Feb. 3, quoted in James, *William Wetmore Story and His Friends* (1903), 1:80; Rice, *Curry*, pp. 13, 15; Coleman, *Priscilla Cooper Tyler and the American Scene, 1816–1889* (1955), p. 94. In 1880, Henry Adams captured the persistent appeal of the custom of visiting Congress in his novel *Democracy*, when he wrote that his heroine, Madeleine Lee, began her study of political "power" by spending two weeks observing legislators at work. See *Democracy: An American Novel* (1880; reprint New York: New American Library, 1961), p. 22. More generally, pilgrimages to political shrines, like hero worship, were deliberately encouraged. When southern women sponsored the restoration of Mount Vernon in the 1850s, orators who praised the project urged their countrymen to journey to Washington's home. See Forgie, *Patricide in the House Divided*, p. 172.

[8] David Terry to Cornelia Runnels Terry, June 30, David Smith Terry Papers. Carl F. Kaestle argues that a primary aim of common schools was to form good citizens, but he also suggests that religious teaching, not history, was the preferred vehicle for shaping republican character, in *Pillars of the Republic: Common Schools and American Society, 1780–1860* (1983), pp. 100–1. Anne M. Boylan adds that there was a movement in some places by the 1820s and 1830s to exclude religious instruction seen as sectarian from public schools, in *Sunday School: The Formation of an American Institution, 1790–1880* (1988), pp. 52–9. But there is little evidence that the Bible was widely displaced and replaced by formal tuition in the principles of American government.

by a combination of explicit instruction from guardians and informal exposure to patriotic oratory, stump speaking, and political discussion. For better or worse, ideas in nearly all of these settings were conveyed with passion or bias or both. Unless the fact is acknowledged that American republican values were subject to many interpretations, it is difficult to explain Terry's movement from these words of unexceptionable loyalty in 1856 to his decision to fight for the Confederacy in 1861. Nor was Terry alone in having his patriotism nurtured from a particular viewpoint. The political meetings Curry sought out in Boston were those of his father's party, the Democrats. At nineteen, Josiah Grinnell in Vermont was initiated into civic life as a Whig, when he marched twenty miles to Burlington behind an ox-drawn log cabin. In sum, young Victorians' political lessons were decidedly partisan. The excitement of taking a stand was probably one reason their interest was stirred.[9]

Perhaps the most persuasive influence that attracted the Victorians to politics was the civic participation of their fathers. Politics ranked close behind agriculture and entrepreneurship as an occupation that engaged the Victorians' fathers, since about one-third of the fathers whose employment is known (twenty-one of sixty-five) held public office at one time.[10] This was a proportion higher than the national average, reflecting the prominence of the Victorians' families. Despite their greater access to political power, however, the fathers' attitude toward office holding was representative of the view of public service widely held in the early republic. Most fathers must be designated political "amateurs," men who considered occupations besides politics as their principal careers.

The political activity of the Victorians' fathers ran a spectrum from

[9] Rice, *Curry*, pp. 11, 13; Payne, *Josiah Bushnell Grinnell* (1938), p. 8. Despite the growing acceptance of partisanship, suspicion of political contention remained, as Major Wilson points out in "Republicanism and the Idea of Party in the Jacksonian Period."

[10] For a list of occupations of the Victorians' fathers, see Appendix B, Tables 1 and 2. The totals cited in the text include the fathers of both male and female Victorians. Especially for the fathers, politics was not necessarily an occupation that they depended on for sustained financial support. To view politics as a career required a specialized view of civic activity that was in the early stages of development in the nineteenth century. Still, to demonstrate how widespread office holding was in the middle classes, it is helpful to compare political participation numerically to other occupations. See Appendix D, "Political Affiliations and Views," for a more detailed tabulation of the political sympathies and/or activities of the Victorians' childhood families, in nearly all cases determined by the father's initiative. I have listed the political position of twenty-eight of the families of Victorian men and three families of women as "unknown." In fourteen cases, the reason for the classification was insufficient information, especially due to manuscript collections that include little material on an individual's childhood. In the other seventeen cases, it is likely that political activity was not important enough in the parents' lives to merit comment by biographers. Among the Victorians themselves, only two men and one woman showed almost no interest in politics. This pattern of development stands in contrast to the Victorians' changing religious loyalties. Biographers conscientiously comment on their subjects' early religious exposure because most received some training. In only twelve cases was the childhood religious experience classified in Appendix A as "unknown" or "none." These totals suggest that politics gained authority over time, whereas religious convictions and practice declined.

nonpartisan community service to office holding aimed at advancing specific interests, as old and new premises about public life overlapped. A colonial ideal of nonpartisan civic duty still impelled men, North and South, to fill local offices at the turn of the nineteenth century. John Wentworth's father, a farmer and merchant, was a selectman and justice of the peace in Sandwich, New Hampshire, after he moved there in 1812. Sanders Guignard, the father of two of these Victorians, earned his living in Columbia, South Carolina, by planting, running a ferry, and manufacturing bricks. He also served as an alderman.[11] Perhaps even these appointments reflected factional loyalties in local societies that so often marred prescriptions for consensus. But it is more certain that the same men who participated in traditional town politics sometimes sought state office as well in explicitly partisan contests. Thus by the 1830s, Paul Wentworth identified himself as a Democrat and won a seat in the legislature.[12] As amateurs, these men did not think of politics as a career, and they sometimes served no longer than needed to promote a particular project. The father of Lewis Henry Morgan, for example, a merchant from Aurora, New York, apparently went to the legislature in 1823 to push for construction of the Erie Canal.[13] Indeed, too much time given to politics was a distraction from regular business. William Curry of Georgia, a merchant, planter, and militia colonel whose store was a center of partisan debate, spent six years in the state legislature, but he did not let his political interests keep him from moving to the Alabama frontier in 1838 to improve his fortunes.[14] Politics was finally marginal to Curry's life's goals.

Although the political amateurism of the Victorians' fathers did not preclude rising partisan activity, the party system was still loose enough during

[11] Fehrenbacher, *Chicago Giant: A Biography of "Long John" Wentworth* (1957), p. 5; Childs, ed., *Planters and Business Men: The Guignard Family of South Carolina, 1795–1930* (1957), p. 39.

[12] Fehrenbacher, *Chicago Giant*, p. 12. Only five of the fathers of Victorian men and women are listed in Appendix D as participating only in "local politics" or "state politics" because most did eventually ally themselves with a national party, even if they continued to serve exclusively at the state level or below. In other words, more of the fathers' activity was regional, although with an awareness of national politics, than the classification might suggest. On the traditional corporate ideal and the way factionalism in practice marred accord before the nineteenth century, see Robert A. Gross, *The Minutemen and Their World* (New York: Hill and Wang, 1976), ch. 1. For a vivid account of the relation of social to political conflict in the Maine backcountry at the turn of the nineteenth century, see Alan Taylor, *Liberty Men and Great Proprietors: The Revolutionary Settlement on the Maine Frontier, 1760–1820* (Chapel Hill: University of North Carolina Press, 1990). It is probably true, as a number of scholars propose, that a political ethic of nonpartisan public service persisted longer in the South. That belief did not deter elites who held power from playing politics, however, to retain positions of prestige. See, e.g., Greenberg, *Masters and Statesmen*, esp. chs. 1, 3, and 4, and Escott, *Many Excellent People: Power and Privilege in North Carolina, 1850–1900* (1985), esp. pp. 15–20.

[13] Resek, *Lewis Henry Morgan: American Scholar* (1960), pp. 3–4.

[14] Rice, *Curry*, pp. 4, 6, 9. For a study of antebellum politics structured around a similar distinction between political "mavericks," who acted from personal belief, and more modern "conformists," who accepted party discipline, see Shields, *The Line of Duty: Maverick Congressmen and the Development of American Political Culture, 1836–1860* (1985).

the Victorians' childhoods to invite fairly widespread firsthand acquaintance with the political process among the middle classes. This affected young people in two ways. First, men with no special expertise in governing felt that they could try for office with a reasonable chance of success, with the consequence that many children belonged to families with a personal political interest. Probably most of the fathers studied here viewed their social station as a sufficient qualification for public leadership. But on occasion, even a man of slender means interpreted republican theory liberally enough to run for office. Thus Clovis Lowe, a farmer and shoemaker, was so close to poverty that he eventually indentured his son, Thaddeus, to another New Hampshire farmer. Even so, Lowe exercised his right to seek office and went to the state legislature in 1833.[15]

Second, parents intimately involved with politics either created opportunities for their sons or at least nurtured a facility at partisanship that helped to launch young men's political careers. Nearly all antebellum newspapers were party organs, and journalism often gave the Victorians their first chance to influence public affairs. As an undergraduate at Harvard, Edward Everett Hale reported on proceedings at the Massachusetts State House for his father's Whig paper, the *Daily Advertiser.* Although Hale finally chose to become a minister instead of an editor, his grounding in civic culture made possible his single greatest success, the patriotic story of *The Man without a Country,* published in 1863. William Dean Howells worked with his father on a variety of left-leaning utopian and Free Soil papers before he became city editor in Columbus of the Republican *Ohio State Journal,* a job that advanced his literary career when he was asked to write a campaign biography of Lincoln. In addition, Franklin Sanborn in New Hampshire contributed to his brother's *Independent Democrat,* Jabez Curry in Alabama wrote on a free-lance basis for the Democratic press, and John Wentworth's first job in a long political life was as assistant editor of the Chicago *Democrat.*[16]

Young women, too, grew up in these politically active families, and they were as naturally intrigued by politics as were their male kin. Along with more leisure and better education, this childhood exposure to political interest at home helps to explain Victorian women's adult interest in government. Rebecca Felton of Georgia, who became the first female member of the U.S. Senate in 1922 when she was appointed to complete Tom Watson's term after his death, traced her political memories back

---

[15] Block, *Above the Civil War: The Story of Thaddeus Lowe, Balloonist, Inventor, Railway Builder* (1966), pp. 12–13.

[16] Hale, *A New England Boyhood* (1893), p. 43; Lynn, *William Dean Howells: An American Life* (1970), pp. 24–7, 66, 80–3, 89; Sanborn, *Recollections of Seventy Years* (1909), 1:24; Rice, *Curry,* p. 22; Fehrenbacher, *Chicago Giant,* pp. 19–20. McGeer discusses the transformation of journalism in the 1870s from a partisan tool into an independent voice in public life, in *Decline of Popular Politics,* ch. 5.

to the Harrison campaign that took place when she was five and to the habit of her father, a planter, merchant, and Whig, of reading newspapers to his illiterate neighbors. Later married to a politician, Felton declined for many years to attend political rallies for the sake of propriety and did not advocate suffrage until after 1900. But by writing anonymously for the press, composing her husband's speeches, and drafting his proposed legislation, she sustained a high level of political activity even within self-imposed bounds.[17]

Elizabeth Cady Stanton learned of the connection between social and political issues more from her father's law practice, because his office adjoined their house in Johnstown, New York, than from contact with his more distant work as a Federalist politician and, after her marriage, a justice of the New York Supreme Court. Stanton recalled how much her father focused her appreciation of politics when she wrote in her memoirs: " 'When you are grown up, and able to prepare a speech,' said he, 'you must go down to Albany and talk to the legislators; tell them all you have seen in this office . . . , and if you can persuade them to pass new laws, the old ones will be a dead letter.' "[18] Her later insistence that the solution to women's dilemma must be political, rather than simply moral or social, most likely grew from her father's influence as well as from the broader civic influences of her childhood. Most Victorian women remained more on the margin of politics than did Felton and Stanton. Even so, women were aware of public issues to an extent that indicates that political culture, though still not political power, was more inclusive in fact than in law.

Despite strong evidence of the persuasive hold that politics exerted over young people, it is important to question if there was ambiguity in these lessons similar to the mixed message children received from religion. Political nurture did in fact contain dissonant notes. Whereas parents' sporadic religious practice inadvertently informed sons and daughters that they might compromise prescriptions for piety, suspicion of partisanship was voiced without power to quell political interest. Inconsistency robbed religion of credibility, in short, but testified to the seduction of politics.

From the founding of the republic, a host of reservations was expressed about parties as divisive, self-seeking, and low-minded, and young Vic-

---

[17] Felton, *My Memoirs of Georgia Politics* (1911), pp. 17–18; Talmadge, *Rebecca Latimer Felton: Nine Stormy Decades* (1960), pp. 40, 79, 103–4.

[18] *Eighty Years and More: Reminiscences, 1815–1897* (1898), p. 32. On the political background of Stanton's father, see also Banner, *Elizabeth Cady Stanton: A Radical for Woman's Rights* (1980), p. 2. In addition to the reasons cited for Victorian women's rising political interest, Nancy Cott argues that one special aspect of women's socialization, an emphasis on traits associated with their "domesticity," contributed to women's collective self-consciousness that stood behind the demand for their rights. See *The Bonds of Womanhood: "Woman's Sphere" in New England, 1780–1835* (1977), esp. pp. 200–1. Ellen DuBois outlines the development of women's political vision in *Feminism and Suffrage: The Emergence of an Independent Women's Movement in America, 1848–1869* (1978), esp. ch. 1.

torians assimilated the anxieties they heard. According to David Donald, William Herndon had a visceral aversion to strife from his earliest political contests in the 1840s. In 1861, Herndon called most politicians "corrupt-fish – dollar-power seekers – mudhunters – scoundrels."[19] George Templeton Strong complained at age twenty-four that even the conservative Whigs had no "higher aim than the cultivation of tariffs and credit systems."[20] William Story likened the atmosphere of politics to the mythic filth of Hercules' stable. Yet these often vehement feelings did not keep these men away from politics. Herndon was mayor of Springfield, Strong commented assiduously in his diary on political news, and even Story, an expatriate living in Europe, kept up a correspondence with Charles Sumner.[21] The perception of politics as corrupt persisted unabated from the Victorians' childhood through their adulthood. But because they voiced criticism in tandem with rising political interest, articulated misgivings were more a sign of the successful entrenchment of partisanship, never fully trusted, than of its weakness.[22]

Overall, it is not surprising that the Victorians' childhood encounters with politics inspired many to participate in public life as adults. Of the sixty-one men studied, twenty-four held office at some time in their lives. Although the amateur attitudes of some meant that politics was not necessarily a career that demanded a sustained commitment, it is still useful to note for the sake of comparison that more Victorian men worked as public officials than engaged in any other occupation. Half of the women married politicians (seven of fourteen), and Felton and Stanton were active themselves.[23] Just as the Victorians built on their fathers' examples, the basic features of the Second Party system persisted in the midcentury decades. Opportunities to express political feeling and to articulate values were offered within a context of partisan competition. Yet it is no less true that these characteristics took on an exaggerated quality. Debate about fundamental issues proceeded with a passion that was matched by intense ambition among politicians and constituents to make government serve their goals. In this way, the Victorians turned their political inheritance to their own ends.

---

[19] Herndon to Lyman Trumbull, Jan. 27, quoted in Donald, *Lincoln's Herndon* (1948), p. 31. See Donald's discussion of Herndon's aversion to contention, pp. 30–1.

[20] May 27, 1844, *Diary of Strong*, ed. Nevins and Thomas, 1:236.

[21] Donald, *Herndon*, p. 67; *Diary of Strong*, ed. Nevins and Thomas, vols. 1–4; James, *Story*, 1:29–50.

[22] For a summary of early Americans' distrust of political factionalism, see Hofstadter, *Idea of a Party System*.

[23] For occupations of these Victorians, see Appendix B. See Appendix D, Table 1, for further information on the political views and degree of involvement of these Victorian men. For Victorian men, the total number classified as "amateur" and "professional" in Appendix D exceeds the number listed as "politicians" in Appendix B because some served in office so briefly that politics cannot be called a sustained occupation.

POLITICAL PROFESSIONALISM AND
THE ACTIVE STATE

The Victorians' political enthusiasm was most visible in their excitement at partisan contests and their struggle for legislative rewards. Much as individuals in the midcentury generation leaped at their society's promise to supply identity and purpose in other areas of culture, so they asked politics to satisfy substantial ambitions for personal accomplishment and practical gain. With such high expectations, the increasingly structured political system their aspirations produced was doubly disturbing. They did not see how much the roots of a complex state run by professionals lay in their own expectations, but they were aware of a number of their government's problems.

As the Victorians entered politics as adults, amateur attitudes that kept office seeking a sporadic or part-time activity were found side by side with an uncompromising drive to be a politician, an outlook that may be called "professionalism." Yet even amateurs now played for bigger stakes with more determination than had their fathers and, indeed, their mothers. Before turning to the professionals, it is useful to look at three Victorians with modest public commitments, one moved by duty and practicality, another by love of political sport, and the last by frustrated professionalism.

The career of Cyrus Holliday most closely resembled the amateurism of the Victorians' parents, because he pursued politics occasionally from motives of obligation and self-interest. A native of Pennsylvania, Holliday was a founder and promoter of the city of Topeka, Kansas, where his civic and private interests converged. He won a seat in the territorial legislature soon after he arrived in 1854, not only to secure the "brilliant destiny" of Kansas as a free state, but to advance his own ends by making Topeka the capital, "a great triumph," he wrote to his wife after the legislative struggle, that "will greatly enhance the prospects of our town and our property."[24] The three terms Holliday served subsequently as mayor were undertaken in a mood that blended a sense of public duty owed by a prominent citizen and determination to protect his investment. Holliday sought no further offices, however, because his main ambition was to create what became the Atchison, Topeka, and Santa Fe railroad. He worked hard at lobbying Congress when he wanted a land grant for the line in the 1860s, but he did not want a seat for himself that might distract him from business. What was new in Holliday's perspective was his awareness that the national government was a key influence in local and personal prosperity. Otherwise, he would neither have

---

[24] Cyrus Holliday to Mary Holliday, Dec. 10, 1854, July 24, 1859, Cyrus Kurtz Holliday Papers.

returned to Pennsylvania in 1856 to campaign for John C. Frémont, a candidate who promised a Free Soil policy throughout the West, nor would he have later solicited federal aid in the form of land.[25] Amateurism persisted, but to pull government strings effectively required broader vision and sharper political savvy than in the past.

A more unprecedented kind of amateurism consisted of involvement with politics as nearly a hobby, spurred by enthusiasm for the spectacle of speeches, parades, and momentous issues hotly contested. Whereas most Victorians were content to observe from the crowd, these amateurs wished to act as politicians, but were without the drive to make a career of politics that led others to find strategies of survival. Partisanship informed the life of Lew Wallace, one such amateur, in a startling number of ways. Between the 1840s and 1880s, Wallace wrote for two political journals, served one term in the Indiana Senate, tried twice unsuccessfully for Congress, campaigned after 1872 for nearly every Republican candidate for president, supervised the recount in 1876 of contested votes in Florida, and finally found a political niche as a recipient of minor appointments, governor of the New Mexico Territory in 1878, and ambassador to the Ottoman Empire in 1881. Yet it was a sign of Wallace's political marginality that his civic achievements grew as much from his reputation in his ongoing careers as a lawyer and novelist as from his partisan loyalty. His acceptability as an election commissioner in 1876 was due to his legal background. By some logic, moreover, an author of historical novels about Mexico and ancient Palestine, *A Fair God* (1873) and *Ben-Hur* (1880), was a qualified representative to neighboring lands. Thus what is arresting is that a man with so tenuous a political existence participated with unflagging passion and, conversely, that he let go so easily after each episode of engagement. Self-interest in his reappointment helps explain why Wallace campaigned for James G. Blaine during a trip home from Constantinople in 1884. Nonetheless, when Cleveland recalled him in 1885, Wallace simply went about his business as a writer, just as in earlier years he turned back to the law. He waited patiently for a new political opening, which came as the chance to write Harrison's campaign

---

[25] Cyrus Holliday to Mary Holliday, July 30, Oct. 17, 1856; [Fred G. Gurley?], "The Man with the White Hat," in *Cyrus K. Holliday: Dedication of the Cyrus K. Holliday Plaque, Santa Fe Station, Topeka, Kansas, Apr. 3, 1949*, pp. 25–6, Holliday Papers. Others among these Victorians who behaved as this kind of political amateur, engaging periodically in politics to achieve limited ends, include Lewis Henry Morgan, who spent one term in the New York Assembly in the 1860s in a failed effort to gain appointment as federal commissioner of Indian affairs, and Pierre Beauregard, who ran for mayor of New Orleans in the 1850s and later led the short-lived Louisiana Unification Movement in the 1870s. See Resek, *Morgan*, pp. 82–3, and Williams, *Beauregard*, pp. 43–4, 268–71. The persistence of amateurism in the Victorian generation may be seen by comparing the number of amateurs among Victorian men (twenty) to professionals (eight). For a list of individuals, see Appendix D, Table 1. A few women may also be considered political amateurs, as I explain later.

biography in 1888.[26] Politics spiced Wallace's life in an unrelenting fashion but did not finally control his actions.

The political amateurism of Victorian women was most new with respect to past practices and most problematic, among these examples, in its implications for the justice of politics. Far more than their mothers, women of the middle classes whose adulthoods spanned the Civil War followed political developments with informed interest. But in a milieu where political language tended to serve in place of religion as the chosen medium of public debate, it is troubling that women were closed out of full participation by a combination of legal disability, social pressure, and their own consent. One poignant example of deferential yet frustrated amateurism is that of Rebecca Felton. During her long marriage to William Felton from 1853 to 1909, Felton stood as demurely as she was able behind her husband, a reform Democrat, in Georgia politics. But her temper was that of a caged tiger. "Only a few dared to fight them," she wrote fiercely of the ongoing struggle between the state's corrupt bosses and their opponents in her memoir of William in 1911, and although she meant her declaration to eulogize her husband's integrity, she more clearly revealed her own love of a rousing contest.[27] Forever in the wings of William's career, ready to offer advice, drafts of speeches, and letters to the newspapers answering his opponents, Felton nonetheless contained her political passion within his. *My Memoirs of Georgia Politics*, written after her husband's death, observed strict propriety as a tract about William's honesty written at her "husband's request" to inspire "unpurchasable patriotism" in young men.[28] A picture of the seventy-five-year-old author, "Mrs. William H. Felton," wearing widow's black appeared in the preface. Yet even Felton recognized how much her self-effacement was a pose. "My memoirs" were too much about her own life in politics, she observed at the book's end, because "I discover that I should have said more of what my husband did and less of my own toils and tribulations."[29] Not all Victorian women loved politics as thoroughly as did Felton, although some others sought real entry into the political process with fewer scruples than she.[30] Still, Felton's history reveals a kind of am-

---

[26] Wallace, *Lew Wallace: An Autobiography* (1906), 1: chs. 8–28; Morseberger and Morseberger, *Lew Wallace: Militant Romantic* (1980), pp. 21, 37, 51–2, 215–17, 247–9, 256, 295, 344–50, 367. Wallace's excitement highlights the recreational side of politics that Michael McGeer documents in his account of political clubs, rallies, and parades, in *Decline of Popular Politics*, ch. 1.

[27] Felton, *Memoirs of Georgia Politics*, p. 7. Although Felton was the only woman among this group who ever held public office, she and Elizabeth Cady Stanton may still be considered political "amateurs" because of their thorough acquaintance with party politics and/or the legislative process. See my classifications of the political affiliations of Victorian women and their husbands in Appendix D, Table 2.

[28] Ibid., headnote and p. 11.

[29] Ibid., p. 159.

[30] Other southern wives of politicians who were especially active in their husbands' careers were Mary Chesnut and Varina Davis. See *Mary Chesnut's Civil War*, ed. Woodward (1981), and Wiley, *Confederate*

ateurism peculiar to women that involved more strain and restriction than was experienced by contemporary men.

Viewed from the perspective of motive, the difference between Victorian political amateurs, male and female, and professionals was one of degree more than of kind. The professionals went to lengths to sustain their careers, as if exercising power was their life's blood. But the amateurs entered civic affairs with kindred passion at least capable of transforming them into professionals. Indeed, some Victorian men, unburdened by the prohibitive restraints on women, were middle-aged before they embraced politics with an instinctive certainty not unlike finding one's calling. James Garfield spent his early adult years as a teacher and lay preacher before committing himself to politics with single-minded devotion in the last two decades of his life.[31] But to present Victorian professionalism in bold outline, it is best to look at men who seemed to want little else from the first.

On the surface, John Wentworth of Illinois and Zebulon Vance of North Carolina might simply appear more successful than a dogged campaigner such as Wallace. But their tenure in office grew, subjectively, from a desire for politics to anchor their private identities, and objectively, from an appreciation of parties as agents to mobilize votes and execute policy, an understanding that the amateurs often lacked. Both held offices almost continuously over several decades. John Wentworth (1815–88) left New Hampshire for Chicago in the mid-1830s to find a clear political field. He bought a newspaper to secure a voice and rode the circuit as an attorney to cultivate contacts. First elected to Congress in 1843, Wentworth kept his seat for nearly a decade with the help of a Cook County political machine of his own making. The trials of maneuvering in national politics during the party turmoil of the 1850s helps to explain why Wentworth returned to local office, serving two terms as mayor at the end of the decade. He won a final term in Congress in 1864, and in the early 1870s, he essentially retired from politics, devoting his time to experimental farming and managing his properties.[32]

The persistence in politics of Zebulon Vance (1830–94) was even more impressive, particularly in light of his greater liability as a southerner. Entering the North Carolina legislature in 1854, Vance was soon elected to two terms in Congress before the war. He acted as governor of the state from 1862 until the Confederacy's defeat. When his civil rights were restored in 1867, Vance returned to public life, acting as a delegate to the Democratic convention in New York in 1868 and winning a seat in the Senate in 1870,

---

Women (1975), ch. 3. On women bolder than these who campaigned for suffrage, see DuBois, *Feminism and Suffrage*, and Flexner, *Century of Struggle: The Women's Rights Movement in the United States, 1848– 1920* (1975).

[31] For Garfield's transformation, see my subsequent discussion.

[32] Fehrenbacher, *Chicago Giant*, esp. pp. 13, 28, 38, 45, 52, 143–6.

from which he, however, was barred. Vance was reelected governor in 1876 and senator in 1878, and remained in the Senate until his death.[33]

Behind these straightforward accounts of professional development, however, lay the struggles of Wentworth and Vance to keep their political integrity without sacrificing party connections. Their stories were strikingly similar, and in both, party loyalty was the dominant theme. Wentworth, who began his career as a Democrat, repeatedly paid the consequences of adopting a Free Soil position while refusing to leave the Democrats. Denounced by the Free Soil party in 1848 for his lack of support, Wentworth was attacked equally by the Democrats for his opposition to the Compromise of 1850. Although he called himself a Democrat until 1856, he inched toward the Republicans by forming his own coalition of "Republican Democrats" to elect him mayor of Chicago in 1857. By 1860, Wentworth allied himself with Lincoln. But he was neither comfortable with Republican economic principles nor did his new party favor a former Democrat, both circumstances working to limit his career as a Republican officeholder to one term.[34]

Vance held on to the Whig party just as tenaciously. The party was nearly defunct when he entered public life as a Whig in 1854. Well into the 1870s, however, Vance went to great lengths to avoid betrayal of old friends and principles by hedging firm ties with the Democrats. He flirted with the Know Nothings in the mid-1850s as a vehicle for Whig values, but called himself a Whig once again when he ran for Congress at the end of the decade. A group of self-styled "Conservatives," all eager to obscure former differences, elected Vance governor in 1862, and the same impulse to avoid offense accounts for his support by "Conservative Democrats" in 1876. Only as a senator toward the end of his life did Vance stop making bows to his former Whiggery and settle more comfortably with the Democrats.[35]

[33] Tucker, *Zeb Vance: Champion of Personal Freedom* (1965), esp. pp. 57, 67, 79, 147–54, 430, 452, 460, 463.

[34] Fehrenbacher, *Chicago Giant*, pp. 64, 103, 134–40.

[35] Vance to David F. Caldwell, Feb. 19, 1858, in *The Papers of Zebulon Baird Vance, 1843–1862*, ed. Johnston (1963), 1:34; Tucker, *Vance*, pp. 84–5, 91–2, 150, 448, 452, 456. While this analysis explains the persistence of parties from the viewpoint of individual attitudes, there is a substantial literature on the ability of mid-nineteenth-century political organizations to withstand disruption, particularly that of the sectional crisis. See, e.g., Baker, *The Politics of Continuity: Maryland Political Parties from 1858 to 1870* (1973), and Silbey, *A Respectable Minority: The Democratic Party in the Civil War Era, 1860–1868* (1977). Studies indebted to the idea of critical elections similarly downplay the war's importance and assume that party competition itself remained secure through periods of realignment of specific loyalties. See, e.g., Kleppner, *The Third Electoral System, 1853–1892* (1979). Recognized parties did disappear in the Confederacy, as Eric L. McKitrick shows in his excellent comparison, "Party Politics and the Union and Confederate War Efforts," in Chambers and Burnham, eds., *The American Party Systems* (1975), pp. 117–51. But Richard E. Beringer argues that partisan habits were so entrenched that partylike factions began to appear late in the war, in "The Unconscious 'Spirit of Party' in the Confederate Congress." Michael Perman suggests that despite the extraordinary civic conditions of Reconstruction, southern parties behaved as conventional political organizations in the sense that they chose among acknowledged strategies for winning elections. See *Road to Redemption*, esp. pp. 23–4.

Nearly all men eligible to participate in politics had to make choices during these tumultuous decades that balanced the requirements of conscience and practical effectiveness. But professional politicians were distinguished by their use of party affiliations as tools of ambition and their assimilation of partisan positions as extensions of private identities. Wentworth and Vance wished with singular intensity to be politicians and carefully adjusted their loyalties to ensure their political survival.[36] Unlike other callings, however, public service inevitably affected civic life. Habits of professionalism contributed to the stability that party activity provided the nation during this period of crisis. Despite great changes in party alignment, Americans, guided by politicians, chose to act through familiar kinds of partisan organizations during much of the Civil War era. The Democratic party in particular remained faithful to its original principles. But the Victorians' ambivalence about partisanship blocked their appreciation of professionalism's benefits. When they looked out at the changing public landscape, the impression they most frequently voiced was that politics was corrupt.

Denunciations of demagogues have recurred throughout history and have served as a rallying cry for resistance. But among the Victorians, politicians themselves so often exposed wrongdoing that it seemed that the rebellion they sought was safely restricted to a change in political parties. Self-righteous condemnation of opponents resembled the shoptalk of political insiders, who successfully turned their doubts about their own legitimacy into aggressive partisan weapons. Thus Zebulon Vance, of all people, blamed crafty politicians for secession in his correspondence at the outset of the war. In a lecture in Richmond in 1863, Jabez Curry, up for reelection to the Confederate Congress, attacked sycophants who courted popular favor. Across the continent, Charles Maclay called on the people of California in his campaign for the state senate in 1865 to "sweep with one stroke of inde-

---

[36] If sustained party activity and office seeking through at least part of two decades is used as a rough index of professionalism for men, the following individuals can be grouped among political professionals along with Wentworth and Vance: Robert Tyler, Wade Hampton, Ulysses Grant, Abram Hewitt, James Garfield, and Chauncey Depew. Several other marginal choices have been excluded since, in my judgment, they neither conceived of themselves primarily as politicians for a significant part of their lives nor worked with consequent energy to retain power: James Beekman, Josiah Grinnell, Joseph Taylor, Robert Ingersoll. Most of the literature on political professionalism approaches the problem through members of specific institutions and their behavior within those bodies, rather than by scrutiny of the careers of individual men. The best recent studies of Congress are Thompson, *The "Spider Web": Congress and Lobbying in the Age of Grant* (1985), which documents the high turnover rate and inefficient committee system of the House as late as Grant's administrations (ch. 2), and Shields, *Line of Duty*, on the beginnings of party discipline in the late antebellum period. See also Allan Bogue, "Members of the House of Representatives and the Process of Modernization"; H. Douglas Price, "The Congressional Career: Then and Now," in Polsby, ed., *Congressional Behavior* (1971), pp. 14–27; and Nelson W. Polsby, "The Institutionalization of the U.S. House of Representatives." The best general discussion of the impulse of the middle classes to seek sustained careers is Bledstein, *The Culture of Professionalism: The Middle Class and the Development of Higher Education in America* (1976), ch. 5. Kenneth Greenberg argues that although southerners seceded to prevent the spread of political self-seeking, part of their anxiety grew from their inability to achieve their own standard of disinterested rule, in *Masters and Statesmen*, p. 137 and ch. 7.

pendant thought & action away, forever away from public office & trust [these] men who are growing fat & becoming princely rich holding & controlling with such deathlike tenacity the offices of this country."[37] So, too, the liberal Republican movement of 1872 was based on censure of the "office-mongering element," who should be replaced, in the view of Edwin Godkin, by "a strong reform party, led by thoughtful, educated, high-minded men."[38] There was, in fact, little consensus on whether the remedy for self-seeking politicians should be the restoration of democratic control or the election of a disinterested elite. But in the end, both proposals tended to evaporate as rhetoric, because the purpose of all these speakers was to win power themselves.[39]

The broader middle classes shared this perception of politicians as agents of moral compromise and civic contention. This was one sign of the potential inherent in professionalism to alienate the public. Yet bitter words about politicians also registered the Victorians' high expectations for the political process. Scuffling over the behavior of leaders was as much a way to articulate standards and to cope with disappointment as a gesture of permanent, angry withdrawal. The example of John Kinkade in California is revealing. A man who never held office except that of superintendent of schools, Kinkade oscillated between enthusiasm and disgust at partisan contests. Kinkade migrated from Virginia to California as a forty-niner and proud Democrat, "the conservative party," he wrote to his brother in 1856, that he hoped would survive challenges in the West: "Democracy will carry this state [;] negro worshipers will stand no show at all [;] yet I expect that Greel[e]y Seward or those [will] be our next president, and if so [we] will set up for ourselves on this side."[40] Throughout his life, Kinkade stumped for candidates as a matter of conviction and pleasure. But by late 1860, he began his first cycle of antagonism to party politics, when he grew "disgusted" with contentious Democratic leaders who set the party adrift, in his eyes, like a mutinous crew. Although he vowed that "the stump will not bear my weight this fall," Kinkade was too infatuated by the political process to long remain idle.[41] Writing to his brother after Lincoln's death, Kinkade

---

[37] "Reasons for Accepting the Nomination for the State Senate," ms. address, [Aug., 1865], Charles Maclay Papers. Variant spellings in this and subsequent citations appear in the original texts. On Vance and Curry, see Vance to William Dickson, Dec. 11, 1860, in *Papers of Vance*, ed. Johnston, 1:71–3, and Rice, *Curry*, p. 43.

[38] Godkin to Carl Schurz, Apr. 5, 1871, in *The Gilded Age Letters of E.L. Godkin*, ed. Armstrong (1974), p. 171.

[39] On fears of corruption in the postwar period, often connected with the strength of parties, see Thompson, *Spider Web*, ch. 1; McCormick, *Party Period and Public Policy*, ch. 6; and McGeer, *Decline of Popular Politics*, ch. 3.

[40] John Kinkade to James Kinkade, Dec. 28, May 26, 1856, John Thompson Kinkade Papers. All subsequent quotations are taken from letters from John to James, Kinkade Papers. Only the dates will be cited in subsequent notes.

[41] Sept. 23, 1860.

reported, "I stumped my country for him last fall," and he praised Lincoln as "an honest firm and benevolent man and the greatest reformer of modern times."[42] By 1871, however, he had given up once again on "political parties [that] are in the field with their usual energy and bitterness," and set out on a "stumping campaign," as a party of one, to defeat subsidies to railroads.[43] So strong was Kinkade's conviction that the people would hear an honest voice that he did not turn entirely from politics. Yet he was distressed that the actions of political leaders did not match the promise of republican government, and he approached politics with increasing reserve.[44]

The two-faced character of Victorian political criticism, mixing infatuation and impatience with partisanship, showed up more bluntly in charges of government corruption. The activity of city, state, and federal governments swelled to meet rising demand during the Victorians' lifetimes, and suspicions of illicit dealings increased in turn.[45] Simple application to rulers for aid was a practice rooted in the traditional duties of hierarchy, and these pleas continued. Ordinary citizens in North Carolina during the war petitioned their governor, Zebulon Vance, for protection by troops, release from the army, and help in securing scarce goods.[46] Next to these straightforward requests from people who assumed their subordination to government, however, were solicitations initiated by men cognizant of the state's rich potential to advance private goals. Mathew Brady pulled strings in a modest way when he used his acquaintance with the general of the army, Winfield Scott, to secure permission to take battlefield photographs.[47] Other men approached

---

[42] Apr. 26, 1865.

[43] June 28.

[44] Robert Ingersoll, a man sufficiently prominent in the Republican party to deliver the nominating speech for James G. Blaine in 1876, was another person so disillusioned with the political process that he dropped out of political life after the mid-1880s. See Cramer, *Royal Bob*, p. 252. A surfeit of contention and manipulation also contributed to the cyclical pattern of enthusiastic activity followed by weary withdrawal that made Victorian politics resemble religious revivals, a phenomenon to be explained.

[45] Although Richard L. McCormick's assessment that postwar government did not return to a prewar level of activity is persuasive, he and other writers also note influences that contained expansion. Along with the state's new visibility in promoting economic progress and social legislation, Morton Keller cites the limiting power of persistent localism, cultural diversity, laissez-faire theory, and fears of corruption, in *Affairs of State: Public life in Late Nineteenth Century America* (1977), chs. 3–5. In the postwar South, Michael Perman similarly documents an uneasy balance between restriction and recruitment of government, as Democratic "Redeemers" rewrote state constitutions to curb official power, particularly that aimed at developing industry and railroads, but by nearly the same stroke directed government assistance to agriculture. See *Road to Redemption*, esp. chs. 9–10. My analysis suggests that some of the tension about government's growth emerged from the conflict within individuals between desire for rewards and suspicion of power. For McCormick's view, see *Party Period and Public Policy*, p. 213.

[46] See, e.g., John Pool, P. H. Roane, and William Poisson to Vance, Sept. 18, Sept. 23, Nov. 1, 1862, respectively, in *Papers of Vance*, ed. Johnston, 1:198–201, 221–2, 294. Petitioning rulers is consistent with Paul Escott's view of midcentury North Carolina as elite-dominated in society and government. Although there was some rebellion from below, particularly during the war, members of the elite retained power in the end, aided by persistent deference that reinforced their own exertions. See *Many Excellent People*, esp. chs. 1, 3.

[47] Horan, *Mathew Brady: Historian with a Camera* (1955), p. 35.

caricature in their private campaigns for political appointment. Three men among the comparatively small group studied here, for example, vied at one time or another for the office of commissioner of Indian affairs. John Wesley North traveled from Minnesota to Springfield, Illinois, in 1861 to present his credentials to Lincoln, then the president-elect. Lewis Henry Morgan won a seat in the New York Assembly and the chairmanship of its Committee on Indian Affairs in order to establish himself as a credible candidate for the federal job, and he subsequently asked friends to send letters to Lincoln on his behalf. In 1868, Grant's wartime aide, Ely Parker, campaigned for his former commander and, alone of these three, won the coveted prize of commissioner. Grant's choice of Parker was probably due less to the fact that he was a Seneca Indian than to his sincere relations with Grant, who handled the perplexing task of appointments in a setting where suppliants offered ever more varied claims by simply naming his friends.[48]

Few of these men sought public office for the sole purpose of enjoying a salary. Morgan and Parker, for example, intended to institute fairer Indian policies. Although critiques of government corruption phrased the evolving system's flaw as its susceptibility to greed, at least as disturbing was the way an active state invited an ambiguous blend of private and public profit. In fact, personal and public gain commonly overlapped. Thaddeus Lowe, an avid balloonist, certainly had his own needs in view when he petitioned Congress in 1858 to establish a national weather service. Self-interest, however, did not invalidate his claim that climatological data would help farmers and seamen, an argument that helped to bring the project to fruition in 1870. In California in 1864, Charles Maclay presented a bill to the state assembly, of which he was a member, seeking authorization for him and his associates to construct a road through the district he represented. He saw no problem in asking that the builders be allowed to collect tolls for twenty years to repay them for their work.[49]

For men who spent more of their lives in politics than Lowe or Maclay, the line between self-interest and public service became all but impossible to discern. Josiah Grinnell, an Iowa landowner, businessman, and reformer, was active in politics as a Whig and Republican for nearly three decades. During that time, he worked to enhance the value of his enterprises, to

---

[48] Stonehouse, *John Wesley North and the Reform Frontier* (1965), pp. 124–31; Resek, *Morgan*, pp. 82–3; Parker, *The Life of General Ely S. Parker* (1919), p. 146. Grant did not always reduce the problem of appointments to the selection of old friends, but William S. McFeely notes that Parker was "a most typical Grant appointment; Parker was a crony from army days," in *Grant: A Biography* (1981), p. 305. On his use of patronage, see also *Grant*, pp. 290–304. For a broader view of the ambivalence of the middle classes toward government labor, viewed both as restrictive and yet respectable and lucrative, see Aron, *Ladies and Gentlemen of the Civil Service: Middle-Class Workers in Victorian America* (1987), chs. 2–3.

[49] Block, *Above the Civil War*, p. 23; [California Legislature, Draft of an Act to Provide for the Construction of a Turnpike Road in Santa Clara and Santa Cruz Counties, Apr. 4, 1864], Maclay Papers.

assist his constituents, and to advance an assortment of social causes, including land grants to railroads, a national bureau of education, military pensions for constituents, black suffrage, temperance, and aid to Indians and the poor.[50] Among the Democrats, principled opposition to centralized power did little to slow their entry into the race for government favors. Although Jabez Curry of Alabama systematically fought initiatives for a national bank, tariffs, and pensions to War of 1812 veterans during his two terms in Congress in the 1850s, he just as warmly supported projects sponsored during the same decade by his state: aid to railroads, public schools, and a geological survey. During a second career after the war as executive officer of the Peabody Fund for southern education, Curry's scruples about federal activity evaporated as well, and he moved to Washington in 1890 to facilitate his ongoing lobbying of Congress.[51] Neither as a prewar planter nor a postwar bureaucrat did Curry place self-interest before his constituents' good. Neither, however, did he slight government's potential for protecting his livelihood. It was precisely this slippery mix of motives behind growing demand for state aid that fueled charges of political corruption.

Accusations of mismanagement climaxed after the war in the wake of increasingly rapid expansion. Samuel McCullough, superintendent of construction of federal buildings in San Francisco from 1873 to 1878, spent so much of his time deflecting accusations of graft that it must have hampered his work. Under suspicion in 1875, McCullough offered to resign if his conduct were judged inappropriate. The next year, he denied skimming profits from inflated building materials and laborers' salaries, and he took time to expose an "attempt to rob the Government of a large sum of money," most likely in self-defense lest he himself be accused.[52] Finally removed from office "in a very summary manner," as he told a correspondent, McCullough in the meantime somehow built the San Francisco Mint, Marine Hospital, and other public buildings.[53] Because charges against McCullough were leveled in partisan contexts, his opponents probably used suspicion of corruption as a rhetorical weapon in part. Yet images of devious officials would not have been effective political tools if pictured greed had not touched real public anxieties. A state growing in response to eager demands by both the people and political professionals was almost bound to provoke worry about the process of change. A more sophisticated government was not created, in sum, without this displaced and complex debate about its costs that

---

[50] Payne, *Grinnell,* pp. 165, 170–1, 183–5, 215, 217.

[51] Rice, *Curry,* p. 27, 32, 152.

[52] McCullough to Albert Bolt Mullett, Sept. 25, 1876, Samuel McCullough Papers. See also McCullough to Mullett, Oct. 5, 1876, and McCullough to A. A. Sargent, Dec. 21, 1875, Apr. 1, 1876, May 10, 1877, McCullough Papers.

[53] McCullough to James G. Hill, Mar. 6, 1878, McCullough Papers.

worked both to curtail officials' short-term effectiveness and possibly to keep them morally in line.

Perhaps the earliest acknowledgment by one of these Victorians that government was being transformed from a social agency conducted mainly by amateurs into a self-contained institution subject to professionals' rules was Henry Thoreau's "Resistance to Civil Government," written during the Mexican War. Thoreau's ostensible theme was the manipulation of policy by the "slave power." But readers have long been aware that the essay's lasting force lies in thoughts on the limits of individual responsibility to the state. In the course of his argument, Thoreau's language progressed from discussion of "government," to references to the "state," and to allusions to the "State," as a strangely personalized, and forbidding, entity.[54] Thoreau knew that most men would have difficulty standing for principle against actual politics, because the "mass of men," he wrote, "serve the state thus, not as men mainly, but as machines, with their bodies."[55] Yet he saw less clearly how much his fellow citizens called the state into being by their taste for partisan contests and their demands for government's prizes.

Nor did the terms of Thoreau's discussion, centered in the dichotomy between the individual and the state, encourage him to see the difficulties that strong government posed for classes of citizens, such as women and blacks, who were offered less than equal rights for reasons unrelated to their own wills. The Victorians' perspective matched that of Thoreau and shared his viewpoint's shortcomings. Their denunciations of corruption phrased their system's danger as a function of the moral failings of individuals. Absorbed in thoughts of the petty selfishness of politicians, they were slow to reflect on the possibility that government might systematically serve some groups in the polity at the expense of others. This is one explanation for northern Victorians' intellectual acceptance of the abolition of slavery, an initiative that involved an affirmation of personal rights, and their equivocal commitment to political and, even more, social equality for former black slaves.[56] Still, the individualistic focus on the Victorians' political thinking took accurate account of the fact that many of their own political choices were rooted in the dilemmas of personalities. Although they might slight the kind of corruption that consists of the restriction of minority rights, they were aware that character influenced the rising state, even if they saw less clearly how much vexing spiritual questions informed their own political

---

[54] "Resistance to Civil Government" (1849) was later published as "Civil Disobedience," and the phrases referred to appear under that title in *The Portable Thoreau,* ed. Bode, pp. 109, 112, 124. As the essay progressed, Thoreau allowed the traditional meaning of the "State," one political component of the Union, to blend with its more modern meaning as a separate political apparatus.

[55] Ibid., p. 112.

[56] On the way legislative initiatives for racial progress slowed during Reconstruction, see Foner, *Reconstruction.*

decisions. The emerging political system, distinguished by an inner cadre of professionals and by bureaucratic intricacy, posed conditions that threatened public disaffection even among the middle classes whose priorities impelled state formation. In the short run, however, Victorian politics was rocked less by hostile feelings about big government than by ideological questioning.

TRIALS OF POLITICAL CONSCIENCE AND DEFENSES OF SECTIONAL HONOR

Alongside the development of a political structure that satisfied an unprecedented range of ambitions, Victorian politics contained a strain of reflection about basic issues of nationhood that seemed strangely at odds with the impulse toward organization. Despite debts to their fathers' political culture, young people in the North struggled with inherited positions on the civic implications of slavery, as if desperate to settle a troubling moral dilemma. Southerners, too, took up fundamental questions that led to secession. Yet in contrast to their contemporaries in the North, their probing was directed more at preserving communal well-being than at resolving the torments of conscience. The resurgence of emotional debate about the meaning of a nation divided by slavery was a spectacle of public self-examination that historians have often explored. Probably no single theory can account for events that many have felt proceeded with nearly inexorable certainty. But as a critical piece in the puzzle, it is important to draw attention to how much Victorian politics absorbed religion's task of defining life's goals.[57]

Contention about politics between young Victorians and their fathers raises the question of why sons took issues so seriously that they willingly disrupted family peace. The same story of Republicanism emerging in families recurred across the North. In New Hampshire in the 1840s, Franklin Sanborn broke as a teenager with his father and uncles, an assortment of proslavery Democrats and Whigs, to become an "Independent Democrat" opposed to the extension of slavery. In upstate New York, Chauncey Depew returned home from Yale in the 1850s as a Republican, to the dismay, he recalled in his memoirs, of his Democratic father and brothers. In Illinois, William Hern-

---

[57] Eric Foner has been instrumental in calling attention to the unsettling role of ideology in the mounting sectional crisis. See his *Free Soil, Free Labor, Free Men: The Ideology of the Republican Party before the Civil War* (1970), esp. pp. 1–10, and *Politics and Ideology in the Age of the Civil War* (1980), esp. "Politics, Ideology, and the Origins of the American Civil War," pp. 34–53. Kenneth Greenberg points out how important southerners' defense of their version of republicanism was to secession, in *Masters and Statesmen*, p. 143 and ch. 7. William E. Gienapp cautions not to overestimate the role of ideology in the sectional crisis, however. He acknowledges that the high level of voter interest increased the power of ideas in the political process, but writes that they were probably most influential among an articulate minority, in *The Origins of the Republican Party, 1852–1856* (1987), pp. 8–9.

don came back similarly from school with abolitionist leanings that so angered his father, the story is told, that he cast his son out of his home.[58] Within Victorian families as a rule, sons fought for autonomy from domineering fathers in order to satisfy high expectations for separate identities. Rather than interpret political battles across generations as simply a function of family tensions, however, these conflicts may be seen more profitably as disturbances brought by conscience to political allegiances that in the past had bound kin.[59]

Both memoirs and contemporary records help to make the case that the Victorians worked sincerely and often painfully to come to views they could live with on slavery and its consequences for the Union. Perhaps Lew Wallace inflated his idealism when he looked back in his autobiography, published in 1906, at his quest in the 1850s for "a position in ease of my conscience."[60] But his troubled ruminations were almost too sinuous to be fabricated. As Wallace moved through successive party affiliations in Indiana as a Whig, Free Soiler, Democrat, and Republican, he grappled with the problem of slavery, less in its absolute ethical significance, however, than as it affected the nation. Torn between beliefs that freedom was based in natural law and that the Constitution justifiably protected slavery, Wallace stayed with the Democrats in order to avert civil war, a prospect that filled him with "horror."[61] With some inconsistency, the same thought revived his love of military life, striking "with the force of a passion," and he formed a drill company in 1856 that met continuously until war broke out.[62] After Lincoln's election, Indiana's Democratic leaders advised that the state should secede with the South, and Wallace ended his political odyssey by quitting the party.[63] In principles, he was faithful throughout to the Union and arranged his thoughts on slavery and violence to serve the interest of preserving the country's civic integrity. His positions lacked the moral clarity of the message of a hero or martyr, but neither was Wallace unreflective, and his impulse to think and act correctly on questions that he made part of his own identity informed his political activity.

The diaries of George Templeton Strong and James Garfield reveal similar efforts of two very different men to find positions that satisfied conscience. Strong, the New Yorker, was as urbane and attuned to ironies as Garfield,

---

[58] Sanborn, *Recollections*, 1:23–4; Depew, *My Memories of Eighty Years* (1924), pp. 15–16; Donald, *Herndon*, pp. 10–14.

[59] See my discussion of conflict between fathers and sons in Chapters 2 and 4. Richard L. McCormick notes that fathers passed their political affiliations on to their sons, in *Party Period and Public Policy*, p. 164. The extraordinary demands placed on politics by this generation disrupted this pattern.

[60] Wallace, *Wallace*, 1:240.

[61] Ibid., 1:243. For Wallace's retrospective account of his actions in the 1850s, see ibid., 1: chs. 25–6.

[62] Ibid., 1:244–7. The quotation appears on 1:244.

[63] Ibid., 1: ch. 28.

from Ohio, was piously sincere. Both, however, stood aloof from politics until driven by a need to resolve their convictions in debate that nearly irresistibly drew in observers.

George Templeton Strong disdained politics as a young man. In 1844, he rued the lack of an American "conservative party" with elevated objectives, and he never grew used to the pedestrian temper of ward meetings that meant "bad grammar, bad manners, bad taste."[64] Nonetheless, Strong attended local Republican caucuses during Frémont's campaign in 1856 until he was "aweary" of them. His practical devotion was a sign of mounting ethical concerns that he turned over more than once in his journal.[65] Sometimes he phrased the issue as how best to protect civilization. He felt boxed in between disorderly abolitionists and southerners no better than "beggarly barbarians" in 1856, and decided to vote Republican in an effort to protect the "law-abiding and peace-loving" North.[66] At other times, he examined the meaning of slavery, a relationship of dependents to masters not by nature immoral, he thought, but so abused by southerners who denied slaves civil rights and education that in their hands slaveholding was "the greatest crime on the largest scale known in modern history."[67] During the 1850s, Strong came closer to knowing his own mind than to seeing how the available parties might represent his viewpoint. In September 1860, he still wavered between Republican and Constitutional Union candidates.[68] But throughout the foregoing decade, Strong's private reflection and public debate worked to invigorate one another. He wished from the start for a politics capable of moral aspiration, and the tenor of civic dialogue in the years before the war did indeed summon voices, including his own, eager to confront ideals.

James Garfield might not have permitted himself to engage in politics had he not been convinced that partisanship admitted moral gravity. At the time of his religious conversion in 1850 at age eighteen, Garfield disdained politics entirely, writing in his journal when he heard a stump speech that he was "perfectly disgusted with the principle."[69] But two impulses made him reconsider. The first was a desire, repeatedly repressed, to enter a calling more worldly than that of a teacher and lay preacher. On one occasion in 1854, he toyed with the idea of becoming a lawyer and, on another, warned himself that "bookworms are not *men*."[70] The second influence that led Garfield to politics was the conviction that Christianity required opposition to slavery and that politics was an acceptable means, to the point that he

[64] May 27, 1844, Oct. 28, 1856, *Diary of Strong,* ed. Nevins and Thomas, 1:236, 2:306.
[65] Oct. 28, 1856, ibid., 2:306.
[66] May 29, June 17, ibid., 2:275, 281.
[67] Oct. 19, 1856, ibid., 2:305.
[68] Sept. 14, ibid., 3:42.
[69] July 6, *The Diary of James A. Garfield,* ed. Brown and Williams (1967), 1:51.
[70] June 29, July 22, 1854, ibid., 1:256, 268.

allowed his female students to attend political speeches.[71] In 1859, when he ran for Congress at the request of a group of citizens, he admitted that he had long thought of "statesmanship" as a vocation, still warned himself that it was "seductive and dangerous," and yet won office with satisfaction.[72] So ill-contained were Garfield's career aspirations that his moral interest might be interpreted as an excuse for entering politics, had he not begun with such irreproachable piety that his concern for national rectitude almost surely must be read as sincere. More accurately, Garfield's path in the 1850s was that of a man who recognized, a bit sadly, that he was no saint. Precisely because he feared he was "losing spirituality of soul," he looked to politics as a middle ground where he could satisfy ambition and conviction at once.[73]

Few of these Victorians articulated their religious misgivings as clearly as Garfield while they turned in the direction of politics. But for this generation as a whole, spiritual difficulties loomed behind widespread willingness, even eagerness, to rethink civic ideals. Like Garfield, many must have found the political world a more hospitable place to work out a sense of purpose than a religious sphere defined by customs increasingly less compelling.[74] Rarely was the desire to come to terms with the problem of nationhood unconnected with a range of mundane longings, such as Wallace's taste for the military, Strong's maneuvering for social position, and Garfield's need for a challenging

[71] Nov. 2, 1855, Oct. 8, 1857, ibid., 1:273, 291.

[72] Aug. 22 and 23, 1859, ibid., 1:340, 341.

[73] Dec. 10, 1857, ibid., 1:308. Garfield figures largely in Margaret Thompson's account of nascent political professionalism in the 1870s, in *Spider Web*. She relied for evidence on his diaries, which provide an excellent view of the outlook of a Victorian politician. See *Diary of Garfield*, ed. Brown and Williams, vols. 2–4 (1872–81).

[74] Conversely, individuals whose religious convictions stayed most vital remained at a distance from politics. Although ministers and priests might have strong views on the polity, they often participated only marginally in civic contention. Among men of this inclination were Isaac Hecker, James Cardinal Gibbons, Octavius Brooks Frothingham, Edward Everett Hale, Moncure Conway, and Lyman Abbott. Overall, scholars differ about the role of religion in midcentury politics, but most studies suggest that the direct influence of religion was limited to a few issues advocated by specialized groups most vocal at specific times. Most would concur with Eric Foner that comparatively secular Republicanism displaced the "religiously oriented abolitionism of the 1830s," so that evangelical Protestantism most visibly influenced only the Radical Republicans. See *Free Soil, Free Labor, Free Men*, pp. 109–10. Most scholarly dispute centers on the evaluation of nativism, encompassing the religiously charged issues of temperance, sabbatarianism, and common-school curricula. Whereas Foner sees nativism as marginal to the Republican worldview, William Gienapp judges anti-Catholicism the principal "sub-theme" for Republicans after slavery (*Free Soil, Free Labor, Free Men*, p. 241; *Origins of the Republican Party*, p. 365). The ethnocultural analysis of Paul Kleppner makes issues of belief central to partisan conflict in the Third Party system (*Third Electoral System*). Two points must qualify a recognition of the importance of these questions. First, the thrust of nativism from a religious perspective was negative, making anti-Catholicism a gesture by a community of troubled faith to define the boundaries of acceptable belief by exclusion. The prominence of political nativism, in short, may be read as a sign of religious uncertainty. Second, most of these analyses implicitly set religious advocates in competition with comparatively secular voices, whether they were Republicans bent on the progress of free society or Kleppner's "antipietists" who were relatively unconcerned with crusading. The fact that religion tended to be identified with interest groups, in other words, signaled its loss of preeminence as a language for the culture as a whole. For a good summary of the political significance of religion after the war, see Keller, *Affairs of State*, pp. 136–42.

career. But the fact that scrutiny of civic values was mixed up with other ambitions is precisely the point. Trials of conscience in the North were not the crises of zealots, but of morally ordinary people unable to subordinate everything to principle. In this context, the impulse to reach a right understanding could be diverted, but it might equally gain practical power from its close relation to other goals.

Southern Victorians in the 1850s were similarly caught up in debate about first political principles, but there was less private compulsion to find, as Lew Wallace said, "a position in ease of my conscience." Certainly there was discussion, as in the North, on the significance of the Union. From the time Jabez Curry held his first political office in the Alabama legislature in 1847 at age twenty-two, he championed states' rights and the legitimacy of secession. Still, there is little evidence for this generation of southerners, either in memoirs or contemporary documents, of personal struggles to evolve views that afforded inner satisfaction. Rebecca Felton's recollections of the prewar decade focused on secession as an "awful crisis" for a person, such as herself, who was attached to the Union. But she recalled no ongoing effort to deal privately with points raised in heated national dialogue. The letters of Zebulon Vance show him as a thoughtful unionist Whig, yet by no means obsessed with probing and reviewing his position. Mary Chesnut's journal, in structure and language, reveals a woman less interested in weighing ideas than in demonstrating commitments in actions. Because her diary was a record of the odyssey of her section and herself, it is telling that she began with secession, not with earlier verbal contention. She expressed regret in her first entry in 1861 that she kept no journal during the past two "eventful years." But political moves and countermoves, bound up with discussion of theory, were not sufficiently gripping to make one begin to write who concluded, "I wanted them to fight and stop talking."[75]

On the surface, Chesnut's words confirm a stereotype of southerners as hotheaded. More subtly, however, her language calls attention to the communal focus of southern consciousness, one aspect of the notion of honor,

[75] Feb. 18, 1861, *Chesnut's Civil War*, ed. Woodward, pp. 3,4. On Curry, Felton, and Vance, see, respectively, Rice, *Curry*, pp. 23–4, 34–6; Felton, *Memoirs of Georgia Politics*, esp. p. 25; Vance to David F. Caldwell, Feb. 19, 1858, Vance to William Dickson, Dec. 11, 1860, in *Papers of Vance*, ed. Johnston, 1:32–6, 71–3. Felton also recalled that she spent most of the 1850s immersed in care of her growing family, which explains part of her passing concern with public issues (Talmadge, *Felton*, p. 15). But I have turned necessarily to southern women's response to sectional tensions, despite such complications, because the record of men's concern was so thin in comparison to northerners' personal struggles. For example, Wade Hampton served in state and national politics from 1852 until 1861 and spoke out as a moderate on policies connected with slavery. But throughout the 1850s, he never mentioned those issues in correspondence exchanged with his family. No doubt his public stand reflected sincere beliefs, yet Hampton does not seem to have been tormented privately as many northerners were. On Hampton's political career, see Wellman, *Giant in Gray: A Biography of Wade Hampton of South Carolina* (1949), pp. 30–6, and for his family letters, see Cauthen, ed., *Family Letters of the Three Wade Hamptons, 1782–1901* (1953), pp. 37–70.

that is part of the explanation for the slimmer record of private political
reflection than is found in the North.[76] Chesnut gave thought before secession
to the conditions of nationhood, as she was caught between the faith she
inherited from her father, "a South Carolina nullifier," and the opinion of
her husband's family, "equally pledged to the Union party."[77] Yet the activity
of her own mind was not of sufficient interest to Chesnut to merit a journal.
Nor did she use her diary, once begun, as an instrument of private moral
scrutiny, but made it a document to contain the collective experience of
herself and her Confederate neighbors. In short, Chesnut's concern with civic
ideals was inseparable from community dialogue. Like Curry and Vance,
Chesnut was less burdened personally by political issues than were northern
Victorians and less bent on establishing her peace of mind.[78]

Whatever the temper of the Victorians' political inquiry, reassessment of
fundamentals was a volatile process, particularly so because politics inherited
so much of religion's emotional force. Chesnut's preference for fighting over
talking was just one manifestation of the way reflection on basic commitments
strained the limits of reasoned debate. Contrary to the myth of southern
impulsiveness, northerners were at least as susceptible to extreme positions.
Young Harvard-educated men were enamored of violence, as if lawlessness
were an inseparable part of antislavery's appeal. By the late 1850s, Franklin
Sanborn and Thomas Wentworth Higginson had each spent more than a
decade forging principles of opposition to slavery when they helped to form
the "Secret Six" who sponsored John Brown's armed assault at Harpers Ferry,
Virginia.[79] Their antislavery efforts were explosive not simply because of
their taste for practical deeds, but because of their convictions' unsettled

[76] The notion of honor is a useful yet perhaps dangerously protean concept, and I focus here on the
community orientation of people governed by this ethic, as Wyatt-Brown emphasizes in *Southern Honor:
Ethics and Behavior in the Old South* (1982), p. xvi and ch. 2. Wyatt-Brown notes that there was less
soul-searching among southerners, p. 100. This does not mean that they were unconcerned with values,
simply that reflection was intimately connected with dialogue. See also Greenberg, *Masters and Statesmen*,
for discussion of the role of honor in southern politics. I am indebted to Johanna Shields for directing
my attention to the literature that explores the relation of honor to southern political culture.

[77] Feb. 18, 1861, *Chesnut's Civil War*, ed. Woodward, p. 4.

[78] It is also possible that the ethical difficulty of slavery imposed a timidity on the southern conscience.
Although there were many public apologies for servitude, much political theorizing in the South dealt
exclusively with the union's value and not, as in the North, with slavery's relation to nationhood. This
intellectual strategy seemed to leave one component of the dilemma unsaid, as if the implications of
slavery were too troubling to begin to unwind. Kenneth Greenberg has noticed this evasive style in
"The Proslavery Argument as an Antislavery Argument," where he proposes that southern ideologues
defended hierarchy without specifically defending slavery, in *Masters and Statesmen*, ch. 5. On defenses
of slavery, see also Faust, *Sacred Circle*, ch. 6. In contrast to my emphasis on southern communalism,
Faust discusses five southern intellectuals who, she argues, acted to overcome their sense of alienation
from southern society by presenting their contemporaries with defenses of slavery. To explain these
different emphases, it is important to keep in mind that because all of Faust's subjects were older than
these Victorians, it is possible that growing southern defensiveness about slavery worked in younger
people to limit self-scrutiny in psychological self-defense. In other words, perhaps there was less inwardness
among the Victorians because of the greater risk of self-condemnation.

[79] Sanborn, *Recollections*, 1: ch. 7; Edelstein, *Strange Enthusiasm*, ch. 12.

Figure 11. Thomas Wentworth Higginson (1823–1911). Although Higginson began his professional life as a Unitarian minister, he found antislavery activism and military service more suitable to his vigorous temperament. He was photographed here in 1862 as a Union colonel of black troops, an experience he recounted in *Army Life in a Black Regiment* (1870). Reproduced by permission of the Houghton Library, Harvard University, Cambridge, Massachusetts.

and unpredictable character. To follow Higginson through the 1850s is to watch a man who tried out nearly every available strategy: Free Soil politics, daring rescues of fugitive slaves, civil war in Kansas, disunion proposals, and finally a guerrilla-led slave uprising.[80] Against the mental background of Higginson's irresolution, violence was more a function of intelligence casting about for a way to close off difficult speculation than a preferred solution.

This political skittishness was not limited to New Englanders. David Donald portrays William Herndon in Illinois as repeatedly chafing at his friend Lincoln's moderation. Whereas Herndon wished for violence in Kansas and later longed for civil war and emancipation, Lincoln could better dis-

[80] Edelstein, *Strange Enthusiasm*, chs. 6–14.

tinguish between holding antislavery convictions and advocating uncom-promising solutions, and, to an extent, he held Herndon in check.[81] Donald seems to use these tense exchanges between law partners to signify the far more pervasive struggle of impatience with reason. In so doing, he effectively calls attention to the impulsive quality in discussions of nationhood that grew out of the depths of identity this thinking tapped and that brought men around to an attraction to violence that both matched their passion and obviated further thought.[82]

Feverish inclinations generated by ideological debate did coexist with more temperate, and indeed temporizing, influences, however, as Donald shows. Lincoln's counsel to Herndon may be seen as a product of a professional politician's instinct to contain charged issues within routine channels.[83] But the impetuous temper that seemed so eagerly to invite war was also diffused by three forces unrelated to increasingly structured partisanship: cyclical swings of political commitment, benign outlets for emotionalism, and the individualized tenor of inquiry.

A political setting characterized by intense personal involvement was subject to the natural fluctuations of feeling sometimes seen as one cause of religious revivals. An explanation of appealing simplicity to account for the periodic occurrence of revivals is that high-pitched emotion cannot long be sustained.[84] Just so, though American Victorians strained in politics for decisive action, their energy could be strangely ephemeral, leaving not reasonableness but lethargy in its wake. Sometimes attention to public issues varied with the timing of major elections. One year after the

---

[81] Donald, *Herndon*, pp. 83, 104–7, 132–4, 148–9.

[82] Many studies of violence in mid-nineteenth-century America have focused on the South, where much of the literature concerns the ritualized violence of a traditional society rather than outbursts associated with the uncertainties of a society in transition. See Wyatt-Brown, *Southern Honor*, esp. ch. 16; Greenberg, *Masters and Statesmen*, ch. 2; and most broadly, Bruce, *Violence and Culture in the Antebellum South* (1979). Greenberg, however, in effect acknowledges that traditional rituals of combat became particularly explosive in unfamiliar settings, when he proposes that southerners interpreted the events leading to war in terms of insulted honor and reprisal, in *Masters and Statesmen*, pp. 140–6. Studies of mobs and other assaults against minorities, especially in the North, are sensitive to the role of violence in defining boundaries in fluid social contexts. See, e.g., David Brion Davis, "Some Themes of Counter-Subversion: An Analysis of Anti-Masonic, Anti-Catholic, and Anti-Mormon Literature," in his *From Homicide to Slavery: Studies in American Culture* (1986), pp. 137–54, and Leonard Richards, *"Gentlemen of Property and Standing": Anti-abolition Mobs in Jacksonian America* (New York: Oxford University Press, 1970). Consider also Patricia Nelson Limerick's view that conquest was an integral part of westward expansion, in *The Legacy of Conquest: The Unbroken Past of the American West* (1987), as well as Richard Slotkin's kindred argument that acts of destruction were essential to the American identity, in *Regeneration through Violence: The Mythology of the American Frontier, 1600–1860* (1973). American culture's thorough familiarity with violence made it almost inevitable that thoughts of force surfaced in a time of crisis.

[83] That parties bring order to the nation's political culture is a widespread modern assumption, as is the view that the Civil War represented a hiatus in normal competition. See, e.g., Holt, *Political Crisis of the 1850s*, esp. ch. 1, and Foner, "Politics, Ideology, and the Origins of the American Civil War," in *Politics and Ideology*, pp. 35–6.

[84] For a statement of this view, see Martin Marty's "Foreword" to McLoughlin, *Revivals, Awakenings, and Reform: An Essay on Religion and Social Change in America, 1607–1977* (1978), p. vii.

Republicans ran their first presidential candidate, George Templeton Strong wrote: "Twelve months and a crisis have toned down people's interest in politics wonderfully. John C. Frémont is a very insignificant person, and Kansas a very remote insignificant territory."[85] Similarly, although the end of the Civil War at times inspired strategies to hold onto the strenuous life, the cessation of fighting also triggered abrupt withdrawal from political activity. Thomas Wentworth Higginson forcefully began Reconstruction by championing black civil rights, both in print and as a member of the Newport, Rhode Island, school board. But by 1867, he convinced himself that reform could proceed without him and began to write fiction.[86]

Other men's departures from public roles adhered even more bluntly to personal timetables, with little heed to civic interests abandoned by waning commitments. Frederick Law Olmsted was probably in poor health, as he professed, when he left his job as secretary of the Sanitary Commission in 1863. But his eager immersion in his new post as superintendent of a California mining project, far from the war, suggests that at least some of his fatigue was simply the exhaustion of his political energy before the cause was won.[87] In the case of William Herndon, his withdrawal into self-absorption was so radical that his flight from politics corresponded to the departure of respectability and even of sanity. For a decade after the war, Herndon moved with idiosyncratic fervor from issue to issue, including radical Reconstruction, liberal Republicanism, antimonopoly, and hard money. But when he quit politics and left Springfield for the country in 1875, he lived an impoverished and ill-kempt life, surrounded by rumors of drinking and attempted suicide, until, with one stroke, he resolved to reform himself and to run for the Illinois legislature in the early 1880s.[88] In sum, fierce convictions in Victorian politics flourished in a cyclical relation with languid indifference that verged on rebellion against public exertion. This was an atmosphere hospitable to heroic efforts to reach great objects, much less to the sustained pursuit of limited ends.

High-pitched dedication could also be diverted from practical efficacy by rituals that both celebrated, yet contained, emotion. Although George Templeton Strong scorned a "Union" meeting in 1850 as just so "much howling and hurrahing," the uses of dramatic display in Victorian politics were not frivolous.[89] Mass gatherings no doubt stirred feelings that in turn inspired action. Yet Strong was also probably correct that potentially useful energy evaporated in political hoopla. Perhaps the drill companies formed in the

---

[85] Nov. 2, 1857, *Diary of Strong*, ed. Nevins and Thomas, 2:368.

[86] Edelstein, *Strange Enthusiasm*, pp. 298–309. See my discussion in Chapter 2 of attempts by the Victorians to secure war-related employment immediately after the conflict.

[87] Roper, *FLO: A Biography of Frederick Law Olmsted* (1973), chs. 21–4.

[88] Donald, *Herndon*, pp. 260–3, 285–92.

[89] Oct. 31, 1850, *Diary of Strong*, ed. Nevins and Thomas, 2:24.

1850s, such as the Zouave-suited recruits Lew Wallace attracted, heightened a taste for war or perhaps playing soldier satisfied martial longings for a time.[90] But whether raised passions hastened or deferred civil conflict, much interest was consumed on the spot in the costuming, cheering, and marching. Political rituals were almost necessary in a professionalized republican system in order to reassure people that they still had a voice. But to the extent that visible dramas of commitment offered immediate excitement over long-term effectiveness, they guaranteed that much of the fire they generated would be quickly dispelled.

Decades before, Alexis de Tocqueville called attention to the paradox that the homogenized character of mass democracy was a function of its individualism, and he would have appreciated the way political pageantry stood beside private speculation in the Victorian era.[91] In fact, the issues explored were so difficult and the intelligence of the educated middle classes was so sharp that there was a tendency for public concern to dissipate in many separate directions. Changes in opinion over time, inevitable in a tumultuous period, accented the trend toward idiosyncratic positions. On the era's most difficult question, the problem of slavery, individual Victorians formulated and reformulated their judgments. Frederick Law Olmsted's famous trips to the "cotton kingdom" in the 1850s convinced him that "the field-hand negro" was "much worse than I had supposed before I had seen him" and hence less capable of self-government.[92] Charles Maclay, running for the California legislature in 1865, responded both to public pressure and private doubts when he told his constituents that he had changed his mind on black suffrage: "Their old masters would control their votes like the iron masters of Pennsylvania where I was born."[93] Certainly the process of probing values energized politics. But to look one by one at particular cases also leaves the impression that reflection might grow atomized to an extent that could deter the implementation of policy.

Thus the Victorians' political fervor mixed deep thoughtfulness with transient emotionalism and inspired extraordinary, yet ephemeral, activity. Their temperament inhibited reasoned discourse, but their outlook also brought

[90] Wallace belonged to one military company in the early 1840s and formed his own in the next decade. See his autobiography, *Lew Wallace*, 1:93, 245–7. In a social milieu very different from Indiana, Henry Lee Higginson in Boston belonged to a drill club before the war that consisted of friends from his childhood. See Perry, *Life and Letters of Henry Lee Higginson* (1921), p. 145. Marcus Cunliffe writes that as community-based militia units became less common in antebellum America, military companies structured as voluntary associations arose in their place, in *Soldiers and Civilians: The Martial Spirit in America, 1775–1865* (1968), ch. 7. Cunliffe observes that the atmosphere of the companies was clublike, with a strain of "make believe" running through their activities (p. 248).

[91] *Democracy in America* (1835), ed. Mayer (1969), esp. 1: pt. 2, ch. 7, and 2: pt.2, ch. 2.

[92] *The Cotton Kingdom: A Traveller's Observations on Cotton and Slavery in the American Slave States* (1861), ed. Schlesinger, intro. Powell (1984), p. 564.

[93] [Reasons for Accepting the Nomination for the State Senate], ms. address, Aug., 1865, Maclay Papers.

essential questions of nationhood to the forefront of public attention. No doubt concern with ideology seems strangely poised in an increasingly disciplined partisan system, but these developments came alike from the Victorians' determination to make politics satisfy social and intellectual drives of unusual seriousness because they were bound up with self-definition. Both trends conspired, moreover, to invite civil war.

WAR'S GALLERY OF HEROES AND BUREAUCRACY'S REVOLVING DOOR

The Civil War has been seen as a result of the failure of political dialogue, but it is no less true that the sections came to blows because of the kind of political activity in which the Victorians engaged. The impulse of the Victorian middle classes to open fundamental questions of nationhood made politics searching and volatile. Organizational expertise, acting initially as a break on civil disruption by inspiring loyalty to routine, became a tool to forward the campaigns of the warring sides. As scrutiny of basic commitments thus paired with technical facility, however, there was no sure source of rational intelligence capable of resolving differences, and the war reinforced these trends. The intense activity of war at once circumscribed discussion of issues and enhanced the importance of symbols that summoned feeling with little reflection. Bureaucracy expanded, but the crisis recruited many political amateurs unable to make the mechanisms of government work effectively to reach desired ends. That the Civil War heightened emotional engagement and opened new channels of public action was not without value. The conflict neither clarified objectives, however, nor secured a foundation for the use of conciliatory means.[94]

The prevailing impression among American Victorians was that warmaking precluded serious thought. Writing for the *Atlantic Monthly* in 1862, Thomas Wentworth Higginson complained that the war "interrupts all higher avocations."[95] James Garfield, serving in the Union army, complained to a friend that "I am shut out of the great world of doctrines and philos-

[94] Much historiography on the politics of the Civil War era falls into two opposing schools in assessing the impact of the war on the political process. On the one hand, there is an understandable tendency to see the war as a disruption of ordinary partisan competition. Whereas historians once laid blame on the errors of political leaders, more recent interpreters, such as Michael Holt, point to endemic weaknesses in party structure. See Pressley, *Americans Interpret Their Civil War*, sec. 7, and sec. 8, ch. 3; and Holt, *Political Crisis of the 1850s*. On the other hand, writers who stress that the two-party system functioned with little hiatus throughout the Civil War era downplay the conflict's cataclysmic quality, to the point that Eric Foner wrote in a seminal essay that the Civil War as a crisis was disappearing from historical interpretation. See his "Introduction" to *Politics and Ideology*, pp. 3–12. Several works that conform to the tendency to focus on long-term trends are cited in n. 35.
[95] "Letter to a Young Contributor," p. 409.

ophy."[96] This anti-intellectualism, precipitated by wartime conditions of passion and haste, did not altogether block political debate. Indeed, the impetus of civil crisis to an extent energized attempts to comprehend the direction of national development. As a young minister eager to gain a foothold in a new congregation in Terre Haute, Indiana, in 1860, Lyman Abbott cautiously refrained from bold political statements until the sectional crisis, and his pastorate, progressed. But by the time he left the church in 1865, Abbott had probed, in sermons and articles, what he saw as the divine mission of democratic government in its struggle with rebellious tyrants. Once he overcame his fear of dividing a church composed of settlers from the North and South, Abbott used the war as an occasion to clarify social ethics.[97] Similarly, when Edwin Godkin, soon assisted by Frederick Law Olmsted, began to publish the *Nation* in 1865, they made the magazine a vehicle for the examination of republicanism from a Republican perspective. Thus the *Nation* took up matters of equal rights, women's suffrage, the Freedmen's Bureau, and readmission of rebel states.[98] The heady excitement caused by the North's military triumph combined with a sense of the impending difficulty of political reconstruction to move these Victorians to create this new forum for public opinion.

Nonetheless, the disrupted conditions of wartime strongly encouraged intellectual simplification. In one crucial kind of reductionism, broad issues of nationhood tended to be compressed into concern with traits of personality such as loyalty and courage. The immense popularity in 1863 of Edward Everett Hale's story, *The Man without a Country,* must have come in part from the way Hale collapsed difficult political questions into the elemental problem of faithful service. In the fiction, the tale's antihero, Philip Nolan, assists the traitor, Aaron Burr, in 1807, and as punishment is confined to a ship where he may hear no news of his country for the rest of a long life.[99] Hale's lesson in patriotism was not unimportant in light of the ambivalent allegiances of many Americans. Even so, to preach on personal morality at a time when an understanding of public policy increasingly eluded the average

[96] Garfield to J. Harrison Rhodes, Feb. 12, 1862, in *The Wild Life of the Army: Civil War Letters of James A. Garfield,* ed. Williams (1964), p. 66.

[97] Brown, *Lyman Abbott, Christian Evangelist: A Study of Religious Liberalism* (1953), pp. 27–32.

[98] Roper, *FLO,* pp. 294–8. The range of issues discussed in the early years of the *Nation* suggests the way the prospect of Reconstruction vitalized ideological debate, a phase of limited duration as social policy became bogged down in bitter political disputes. On Reconstruction, see Foner, *Reconstruction.*

[99] *The Man without a Country* (1863). Gerald F. Linderman argues that courage, the centerpiece of a value system, was seen as critical for soldiers, in *Embattled Courage: The Experience of Combat in the American Civil War* (1987), esp. ch. 1. I do not disagree that the Victorian emphasis on character transcended the war itself, but the evidence of this study indicates that the focus on personal traits grew more pronounced during the crisis, a comparison over time Linderman does not make since he concentrates on the war itself. On the Victorian insistence on developing inner resources, see Daniel Walker Howe, "Victorian Culture in America," in Howe, ed., *Victorian America* (1976), esp. pp. 24–5.

Figure 12.   Ulysses Grant (1822–85). Grant appeared in this picture as a man of
plain but strong features and penetrating eyes, with his uniform casually unbuttoned.
Collodion glass-plate negative taken at Mathew Brady's studio about 1864. National
Portrait Gallery, Smithsonian Institution.

person's grasp reinforced a tendency to rely on symbols in political discourse
at the expense of reasoned explanation.

The wartime habit of approaching principles through traits of character
was furthered by the popularity of photographs of famous men. A consum-
mate showman, the photographer Mathew Brady may have realized that his
artistry fed a taste for heroes, as his pictures of notables appeared in peri-
odicals, as lithographs, and as separate prints. More clearly, Brady's public
was ready to invest their trust in personalities that shone through visual
images. The political success of Ulysses Grant epitomized the advent of a
public style in which symbols of heroism edged aside mastery of issues, and
it is hardly surprising that Brady scrambled in 1864 to photograph the

226

victorious general of Vicksburg in response to keen interest from political managers and magazine editors alike.[100]

William McFeely's provocative biography of Grant presents a portrait of a leader who was instinctively in tune with a political process oriented, on a popular level, around impressions of character. McFeely's theme is how much the public's image of Grant made possible his political career: more than by his appeal as a military hero, Grant drew people as "an ordinary American man" who sought "to make his mark" in the world and grandly succeeded.[101] He was not a passive symbol. Grant's political genius was his command of appearances. Thus during the tense period of conflict over Reconstruction involving Andrew Johnson and Congress, Grant, then commanding general of the army, crafted a persona for himself as a loyal soldier ready to serve his superiors and the people. That is not to say Grant was simply manipulative to advance his ambition, but his political convictions were narrowly focused and, in the end, lightly worn. In keeping with the Victorians' passionate interest in ideology, Grant felt strongly about a few causes and promoted them tirelessly, most notably devising a just Indian policy and annexing Santo Domingo. Yet he lacked the breadth of vision to set out coherent programs and, if issues grew troublesome, he let them go. In a bold move, he appointed Amos T. Akerman to the position of attorney general in 1870 so that Akerman might vigorously prosecute whites responsible for violence against southern blacks. But Grant fired him less than two years later for his impolitic zeal.[102]

McFeely concludes that Grant had "no sense of statecraft," and he means in part that Grant had no "grand design" based on an understanding of the potential of the American polity.[103] Yet if Grant were more in control of gesture than policy, the consequences were not wholly disadvantageous. The war hero, McFeely writes, presided as a political leader over a period when there was no war.[104] Although Grant did not unite all the people, as some southerners' peculiar alliance with the liberal Republicans in 1872 attests, his administration was at least not dangerously divisive at a time when white southerners remained seriously alienated from national politics. To a significant extent a self-made hero, Grant devised a political style that obscured real issues and fostered emotional resolution, and people turned to his leadership with relief.

Thus the Civil War helped to transform the prominent strain of ideological

---

[100] Horan, *Brady*, p. 55. On Brady's self-appointed role as an arbiter of political images, see Trachtenberg, *Reading American Photographs: Images as History, Mathew Brady to Walker Evans* (1989), chs. 1–2.

[101] *Grant*, p. xiii.

[102] Ibid., chs. 17, 19, 21, 22.

[103] Ibid., p. 385.

[104] Ibid., p. 332.

interest in late antebellum politics into a less intellectually taxing and more emotionally engaging popular reliance on symbols. This aspect of political culture was not unprecedented, because even as children the Victorians were schooled in the importance of heroes. The heightened stresses and passions of wartime, however, made the Victorians more inclined to rest content with allusions to principles rather than to seek the kind of meticulous intellectual command of public ethics so pronounced before the war in northern cases of conscience and southern struggles of honor. In an increasingly separate area of political life, the mechanisms of governing were also changed by the war, though, once again, in predictable ways.

The Civil War underscored the importance of political professionalism and bureaucratic organization in Victorian political culture, yet it also created conditions that challenged the smooth operation of the state. Neither the Union nor the Confederacy could have mobilized armies so quickly without the seasoned expertise of men familiar with the channels of power. The dependency of the war effort on professionals' experience was clearest in the South. Not only was the Confederate government created from scratch, but by nearly the same stroke, the new heads of state put armies in the field. Among the Victorians studied here, the men who figured prominently in the activity of Montgomery, Richmond, and the Confederate state capitals were seasoned party politicians. Most had served in Congress and a few elsewhere, such as Robert Tyler, who left his post as chairman of Pennsylvania's Democratic party to become Register of the Confederate Treasury.[105] Their years in the American government now made possible their resistance to it.

Yet the unsettlement of war also revealed the tenuous hold of statecraft on Victorian political affairs. At the same time that the responsibilities of government became more complex, people entrusted with power either disregarded established practices or were unfamiliar with them. Amateurism, in the worst sense of pettiness or ignorance or both, remained a real possibility in a political system poised between informal public service and a potentially responsive and responsible state. Southern politics during the war was particularly disordered and contentious. Across the South, political parties, in disarray in the late 1850s, disappeared altogether. In Richmond, policies were initiated nearly as much in drawing rooms as in the offices of state. The most visible result of the erosion of binding procedures was the high

---

[105] Jabez Curry and Zebulon Vance served in the House of Representatives from 1857 to 1861. The husbands of Mary Chesnut, Virginia Clay, and Varina Davis, all older than their wives, held seats in the Senate in the 1850s, while Jefferson Davis was also Franklin Pierce's secretary of war. Wade Hampton, appointed to the Senate in 1858, was the only one of this group who never entered Confederate politics, choosing instead to serve in the army, perhaps because of his cool support of secession. In all of these cases, experience in the federal government followed participation in state politics. See Rice, *Curry*, pp. 27, 34; Tucker, *Vance*, chs. 5–7; and Wiley, *Confederate Women*, pp. 8, 47, 91–3. On Robert Tyler, see Coleman, *Tyler*, pp. 135–8.

incidence of feuding. A governor such as Zebulon Vance, who withheld North Carolina's support from Richmond, seemed to be moved as much by petty jealousy as by principle or self-interest. More dramatically, the Confederate capital was a web of alliances that centered on feelings about Jefferson Davis. Almost from the beginning of the war, Mary Chesnut recorded conversations such as these remarks she heard in August 1861: "Mrs. Wigfall said triumphantly [that] Cobb, Hammond, Keitt, Boyce, and Banks were in the coalition against Jeff Davis. . . . She says – unless it be Clay of Alabama – that Davis has not a personal friend."[106]

Historians of Confederate politics have been aware of how difficult it was to resolve differences once traditional guideposts, such as parties, were obscured. But they have said less about possible reasons for this pattern of change. Southerners' wish to appear united has been offered as one motive for their disinclination to revive parties. In addition, structured institutions disengaged from community customs were rooted less deeply in southern society, so that southerners were often content, for example, to pursue religion without regular church attendance and to enjoy leisure outside formal clubs. Just so, parties may have been considered superfluous or even intrusive in a political culture with implicit rules.[107]

A third source of contention corresponds to a trend also found in the wartime North, the recruitment of amateurs during the political crisis. In the South, antiprofessionalism, an emphasis on pure principles, and the rising influence of women all contributed to the resurgence of amateurism. Despite the Confederacy's initial reliance on political professionals, popular doubts of leaders' abilities combined with the disruption of entrenched channels of power to allow the election of progressively less experienced men, as Thomas Alexander and Richard Beringer have shown.[108] Suspicion of manipulative professionals, frequently articulated before the war, now fueled open rebellion by the voting public as wartime hardships increased. In a shift of values, moreover, loyalty could be as important a criterion of selection for public office as expertise. When William Montague Browne, a native of Ireland and the editor of the Democratic *Washington Constitution* before the war, sided with the Confederacy in 1861, he was rewarded with the post of assistant secretary of state.[109] As politics spilled over official channels to

[106] Aug. 8, *Chesnut's Civil War*, ed. Woodward, pp. 138–9.

[107] See citations on partisanship in the Confederacy in n. 35. The most thorough study is Alexander and Beringer, *The Anatomy of the Confederate Congress: A Study of the Influences of Member Characteristics on Legislative Voting Behavior, 1861–1865* (1972), esp. chs. 2, 12. Although national parties functioned in the South before and after the war, Kenneth Greenberg argues that the southern commitment to statesmanship, understood as nonpartisan rule by an elite, was an attitude at odds with competition that limited the impact of party behavior, in *Masters and Statesmen*, esp. ch. 3. Whether or not this is the whole answer, the structure of Confederate politics indicates that southerners' attachment to parties was somewhat superficial.

[108] *Anatomy of the Confederate Congress*, p. 25.

[109] Coulter, *William Montague Browne: Versatile Anglo-Irish American, 1823–1883* (1967), pp. 80–2.

involve Richmond society, finally, women were drawn into the political process. Intelligent but undisciplined by political experience, included in discussions yet excluded from active roles, Confederate wives must have stirred fires that gave the Confederate government a tone of intrigue. Although women alone were clearly not responsible for Richmond's factionalism, Mary Chesnut must have appreciated the danger of their unregulated political enthusiasm when she contrasted the behavior of the gossiping Mrs. Wigfall with that of her husband: "Wigfall, fresh from the army and 'bearded like the pard,' stroked his beard and said nothing. He has too much common sense not to see how quarreling among ourselves must end."[110]

In the North, the dilemma of an expanding bureaucracy managed by political amateurs resembled the South's situation. Much as the Confederate government was opened to a wider range of community voices as professionalism was questioned and loyalty honored, the Union gained followers due to the high esteem granted within the party system to ideological fervor. In the 1850s, the Republican party took shape to a great extent around the single principle of the containment of slavery. During the war, the Republican administration absorbed people who qualified mainly by their ability to think correctly on antislavery and the need to fight to achieve that goal.[111] There were real benefits gained by this infusion of amateurism. Fresh idealism may have reinforced the ethical interests of government, although to pass party approval, an individual's values had to conform to standardized phrasing that may also have compromised his integrity. In addition, some amateurs brought valuable organizational talent from enterprises outside politics. George Templeton Strong must have aided the quasi-official Sanitary Commission by managerial techniques learned as a college and church trustee.[112]

---

[110] Aug. 8, 1861, *Chesnut's Civil War*, ed. Woodward, p. 139. In light of the more traditional attitude toward women in the South (see Chapter 4), it seems ironic that they so easily crossed over from private to public life during the war. But the puzzle is perhaps resolved by the observation that a more traditional community may also be less tightly structured, making the barriers between different spheres of activity less rigid. Laurel Thatcher Ulrich thus argues that boundaries in colonial society were more permeable for women than they would later become, in *Good Wives: Image and Reality in the Lives of Women in Northern New England, 1650–1750* (1982), esp. pp. 35–6, 49–50. Although these southern women remained active on the margin of politics after the war, by participating in Confederate commemorative organizations for example, they did not exert so strong an influence on governing itself as during the time of crisis.

[111] In a revisionist challenge to the long-standing assumption that antislavery principles were central to the formation of the Republican party, William Gienapp argues that the party took shape around a variety of issues and conformed to ordinary assumptions about the behavior of parties, in *Origins of the Republican Party*, esp. pp. 8–9. Eric Foner, in contrast, emphasizes the importance of ideology, in *Free Soil, Free Labor, Free Men*.

[112] By 1861, Strong had been recruited as a trustee of several New York churches and schools, including Columbia College. His first appointment was as a vestryman at the Church of the Redemption in 1843, when he was twenty-three years old. By 1857, he served so many organizations that he wrote with bemusement of his latest post as "a trustee or director or something" of Trinity School. See Apr. 25, 1843, May 11, 1857, *Diary of Strong*, ed. Nevins and Thomas, 1:201, 2:334. Probably voluntary

Yet there were also ambitious government projects run by individuals with little relevant experience. As the war progressed, military service blended with right thinking as requirements for Republican posts and Union victories increased the social jurisdiction of civil authority. In these challenging circumstances, soldiers such as U. S. Grant, O. O. Howard, and Ely Parker found themselves responsible for major social programs. Charges of corruption directed at the Grant administrations, the Freedman's Bureau, and the Bureau of Indian Affairs, forcing the resignation of Howard and Parker, were probably exaggerated, given pervasive Victorian suspicions of bureaucracy. But the presence of enough wrongdoing to foster misgivings and to justify formal investigations indicates that these three men were not altogether in command of the agencies of which they had formal control.[113]

Perhaps all major American wars have drawn inexperienced people into the political arena because of the disruption of established routines, the extraordinary need for talent, and the high pitch of conviction in the population at large. Victorian politics, combining elements of amateur and professional outlooks, was sufficiently unsophisticated to allow wartime amateurism to stir contention and to block effective implementation of policy. Over time, the Victorian party system and bureaucracy had an independent momentum, however, that limited the impact of amateurism. The impulse among Republicans to let Reconstruction go, to allow the return to office of former Confederates, and once again to take up economic and social issues related to national development was an endorsement of government as usual. In a political system rapidly becoming professionalized, the norm was perceived as a state controlled by men adept at manipulating the mechanisms of government.[114] Accusations of greed and corruption, voiced loudly in the 1870s, reflected second thoughts about the direction of change. But because attacks were often launched by professionals themselves, denunciation acted as a ritual expiation that contained anxiety and protected the status quo. So eager were the Victorians for government's benefits that it is unlikely that many would have chosen to return, if they could, to an amateur system, however ethically superior it might be. Thus when Garfield was elected president in 1880, voters were less swayed by the moral commitments that

associations were more tightly organized in cities than elsewhere, but Gregory Singleton has proposed that such experience in benevolent activities was sufficiently widespread to assist, by overlapping personnel, the development of American business, in "Protestant Voluntary Associations and the Shaping of Victorian America," in Howe, ed., *Victorian America*, pp. 47–58. The same argument can be made with respect to the organization of American government.

[113] On the charges of corruption, see McFeely, *Grant*, chs. 20, 24; Howard, *Autobiography of Oliver Otis Howard* (1907), 2: ch. 61; Parker, *Parker*, ch. 14.

[114] Perhaps the very profundity of the social and ethical issues raised by Reconstruction guaranteed that discussion and action would be limited. For recent interpretations, see Foner, *Reconstruction*, and Keller, *Affairs of State*, chs. 2, 6.

lured him toward politics in 1859 than by the narrower party loyalty and the degree of mastery of the legislative process that he had later acquired.[115]

Recollections of Garfield's service in the Union army were also important, a sign of the persistent influence in politics of symbols generated by the war. At the same time that the Victorians coped with self-doubt by condemning corruption, they reinforced their self-esteem by bringing Civil War commemoration to bear on politics. North and South, the Victorians relied on celebration of war to soften the pragmatism of political professionalism and to take part, at least emotionally, in a civic culture increasingly handled by experts.[116] Sometimes political managers carefully orchestrated efforts to connect recollections of wartime idealism with partisan campaigning. They invited organizations of uniformed veterans, for example, to attend party events. Other demonstrations of loyalty to a past where military and political achievement blended together were more spontaneous. The rapt nationwide deathwatch for Ulysses Grant, dying of cancer during the summer of 1885, was surely fueled by detailed daily accounts of his health in a profit-seeking press. More deeply, however, people wished to honor a man who, despite his mediocre presidency, seemed to stand for an elemental democratic virtue needed, in the eyes of many, to sustain the party system. As Grant commanded the loyalty of his countrymen and countrywomen near death as he had in earlier life, he inadvertently taught a final lesson: that symbols had the power to obscure such political problems as inequalities, concentrated power, and shallow emotionalism, and thereby to unite diverse citizens in a political culture that allowed an imperfect system to continue to function.[117]

However one judges mass politics, study of these Victorians suggests that the Civil War, as an event and a symbol, helped to entrench collective rituals in American political life. As the "howling and hurrahing" heard by George Templeton Strong became increasingly audible, however, the soul-searching quality that marked politics in the 1850s all but disappeared in the middle classes. Postbellum public leaders engaged in passionate discussion of monetary policy, national expansion, and civil service reform. Voices on the

[115] This is the judgment of Garfield's biographers, Leech and Brown, *The Garfield Orbit* (1978), p. 219 and ch. 10.

[116] Two recent interpretations of Civil War commemoration that stress its compensatory functions are Foster, *Ghosts of the Confederacy: Defeat, the Lost Cause, and the Emergence of the New South, 1865–1913* (1987), esp. pt. 2, and Linderman, *Embattled Courage*, pp. 179–84. Both writers see war remembrance as the way Americans coped with disturbing socioeconomic change. In light of the argument in this chapter, celebrations of the war also served to offset ambiguous developments in republican government. Mary R. Dearing, on the other hand, proposes that veterans' organizations played a direct political role as practical interest groups intended to win political favors for members, in *Veterans in Politics: The Story of the G.A.R.* (1952).

[117] McFeely, *Grant*, ch. 28. The Civil War was not the first event to bring patriotic pageantry into political culture. Fourth of July celebrations throughout the antebellum decades and oratory glorifying the Mexican War are two earlier examples of the importance of drama in the American political system. See Somkin, *Unquiet Eagle*, ch. 4; and Johanssen, *To the Halls of the Montezumas*, esp. ch. 5. The Civil War simply increased Americans' reliance on collective emotional display.

margin of politics, such as those of farmers, workers, and women, increasingly raised questions about their civil rights and political power. But the Victorians themselves, for the most part, were no longer as troubled about their basic commitments as they had been.[118] The simple need for rest from taxing efforts after two decades of debate and struggle explains their loss of intensity to an extent. Perhaps, too, they felt that the key issue, the place of human bondage in society, was settled. But it is also important to remember that the change in their political temper took place in the midst of a decisive, though muted, spiritual crisis. The moral fervor that informed late antebellum civil life represented a search for meaning in politics undertaken because religion spoke less clearly to longings for both personal and common direction. But the Victorians' loss of vital faith was a process in time, and this insistent probing had an end as well as a beginning. The extraordinary demands placed on politics by the sectional crisis worked inadvertently as a vehicle to set the Victorians more comfortably in the secular world. If they had stopped asking altogether what sense they could make of their experience, they would have scarcely been human. Yet the poignancy of those questions, now posed in a political context, would never be greater than during the first decades when religious conceptions lost a firm hold on the outlook of the middle classes.

Many features of Victorian politics may be judged problematic from the viewpoint of vital republicanism. Professionals' handle on power, popular reliance on emotionalism for public involvement, the divisive individualism of a polity that allowed wide-ranging private reflection, and inattention to collective rights all inhibited democratic dialogue. Nonetheless, the Victorians made politics a serviceable tool for a complex community, capable of responding to pragmatism and idealism alike. Strangely, however, the Victorians' thinking was changed less by the virtues of the political process than by its breakdown. Despite all the strengths of the peacetime culture they created, the Victorians' attitude toward themselves was affected most critically by the Civil War.

[118] Keller concurs that politics after the war was less ideologically charged and more committed to maintaining party identity, in *Affairs of State*, p. 238. Key studies that explore the social and political roots of postbellum populism and labor agitation are Hahn, *The Roots of Southern Populism: Yeoman Farmers and the Transformation of the Georgia Upcountry, 1850–1890* (1983), and Montgomery, *Beyond Equality: Labor and the Radical Republicans, 1862–72* (1967). Though women (mainly of the middle classes) became more vocal in public life, the reform they sought narrowed from women's rights, broadly conceived, to women's suffrage. They continued to agitate for basic principles, but, like the Victorians overall, they lost much of the original adventurous quality in their thinking. On this transformation, see Flexner, *Century of Struggle*.

Figure 13. Henry Lee Higginson (1834–1919). As a wealthy Boston stockbroker and the founder of the Boston Symphony Orchestra, Higginson sat for this portrait by John Singer Sargent in 1903. So painfully indecisive about his vocation as a young man, Higginson's commanding presence in Sargent's painting conveyed the self-esteem Higginson finally achieved. Courtesy of the Harvard University Portrait Collection, Harvard University, Cambridge, Massachusetts.

6

Victorian America and the Civil War

> War feels to me an oblique place—
> *Emily Dickinson, 1863*

There are few more moving declarations of the romantic's hope that the temporal world will satisfy transcendent longings than this passage from Henry Thoreau's essay, "Walking," published in 1862, the year of his death:

So we saunter toward the Holy Land, till one day the sun shall shine more brightly than ever he has done, shall perchance shine into our minds and hearts, and light up our whole lives with a great awakening light, as warm and serene and golden as on a bankside in autumn.[1]

As a pilgrimage became a contemplative saunter and revelation came through the sun's natural rays and salvation blended indistinguishably with a hillside beckoning the sojourner to reflection and rest, nature's splendor, in Thoreau's eyes, fully answered the needs of the human spirit for inspiration and rest. Had Thoreau looked beyond nature to Victorian society, he would have found that his contemporaries, moved by their unsettling distance from traditional religious truths and their excitement at the tangible world's potential gifts, had created a culture as vibrant and rich as his autumn landscape. What Thoreau did not live to see and perhaps would have scarcely believed was the critical role played by the Civil War in bringing the Victorians to value their experience.

The characteristics of American Victorian culture that made it a source of fulfillment to the middle classes were well established by 1861. Promising careers, varied leisure, families steeped in emotion, and politics involving high drama all offered the Victorians attainable rewards. Even religion, viewed as a social pursuit, held sources of interest – visits to non-Protestant services, intriguing superstitions, reflections on the implications of science. Yet on the verge of war, the Victorians were unable to find contentment. The disturbing problems that were mixed with their society's virtues were

---

[1] "Walking," *The Portable Thoreau,* ed. Bode (1964), p. 630.

part of the reason. Personal isolation, the routinization of public enterprises, and the anonymity of mass activities were conditions sufficient to make the Victorians pause. But their discontent grew, too, from a half-formed but compelling wish for a defining event, an experience like a religious conversion that would allow flawed human beings to come to terms with themselves. By itself, the Civil War could not have fulfilled this difficult task, no matter how significant the social, political, and intellectual issues raised by the crisis were. Instead, it was the Victorians' determination to make the war a vehicle of spiritual resolution that gave it such a central place in their lives.[2]

Whereas the previous chapters interpret American Victorian culture through the actions and varied writings of individuals, this conclusion concentrates on memoirs as a narrative form with religious and philosophical implications. Because this is the book's most literary discussion, it is necessary to clarify my view of how these recollections relate to Victorian values more broadly. The analysis assumes that the Victorians' published reminiscences were selective readings of the past inspired by this generation's shared cultural dilemma. The perspective produced inhered not only in formal literary works, in my judgment. Rather, those crafted writings precisely articulated a widespread sensibility. The memoirs may be used to approach that state of mind. The outlook consisted of an affirmation of temporal possibilities. As a matter of subjective thoughts and feelings, this posture of resolution stood in tension with some troubling aspects of Victorian society, such as personal restriction and social fragmentation, and in accord with more promising trends toward self-determination and emotional reward. To explore the many consequences of Victorian culture's sometimes strained external relationships is beyond this study's intent. In keeping with my original purpose to investigate the inward dynamics of Victorian personalities, the focus of this chapter is the process whereby the Victorians quelled their restlessness.[3]

---

[2] Among studies that assess the mutual influence of the Civil War and American culture, the most comprehensive are Fredrickson, *The Inner Civil War: Northern Intellectuals and the Crisis of the Union* (1965); Barton, *Goodmen: The Character of Civil War Soldiers* (1981); Linderman, *Embattled Courage: The Experience of Combat in the American Civil War* (1987); Jimerson, *The Private Civil War: Popular Thought During the Sectional Conflict* (1988); Mitchell, *Civil War Soldiers* (1988); Paludan, *"A People's Contest": The Union and the Civil War, 1861–1865* (1989); and Rable, *Civil Wars: Women and the Crisis of Southern Nationalism* (1989). There are also provocative analyses of the relationship of war and culture that pertain to other conflicts through which some or all of the Victorians lived. On the Mexican War, see Johanssen, *To the Halls of the Montezumas: The Mexican War in the American Imagination* (1985), and on the Spanish-American War, Linderman, *The Mirror of War: American Society and the Spanish-American War* (1974). Some of these Victorians also lived through World War I. There is much debate among historians about the role of World War I in undermining the attitudes commonly seen as Victorian. See esp. Kennedy, *Over Here: The First World War and American Society* (1980), ch. 4, and May, *The End of American Innocence: A Study of the First Years of Our Own Time, 1912–1917* (1959). On the same process in Europe, see Fussell, *The Great War and Modern Memory* (1975), and Eksteins, *Rites of Spring: The Great War and the Birth of the Modern Age* (1989).

[3] For critical overviews of the writing inspired by the Civil War, including memoirs, see Wilson,

The Civil War

A VICTORIAN TALE OF WAR

How thoroughly the Victorians' questions shaped their experience of war and later their recollections may be seen in the idiosyncratic story about the conflict they told. From the Civil War until the present day, perhaps two issues have commanded most attention, the meaning of mass suffering and of emancipation, race, and racism. These moral concerns have evoked many interpretations. For Ambrose Bierce, born in 1842 and thus slightly younger than these Victorians, war's horrors became tokens, in his stories in the 1890s, of the gruesome tricks of fate that mercilessly tested human endurance.[4] For W. E. B. DuBois, writing in *The Souls of Black Folk* in 1903, the Civil War was "the dawn of freedom," but so limited in the generosity and justice of whites that "despite compromise, war, and struggle, the Negro is not free."[5] Neither of these points of view represented the Victorians' perspective. Instead, their pressing need to turn the Civil War into a tool of self-validation made them emphasize mastery of self and circumstance in tales of dogged optimism that pertained to whites only.

The Victorians began the work of tailoring the facts of war to their own cultural ends in their handling of suffering. Not unaware of war's many kinds of pain, they moved to subsume evidence of ill fortune and portended despair in narratives of moral triumph. Two accounts composed close in time to the war, one by John DeForest and one by Mary Chesnut, reveal the Victorians' deep sensibility to suffering, as well as their equally strong will to struggle against the temptation to succumb to desolation. In a description of battle first published in *Harper's New Monthly* magazine in 1867, DeForest offered this view of war's sadness:

That man lay near me, dying from a terrible wound through the abdomen, his fair face growing whiter with every laboring breath and his light blue eyes fixed vacantly

---

Patriotic Gore: Studies in the Literature of the American Civil War (1962), and Aaron, *The Unwritten War: American Writers and the Civil War* (1973).

[4] See, e.g., "An Occurrence at Owl Creek Bridge," "Chickamauga," and "One of the Missing," all originally published in 1892, in *The Collected Writings of Ambrose Bierce*, ed. Clifton Fadiman, 3d ed. (New York: Citadel Press, 1966), pp. 9–23, 30–40. Writers younger than the Victorians often lost hold of the older generation's resilient optimism. Like Bierce, Stephen Crane (1871–1900) was another naturalistic writer who used the Civil War as a setting in which to explore human trials. On the Civil War fiction of Bierce and Crane, see Aaron, *Unwritten War*, chs. 12, 14. But age was not a simple determinant of how observers responded to the conflict. Henry James (1843–1916) neither took for granted that war-making contained hidden sources of value, as did the Victorians, nor assumed that violence forced enduring doubts about life's meaning, as did the naturalists, but set up a contrast in his Civil War fiction between the battlefield and the home as an ordering device to help himself and his readers organize their perceptions. With the fighting as a distant background, James wrote of the domestic consequences of war, in effect staking out a sphere of social intercourse of which he could make sense and on which he would build his subsequent career. See "The Story of a Year" (1865), "Poor Richard" (1867), and "A Most Extraordinary Case" (1868), in *The Complete Tales of Henry James*, ed. Leon Edel (London: Rupert Hart-Davis, 1962), 1:49–98, 191–258, 321–68.

[5] *The Souls of Black Folk* (New York: Penguin, 1989), p. 34.

Figure 14.   Mary Boykin Chesnut (1823–86). A passionate chronicler of the Confederate cause in the voluminous diary she kept during the Civil War, Chesnut repeatedly returned to the literary, and highly personal, task of revising her journal during the postwar years she spent in Camden, South Carolina. South Caroliniana Library, University of South Carolina.

on the glaring sky. He was about twenty-seven and looked to me like a respectable, intelligent American mechanic, probably a husband and father. I glanced at him pitifully from time to time as he patiently and silently drew towards his end. Such individual cases of suffering are far more moving than a broad spectacle of slaughter.[6]

Mary Chesnut did not have to go near the battlefield to hear similar tales of loss. Although she destroyed her original diary of 1863, she later reproduced this scene with undiminished pathos in her revised journal of the early 1880s:

Then came fatal Sharpsburg. My friend Colonel Means – killed on the battlefield, his only son wounded and a prisoner. His wife had not recovered from the death of her other child, Emma, who had died of consumption early in the war. She was lying on a bed when they told her of her husband's death – and then they tried to keep Stark's condition from her. They think now that she misunderstood and believed him dead, too. She threw something over her face. She did not utter one word. She remained quiet so long, someone removed the light shawl which she had drawn

[6] *A Volunteer's Adventures: A Union Captain's Record of the Civil War*, ed. Croushore (1946), p. 138.

over her head. She was dead. Miss Mary Stark said afterward: "No wonder! how was she to face life without her husband and children. That was all she had ever lived for."[7]

For both writers, the sorrow of war was less a matter of masses of dead than of trials of personality, as circumstances assaulted the wills of individuals and tested their strength. In the scenes recorded here, the resources to combat hopelessness that threatened both the victims and the Victorians who observed them were tested together.

The Victorians' impulse to contain suffering in dominant messages of human resilience prevailed in both cases. Neither DeForest nor Chesnut let the torment of helplessly witnessing sadness overwhelm their narratives. Instead, they emphasized people's ability to surmount distress. The theme centering the letters and articles that DeForest produced as a Union officer was the heroism of ordinary men, evoked less often by catastrophe than by unrelenting and unglamorous discomforts. Battle scenes filled just a small part of the collection of war writings eventually published as *A Volunteer's Adventures*. The fatigue of forced marches, the risks of illness, and the oppression of boredom more severely tried his troops. As a court martial judge, DeForest saw drunkenness and desertion. But a reader still comes away with the sense that his men generally rose to the challenges war imposed. " 'Grand is the heart which is ennobled, not crushed by sorrow,' " said the hero of DeForest's novel, *Miss Ravenel's Conversion from Secession to Loyalty*, Captain Colburne.[8] Just so, DeForest's tenacious optimism was based on his acceptance of loss as a provocation to find deeper sources of strength.

"These sad, unfortunate memories – let us run away from them," declared Chesnut at the end of her chronicle of Mrs. Means. Her words were in part simple evasion, but also an invitation to recollect what made life endurable after all.[9] Chesnut never gave precisely the same answer twice in her long wartime journal, but she succeeded time and again in fighting off the desolation that threatened her by summoning thoughts of redeeming things. In this instance, she called to mind her friendship with two vibrant young women, Buck and Mamie Preston: "There was nothing then or ever in the

[7] Sept. 23, 1863, *Mary Chesnut's Civil War,* ed. Woodward (1981), p. 426. This date and all others used in reference to this volume denote diary entries.

[8] *Miss Ravenel's Conversion from Secession to Loyalty* (1867), ed. Haight (1955), p. 457. For instances of human weakness that DeForest witnessed as an officer and particularly as a court martial judge, see *Volunteer's Adventures*, pp. 41–6. For his sense of the soldiers' tenacity, see his report of the siege of Port Hudson (pp. 103–46). DeForest oscillated between elevated and mundane images to describe people's capacity for spiritual survival, as if uncertain about the source of their resilience. Whereas the passage quoted from *Miss Ravenel* blended the language of romance with allusions to Christian "sorrow," his soldiers in *Volunteer's Adventures* survived with a "surly patience, reminding me of bulldogs and bloodhounds" and, again, "the patience of cats" waiting for prey (pp. 108, 118). Compelled by a private imperative to locate reserves of inner strength, DeForest wrote in an intellectual context where it was unclear if man inherited the means of self-renewal from angels or beasts.

[9] *Chesnut's Civil War,* ed. Woodward, p. 426.

Confederacy so sweet, so lovely, so stately, so accomplished as these interesting friends of mine."[10] Not only was Chesnut enlivened by their friendship but awed by the irrepressible vitality of Buck herself. "She wore the black mantle several days," Chesnut observed after the death in a duel of Buck's friend: "But the days were beautiful, and she so young and lighthearted, her grief was but a summer cloud − fleeting and leaving no trace behind for any of them."[11] In temperament, Chesnut was nearly the antithesis of Buck, forever verging on "a sad, an anxious, state" when not actually taking to bed as attacks of nerves compounded real illness. For all her love of Buck, she sensed that her young friend's sunniness was immature.[12] "We went to our brave boy's funeral," Chesnut wrote after the death of Preston Hampton: "Buck ran away. 'I can't bear to think of Preston,' she said, 'Can't bear to hear any more moaning, and weeping and wailing − if I do, I shall die.' "[13] Yet Chesnut saw just as clearly how much she needed the proximity of Buck's feisty resilience to protect her from her own impulse to despair. Were Chesnut's diary simply one woman's view, it might have been an unqualified dirge for a dying culture. But she deliberately invited voices besides her own to respond to events because she knew that dialogue, in her life and in her narrative, infused essential notes of hopefulness that would have eluded her grasp were she alone.[14]

Why did DeForest and Chesnut absorb the pain of war in tales of resistance to demoralization? The Victorians encountered war's trials as a special instance of the challenge to comfortable and secure meaning that informed their lives. Scarcely ready as civilians to watch religion's power diminish without scrambling to forge new values, no more were they ready to let suffering stand in war as the final word. The will to recover a positive message threaded equally through peace and war because they perceived the conflict's trials to be spiritual as much as physical and thus akin to the uncertainties they contested everyday. What shook DeForest's courage as he watched the dying soldier was less the sight of pain than DeForest's empathy with what the man must be thinking as he left behind a life as a worker, husband, and father in the dehumanizing circumstances of battle. Similarly, not only was the despair of Mrs. Means the result of

[10] Ibid., p. 430. Gay social life was another resource that counterbalanced sadness for Chesnut, but she recurred most often to the company of women. For another example of her solace in the friendship of young women, see ibid., p. 91. When she reworked her journal in the 1880s, she set some of her most valued observations in a dramatic setting consisting of dialogue among "our party of matrons," p. 171. See also ibid., ch. 8.

[11] Ibid., pp. 430–1.

[12] Ibid., p. 663.

[13] Ibid., p. 665.

[14] Woodward writes in his introduction that Chesnut's "story is predominantly one of grief, anguish, pessimism, and anxiety, and her role increasingly Cassandra-like rather than one of Gallic gaiety" (ibid., p. xl). While I agree that elements of sorrow and joy in the diary are mixed, I think that the narrative is more a movement among moods rather than an expression of one principal temper or another.

an assault on her will, but Chesnut's own sadness at hearing the story grew from a cluster of subjective components: pain at separation from friends by death, sorrow at a tragedy provoked by one of war's misunderstandings, and anger at a woman's belief that she had no more than family to live for.

Overall, the war strangely reinforced the Victorians' optimism. DeForest and Chesnut wrote with excitement at having found a dramatic situation and a cast of characters so appropriate to their questions about life's significance, as if possessing the right tools for inquiry promised satisfying answers. Although the extreme demands of war could not help but disturb them, neither could they turn away from what the crisis showed them about their contemporaries and about themselves. Through narratives of resistance to suffering, they moved toward a broader confidence in their ability to construct positive meanings.

Less literary Victorians than these told a slightly different story about suffering, where pain was contained not by intellectual determination but by action. The memoirs of generals were not a transparent lens on their war experience. But precisely because their recollections reflected what was important to them, their accounts show the tense relationship between their awareness of suffering and their exhilaration at control.

The *Personal Memoirs* of Ulysses Grant, completed just before his death in 1885, contained this terse yet in a way starkly horrifying description of the human cost of the Battle of the Wilderness in 1864:

The ground fought over had varied in width, but averaged three-quarters of a mile. The killed, and many of the severely wounded, of both armies, lay within this belt where it was impossible to reach them. The woods were set on fire by the bursting shells, and the conflagration raged. The wounded who had not strength to move themselves were either suffocated or burned to death. Finally the fire communicated with our breastworks, in places. Being constructed of wood, they burned with great fury. But the battle still raged, our men firing through the flames until it became too hot to remain longer.[15]

Although Grant's simple report of the terrible facts suggests that he stood aghast at the magnitude of human destruction, his words also intimated that he allowed himself to feel no pity. A commander's need for dispassion, his personal immunity from harm, and the distance in time of two decades must have worked to restrict Grant's acknowledgment of the grief caused by the devastation. Yet his measured portrayal arose, too, from the preeminent importance in his autobiography of another theme, the possibility of controlling one's circumstances.

Grant's language reflected his thrill at discovering his superior ability to manipulate military resources. "I now determined upon a regular siege," he

---

[15] *Personal Memoirs of U.S. Grant* (1885), ed. Long (1982), p. 407.

wrote about Vicksburg in his *Memoirs,* and again, "I determined to explode no more mines."[16] With proud assurance, he was consistently in possession of an understanding of his effort's precise needs. "Upon the surrender of the garrison of Vicksburg there were three things that required immediate attention," and later, "two things connected with all movements of the Army of the Potomac" were essential.[17] Grant's intellectual command of the requisites of combat must have been sharpened by retrospect and by the organizational requirements of writing itself. Yet his ability to envision complex maneuvers was still the real source of his astounding success at ordering battles, so unlike his failure at turning the opportunities of civilian society to his will. Against this chronicle of mastery, it is telling that Grant slipped into a passive and impersonal voice when he spoke of the destructive consequences of his decisions for his men. Twice in one paragraph he wrote, "the losses inflicted, and endured, were destined to be severe," and, "the campaign now begun was destined to result in heavier loses, to both armies, in a given time, than any previously suffered."[18] Perhaps Grant's twisted language betrayed guilty denial of complicity by a sensitive man. More surely, the change in his tone showed how pain must be mastered, in part by obfuscation, in a narrative of personal triumph.[19]

Just as the enduring concerns of Victorian culture predisposed DeForest and Chesnut to subsume war's anguish in affirmations of spiritual recovery, the Victorians' preoccupation with making their actions serve inner needs meant that soldiers like Grant grasped the chance to make effectual decisions. All of them transformed the war into an odyssey on preestablished cultural terms. To approach the war as an opportunity for self-definition was a possibility, from the Victorians' perspective, available to whites only.

Victorians in the North and South were involved in legislative efforts and social programs after emancipation that affected former slaves. But within their voluminous personal writings on wartime, blacks were scarcely mentioned, as if the freedmen's dilemma failed to grip the Victorians' consciousness in an affecting way. When they did describe former slaves, they projected their own traits of character onto them and, in ignorance more than malice, erased blacks' autonomy. With the Civil War so important to the Victorians' larger cultural struggle, it is sadly ironic that they could not see that blacks,

---

[16] *Memoirs of Grant*, pp. 278, 288.
[17] Ibid., pp. 301, 409.
[18] Ibid., p. 391.
[19] William McFeely concurs that Grant was able to push war's destructiveness out of his consciousness, in his *Grant: A Biography* (1981). While the wounded at Cold Harbor lay dying on the battlefield due to the inefficient diplomacy of Grant and Lee, Grant sat down to write a letter to his daughter and "retreated into a fantasy of comfortable domesticity," p. 173.

clothed in their view in white middle-class aspirations, needed to make their independent way in the postwar world.[20]

When John DeForest became an agent of the Freedman's Bureau in postwar South Carolina, an experience presented in essays later collected as *A Union Officer in the Reconstruction,* his encounters with former slaves were controlled by his own preoccupations. Having left his family once again after four years in combat, DeForest described himself in his narrative in light comic caricature: he was a civil servant who rarely had enough work to keep him in the office beyond two o'clock and who, after dining at his hotel, might be seen taking walks, less often joining the local literary circle for discussion.[21] Yet there was another man hidden by this portrait who was far less relaxed and free, one driven to the South by a professional's need for literary material, a bourgeois's taste for adventure, and a bureaucrat's pleasure at command. This set of needs, not unlike those of his Victorian contemporaries, impelled DeForest to think hard about how best to order his own destiny and tended to trap him in his private point of view.

On the surface, DeForest judged his black clients as "simple and childish."[22] Yet less consciously, he portrayed them as unexpectedly like himself. DeForest presented his freedmen to his readers as they appeared to him, coming singly or in pairs to his office with questions, complaints, and requests. Certainly a writer could not be faulted for adopting this procession of petitioners as a literary device to introduce the objects of his interest. But DeForest's excitement at spinning stories about these disengaged characters signaled his lack of appreciation of an integrated and autonomous black culture. He listened to the freedmen explain their frequent moves as part of their search for kin. Yet he could not quite believe that their traveling was not frivolous, akin to his own yen to see new places, and so he denied government funding for "favors" that he deemed unconnected with "jus-

---

[20] On northern Victorians in this study who participated in Reconstruction either as politicians, civil servants, reformers, or journalists, see McFeely, *Grant,* ch. 22; *Diary of Garfield,* ed. Brown and Williams, 1:xxxviii–xxxix; McFeely, *Yankee Stepfather: General O. O. Howard and the Freedmen* (1968); Light, *John William DeForest* (1965), ch. 3; Edelstein, *Strange Enthusiasm: A Life of Thomas Wentworth Higginson,* pp. 302–8; Perry, *Henry Lee Higginson,* ch. 8; Roper, *FLO: A Biography of Frederick Law Olmsted,* ch. 25; *The Gilded Age Letters of E. L. Godkin,* ed. Armstrong (1974), chs. 3–4; "Franklin Benjamin Sanborn," *Dictionary of American Biography,* ed. Dumas Malone (New York: Scribner's, 1935), 16:326–7. Southerners obviously had less influence on Reconstruction policies and tended not to voice their views of emancipation because of their tenuous political position and fear of reprisals as well as their necessary preoccupation with rebuilding their own lives. But when they regained power as part of Restoration governments, they were involved in the implementation of racial policies. Consider, e.g., the attention to race in the postwar career of the North Carolina politician, Zebulon Vance, in Tucker, *Zeb Vance: Champion of Personal Freedom* (1965), chs. 27–8. On racial bias during this period, see Fredrickson, *The Black Image in the White Mind: The Debate on Afro-American Character and Destiny, 1817–1914* (1971), esp. chs. 4–11.

[21] *A Union Officer in the Reconstruction,* ed. Croushore and Potter (1948), pp. 44–7.

[22] Ibid., p. 91.

tice."[23] Similarly, he convinced a woman to let her daughter work for a white man at a distance from home because he was sure that the mother's woeful plaint grew from laziness and that the daughter might profit more in a prosperous household. "I wants to see her," cried the mother, "She's my little gal, an' I has a right to hev her, an' I wants her." "Ah, aunty," DeForest replied, "All you want of her is to wait on you while you sit and tattle."[24] To DeForest, the issue hinged on outward advantage, the standard of value of an ambitious man: "The result was that, by dint of ridicule, coaxing, and arguing, I prevailed upon her to leave her child with Mr. Jack Bascom, in whose care the pickaninny was of course far better off than she could have been with her poverty-stricken parent."[25] Precisely because DeForest's attachment to family and community was mediated and indeed compromised by his personal initiatives, he presumed that the freed slaves he pledged to help were similarly moved.[26]

Nearly four decades later, Virginia Clay of Alabama likewise cast white-faced blacks in a supporting role in her own Victorian saga of material aspirations and fashionable display in *A Belle of the Fifties,* published in 1905. She viewed blacks with unrelenting condescension, recalling "that throng of well-fed, plump and happy coloured people" of prewar days. But the blacks who appeared in Clay's narrative also resembled herself, more concerned with comfort and status than with liberty. "Poor Alfred," she wrote of a former house servant, "he eked out a scanty living at a meagre little luncheon-stand on the corner of a thoroughfare." He regained respect for his former master after a time "and with it, I doubt not, a longing for the days when, in his fresh linen suits, laundered by the laundress of the Governor's household, a valued servant, he had feasted on the good things he himself had assisted in concocting!"[27] Clay could not imagine that Alfred might be compensated for his diminished comforts by his freedom, so thoroughly was she trapped by a blinding combination of racism and materialism.

Neither the account of Clay nor DeForest admitted a black Civil War, an experience distinct from that of the Victorians in goals and mood. The Victorians so intently crafted the war into a tale of spiritual struggle that essential facts and alternative viewpoints were obscured. That is not to say that other interpretations of the war were not publicly voiced, but simply to underscore the power of middle-class culture to inspire a certain

[23] Ibid., p. 38. For DeForest's discussion of black mobility, see pp. 36–8.

[24] Ibid., pp. 112, 113.

[25] Ibid., p. 113.

[26] Recent historiography generally acknowledges the strength that slave society gained from both traditional community customs and emotional ties among kin. See, e.g., Blassingame, *The Slave Community: Plantation Life in the Antebellum South* (1979). These were the interconnections that DeForest could not see.

[27] Clay-Clopton, *A Belle of the Fifties: Memoirs of Mrs. Clay of Alabama,* ed. Sterling (1905), p. 284.

vision. In the postwar decades, the optimism that the Victorians constructed through reflection on the conflict became the core of a broader humanism.

FROM WAR NARRATIVES TO AUTOBIOGRAPHY

As important as the content of the Victorians' Civil War stories was their narrative form. First-person memoirs, focused at first on the war years and later more broadly autobiographical, were so widely produced as to merit designation as the Victorians' characteristic written expression. Rather than the antithesis of romanticism, these recollections reflected the Victorians' cautious wonder that the war came as close to satisfying their longing for purposive action as they were bold enough to hope it would. How better to celebrate history's ability to approach aspirations than to tell one's own story, pruned of horrors and uncomplicated by competing interpretations, but otherwise unembellished. Reminiscences were thus a gesture of reconciliation with the rewards society offered and a medium for affirming the value of secular accomplishments. Although the authority of a personal voiced edged aside transcendent validation as a warranty of meaning, the Victorians who constructed retrospective views did not doubt that self-reflection would produce moral clarity. Thus the Civil War tempered the Victorians' spirit of insistent striving with a confident humanism, as they looked back with satisfaction on events inspired by their determination to engage life's basic questions.[28]

Perhaps like many momentous events, the Civil War deepened in importance to the Victorians after the fighting ceased. Remembering the war became a habitual occupation, and recollections did not have to be pleasant to become cherished intellectual possessions. Petty quarrels about wartime decisions, for example, ran through soldiers' memoirs as a persistent theme. William Tecumseh Sherman lit out in his *Memoirs* of 1875 against meddlesome politicians, particularly Edwin Stanton, Lincoln's secretary of war. John Bell Hood wrote *Advance and Retreat*, issued in 1880, in large measure to refute allegations of poor leadership initiated by his former Confederate

---

[28] Despite my focus on memoirs as the Victorians' central literary form, it is essential to note that Americans also chronicled the war in fiction and poetry. On Civil War fiction, see Wilson, *Patriotic Gore,* and Aaron, *Unwritten War.* The most sustained poetic efforts that dealt with the war were Walt Whitman, "Drum Taps" (1861–65), in *The Portable Walt Whitman,* rev. ed. (New York: Viking, 1974), pp. 216–34, and Herman Melville, *Battle-Pieces and Aspects of the War* (1860–66) (Gainesville, Florida: Scholars' Facsimiles and Reprints, 1960). It is also significant that Emily Dickinson's most productive years occurred during the Civil War. Consider the dates of Dickinson's poems included in Cleanth Brooks, R. W. B. Lewis, and Robert Penn Warren, eds., *American Literature: The Makers and the Making* (New York: St Martin's Press, 1973), 2:1236–51. Though her imagination may have been stirred as well by the end of her romantic involvement with Rev. Charles Wadsworth in 1862, it is likely that the distant excitement of war touched even this reclusive writer, as Daniel Aaron suggests in *Unwritten War,* pp. 355–6.

Figure 15. William Tecumseh Sherman (1820–91). Photograph of Sherman as an old man, taken around 1890 by George C. Cox. National Portrait Gallery, Smithsonian Institution.

colleague, Joseph Johnston. In 1885, Ulysses Grant recurred repeatedly in his memoirs to the irksome resistance that Henry Halleck, his superior, posed to his strategies. Lew Wallace tried hard to explain in his autobiography of 1906 why he got lost with his troops on the way to Shiloh and missed the battle's opening day. O. O. Howard undertook his memoir of 1907 in part to dispel suspicions that the Freedman's Bureau was corrupt, a worry that must have disturbed his old age nearly four decades after the agency was dissolved.[29]

The polemical intent of these memoirs is arresting less because the issues were insignificant than because this discussion must be imagined against a background of massive immigration, urban growth, and industrialization,

---

[29] *Memoirs of General William T. Sherman by Himself* (1875), 2:85–6, 245, 361–6, 377; *Advance and Retreat: Personal Experiences in the United States and Confederate States Armies* (1880), ed. Current (1959), esp. pp. vii–viii; *Memoirs of Grant*, e.g., ch. 39; Wallace, *Lew Wallace: An Autobiography* (1906), 1: esp. ch. 53; *Autobiography of Oliver Otis Howard* (1907), 2: chs. 60–1.

developments that should have consumed the nation's attention. Why would anyone care about the feuds of bygone days? Why these works appealed to a wide audience is beyond the scope of this study, though other research suggests that they were popular. More clearly, the Victorians fought old battles in print both to carry themselves back in imagination to a time when they wielded great power and to assert their continuing importance as arbiters of debate that, they implicitly argued, still made a difference.[30] Perhaps a war of words was a pale copy of actual combat in terms of excitement. But the acerbic tone of verbal contention still lent spirit to the process of looking back for people who savored defending a cause.

Although self-dramatization to bolster demanding egos gave a theatrical flourish to the Victorians' memoirs, it would be mistaken to think that reminiscing was a frivolous indulgence tangential to their serious pursuits. Rather, the Victorians' difficulty completing projects that involved recollection underscores the high emotional stakes at risk when they plunged into the past. How could they reconcile themselves to painful events? How could they accept the fact that their days of glory were over? How could they in effect alienate themselves from their memories by turning them out as publications? Stories abound about the Victorians' stalled and abortive efforts to issue works about their lives. Ulysses Grant put off requests for his memoirs until he knew that he was dying of cancer and determined to leave his family an income. Julia, his widow, dictated her recollections to her son around 1890. But she never decided where to publish them, and they remained in manuscript until 1975. William Herndon began compulsively collecting facts about his friend, Abraham Lincoln, soon after the assassination, and he lectured widely, and controversially, about what he found out. Yet not until a young writer named Jesse Weik offered to help

---

[30] Gaines Foster writes suggestively about the popular appeal of Civil War commemoration, in *Ghosts of the Confederacy: Defeat, the Lost Cause, and the Emergence of the New South, 1865–1913* (1987), pp. 6, 105–9, 133–6. He argues that the social identity of both the organizers of and participants in commemorative efforts in the South changed over time. Whereas prominent Civil War officers who belonged to the antebellum slaveholding class initiated memorial activities in the 1860s, the reunions at the turn of the century were the work of younger urban middle-class men who, if they fought in the war at all, served as rank-and-file soldiers. Women also helped to organize these occasions, and people of both sexes who did not participate in the war attended the festivities. Although I am not sure that these precise trends applied throughout the nation, I think Civil War celebration drew an increasingly broad audience who read memoirs, attended veterans' reunions, and belonged to military clubs such as the Grand Army of the Republic. Beyond their interest in the Civil War in particular, Americans at the turn of the century were attracted both to war and to the past as sources of ideals and avenues of emotional escape. Consider William James's paean to the high-minded discipline of war-making, "The Moral Equivalent of War" (1910), in *William James: The Essential Writings*, ed. Bruce W. Wilshire (New York: Harper and Row, 1971), pp. 349–61. On the other hand, Jackson Lears emphasizes the appeal of premodern activities such as handicraft industry and chivalric combat as both a protest and a corrective to the constraints of a routinized society, in *No Place of Grace: Antimodernism and the Transformation of American Culture, 1880–1920* (1981), esp. p. xiii. In sum, Civil War commemoration was influenced by and, in turn, strengthened a broader mood of cultural criticism that centered on similar attention to warfare and history.

Herndon pull the pieces together in a coauthored book did *Herndon's Life of Lincoln* appear in 1889. Mary Chesnut revised her Civil War diary on and off after the war, but when she died in 1886, she still had not brought to fruition her plan for the journal's publication. John DeForest published numerous articles in the late 1860s on his life as a Union officer during and after the war. Yet despite a growing market for memoirs and his own financial need, he gave up on his effort to revise them in the 1880s, and it was not until the 1940s that his essays were put together as books.[31]

Certainly pragmatic reasons such as pressures to make a living or to cope with ill health contributed to these protracted literary histories. But self-generated inhibitions were at least as decisive. First, stories had to be told carefully so that pleasant memories prevailed. It was easy for Julia Grant to tell a newspaper in 1900 that memoirs were "a panacea for loneliness, a tonic for old age," since she had already figured out how to deal with her husband's alleged drinking and corruption, first by attacking his detractors and then by skimming over the rest, in fact filling one-third of her reminiscence with a report of her two-year around-the-world trip.[32] Nonetheless, strategies for handling disturbing thoughts, less by deception than by emphasis or by finding the right words to contain the truth, were rarely devised without struggle, as Julia most likely privately knew. Victorian writers must have been deterred by this taxing emotional process. Second, setting down one's memories was at best an ambiguous act, since language made thoughts not only tangible possessions, but autonomous objects. Perhaps Julia stewed so long about where to publish her memoirs because she wanted to strike a good bargain or because she worried that her narrative's reception might not do justice to her self-esteem. But it is equally possible that she could not quite hand them over to a publisher and to the public, thereby jeopardizing her intimate relation with her memories that, as a widow, bound her to her life with Ulysses. There was an emotional safety for the Victorians in working and reworking autobiographical material. If they finished their books, they would have to face the future unprotected by identities they forged in the past.

Nevertheless, the psychological hazards of producing memoirs were finally less decisive than the persuasive advantages of constructing one's own history. One-third of these Victorians, twenty-five of seventy-five, left one or more reminiscences intended for the public.[33] Younger members of this generation

---

[31] McFeely, *Grant*, ch. 28; Herndon and Weik, *Herndon's Life of Lincoln*, ed. Angle (1930), pp. xxi–xlv; Chesnut to Varina Davis, June 18, 1883, cited in *Chesnut's Civil War*, ed. Woodward, p. xxiv; Light, *DeForest*, pp. 65, 76–7; *Volunteer's Adventures*, ed. Croushore, p. xii.

[32] John Y. Simon discusses Julia's defensive strategies in his "Foreword" to *The Personal Memoirs of Julia Dent Grant*, ed. Simon (1975), p. 22. Her public praise of writing memoirs is cited in ibid., p. 20.

[33] The memoirs cited are listed in order of the author's date of birth, given in parenthesis after his or her name. If a person left more than one reminiscence, all of the titles are listed. A subtitle is cited only if essential for understanding a book's theme. Although only reminiscences intended for publication

were more inclined to engage in personal retrospect. Only 12 percent (two of seventeen) of the men and women born between 1815 and 1819 wrote a memoir, but 36 percent (twelve of thirty-three) did of those born between 1820 and 1829, as did 28 percent (seven of twenty-five) born between 1830 and 1837. This trend suggests that Victorians who were farther removed from the heyday of evangelicalism invested their trust more readily in temporal sources of authority, time and self. The works produced included recollections of war, memoirs of childhood, inclusive autobiographies, and biographies of intimate friends. Two trends emerged over time, the increasingly circumscribed place of the Civil War in the Victorians' memoirs and their mounting enthusiasm for reminiscence as a narrative form. To an extent, this was simply the result of the Victorians' advancing age and broader achievements. But the change also suggests how crucial the Civil War was in inspiring a mood of rising appreciation for the value of temporal endeavor.

Although the Victorians strove all along to make their everyday lives reproduce the excitement of intimacy with spiritual things, they never quite believed that their experience might match their dreams until they looked back on the war. Their first reminiscences in the postwar years focused squarely on the conflict. The magazine pieces of John DeForest, published

are included, a few were not published; for those, the date of composition is listed instead, designated by an asterisk(*). Elizabeth Cady Stanton (1815), *Eighty Years and More: Reminiscences, 1815–1897* (1898); William Herndon (1818) and Jesse Weik, *Herndon's Life of Lincoln* (1889); William Tecumseh Sherman (1820), *Memoirs of General William T. Sherman by Himself* (1875); Octavius Brooks Frothingham (1822), *Recollections and Impressions* (1891); Ulysses Grant (1822), *Personal Memoirs of U.S. Grant* (1885); Edward Everett Hale (1822), *A New England Boyhood* (1893) and *Memories of a Hundred Years* (1902); Jeanne Carr (1823), "My Own Story" (ms. ca. 1886*); Mary Chesnut (1823), Civil War diary [*Mary Chesnut's Civil War*] (1880s version*); Thomas Wentworth Higginson (1823), *Army Life in a Black Regiment* (1870) and *Cheerful Yesterdays* (1898); Lucy Larcom (1824), *A New England Girlhood* (1889); Virginia Clay-Clopton (1825), *A Belle of the Fifties* (1905); John William DeForest (1826), *A Volunteer's Adventures: A Union Captain's Record of the Civil War* (as articles, 1860s) and *A Union Officer in the Reconstruction* (as articles, 1860s); Julia Grant (1826), *The Personal Memoirs of Julia Dent Grant* (ca. 1890*); Lew Wallace (1827), *Lew Wallace: An Autobiography* (1906); Oliver Otis Howard (1830), *Autobiography of Oliver Otis Howard* (1907); John Bell Hood (1831), *Advance and Retreat: Personal Experiences in the United States and Confederate States Armies* (1880); Franklin Sanborn (1831), *Recollections of Seventy Years* (1909); Moncure Conway (1832), *Autobiography, Memories and Experiences of Moncure Daniel Conway* (1904); Chauncey Depew (1834), *My Memories of Eighty Years* (1924); James Cardinal Gibbons (1834), *A Retrospect of Fifty Years* (1916); Lyman Abbott (1835), *What Christianity Means to Me: A Spiritual Autobiography* (1921); Andrew Carnegie (1835), *Autobiography of Andrew Carnegie* (1920); Rebecca Felton (1835), *My Memoirs of Georgia Politics* (1911) and *Country Life in Georgia in the Days of My Youth* (1919); John Burroughs (1837), *Whitman: A Study* (1896), and *My Boyhood* (1922); William Dean Howells (1837), *A Boy's Town* (1890) and *Years of My Youth* (1916). While nearly all of the works listed conform to what are now recognized as conventions of reminiscences, including a personal voice and a retrospective view, three narratives have been included that I think functioned for their writers as memoirs, despite their different form, by enabling the authors to review and order the past. Mary Chesnut retained the temporal immediacy of her journal when she rewrote much of it two decades after the war, but she still used the process of writing to come to terms with her history. The composition of biographies of friends and relatives was a more conventional enterprise than a story about oneself. Still, I include two biographies (Herndon's of Lincoln and Burroughs's of Whitman) about friends so close to the author that the books served as self-exploration. Many other biographies of kin and friends written by the Victorians have been omitted because I judged them more outwardly focused.

between 1864 and 1869, and *Army Life in a Black Regiment* by Thomas Higginson, appearing in 1870, drew their readers close to combat by building narratives around quotations from wartime letters, journals, and official reports.[34] But in the next two decades, writers and readers of memoirs grew more curious about the earlier part of a hero's or heroine's life that brought him or her to prominence. Whereas John Bell Hood diverged only slightly from established usage by beginning *Advance and Retreat* of 1880 with his appointment to West Point and spending ten subsequent pages on his army service prior to secession, William Tecumseh Sherman and Ulysses Grant reviewed their childhoods and prewar careers at considerably more leisure in their respective memoirs of 1875 and 1885. The war remained firmly at the center of each man's attention, because it was the source of his achievement. But both moved decisively in the direction of autobiography, as Sherman spent eight of twenty-four chapters recounting his family background and early struggles and Grant did the same in sixteen chapters of seventy.[35]

By the turn of the century, these Victorians immersed themselves in an expanding number of retrospective genres. Perhaps only a society already attached to personal recollection as window on experience could have tolerated the sentimental turn that memoirs took around 1890 when writers chose to look back on the simpler world of their childhoods in books such as Lucy Larcom's *A New England Girlhood* (1889), William Dean Howells's *A Boy's Town* (1890), and Edward Everett Hale's *A New England Boyhood* (1893).[36] Why authors veered away for a time from the aggressive idealism of warfare to nostalgic visions of social peace is not altogether clear. But these factors probably influenced the change of theme: mounting urban and industrial tensions that made people seek a refuge instead of inspiration, the advancing age of writers that made them favor restful thoughts over provocation, and the entry of women, schooled to observe the domestic and the emotional, into the ranks of commentators on the past.

The lighthearted tone of memoirs that shaded toward fantasy persisted to an extent, as Thomas Higginson abandoned war stories for his *Cheerful Yesterdays* of 1898 and Virginia Clay treated her readers to pictures of the antebellum South's "Arcadias of beauty" and Washington's "fashion and mirth, beauty and wit" in *A Belle of the Fifties* in 1905.[37] But after the turn

---

[34] DeForest quoted letters to his wife in *A Volunteer's Adventures*, Higginson cited his journal in *Army Life in a Black Regiment* (1870), and DeForest drew information from his reports as an agent of the Freedman's Bureau in *A Union Officer in the Reconstruction*.

[35] *Advance and Retreat*, pp. 5–15; *Memoirs of Sherman*, 1: chs. 1–8; *Memoirs of Grant*, chs. 1–16.

[36] *A New England Girlhood* (1889); *A Boy's Town* (1890); and *A New England Boyhood* (1889).

[37] *Belle of the Fifties*, pp. 19, 87. Other memoirs limited in theme to the authors' early years include W[illiam]. D[ean]. Howells, *Years of My Youth*, and Rebecca Felton, *Country Life in Georgia in the Days of My Youth*. People younger than the Victorians also wrote childhood recollections contemporaneously. Consider Henry James, *Notes of a Son and Brother* (New York: Scribner's, 1914). Beyond the element of escapism in these recollections, the genre was also based on a sense of the formative influence of childhood on an adult's personality, an idea developed with most sophistication by Sigmund Freud during pre-

of the century, there was also a reassertion of a tougher core that made reminiscences strenuous in the sense that they dealt with issues that engage adults. In stark contrast to her idyllic prewar scenes, Clay devoted one-third of her memoir to the postwar imprisonment of her husband, a Confederate statesman, and her efforts to have him freed.[38] Similarly, autobiographies found their emotional center less in childhood than in a wide range of their author's mature efforts, including the abolitionism of Moncure Conway and Franklin Sanborn, the political activity of Lew Wallace and Rebecca Felton, and the religious causes of James Cardinal Gibbons and Lyman Abbott.[39] The Civil War still tended to dominate the Victorians' vision, as they wrote with lucidity and force of this key personal event. Although Franklin Sanborn turned out two volumes of his *Recollections of Seventy Years* in 1909, he seemed scarcely to match in later life the thrill of engineering John Brown's raid as one of the "Secret Six," so vividly did he tell his tale.[40] Nonetheless, the war stood alongside the Victorians' other accomplishments in these later autobiographies, as this generation in effect asserted, by crafting expansive self-portraits, that their lives had significance as a whole.[41]

All of these memoirs, ranging in time from the end of the war through the early twentieth century, were characterized by their realistic intentions and their possession of a personal voice. Scholars have wondered why the Civil War did not generate more works of fiction. But the Victorians' preference for nonfiction is not surprising in light of this book's argument.[42]

cisely these years. See Peter Gay, *Freud: A Life for Our Time* (New York: Doubleday, 1988), esp. chs. 2–3.

[38] *Belle of the Fifties*, pp. 246–379.

[39] *Autobiography, Memories and Experiences of Moncure Daniel Conway* (1904), vol. 1; Sanborn, *Recollections of Seventy Years* (1909), vol. 1; Wallace, *Wallace*, vol. 1; Felton, *My Memoirs of Georgia Politics;* Gibbons, *A Retrospect of Fifty Years;* Abbott, *What Christianity Means to Me: A Spiritual Autobiography.* James Cardinal Gibbons's book is perhaps the least personal of these memoirs. Although it represents one man's view of events in his time, Gibbons's retrospect is primarily an anthology of articles and sermons he wrote over the years, given coherence by a first-person explanatory introduction. He also included approximately 150 pages of the private journal he kept at the Vatican Council in Rome in 1869. Gibbons's personal reserve may be explained both by Catholicism's insistence on the subordination of the individual to the church and by the comparative vitality in Catholicism of the notion of transcendent authority. Nevertheless, Gibbons did conform to contemporary custom to the extent that he saw the utility of writing a reminiscence as a way of organizing his thoughts and reaching an audience.

[40] Sanborn explained in his *Recollections* that he would cover four of his careers – politics, literature, reform, and journalism – and omit, for no apparent reason, his substantial work in organized charity (1:xiii, 20). But in fact almost all of his first volume was devoted to antislavery and most of his second to his acquaintance with writers living in Concord, Massachusetts. Events leading up to John Brown's raid are described in *Recollections*, 1:75–252.

[41] It is possible that the Spanish–American War helped to redirect the Victorians' attention in the late 1890s from childhood recollections to military and broader adult interests. Reciprocally, moreover, the vitality of Civil War commemoration throughout the late nineteenth century fanned popular enthusiasm for the Spanish–American conflict. See Linderman, *Mirror of War*, esp. ch. 4.

[42] Edmund Wilson opens his *Patriotic Gore* with this evaluation: "The period of the American Civil War was not one in which belles lettres flourished, but it did produce a remarkable literature which mostly consists of speeches and pamphlets, private letters and diaries, personal memoirs and journalistic

The Civil War was so bound up with questions about the meaning of human efforts that the Victorians were hardly inclined to confront them through fiction's indirection and self-conscious effects. Instead, serious issues called for eyes ready to penetrate events and for words equipped to report the answers in plain prose. Eager to see if their society might yield traces of transcending brilliance, they reviewed their histories to determine the extent of their success. In the war, they found a cause of their own making so monumental that they needed simply to tell a straightforward story to convey its importance. As they came to see the romance hidden in common pursuits, unadorned narratives, once again, served to expose their discovery. Finding one's own words to tell the story was essential, too, because the critical problem of this generation was identity. If a person could no longer center himself or herself in absolute truth, he or she had to find a new source of authority. Certainly an individual voice lacked the resonance of religious tradition. But when an inherited frame of reference lost its persuasion, the personal perspective not only presented itself as a tool for ordering experience, but gained credibility by successful and repeated use.[43]

The Victorians were not the first Americans to look for meaning in their private histories and to explain what they found in first-person accounts. During the previous century, there were instances as dissimilar as Indian captivity narratives, widely read around 1700, and Benjamin Franklin's classic autobiography, first published in 1791. The Victorians' retrospects differed from both, however, in revealing ways. Stories of Indian abductions were composed to embody the struggle of invisible forces of good and evil. The captive's human adventure mattered only to the extent that it taught the lesson of God's power. So, too, the writers' voluntary submission to a literary formula, whereby the captive's journey through the wilderness was made to reflect the trials of the soul, tacitly acknowledged the cohesiveness of a Christian point of view. Neither curious to look beyond a single experience nor hospitable to departures from convention, these tales of one person's trials ironically denied the legitimacy of a private identity.[44]

Franklin's autobiography jettisoned these assumptions. With no more than a cursory salute to a religious tradition that would have branded as egotism

---

reports" (p. ix). Daniel Aaron likewise observes that American writers produced few literary masterpieces that probed the war's meaning, in *Unwritten War*, pp. xviii–xix.

[43] Daniel Calhoun argues similarly that the intellectual strenuousness of colonial preaching, made possible by the shared assumptions of the speaker and listeners, was replaced by the mid-nineteenth century by a personal style of religious discourse that grounded ideas in experience and aimed at the heart, in *The Intelligence of a People* (1973), esp. pp. 210–30, 256–91. Personalism, he continues, stood side by side with the analytic and bureaucratic as another new source of authority, a conclusion with which this study is also much in accord.

[44] On the conventions that structured captivity narratives, see Slotkin, *Regeneration through Violence: The Mythology of the American Frontier, 1600–1860* (1973), ch. 4. Slotkin notes that archetypes emerged gradually from personal narratives; but the ready formation of conventions still depended on the vitality of shared religious assumptions. See ibid., p. 95.

his self-confident presentation of self, Franklin filled page after page with testimony of his own inventiveness, intelligence, and, in short, value. So self-assured was Franklin that he left the discerning reader humorous asides as an assertion of his complete control, at least in retrospect, of his foibles as well as his achievements. Thus in the technical language of printing, Franklin's original craft, he confessed to the "errata" of his life, as if to call attention all the more proudly to his ability to correct his own errors.[45] With no apparent doubts about the capacity of human beings to use reason to shape their own destinies, Franklin's autobiography was as worldly and realistic as the captivity narratives were otherworldly and typological.

Perhaps because few people dismissed religion as easily as Franklin or because the Second Great Awakening so strongly reaffirmed Christianity's claims at the turn of the nineteenth century, Franklin's unashamedly assertive narrative was followed by first-person writings that equivocated on the authority of the self. Diary keeping, an exercise in private reflection rooted in classic Protestantism, continued in antebellum America in various moods. For those who kept a journal to monitor the progress of the soul, attention to the personal remained a gesture of spiritual submission. For a far bolder diarist such as Ralph Waldo Emerson, fascinated by the encounters of the individual with the world, extended explorations of identity still remained largely private. When Emerson translated his reflections into public lectures and essays, narrated in the first person, his offerings were short, stylized, and modest in comparison with the detailed and imposing Victorian celebrations of one person's achievement.[46]

Toward the middle of the nineteenth century, realistic first-person accounts reporting adventures or trials that were limited in time began to appear in growing numbers. Among these Victorians, Richard Henry Dana, Jr., and Henry Thoreau produced such chronicles. Dana's *Two Years before the Mast,* the story of his voyage from Boston to California as a common seaman, was issued in 1840. Thoreau published *Walden* in 1854 to explain his two-year experiment in social reconstruction and spiritual growth.[47] Outside white

---

[45] Among several "errata" of his life, one that Franklin later changed concerned his tardy decision to marry Deborah Read. See *The Autobiography of Benjamin Franklin,* ed. Leonard W. Labaree et al. (New Haven: Yale University Press, 1964), p. 129. With respect to religion, Franklin was a liberal who appreciated the contribution of morality to social order, but who rejected the dogmatism of the Calvinism of his youth. He opened his autobiography in a way that revealed his understanding of how thoroughly he challenged Puritanism, thanking God for his "Vanity" and "kind Providence, which led me to the Means I us'd and gave them Success." See pp. 44, 45.

[46] Among diaries that treat the self in restrained and conventional terms, there has been more critical study of the records of women than men. See, e.g., Cott, *The Bonds of Womanhood: "Woman's Sphere" in New England, 1780–1835* (1977), and Ulrich, *A Midwife's Tale: The Life of Martha Ballard, Based on Her Diary, 1785–1812* (1990). For an excellent discussion of the view of self that appears in the writings of Emerson and other transcendentalists, see Buell, *Literary Transcendentalism: Style and Vision in the American Renaissance* (1973), chs. 10–11.

[47] *Two Years before the Mast: A Personal Narrative of Life at Sea* (1840), ed. Thomas Philbrick (1981); *Walden,* ed. Shanley, *The Writings of Henry D. Thoreau* (1971), vol. 1.

culture, *The Narrative of the Life of Frederick Douglass,* appearing in 1845, was the best-known of a number of accounts by escaped slaves written to document their enslavement and flight. Douglass's exuberance at self-possession underwrote his descriptions of repeated past afflictions and gave his book a subtly triumphant tone not unlike the mood of the Victorians' later memoirs.[48] All of these personal narratives were focused in terms of the time period covered and the themes developed. In that sense, they were forerunners of the still-narrow soldiers' memoirs written soon after the Civil War. They drew attention more to the unusual occurrences recorded than to the narrators witnessing the evolution of events. To move from the production of such crafted episodes to a willingness to write full-scale autobiography required not simply longer texts but a conviction that the entirety of one's life was of public interest.

In the demanding and dynamic context of Victorian culture, fascination with the self and human experience finally established the acceptability and, indeed, the intellectual and emotional necessity of personal memoirs. Unlike Franklin a century before, the Victorians wrote not as rationalists but as romantics. Far less certain than Franklin of the existence of cosmic order in the largest sense, the Victorians found it impossible to settle without struggle in a world where a single definition of meaning was replaced by a challenge to individuals to make sense of their own lives. Franklin was easily satisfied that his efforts, backed up by lawful regularity, were consequential. But the Victorians were never quite sure whether the freedom they gained equaled the certainty they lost. They pushed themselves to extremes in search of the grandiose, the idealistic, and the heroic, as if strenuous aspirations and great events would quiet doubts. It is hard to imagine Franklin rhapsodizing about a warrior's exploits, unless he deflated his pretensions in the next breath. The Victorians' self-esteem, in contrast, was grounded in the Civil War, conceived in high seriousness as a momentous cause, and for that reason the conflict so often centered their memoirs.

Later generations of Americans perceived Victorianism as a system of culture notable for its self-assured, even smug, idealism. Religious conservatives, first the fundamentalists and later neoorthodox thinkers, reacted strongly against the spiritual laxity, doctrinal carelessness, and human self-confidence they sensed pervaded Victorian Protestantism. Cultural modernists, on the other side, chafed at the affirmative mood that impelled the Victorians to replace supernatural truth with equally certain, and in the modernists' eyes, self-limiting natural values. For modernists attracted to process in lieu of stability, relativism instead of resolution, questioning rather than faith, and the irrational in place of the knowable, Victorianism became

---

[48] *Narrative of the Life of Frederick Douglass, An American Slave* (New York: Signet, 1968).

the cultural enemy to be dislodged.[49] Although the work of rethinking basic commitments proceeded slowly, World War I sharply focused intellectual contention. Victorian spokesmen and their increasingly vocal modernist critics battled over how to interpret destruction on an international scale. The Victorian viewpoint, an outlook that based its faith in the significance of human efforts in an image of the Civil War as a worthy cause, was now contested by competing evidence for pessimism supplied to dissenters by another war.[50]

Perhaps like any opponent, Victorianism appeared more solid and less intelligent to both religious conservatives and cultural radicals than it in fact was. So often was Victorianism conceived as an impersonal set of beliefs that it was easy to forget that its resolutions evolved through individuals' trials. Nor did the Victorians' critics see that their predecessors' insistent search for ideals grew out of their frightening sense that traditional Christian truths might no longer fully answer society's needs. Perhaps the difficulty of the questions the Victorians asked was obscured by their affirmation of people's capacity to surmount the cultural crisis they faced. Poised in time and in thought between Christian revivalism and the twentieth-century's divided impulse to reassert traditionalism or to entertain searching doubts, American Victorians countered their own uncertainty with a resilient humanism built on the sense of personal triumph they first achieved in the Civil War.

[49] On fundamentalism's departure from the assumptions of mainstream Protestantism, see Marsden, *Fundamentalism and American Culture: The Shaping of Twentieth Century Evangelicalism, 1870–1925* (1980). For a good account of how the neoorthodox sensibility in the twentieth century rejected the optimism of nineteenth-century religious and, more generally, cultural liberalism, see Hutchinson, *The Modernist Impulse in American Protestantism* (1976), pp. 288–311. Perhaps the seminal work expressing such skepticism is Reinhold Niebuhr, *Moral Man and Immoral Society: A Study in Ethics and Politics* (New York: Scribner's, 1932), esp. pp. xi–xxv. On the cultural conflict between modernism and Victorianism, see Lears, *No Place of Grace;* John Higham, "The Reorientation of American Culture in the 1890s," in Weiss, ed., *The Origins of Modern Consciousness* (1965), pp. 25–48; May, *End of American Innocence;* David Kennedy, *Over Here;* Singal, *The War Within: From Victorian to Modernist Thought in the South, 1919–1945* (1982); Daniel Joseph Singal, "Towards a Definition of American Modernism," *American Quarterly* 39 (1987): 7–26; and Coben, *Rebellion against Victorianism: The Impetus for Cultural Change in 1920s America* (1991).

[50] David Kennedy in particular argues that World War I occasioned open debate between these different cultural spokespeople, in *Over Here,* ch. 4. Whereas Kennedy suggests that the heroic view of combat advanced by cultural traditionalists drew on the storybook images of G. A. Henty or Walter Scott, a more immediate source of grandiose ideas of war were the many Civil War memoirs produced more or less continuously during the half-century between the two wars. For a provocative interpretation of the way World War I in Europe advanced modernism, not simply as a cultural movement, but as a political one ultimately expressed in Nazism, see Eksteins, *Rites of Spring.* Eksteins also argues suggestively that modernism had roots in romanticism, specifically, in the romantics' fascination with the subjective, idealistic, and symbolic (p. 314).

Appendixes

The appendixes provide tabulated information to clarify and support conclusions reached in the text. The significance of the categories and terms used in the appendixes can be fully grasped only in conjunction with extended discussions that appear in the text of the book. The notes to the text direct the reader's attention to relevant appendixes in order to facilitate the process of interpreting the text and the appendixes together.

The principal source of information for all the appendixes is the biographical primary and secondary sources on the seventy-five Victorians whose lives are the basis of this study. A list of those texts may be found in the bibliography. The information provided by the biographical material has been checked against their biographies in Allen Johnson et al., eds., *Dictionary of American Biography,* 20 vols. (New York: Scribner's, 1928–36), and Edward T. James, Janet Wilson James, and Paul S. Boyer, eds., *Notable American Women, 1607–1950,* 3 vols. (Cambridge, Mass.: Harvard University Press, 1971). Not all of these individuals appear in the latter two reference works, however, nor did all of these sources together provide complete and consistent biographical facts in all cases. The information in the tables represents my best judgment in light of these sources. Errors in evaluation or in fact are wholly mine.

In all the appendixes, the individuals are listed in chronological order by date of birth. In two appendixes, B (occupations) and D (political affiliations and views), separate lists have been compiled for men and women since there were intrinsic differences in their experiences in these areas of Victorian culture.

Due to the heterogeneity and heterodoxy of the Victorians' religious beliefs, particularly in adulthood, several categories have been devised in addition to standard denominations.

"Liberal" signifies individually formulated views that still centered on a belief in Christ. "Radical" connotes a more eclectic and pantheistic perspective, often influenced by transcendentalism. "Religious" means that a person held religious views, but not enough is known to characterize them. A slash between two denominations (e.g., Unitarian/Episcopal) indicates that the individual practiced each one at different times. A slash between a belief system and "none" (e.g., Unitarian/none) signifies that the individual held certain beliefs, but rarely attended public services. A denomination in brackets (e.g., [Catholic]) means that an individual had formal ties with a religious group or attended services, but had little private interest in religion. In cases where the individual's funeral service was conducted by a clergyman, but where the person showed no other interest in that denomination, I have not modified my evaluation of the individual's overall adult religious commitment in light of the single ceremony.

	Childhood Religion	Adult Religion
Beekman, James (1815–77)	Dutch Reformed/ German Reformed/ Presbyterian	Presbyterian
Dana Richard (1815–82)	Congregationalist	Episcopalian
North, John (1815–90)	Methodist	Unitarian/ Episcopalian
Stanton, Elizabeth (1815–1902)	Presbyterian	radical/none
Wentworth, John (1815–88)	Congregationalist	Baptist
Cushman, Charlotte (1816–76)	Unitarian	Unitarian
Tyler, Priscilla (1816–89)	Episcopalian	Episcopalian
Tyler, Robert (1816–77)	Episcopalian	Episcopalian
Thoreau, Henry (1817–62)	Congregationalist	radical/none
Beauregard, Pierre (1818–93)	Catholic	[Catholic]
Hampton, Wade (1818–1902)	Episcopalian	Episcopalian
Herndon, William (1818–91)	Congregationalist	radical/none
Morgan, Lewis (1818–81)	Presbyterian	Presbyterian
Atkinson, George (1819–89)	Congregationalist	Congregationalist
Hecker, Isaac (1819–88)	Methodist/none	Catholic
Mowatt, Anna (1819–70)	Episcopalian	Swedenborgian
Story, William (1819–95)	Unitarian	none
Boucicault, Dion (1820–90)	unknown	none

	Childhood Religion	Adult Religion
Sherman, William (1820–91)	Presbyterian/ Catholic/none	[Catholic]
Strong, George (1820–75)	Presbyterian	Episcopalian
Cooke, Jay (1821–1905)	Methodist	Methodist/ Episcopalian
Grinnell, Josiah (1821–91)	unknown	Congregationalist
Maclay, Charles (1821–90)	Methodist	Methodist
Frothingham, Octavius (1822–95)	Unitarian	radical
Grant, Ulysses (1822–85)	none	none
Hale, Edward (1822–1909)	Unitarian	Unitarian
Hewitt, Abram (1822–1903)	Methodist	Episcopalian
Olmsted, Frederick (1822–1903)	Congregationalist	none
Brady, Mathew (1823–96)	unknown	none
Browne, William (1823–83)	Episcopalian	Methodist
Carr, Jeanne (1823–1903)	Congregationalist	liberal
Chesnut, Mary (1823–86)	Presbyterian	Presbyterian
Higginson, Thomas (1823–1911)	Unitarian	radical
Terry, David (1823–89)	unknown	none
Larcom, Lucy (1824–93)	Congregationalist	Episcopalian
Sherman, Ellen (1824–88)	Catholic	Catholic
Clay, Virginia (1825–1915)	unknown	[Episcopalian]
Curry, Jabez (1825–1903)	Baptist	Baptist
Pickett, George (1825–75)	Episcopalian	Episcopalian
Davis, Varina (1826–1906)	Episcopalian	Episcopalian
DeForest, John (1826–1906)	Congregationalist	[Episcopalian]
Grant, Julia (1826–1902)	Methodist	Methodist
Holliday, Cyrus (1826–1921)	Methodist?	Episcopalian
McCullough, Samuel (1826–1900)	unknown	Presbyterian
Damon, John (1827–1904)	Congregationalist	liberal
Moore, William (1827–91)	unknown	none
Wallace, Lew (1827–1905)	none	liberal/none
Kinkade, John (1828–1904)	unknown	religious
Parker, Ely (1828–95)	Baptist	liberal/none
Potter, William (1829–93)	Quaker	Unitarian/radical
Dickinson, Emily (1830–86)	Congregationalist	liberal/none
Howard, Oliver (1830–1909)	unknown	Methodist/ Congregationalist
Taylor, Joseph (1830–99)	Methodist	Methodist

	Childhood Religion	Adult Religion
Vance, Zebulon (1830–94)	Baptist/Methodist	none/later Presbyterian
Garfield, James (1831–81)	Disciples of Christ	Disciples of Christ
Gilman, Daniel (1831–1908)	Congregationalist	Congregationalist/ none?
Godkin, Edwin (1831–1902)	Congregationalist	Unitarian/ Episcopalian
Guignard, James (1831–1901)	Episcopalian	Episcopalian
Hood, John (1831–79)	Baptist	Episcopalian
Sanborn, Franklin (1831–1912)	Universalist	radical
Alcott, Louisa (1832–88)	radical	radical/none
Conway, Moncure (1832–1907)	Methodist	Unitarian/radical
Guignard, John (1832–1913)	Episcopalian	Episcopalian
Lowe, Thaddeus (1832–1913)	unknown	unknown
Ingersoll, Robert (1833–99)	Presbyterian	none
Depew, Chauncey (1834–1928)	Dutch Reformed	Dutch Reformed
Gibbons, James (1834–1921)	Catholic	Catholic
Higginson, Henry (1834–1919)	Unitarian	Unitarian/none
Abbott, Lyman (1835–1922)	Congregationalist	Congregationalist
Agassiz, Alexander (1835–1910)	unknown	none
Carnegie, Andrew (1835–1919)	Swedenborgian	radical/none
Felton, Rebecca (1835–1930)	Methodist	Methodist
Howells, William (1837–1920)	Swedenborgian	none
Roebling, Washington (1837–1926)	Lutheran/ Presbyterian/radical	Episcopalian
Burroughs, John (1837–1921)	Congregationalist	radical/none

APPENDIX B: OCCUPATIONS

Occupations over three generations, including the Victorians' grandfathers (father's father), fathers, and the Victorians themselves, are listed for the individuals studied. Separate tables have been made for men and women because of the considerably different nature of the sexes' work in mid-nineteenth-century America. In the table on women (Table 2), the woman's husband's occupation is noted in addition to her own, if indeed she had activities besides homemaking. Women who were married are identified by an asterisk (*) next to their names. Both tables are intended to be inclusive, that is, to show the varied pursuits of an individual rather than to identify him or her with a single occupation.

To facilitate comparisons, I have tried to subsume the Victorians' occupations in standardized categories. Although most categories listed are self-explanatory, the text provides a more complete view of the kinds of work in which the Victorians engaged. Several notes on the use of terms will assist interpretation of these tables, however. "Military" only refers to men who served in the army beyond the temporal bounds of the Civil War. "Writer" connotes someone who thought of himself or herself as a writer outside of the context of another career. Many of these people wrote in the course of other occupations, such as the ministry, but they have not been designated "writers" here. "Politicians" are mainly those who held electoral office. "Civil servants" refer to those with appointed public offices. In a few cases, I have listed as "politicians" people who campaigned frequently (and lost) and achieved only appointed office. The reasoning is that they were still closely associated with the political process.

Table 1. *Occupations of Victorian Men*

	Grandfather's Occupation	Father's Occupation	Own Occupation
Beekman, James (1815–77)	merchant	gentleman	politician
Dana, Richard (1815–82)	attorney/politician	attorney/writer	attorney/politician/writer
North, John (1815–90)	unknown	sawmill owner	minister/attorney/entrepreneur/reformer/politician
Wentworth, John (1815–88)	politician	farmer/merchant/politician	attorney/politician/journalist/entrepreneur
Tyler, Robert (1816–77)	planter/politician	planter/politician	attorney/politician/journalist
Thoreau, Henry (1817–62)	merchant	pencilmaker	writer
Beauregard, Pierre (1818–93)	unknown	planter	military/engineer/planter/entrepreneur
Hampton, Wade (1818–1902)	planter/politician	planter/politician	planter/politician/entrepreneur

	Grandfather's Occupation	Father's Occupation	Own Occupation
Herndon, William (1818–91)	unknown	tavern owner/ politician	attorney/ politician/ writer
Morgan, Lewis (1818–81)	farmer	merchant/ politician	attorney/social scientist
Atkinson, George (1819–89)	unknown	unknown	minister
Hecker, Isaac (1819–88)	brewer	brassfounder	priest
Story, William (1819–95)	physician	attorney/ politician (judge)	attorney/ sculptor
Boucicault, Dion (1820–90)	unknown	merchant	engineer/actor/ writer
Sherman, William (1820–91)	civil servant	attorney/ politician (judge)	military/ entrepreneur
Strong, George (1820–75)	unknown	attorney	attorney
Cooke, Jay (1821–1905)	unknown	attorney/ merchant/ politician	entrepreneur
Grinnell, Josiah (1821–91)	farmer	farmer/teacher	minister/ reformer/ politician/ entrepreneur
Maclay, Charles (1821–90)	unknown	unknown	minister/ entrepreneur/ politician
Frothingham, Octavius (1822–95)	coachmaker	minister	minister/writer
Grant, Ulysses (1822–85)	shoemaker	tanner/politician	military/ politician
Hale, Edward (1822–1909)	minister	journalist	minister/writer
Hewitt, Abram (1822–1903)	unknown	cabinetmaker/ mechanic/ entrepreneur	manufacturer (entrepreneur)/ politician
Olmsted, Frederick (1822–1903)	merchant	merchant	reformer/ landscape architect
Brady, Mathew (1823–96)	unknown	unknown	photographer

	Grandfather's Occupation	Father's Occupation	Own Occupation
Browne, William (1823–86)	unknown	unknown	journalist/ politician/ attorney/ educator
Higginson, Thomas (1823–1911)	merchant/college bursar	merchant	minister/ reformer/writer
Terry, David (1823–89)	unknown	unknown	attorney/ politician (judge)
Curry, Jabez (1825–1903)	planter	planter/merchant/ politician	planter/ attorney/ politician/ minister/ educator
Pickett, George (1825–75)	planter	planter	planter/ military/ entrepreneur
DeForest, John (1826–1906)	unknown	merchant/ politician	writer
Holliday, Cyrus (1826–1921)	unknown	teacher/cashier	attorney/ politician/ entrepreneur
McCullough, Samuel (1826–1900)	unknown	unknown	carpenter/hotel owner (entrepreneur)/ miner/ politician/civil servant
Damon, John (1827–1904)	unknown	unknown	printer/ journalist/ minister
Moore, William (1827–91)	unknown	unknown	surveyor/civil servant/farmer
Wallace, Lew (1827–1905)	tavern owner	attorney/ politician	attorney/ politician/ writer
Kinkade, John (1828–1904)	unknown	unknown	teacher/ attorney/miner/ school principal
Parker, Ely (1828–95)	farmer	farmer	engineer/civil servant

	Grandfather's Occupation	Father's Occupation	Own Occupation
Potter, William (1829–93)	farmer	farmer	minister
Howard, Oliver (1830–1909)	unknown	farmer	military/civil servant
Taylor, Joseph (1830–99)	unknown	unknown	attorney/ entrepreneur/ politician
Vance, Zebulon (1830–94)	surveyor/teacher/ farmer/politician	merchant/planter	attorney/ politician
Garfield, James (1831–81)	unknown	entrepreneur/ politician	teacher/school administrator/ politician
Gilman, Daniel (1831–1908)	unknown	manufacturer (entrepreneur)	college administrator
Godkin, Edwin (1831–1902)	unknown	minister/ journalist	journalist
Guignard, James (1831–1901)	planter/surveyor/ politician	planter/surveyor/ politician	planter/ entrepreneur/ politician
Hood, John (1831–79)	physician/planter	physician/planter	military/ entrepreneur
Sanborn, Franklin (1831–1912)	farmer	farmer/civil servant	teacher/ reformer/ journalist/ writer
Conway, Moncure (1832–1907)	unknown	cotton manufacturer (entrepreneur)	minister/ reformer
Guignard, John (1832–1913)	planter/surveyor/ politician	planter/surveyor/ politician	planter/ entrepreneur/ politician
Lowe, Thaddeus (1832–1913)	unknown	farmer/politician	engineer/ inventor/ entrepreneur
Ingersoll, Robert (1833–99)	unknown	minister	attorney/ lecturer/ politician
Depew, Chauncey (1834–1928)	unknown	farmer/merchant	attorney/ politician/ entrepreneur
Gibbons, James (1834–1921)	farmer	farmer/ shopkeeper	priest

	Grandfather's Occupation	Father's Occupation	Own Occupation
Higginson, Henry (1834–1919)	unknown	merchant	entrepreneur
Abbott, Lyman (1835–1922)	unknown	minister/writer	minister/writer
Agassiz, Alexander (1835–1910)	minister	professor/scientist	scientist/ entrepreneur
Carnegie, Andrew (1835–1919)	unknown	weaver	entrepreneur/ manufacturer
Howells, William (1837–1920)	mill manager	printer/journalist/ politician	journalist/ writer
Roebling, Washington (1837–1926)	tobacconist	engineer/ reformer/ entrepreneur	engineer/ entrepreneur
Burroughs, John (1837–1921)	farmer	farmer	writer

Table 2. *Occupations of Victorian Women (and Their Husbands)*

	Grandfather's Occupation	Father's Occupation	Own Occupation	Husband's (or Successive Husbands') Occupation(s)
Stanton, Elizabeth* (1815–1902)	unknown	attorney/ politician	reformer	attorney/ reformer/ politician
Cushman, Charlotte (1816–76)	unknown	merchant	actress	
Tyler, Priscilla* (1816–89)	writer/ reformer	actor	actress	attorney/ politician/ journalist
Mowatt, Anna* (1819–70)	minister	merchant	actress/ writer	attorney/ entrepreneur (1st); journalist (2d)
Carr, Jeanne* (1823–1903)	innkeeper	physician	none	physician/ professor
Chesnut, Mary* (1823–86)	farmer	planter/attorney/ politician	none	planter/attorney/ politician
Larcom, Lucy (1824–93)	unknown	merchant	teacher/ writer	

	Grandfather's Occupation	Father's Occupation	Own Occupation	Husband's (or Successive Husbands') Occupation(s)
Sherman, Ellen* (1824–88)	unknown	attorney/politician	none	military/ entrepreneur
Clay, Virginia* (1825–1915)	unknown	physician	reformer	planter/politician (1st); politician (judge) (2d)
Davis, Varina* (1826–1906)	politician	planter	none	planter/ politician/writer
Grant, Julia* (1826–1902)	unknown	merchant/planter	none	military/ politician
Dickinson, Emily (1830–86)	entrepreneur	attorney/politician	writer	
Alcott, Louisa (1832–88)	farmer	reformer/writer	writer	
Felton, Rebecca* (1835–1930)	unknown	tavern owner/ planter	reformer/ politician	minister/planter/ politician

APPENDIX C: RESIDENCES

The places of residence listed here represent only those where the Victorians spent a sustained length of time. I have generally omitted place of birth if the person lived there only briefly, as well as residences of short duration and seasonal residences such as summer houses. I include seasonal residences if the person spent many months a year there over a long period of time.

	Childhood Residence(s)	Adulthood Residence(s)
Beekman, James (1815–77)	New York City	New York City
Dana, Richard (1815–82)	Cambridge, Mass.	Cambridge, Mass.
North, John (1815–90)	New York state	Northfield, Minn./Knoxville, Tenn./Riverside, Calif.
Stanton, Elizabeth (1815–1902)	Johnstown, N.Y.	Boston/Seneca Falls, N.Y./Tenafly, N.J./New York City
Wentworth, John (1815–88)	Sandwich, N.H.	Chicago/Troy, N.Y.
Cushman, Charlotte (1816–76)	Boston	London/Rome

	Childhood Residence(s)	Adulthood Residence(s)
Tyler, Priscilla (1816–89)	Bristol, Pa.	Bristol, Pa./Philadelphia/Richmond/Montgomery, Ala.
Tyler, Robert (1816–77)	Charles City County, Va.	Bristol, Pa./Philadelphia/Richmond/Montgomery, Ala.
Thoreau, Henry (1817–62)	Concord, Mass.	Concord, Mass.
Beauregard, Pierre (1818–93)	St. Bernard parish, La./New Orleans	New Orleans
Hampton, Wade (1818–1902)	Millwood plantation (near Columbia, S.C.)	Wild Woods, Miss./Columbia, S.C.
Herndon, William (1818–91)	Springfield, Ill.	Springfield, Ill.
Morgan, Lewis (1818–81)	Aurora, N.Y.	Rochester, N.Y.
Atkinson, George (1819–89)	Newberry, Vt.	Oregon City, Portland, Ore.
Hecker, Isaac (1819–88)	New York City	New York City
Mowatt, Anna (1819–70)	New York City	New York City/Richmond/London
Story, William (1819–95)	Cambridge, Mass.	Rome
Boucicault, Dion (1820–90)	Dublin/London	New York City/London
Sherman, William (1820–91)	Lancaster, Ohio	San Francisco/Washington, D.C./St. Louis/New York City
Strong, George (1820–75)	New York City	New York City
Cooke, Jay (1821–1905)	Sandusky, Ohio	Philadelphia
Grinnell, Josiah (1821–91)	New Haven, Vt.	Grinnell, Iowa
Maclay, Charles (1821–90)	Concord, Pa.	Santa Clara, San Fernando, Calif.
Frothingham, Octavius (1822–95)	Boston	New York City/Boston
Grant, Ulysses (1822–85)	Georgetown, Ohio	Washington, D.C./New York City
Hale, Edward (1822–1909)	Boston	Roxbury, Mass.
Hewitt, Abram (1822–1903)	New York City	New York City/Ringwood, N.J.
Olmsted, Frederick (1822–1903)	Hartford	New York City/Brookline, Mass.
Brady, Mathew (1823–96)	Warren County, N.Y.	New York City

	Childhood Residence(s)	Adulthood Residence(s)
Browne, William (1823–83)	unknown	Washington, D.C./Athens, Macon, Ga.
Carr, Jeanne (1823–1903)	Castleton, Vt.	Castleton, Vt./Philadelphia/Madison, Wis./Chicago/Pasadena, Calif.
Chesnut, Mary (1823–86)	Statesburg, S.C.	Camden, S.C.
Higginson, Thomas (1823–1911)	Cambridge, Mass.	Cambridge, Mass.
Terry, David (1823–89)	Kentucky; Texas	Stockton, Calif./Casa de Tija, Mexico/Hamilton, Nev./ Stockton
Larcom, Lucy (1824–93)	Beverly, Lowell, Mass.	Norton, Beverly, Boston, Mass.
Sherman, Ellen (1824–88)	Lancaster, Ohio	Washington, D.C./St. Louis/New York City
Clay, Virginia (1825–1915)	Tuscaloosa, Ala.	Huntsville, Ala.
Curry, Jabez (1825–1903)	Georgia/Alabama frontier	Talladega County, Ala./Richmond/Washington, D.C.
Pickett, George (1825–75)	Turkey Island plantation (near Richmond)	Turkey Island
Davis, Varina (1826–1906)	Natchez, Miss.	Beauvoir plantation, Miss./New York City
DeForest, John (1826–1906)	Humphreville, Seymour, New Haven, Conn.	New Haven
Grant, Julia (1826–1902)	White Haven, Mo.	Washington, D.C./New York City
Holliday, Cyrus (1826–1921)	Carlisle, Pa.	Meadville, Pa./Topeka, Kan.
McCullough, Samuel (1826–1900)	Somerset County, N.J.	San Francisco
Damon, John (1827–1904)	Waltham, Mass.	Cambridge, Lynn, Mass./northern California (mining districts)/San Diego/Port Townsend, Portland, Ore./Seattle, Wash.
Moore, William (1827–91)	Augusta, Me.	Los Angeles
Wallace, Lew (1827–1905)	Covington, Indianapolis, Crawfordsville, Ind.	Covington, Crawfordsville, Ind.
Kinkade, John (1828–1904)	Marysville, Ohio	Washington County, Iowa/Holliday's Cove, Va./Indian Valley, Secret Ravine, Rocklin, Auburn, Calif.

	Childhood Residence(s)	Adulthood Residence(s)
Parker, Ely (1828–95)	Tonawanda reservation (near Buffalo, N.Y.)	Washington, D.C./New York City
Potter, William (1829–93)	North Dartmouth, Mass.	New Bedford, Boston, Mass.
Dickinson, Emily (1830–86)	Amherst, Mass.	Amherst, Mass.
Howard, Oliver (1830–1909)	Leeds, Me.	Washington, D.C./Portland, Ore./ West Point, N.Y./Omaha/San Francisco/New York City
Taylor, Joseph (1830–99)	Cambridge, Ohio	Cambridge, Ohio
Vance, Zebulon (1830–94)	Asheville, N.C.	Raleigh, Charlotte, Asheville, N.C.
Garfield, James (1831–81)	Orange, Ohio	Hiram, Mentor, Ohio/Washington, D.C.
Gilman, Daniel (1831–1908)	Norwich, Conn.	New Haven, Conn./Berkley, Calif./Baltimore
Godkin, Edwin (1831–1902)	Belfast, Ireland/ London.	New York City
Guignard, James (1831–1901)	Edgefield plantation, S.C.	Columbia, S.C.
Hood, John (1831–79)	Montgomery County, Ky.	New Orleans
Sanborn, Franklin (1831–1912)	Hampton Falls, N.H.	Boston, Concord, Springfield, Mass.
Alcott, Louisa (1832–88)	Concord, Mass.	Concord, Mass.
Conway, Moncure (1832–1907)	Fredericksburg, Va.	Washington, D.C./Cincinnati/ London
Guignard, John (1832–1913)	Edgefield plantation, S.C.	Evergreen, S.C.
Lowe, Thaddeus (1832–1913)	Coos County, N.Y.	Norristown, Pa./Pasadena, Calif.
Ingersoll, Robert (1833–99)	Midwestern towns	Peoria, Ill./Washington, D.C./ New York City
Depew, Chauncey (1834–1928)	Peekskill, N.Y.	Peekskill, N.Y./New York City
Gibbons, James (1834–1921)	Baltimore, Ireland, New Orleans	Baltimore
Higginson, Henry (1834–1919)	Boston	Boston
Abbott, Lyman (1835–1922)	Farmington, Me./ New York City	Terre Haute, Ind./Brooklyn
Agassiz, Alexander (1835–1910)	Switzerland/ Cambridge, Mass.	Cambridge, Mass.

	Childhood Residence(s)	Adulthood Residence(s)
Carnegie, Andrew (1835–1919)	Scotland/Allegheny, Pa.	Pittsburgh/Scotland
Felton, Rebecca (1835–1930)	DeKalb County, Ga.	Cartersville, Ga./Washington, D.C.
Howells, William (1837–1920)	Ohio towns	Boston/New York City
Roebling, Washington (1837–1926)	Saxonburg, Pa.	Trenton, N.J./New York City
Burroughs, John (1837–1921)	Roxbury, N.Y.	Washington, D.C./Esopus, N.Y.

APPENDIX D: POLITICAL AFFILIATIONS AND VIEWS

Entries in this appendix represent the most formal level of political activity an individual achieved. If, for example, a person sympathized with Republican party ideas but had few ties with the party, his stance is characterized in brackets as [Republican]. If an individual participated only in local politics, with no discernible national party affiliation, his political activity is designated "local politics." If an individual strongly supported one or successive national parties, that party or those parties are listed successively. In other words, entries specifying party affiliation are most inclusive, and one may assume that men so classified both held the opinions of their parties and participated in local, state, and/or national elections as voters and/or candidates. "Civil War" signifies that participation was limited to wartime civic affairs.

The political positions of Victorian men and women are listed separately (Tables 1 and 2) because the experience of the sexes differed by law and custom. For married women, I have listed the opinions of their husbands. Although many of the wives were thoughtful about politics and a few were active in the political process, their views generally remained within a range defined by the outlook of male kin. When married women differed significantly from their husbands, I have noted their own positions in addition. Women who were married are identified by an asterisk (*) next to their names.

Classification under "professional status" as "amateur" and "professional" is provided to help readers understand the evidential basis of conclusions drawn in Chapter 5, "Politics." Extended explanations of the use of terms may be found in the text. Briefly, "amateur" refers to a man or woman who was involved in electoral politics and perhaps held office, but who did not consider politics his or her principal career through most of that person's lifetime. A "professional" is a person who wished to make politics his career and successfully held public office through many years. Individuals classified under neither category were not as directly involved in politics.

Table 1. *Political Activity of Victorian Men*

	Childhood Influences/ Father's Activity	Adult Participation	Professional Status
Beekman, James (1815–77)	none	Whig/Republican	amateur
Dana, Richard (1815–82)	[Federalist/ Whig]	Whig/Free Soil/ Republican	amateur
North, John (1815–90)	unknown	Liberty/Republican	amateur
Wentworth, John (1815–88)	Democratic	Democratic/Republican	professional
Tyler, Robert (1816–77)	Jeffersonian Republican/ Democratic/ Whig	Whig/Democratic	professional
Thoreau, Henry (1817–62)	[abolitionist]	radical	
Beauregard, Pierre (1818–93)	unknown	Democratic/ liberal Republican/Louisiana Unification Movement/ Democratic	amateur
Hampton, Wade (1818–1902)	state politics	Democratic	professional
Herndon, William (1818–91)	Democratic	Whig/Republican/liberal Republican/Democratic	amateur
Morgan, Lewis (1818–81)	state politics	Whig/Republican	amateur
Atkinson, George (1819–89)	unknown	[Civil War: Union sympathies]	
Hecker, Isaac (1819–88)	Democratic	Democratic/Catholic	
Story, William (1819–95)	Jeffersonian Republican	Civil War	
Boucicault, Dion (1820–90)	unknown	none	
Sherman, William (1820–91)	Whig	Constitutional Union/ Republican	
Strong, George (1820–75)	[Federalist/ Whig]	[Whig]/Republican	
Cooke, Jay (1821–1905)	Whig	Republican	
Grinnell, Josiah (1821–91)	unknown	Whig/Republican/ liberal Republican/ Republican	amateur

Table 1. (*cont.*)

	Childhood Influences/ Father's Activity	Adult Participation	Professional Status
Maclay, Charles (1821–90)	unknown	Republican	amateur
Frothingham, Octavius (1822–95)	[Federalist/ Whig]	[Republican]	
Grant, Ulysses (1822–85)	Democratic/ Whig	Democratic/Republican	professional
Hale, Edward (1822–1909)	Whig	Republican	
Hewitt, Abram (1822–1903)	[Democratic]	Whig/Democratic	professional
Olmsted, Frederick (1822–1903)	unknown	Republican	amateur
Brady, Mathew (1823–96)	unknown	Civil War	
Browne, William (1823–83)	unknown	Democratic	amateur
Higginson, Thomas (1823–1911)	[Federalist]	Free Soil/Republican	amateur
Terry, David (1823–89)	unknown	Know Nothing/ Democratic	amateur
Curry, Jabez (1825–1903)	Democratic	Democratic	amateur
Pickett, George (1825–75)	unknown	Civil War	
DeForest, John (1826–1906)	state politics	Republican	
Holliday, Cyrus (1826–1921)	unknown	Republican	amateur
McCullough, Samuel (1826–1900)	unknown	state politics	amateur
Damon, John (1827–1904)	unknown	local politics	
Moore, William (1827–91)	unknown	Republican	
Wallace, Lew (1827–1905)	Whig	Whig/Free Soil/ Democratic/Republican	amateur
Kinkade, John (1828–1904)	unknown	Democratic/Republican	

	Childhood Influences/ Father's Activity	Adult Participation	Professional Status
Parker, Ely (1828–95)	unknown	Republican	
Potter, William (1829–93)	unknown	Civil War	
Howard, Oliver (1830–1909)	Whig	Republican	
Taylor, Joseph (1830–99)	unknown	Republican	amateur
Vance, Zebulon (1830–94)	unknown	Whig/Know Nothing/ Constitutional Union/ Democratic	professional
Garfield, James (1831–81)	unknown	Republican	professional
Gilman, Daniel (1831–1908)	unknown	{Republican}	
Godkin, Edwin (1831–1902)	European republicanism	European republicanism/ Republican	
Guignard, James (1831–1901)	local politics	Democratic	amateur
Hood, John (1831–79)	unknown	Civil War	
Sanborn, Franklin (1831–1912)	Democratic	Independent Democrat/ Free Soil/Republican	
Conway, Moncure (1832–1907)	Democratic	radical	
Guignard, John (1832–1913)	local politics	Democratic	amateur
Lowe, Thaddeus (1832–1913)	state politics	Civil War	
Ingersoll, Robert (1833–99)	abolitionism	Democratic/Republican	amateur
Depew, Chauncey (1834–1928)	Democratic	Republican/Liberal Republican/Republican	professional
Gibbons, James (1834–1921)	unknown	Catholic	
Higginson, Henry (1834–1919)	{Federalist/ Whig}	{Republican}	
Abbott, Lyman (1835–1922)	unknown	{Republican}	
Agassiz, Alexander (1835–1910)	unknown	none	

Table 1. (*cont.*)

	Childhood Influences/ Father's Activity	Adult Participation	Professional Status
Carnegie, Andrew (1835–1919)	European republicanism	[Republican]	
Howells, William (1837–1920)	radical/Whig/ Free Soil/ Republican	Republican	
Roebling, Washington (1837–1926)	European republicanism	Civil War	
Burroughs, John (1837– 1921)	unknown	Civil War	

Table 2. *Political Views of Victorian Women*

	Childhood Influences/ Father's Activity	Own Views and Activity	Husband's (or Successive Husbands') Views and Activity	Professional Status
Stanton, Elizabeth* (1815–1902)	Federalist	women's suffrage	Republican	both amateur
Cushman, Charlotte (1816–76)	unknown	Civil War		
Tyler, Priscilla* (1816–89)	European republicanism		Whig/ Democratic	husband: professional
Mowatt, Anna* (1819–95)	liberal (aided South American revolutions)		none (1st); Democratic (2d)	2d husband: professional
Carr, Jeanne* (1823–1903)	unknown	active with husband	state politics (Grange movement)	husband: amateur
Chesnut, Mary* (1823–86)	States Rights party (S.C.)		Democratic	husband: amateur
Larcom, Lucy (1824–93)	unknown	[working-class republicanism/ abolitionism]		

275

	Childhood Infuences/ Father's Activity	Own Views and Activity	Husband's (or Successive Husbands') Views and Activity	Professional Status
Sherman, Ellen* (1824–88)	Whig		Constitutional Union/ Republican	
Clay, Virginia* (1825–1915)	Democratic	women's suffrage	Democratic (1st); Democratic (2d)	both husbands amateur
Davis, Varina* (1826–1906)	Whig		Democratic	husband: professional
Grant, Julia* (1826–1902)	Democratic		Democratic/ Republican	husband: professional
Dickinson, Emily (1830–86)	Whig			
Alcott, Louisa (1832–88)	radical	Civil War		
Felton, Rebecca* (1835–1930)	Whig	Democratic (as 1st woman Senator)	Whig/ Independent Democrat/ Populist/ Democratic	self: amateur; husband: professional

Selected Bibliography

VICTORIANS

1. Manuscript Collections.*

Atkinson, George Henry. Letters. George Henry Atkinson Papers, HL.
Carr, Jeanne. Miscellaneous Writings. Jeanne Carr Papers, HL.
Damon, John Fox. Letters. John Fox Damon Papers, HL.
DeForest, John William. Letters. John William DeForest Papers. Beinecke Library, Yale University, New Haven, Conn.
Holliday, Cyrus Kurtz. Letters. Cyrus Kurtz Holliday Papers, HL.
Kinkade, John Thompson. Letters. John Thompson Kinkade Papers, HL.
Maclay, Charles. Letters and Addresses. Charles Maclay Papers, HL.
McCullough, Samuel. Letters. Samuel McCullough Papers, HL.
Moore, William. Diaries. William Moore Papers, HL.
North, John Wesley. Letters. John Wesley North Papers, HL.
Parker, Ely. Letters and Miscellaneous Writings. Ely Parker Papers, HL.
Potter, William. Letters and Journals. William Potter Papers, HL.
Taylor, Joseph Danner. Letters. Joseph Danner Taylor Papers, HL.
Terry, David Smith. Letters. David Smith Terry Papers, HL.
Vance, Zebulon Baird. Letters. Zebulon Baird Vance Papers. North Carolina State Archives, Raleigh, N.C.
Wallace, Lew. Letters. Lew Wallace Papers, Indiana Historical Society, Indianapolis, Ind.

2. Published Primary Sources: General Subjects

Agassiz, Alexander. *Letters and Recollections of Alexander Agassiz.* Ed. G. R. Agassiz. Boston: Houghton Mifflin, 1913.
Alcott, Louisa May. *Alternative Alcott.* Ed. Elaine Showalter. New Brunswick, N.J.: Rutgers University Press, 1988.
Burroughs, John. *Whitman: A Study.* Boston: Houghton Mifflin, 1896.
Cauthen, Charles E., ed. *Family Letters of the Three Wade Hamptons, 1782–1901.* Columbia: University of South Carolina Press, 1953.

*The abbreviation "HL" refers to the Henry E. Huntington Library, San Marino, Calif.

Chesnut, Mary Boykin. *Mary Chesnut: The Unpublished Civil War Diaries.* Ed. C. Vann Woodward and Elisabeth Muhlenfeld. New York: Oxford University Press, 1984.

Mary Chesnut's Civil War. Ed. C. Vann Woodward. New Haven: Yale University Press, 1981.

Childs, Arney R., ed. *Planters and Business Men: The Guignard Family of South Carolina, 1795–1930.* Columbia: University of South Carolina Press, 1957.

Curry, J. L. M. *The Constitutional Rights of the States: Speech in the House of Representatives, Mar. 14, 1860.* [Washington]: T. McGill, [1860].

Dana, Richard Henry, Jr. *The Journal of Richard Henry Dana, Jr.* Ed. Robert F. Lucid. 3 vols. Cambridge, Mass.: Harvard University Press, 1968.

Two Years before the Mast: A Personal Narrative of Life at Sea. 1840. Reprint. Ed. Thomas Philbrick. New York: Penguin, 1981.

DeForest, John William. *Miss Ravenel's Conversion from Secession to Loyalty.* 1867. Reprint. Ed. Gordon S. Haight. New York: Holt, Rinehart and Winston, 1955.

Dickinson, Emily. *Emily Dickinson: Selected Letters.* Ed. Thomas H. Johnson. Cambridge, Mass.: Harvard University Press, 1971.

Final Harvest: Emily Dickinson's Poems. Ed. Thomas H. Johnson. Boston: Little, Brown, 1961.

Frothingham, Octavius Brooks. *Boston Unitarianism, 1820–1850: A Study of the Life and Work of Nathaniel Langdon Frothingham.* 1890. Reprint. Hicksville, N.Y.: Regina Press, 1975.

[Frothingham, Octavius Brooks]. "The Order of Saint Paul the Apostle; and the New Catholic Church." *Christian Examiner* 78 (1865): 1–26.

"Renan's Life of Jesus." *Christian Examiner* 75 (1863): 313–39.

Garfield, James A. *The Diary of James A. Garfield.* Ed. Harry James Brown and Frederick D. Williams. 4 vols. East Lansing: Michigan State University Press, 1967.

The Wild Life of the Army: Civil War Letters of James A. Garfield. Ed. Frederick D. Williams. East Lansing: Michigan State University Press, 1964.

Godkin, Edwin. *The Gilded Age Letters of E. L. Godkin.* Ed. William M. Armstrong. Albany: State University of New York Press, 1974.

Grant, Ulysses S. *The Papers of Ulysses S. Grant.* Ed. John Y. Simon. 18 vols. to date. Carbondale: Southern Illinois University Press, 1967–.

Hale, Edward Everett. *The Man without a Country.* 1863. Reprint. Boston: Houghton Mifflin, 1951.

Herndon, William H., and Jesse W. Weik. *Herndon's Life of Lincoln.* 1889. Reprint. Ed. Paul M. Angle. Cleveland: Fine Editions Press, 1930.

[Higginson, Thomas Wentworth]. "Gymnastics." *Atlantic Monthly* 7 (1861): 283–302.

"Letter to a Young Contributor." *Atlantic Monthly* 9 (1862): 401–11.

"The Maroons of Surinam." *Atlantic Monthly* 5 (1860): 549–57.

Ingersoll, Robert G. "The Liberty of Man, Woman and Child." In *The Works of Robert G. Ingersoll,* vol. 1. [Ed. C. P. Farrell]. New York: Dresden Publishing Company, 1909.

Morgan, Lewis Henry. *The League of the Ho-De-No-Sau-Nee or Iroquois.* 1851. Reprint. Ed. Herbert M. Lloyd. New York: Dodd, Mead, 1922.

Olmsted, Frederick Law. *The Cotton Kingdom: A Traveller's Observations on Cotton and Slavery in the American Slave States.* 1861. Reprint. Ed. Arthur M. Schlesinger, Sr., introd. Lawrence N. Powell. New York: Random House, 1984.

"Public Parks and the Enlargement of Towns." 1870. In *Civilizing American Cities: A Selection of Frederick Law Olmsted's Writings on City Landscapes,* ed. S. B. Sutton. Cambridge, Mass.: MIT Press, 1971.

Pickett, George. *Soldier of the South: General Pickett's War Letters to His Wife.* Ed. Arthur Crew Inman. Boston: Houghton Mifflin, 1928.

Sherman, William Tecumseh. *Home Letters of General Sherman.* Ed. M. A. DeWolfe Howe. New York: Scribner's, 1909.

Stanton, Elizabeth Cady. *The Woman's Bible.* 1895. Reprint. New York: Arno Press, 1972.

Strong, George Templeton. *The Diary of George Templeton Strong.* 4 vols. Ed. Allan Nevins and Milton Halsey Thomas. New York: Macmillan, 1952.

Thoreau, Henry David. "Civil Disobedience." In *The Portable Thoreau,* ed. Carl Bode. New York: Viking, 1964.

Walden. Ed. J. Lyndon Shanley. In *The Writings of Henry D. Thoreau,* vol. 1. Princeton: Princeton University Press, 1971.

"Walking." In *The Portable Thoreau,* ed. Carl Bode. New York: Viking, 1964.

Vance, Zebulon Baird. *The Papers of Zebulon Baird Vance, 1843–1862.* Ed. Frontis W. Johnston. 1 vol. to date. Raleigh, N.C.: State Department of Archives and History, 1963–.

3. Published Primary Sources: Memoirs

Abbott, Lyman. *What Christianity Means to Me: A Spiritual Autobiography.* New York: Macmillan, 1921.

Burroughs, John. *My Boyhood.* Garden City, N.Y.: Doubleday, Page and Company, 1922.

Carnegie, Andrew. *Autobiography of Andrew Carnegie.* 1920. Reprint. Boston: Houghton Mifflin, 1948.

Clay-Clopton, Virginia. *A Belle of the Fifties: Memoirs of Mrs. Clay of Alabama.* Ed. Ada Sterling. New York: Doubleday, Page and Company, 1905.

Conway, Moncure Daniel. *Autobiography, Memories and Experiences of Moncure Daniel Conway.* 2 vols. London: Cassell and Company, 1904.

DeForest, John William. *A Union Officer in the Reconstruction.* Ed. James H. Croushore and David Morris Potter. New Haven: Yale University Press, 1948.

A Volunteer's Adventures: A Union Captain's Record of the Civil War. Ed. James H. Croushore. New Haven: Yale University Press, 1946.

Depew, Chauncey. *My Memories of Eighty Years.* New York: Scribner's, 1924.

Felton, Rebecca. *Country Life in Georgia in the Days of My Youth.* Atlanta: Index Printing Company, 1919.

Felton, Mrs. William H. [Rebecca]. *My Memoirs of Georgia Politics.* Atlanta: Index Printing Company, 1911.

Frothingham, Octavius Brooks. *Recollections and Impressions.* New York: G. P. Putnam's Sons, 1891.

Gibbons, James Cardinal. *A Retrospect of Fifty Years.* 1916. Reprint. 2 vols. in one. New York: Arno Press, 1972.

Grant, Julia. *The Personal Memoirs of Julia Dent Grant.* Ed. John Y. Simon. New York: G. P. Putnam's Sons, 1975.

Grant, Ulysses S. *Personal Memoirs of U.S. Grant.* 1885. Reprint. Ed. E. B. Long. New York: DeCapo Press, 1982.

Hale, Edward Everett. *Memories of a Hundred Years.* 2 vols. New York: Macmillan, 1902.

A New England Boyhood. 1893. Reprint. Upper Saddle River, N.J.: Literature House/Gregg Press, 1970.

Higginson, Thomas Wentworth. *Army Life in a Black Regiment.* 1870. Reprint. Williamstown, Mass.: Corner House Publishers, 1971.

Cheerful Yesterdays. Boston: Houghton Mifflin, 1898.

Hood, John Bell. *Advance and Retreat: Personal Experiences in the United States and Confederate States Armies.* 1880. Reprint. Ed. Richard N. Current. Bloomington: Indiana University Press, 1959.

Howard, Oliver Otis. *Autobiography of Oliver Otis Howard.* 2 vols. New York: Baker and Taylor, 1907.

Howells, William Dean. *A Boy's Town, Described for "Harper's Young People."* New York: Harper and Brothers, 1890.

Years of My Youth. New York: Harper and Brothers, 1916.

Larcom, Lucy. *A New England Girlhood: Outlined from Memory.* Boston: Houghton Mifflin, 1889.

Sanborn, F[ranklin] B[enjamin]. *Recollections of Seventy Years.* 2 vols. Boston: Richard G. Badger, 1909.

Sherman, William Tecumseh. *Memoirs of General William T. Sherman by Himself.* 1875. Reprint. 2 vols. in one. Bloomington: Indiana University Press, 1957.

Stanton, Elizabeth Cady. *Eighty Years and More: Reminiscences, 1815–1897.* 1898. Reprint. New York: Schocken Books, 1971.

Wallace, Lew. *Lew Wallace: An Autobiography.* 2 vols. New York: Harper and Brothers, 1906.

4. Biographies

Armstrong, William. *Warrior in Two Camps: Ely S. Parker, Union General and Seneca Chief.* Syracuse: Syracuse University Press, 1978.

Banner, Lois W. *Elizabeth Cady Stanton: A Radical for Woman's Rights.* Boston: Little, Brown, 1980.

Barnes, Eric Wollencott. *The Lady of Fashion: The Life and the Theatre of Anna Cora Mowatt.* New York: Scribner's, 1954.

Block, Eugene B. *Above the Civil War: The Story of Thaddeus Lowe, Balloonist, Inventor, Railway Builder.* Berkeley, Calif.: Howell-North Books, 1966.

Boucher, Arlene, and John Tehan. *Prince of Democracy: James Cardinal Gibbons.* Garden City, N.Y.: Doubleday, 1962.

Brown, Ira V. *Lyman Abbott, Christian Evangelist: A Study in Religious Liberalism.* 1953. Reprint. Westport, Conn.: Greenwood Press, 1970.

Burton, Katherine. *Three Generations: Maria Boyle Ewing (1801–1864), Ellen Ewing Sherman (1824–1888), Minnie Sherman Fitch (1851–1913).* New York: Longmans, Green, 1947.

Caruthers, J. Wade. *Octavius Brooks Frothingham: Gentle Radical.* University: University of Alabama Press, 1977.

Coleman, Elizabeth Tyler. *Priscilla Cooper Tyler and the American Scene, 1816–1889.* University: University of Alabama Press, 1955.

Coulter, E. Merton. *William Montague Browne: Versatile Anglo-Irish American, 1823–1883.* Athens: University of Georgia Press, 1967.

Cramer, C. H. *Royal Bob: The Life of Robert G. Ingersoll.* Indianapolis: Bobbs-Merrill, 1952.

Donald, David. *Lincoln's Herndon.* New York: Knopf, 1948.

Dowd, Clement. *Life of Zebulon B. Vance.* Charlotte: Observer Printing and Publishing House, 1897.

Dyer, John P. *The Gallant Hood.* Indianapolis: Bobbs-Merrill, 1950.

Edelstein, Tilden G. *Strange Enthusiasm: A Life of Thomas Wentworth Higginson.* New Haven: Yale University Press, 1968.

Elliott, Walter. *The Life of Father Hecker.* 2d ed. New York: Columbia University Press, 1894.

Fehrenbacher, Don E. *Chicago Giant: A Biography of "Long John" Wentworth.* Madison, Wis.: American Historical Research Center, 1957.

Flexner, Abraham. *Daniel Coit Gilman: Creator of the American Type of University.* New York: Harcourt, Brace, and Company, 1946.

Holden, Vincent F. *The Early Years of Isaac Thomas Hecker (1819–1844).* Washington, D.C.: Catholic University Press, 1939.

Holloway, Jean. *Edward Everett Hale: A Biography.* Austin: University of Texas Press, 1956.

Horan, James D. *Mathew Brady: Historian with a Camera.* New York: Crown Publishers, 1955.

James, Henry. *William Wetmore Story and His Friends.* 1903. Reprint. 2 vols. in one. New York: Grove Press, n.d.

Larson, Henrietta M. *Jay Cooke: Private Banker.* 1936. Reprint. New York: Greenwood Press, 1968.

Leech, Margaret, and Harry J. Brown. *The Garfield Orbit.* New York: Harper and Row, 1978.

Light, James F. *John William DeForest.* New Haven: College and University Publishers, 1965.

Livesay, Harold C. *Andrew Carnegie and the Rise of Big Business.* Boston: Little, Brown, 1975.

Lynn, Kenneth S. *William Dean Howells: An American Life.* New York: Harcourt, Brace, Jovanovich, 1970.

McFeely, William S. *Grant: A Biography.* New York: Norton, 1981.

    Yankee Stepfather: General O. O. Howard and the Freedmen. New Haven: Yale University Press, 1968.

Merrill, James M. *William Tecumseh Sherman.* Chicago: Rand McNally, 1971.

Morseberger, Robert E., and Katharine M. Morseberger. *Lew Wallace: Militant Romantic.* New York: McGraw-Hill, 1980.

Muhlenfeld, Elisabeth. *Mary Boykin Chesnut: A Biography.* Baton Rouge: Louisiana State University Press, 1981.

Nevins, Allan. *Abram S. Hewitt, with Some Account of Peter Cooper.* New York: Harper Brothers, 1935.

Parker, Arthur C. *The Life of General Ely S. Parker.* Buffalo: Buffalo Historical Society, 1919.

Payne, Charles E. *Josiah Bushnell Grinnell.* Iowa City: State Historical Society of Iowa, 1938.

Perry, Bliss. *Life and Letters of Henry Lee Higginson.* Boston: Atlantic Monthly Press, 1921.

Resek, Carl. *Lewis Henry Morgan: American Scholar.* Chicago: University of Chicago Press, 1960.

Rice, Jessie Pearl. *J. L. M. Curry: Southerner, Statesman, and Educator.* New York: Columbia University, King's Crown Press, 1949.

Roper, Laura Wood. *FLO: A Biography of Frederick Law Olmsted.* Baltimore: Johns Hopkins University Press, 1973.

Saxton, Martha. *Louisa May: A Modern Biography of Louisa May Alcott.* Boston: Houghton Mifflin, 1977.

Sewall, Richard B. *The Life of Emily Dickinson.* 2 vols. New York: Farrar, Straus, and Giroux, 1974.

Stebbins, Emma. *Charlotte Cushman: Her Letters and Memories of Her Life.* Boston: Houghton, Osgood and Company, 1879.

Steinman, David Barnard. *The Builders of the Bridge: The Story of John Roebling and His Son.* New York: Harcourt, Brace, and Company, 1945.

Stonehouse, Merlin. *John Wesley North and the Reform Frontier.* Minneapolis: University of Minnesota Press, 1965.

Talmadge, John E. *Rebecca Latimer Felton: Nine Stormy Decades.* Athens: University of Georgia Press, 1960.

Tucker, Glenn. *Zeb Vance: Champion of Personal Freedom.* Indianapolis: Bobbs-Merrill, 1965.

Wellman, Manly. *Giant in Gray: A Biography of Wade Hampton of South Carolina.* New York: Scribner's, 1949.

Westbrook, Perry. *John Burroughs.* New York: Twayne, 1974.

White, Philip L. *The Beekmans of New York in Politics and Commerce, 1647–1887.* New York: New-York Historical Society, 1965.

Wiley, Bell Irvin. *Confederate Women*. Westport, Conn.: Greenwood Press, 1975.

Williams, T. Harry. *P. G. T. Beauregard: Napoleon in Grey*. Baton Rouge: Louisiana State University Press, 1954.

NINETEENTH-CENTURY AND EARLY TWENTIETH-
CENTURY CULTURE

1. General Studies

Abrams, M. H. *Natural Supernaturalism: Tradition and Revolution in Romantic Literature*. New York: Norton, 1971.

Billington, Ray. *The Protestant Crusade, 1800–1860: A Study in the Origins of American Nativism*. Chicago: Quadrangle, 1964.

Bode, Carl. *The Anatomy of American Popular Culture, 1840–1861*. Berkeley: University of California Press, 1959.

Bruce, Dickson D., Jr. *Violence and Culture in the Antebellum South*. Austin: University of Texas Press, 1979.

Buell, Lawrence. *Literary Transcendentalism: Style and Vision in the American Renaissance*. Ithaca: Cornell University Press, 1973.

New England Literary Culture: From Revolution through Renaissance. Cambridge University Press, 1986.

Calhoun, Daniel. *The Intelligence of a People*. Princeton: Princeton University Press, 1973.

Coben, Stanley. *Rebellion against Victorianism: The Impetus for Cultural Change in 1920s America*. New York: Oxford University Press, 1991.

Cohen, Patricia Cline. *A Calculating People: The Spread of Numeracy in Early America*. Chicago: University of Chicago Press, 1982.

Crouse, Russell. *Mr. Currier and Mr. Ives: A Note on Their Lives and Times*. Garden City, N.Y.: Doubleday, Doran, 1930.

Cunliffe, Marcus. *Soldiers and Civilians: The Martial Spirit in America, 1775–1865*. Boston: Little, Brown, 1968.

Davis, David Brion. *From Homicide to Slavery: Studies in American Culture*. New York: Oxford University Press, 1986.

Douglas, Ann. *The Feminization of American Culture*. New York: Knopf, 1977.

Eksteins, Modris. *The Rites of Spring: The Great War and the Birth of the Modern Age*. Boston: Houghton Mifflin, 1989.

Elias, Norbert. *The Civilizing Process: The History of Manners*. Trans. Edmund Jephcott. 1939. Reprint. New York: Urizen Books, 1978.

Forgie, George B. *Patricide in the House Divided: A Psychological Interpretation of Lincoln and His Age*. New York: Norton, 1979.

Fussell, Paul. *The Great War and Modern Memory*. New York: Oxford University Press, 1975.

Green, Constance McLaughlin. *Washington: Village and Capital, 1800–1878*. Princeton: Princeton University Press, 1962.

Hall, David. "Introduction: The Uses of Literacy in New England, 1600–1850." In *Printing and Society in Early America,* ed. William L. Joyce et al. Worcester, Mass.: American Antiquarian Society, 1983.

Halttunen, Karen. *Confidence Men and Painted Women: A Study of Middle-Class Culture in America, 1830–1870.* New Haven: Yale University Press, 1982.

Harris, Neil. *The Artist in American Society: The Formative Years, 1790–1860.* New York: George Braziller, 1966.

Higham, John. "The Reorientation of American Culture in the 1890s." In *The Origins of Modern Consciousness,* ed. John Weiss. Detroit: Wayne State University Press, 1965.

Strangers in the Land: Patterns of American Nativism, 1860–1925. Rev. ed. New York: Atheneum, 1971.

Hobsbawm, Eric. *The Age of Capital, 1848–1875.* London: Weidenfeld and Nicolson, 1975.

The Age of Empire, 1875–1914. New York: Pantheon, 1987.

The Age of Revolution, 1789–1848. New York: Praeger, 1962.

Houghton, Walter E. *The Victorian Frame of Mind, 1830–1870.* New Haven: Yale University Press, 1957.

Howe, Daniel Walker, ed. *Victorian America.* Philadelphia: University of Pennsylvania Press, 1976.

Isaac, Rhys. *The Transformation of Virginia, 1740–1790.* Chapel Hill: University of North Carolina Press, 1982.

Johannsen, Robert W. *To the Halls of the Montezumas: The Mexican War in the American Imagination.* New York: Oxford University Press, 1985.

Kaestle, Carl F. *Pillars of the Republic: Common Schools and American Society, 1780–1860.* New York: Hill and Wang, 1983.

Kennedy, David M. *Over Here: The First World War and American Society.* New York: Oxford University Press, 1980.

Kern, Louis J. *An Ordered Love: Sex Roles and Sexuality in Victorian Utopias – The Shakers, the Mormons, and the Oneida Community.* Chapel Hill: University of North Carolina Press, 1981.

Kuklick, Bruce. *The Rise of American Philosophy: Cambridge, Massachusetts, 1860–1930.* New Haven: Yale University Press, 1977.

Lears, T. J. Jackson. *No Place of Grace: Antimodernism and the Transformation of American Culture, 1880–1920.* New York: Pantheon, 1981.

Limerick, Patricia Nelson. *The Legacy of Conquest: The Unbroken Past of the American West.* New York: Norton, 1987.

Linderman, Gerald F. *The Mirror of War: American Society and the Spanish–American War.* Ann Arbor: University of Michigan Press, 1974.

Lynd, Robert, and Helen Merrill Lynd. *Middletown: A Study in Modern American Culture.* New York: Harcourt, Brace, Jovanovich, 1929.

May, Henry F. *The End of American Innocence: A Study in the First Years of Our Own Time, 1912–1917.* Chicago: Quadrangle Books, 1959.

Miller, Perry. *The Life of the Mind in America: From the Revolution to the Civil War.* New York: Harcourt, Brace and World, 1965.

Mumford, Lewis. *The Brown Decades: A Study of the Arts in America, 1865–1895.* 2d rev. ed. New York: Dover, 1955.

Pattee, Fred Lewis. *The Feminine Fifties*. New York: D. Appleton-Century Company, 1940.

Persons, Stow. *The Decline of American Gentility*. New York: Columbia University Press, 1973.

Reynolds, David S. *Beneath the American Renaissance: The Subversive Imagination in the Age of Emerson and Melville*. New York: Knopf, 1988.

Rose, Anne C. *Transcendentalism as a Social Movement, 1830–1850*. New Haven: Yale University Press, 1981.

Samuels, Ernest. *Bernard Berenson: The Making of a Connoisseur*. Cambridge, Mass.: Harvard University Press, 1979.

Saum, Lewis O. *The Popular Mood of Pre–Civil War America*. Westport, Conn.: Greenwood Press, 1980.

Schlereth, Thomas J. *Victorian America: Transformations in Everyday Life*. New York: Harper Collins, 1991.

Singal, Daniel Joseph. *The War Within: From Victorian to Modernist Thought in the South, 1919–1945*. Chapel Hill: University of North Carolina Press, 1982.

Slotkin, Richard. *Regeneration through Violence: The Mythology of the American Frontier, 1600–1860*. Middletown, Conn.: Wesleyan University Press, 1973.

Somkin, Fred. *Unquiet Eagle: Memory and Desire in the Idea of American Freedom, 1815–1860*. Ithaca: Cornell University Press, 1967.

Taylor, William R. *Cavalier and Yankee: The Old South and American National Character*. New York: Harper and Row, 1957.

Trachtenberg, Alan. *Reading American Photographs: Images as History, Mathew Brady to Walker Evans*. New York: Hill and Wang, 1989.

Turner, James. *Reckoning with the Beast: Animals, Pain, and Humanity in the Victorian Mind*. Baltimore: Johns Hopkins University Press, 1980.

Walters, Ronald G. *American Reformers, 1815–1860*. New York: Hill and Wang, 1978.

2. Religion

Ahlstrom, Sydney E. *A Religious History of the American People*. New Haven: Yale University Press, 1972.

"The Romantic Religious Revolution and the Dilemmas of Religious History." *Church History* 46 (1977): 149–70.

Atkinson, Clarissa W., Constance H. Buchanan, and Margaret R. Miles, eds. *Immaculate and Powerful: The Female in Sacred Image and Social Reality*. Boston: Beacon Press, 1985.

Bihartz, Terry D. *Urban Religion and the Second Great Awakening: Church and Society in Early National Baltimore*. Rutherford, N.J.: Fairleigh Dickinson University Press, 1986.

Boylan, Anne M. *Sunday School: The Formation of an American Institution, 1790–1880*. New Haven: Yale University Press, 1988.

Bozeman, Theodore Dwight. *Protestants in an Age of Science: The Baconian Ideal and Antebellum Religious Thought*. Chapel Hill: University of North Carolina Press, 1977.

Butler, Jon. *Awash in a Sea of Faith: Christianizing the American People*. Cambridge, Mass.: Harvard University Press, 1990.

Bynum, Carolina Walker, Stevan Harrell, and Paula Richman, eds. *Gender and Religion: On the Complexity of Symbols*. Boston: Beacon Press, 1986.

Carter, Paul. *The Spiritual Crisis in the Gilded Age*. DeKalb: Northern Illinois University Press, 1971.

Chadwick, Owen. *The Secularization of the European Mind in the Nineteenth Century*. Cambridge University Press, 1975.

Dawson, Jan C. *The Unusable Past: America's Puritan Tradition, 1830 to 1930*. Chico, Calif.: Scholar's Press, 1984.

Dolan, Jay P. The *American Catholic Experience: A History from Colonial Times to the Present*. Garden City, N.Y.: Doubleday, 1985.

Gardella, Peter. *Innocent Ecstasy: How Christianity Gave America an Ethic of Sexual Pleasure*. New York: Oxford University Press, 1985.

Goen, C. C. *Broken Churches, Broken Nation: Denominational Schisms and the Coming of the American Civil War*. Macon, Ga.: Mercer University Press, 1985.

Hatch, Nathan O. *The Democratization of American Christianity*. New Haven: Yale University Press, 1989.

Hennesey, James. *American Catholics: A History of the Roman Catholic Community in the United States*. New York: Oxford University Press, 1981.

Holifield, E. Brooks. *The Gentlemen Theologians: American Theology in Southern Culture, 1795–1860*. Durham, N.C.: Duke University Press, 1978.

Hutchinson, William R. *Errand to the World: American Protestant Thought and Foreign Missions*. Chicago: University of Chicago Press, 1987.

The Modernist Impulse in American Protestantism. Cambridge, Mass.: Harvard University Press, 1976.

Johnson, Paul E. *A Shopkeeper's Millennium: Society and Revivals in Rochester, New York, 1815–1837*. New York: Hill and Wang, 1978.

Kuklick, Bruce. *Churchmen and Philosophers: From Jonathan Edwards to John Dewey*. New Haven: Yale University Press, 1985.

McLoughlin, William. *Revivals, Awakenings, and Reform: An Essay on Religion and Social Change in America, 1607–1977*. Chicago: University of Chicago Press, 1978.

Marsden, George M. *Fundamentalism and American Culture: The Shaping of Twentieth Century Evangelicalism, 1870–1925*. New York: Oxford University Press, 1980.

Mathews, Donald. *Religion in the Old South*. Chicago: University of Chicago Press, 1977.

Moorhead, James H. *American Apocalypse: Yankee Protestants and the Civil War, 1860–1869*. New Haven: Yale University Press, 1978.

Persons, Stow. *Free Religion: An American Faith*. New Haven: Yale University Press, 1947.

Rabinowitz, Richard. *The Spiritual Self in Everyday Life: The Transformation of Personal Religious Experience in Nineteenth-Century New England*. Boston: Northeastern University Press, 1989.

Reynolds, David S. *Faith in Fiction: The Emergence of Religious Literature in America*. Cambridge, Mass.: Harvard University Press, 1981.

Sandeen, Ernest. *The Roots of Fundamentalism: British and American Millenarianism, 1800–1930.* Chicago: University of Chicago Press, 1970.

Scott, Donald M. *From Office to Profession: The New England Ministry, 1750–1850.* Philadelphia: University of Pennsylvania Press, 1978.

Shattuck, Gardiner H. *A Shield and Hiding Place: The Religious Life of the Civil War Armies.* Macon, Ga.: Mercer University Press, 1987.

Smith, Timothy. *Revivalism and Social Reform: American Protestantism on the Eve of the Civil War.* New York: Harcourt, Brace and World, 1965.

Stevenson, Louise L. *Scholarly Means to Evangelical Ends: The New Haven Scholars and the Transformation of Higher Learning in America, 1830–1890.* Baltimore: Johns Hopkins University Press, 1986.

Taves, Ann. *The Household of Faith: Roman Catholic Devotions in Mid-Nineteenth-Century America.* Notre Dame, Ind.: University of Notre Dame Press, 1986.

Turner, James. *Without God, Without Creed: The Origins of Unbelief in America.* Baltimore: Johns Hopkins University Press, 1985.

Weisenburger, Francis P. *Ordeal of Faith: The Crisis of Church-Going America, 1865–1900.* New York: Philosophical Library, 1959.

3. Work and Social Structure

Aron, Cindy Sondik. *Ladies and Gentlemen of the Civil Service: Middle-Class Workers in Victorian America.* New York: Oxford University Press, 1987.

Bledstein, Burton J. *The Culture of Professionalism: The Middle Class and the Development of Higher Education in America.* New York: Norton, 1976.

Blumin, Stuart M. *The Emergence of the Middle Class: Social Experience in the American City, 1760–1900.* Cambridge University Press, 1989.

Clark, Christopher. *The Roots of Rural Capitalism: Western Massachusetts, 1780–1860.* Ithaca: Cornell University Press, 1990.

Faragher, John Mack. *Sugar Creek: Life on the Illinois Prairie.* New Haven: Yale University Press, 1986.

Hahn, Steven, and Jonathan Prude, eds. *The Countryside in the Age of Capitalist Transformation: Essays in the Social History of Rural America.* Chapel Hill: University of North Carolina Press, 1983.

Hall, Peter Dobkin. *The Organization of American Culture, 1700–1900: Private Institutions, Elites, and the Origins of America.* New York: New York University Press, 1982.

Pease, William H., and Jane H. Pease. *The Web of Progress: Private Values and Public Style in Boston and Charleston, 1828–1843.* New York: Oxford University Press, 1985.

Rogers, Daniel T. *The Work Ethic in Industrial America, 1850–1920.* Chicago: University of Chicago Press, 1978.

Soltow, Lee. *Men and Wealth in the United States, 1850–1870.* New Haven: Yale University Press, 1975.

Stansell, Christine. *City of Women: Sex and Class in New York, 1789–1860.* New York: Knopf, 1986.

Trachtenberg, Alan. *The Incorporation of America: Culture and Society in the Gilded Age*. New York: Hill and Wang, 1982.

Wilentz, Sean. *Chants Democratic: New York City and the Rise of the American Working Class, 1788–1850*. New York: Oxford University Press, 1984.

4. Leisure

DeGrazia, Sebastian. *Of Time, Work, and Leisure*. Garden City, N.Y.: Doubleday, 1962.

Donegan, Jane B. *"Hydropathic Highway to Health": Women and Water-Cure in Antebellum America*. New York: Greenwood Press, 1986.

Gilkeson, John S., Jr. *Middle-Class Providence, 1840–1940*. Princeton: Princeton University Press, 1986.

Green, Harvey. *Fit for America: Health, Fitness, Sport, and American Society*. New York: Pantheon, 1986.

Harris, Neil. *Humbug: The Art of P. T. Barnum*. Chicago: University of Chicago Press, 1973.

Lender, Mark Edward, and James Kirby Martin. *Drinking in America: A History*. Rev. ed. New York: Free Press, 1987.

Peiss, Kathy. *Cheap Amusements: Working Women and Leisure in Turn-of-the-Century New York*. Philadelphia: Temple University Press, 1986.

Rosenzweig, Roy. *Eight Hours for What We Will: Workers and Leisure in an American Industrial City, 1870–1920*. Cambridge University Press, 1983.

5. Family and Gender

Ariès, Philippe. *Centuries of Childhood: A Social History of Family Life*. Trans. Robert Baldick. New York: Random House, 1962.

Baker, Jean H. *Mary Todd Lincoln: A Biography*. New York: Norton, 1987.

Barker-Benfield, G. J. *The Horrors of the Half-Known Life: Male Attitudes toward Women and Sexuality in Nineteenth-Century America*. New York: Harper and Row, 1976.

Blair, Karen J. *The Clubwoman as Feminist: True Womanhood Redefined, 1868–1914*. New York: Holmes and Meier, 1980.

Clinton, Catherine. *The Plantation Mistress: Women's World in the Old South*. New York: Pantheon, 1982.

Cott, Nancy F. *The Bonds of Womanhood: "Woman's Sphere" in New England, 1780–1835*. New Haven: Yale University Press, 1977.

Cowan, Ruth Schwartz. *More Work for Mother: The Ironies of Household Technology from the Open Hearth to the Microwave*. New York: Basic Books, 1983.

DuBois, Ellen. *Feminism and Suffrage: The Emergence of an Independent Women's Movement in America, 1848–1869*. Ithaca: Cornell University Press, 1978.

Easterlin, Richard A. "The Economics and Sociology of Fertility: A Synthesis." In *Historical Studies in Changing Fertility*, ed. Charles Tilly. Princeton: Princeton University Press, 1978.

Selected Bibliography

Epstein, Barbara Leslie. *The Politics of Domesticity: Women, Evangelism, and Temperance in Nineteenth-Century America.* Middletown, Conn.: Wesleyan University Press, 1981.

Faragher, John Mack. *Women and Men on the Overland Trail.* New Haven: Yale University Press, 1979.

Flexner, Eleanor. *Century of Struggle: The Woman's Rights Movement in America, 1848–1920.* Rev. ed. Cambridge, Mass.: Harvard University Press, 1975.

Fox-Genovese, Elizabeth. *Within the Plantation Household: Black and White Women of the Old South.* Chapel Hill: University of North Carolina Press, 1988.

Gay, Peter. *The Bourgeois Experience: From Victoria to Freud.* Vol. 1, *The Education of the Senses.* New York: Oxford University Press, 1984.

The Bourgeois Experience: From Victoria to Freud. Vol. 2, *The Tender Passion.* New York: Oxford University Press, 1986.

Ginzberg, Lori D. *Women and the Work of Benevolence: Morality, Politics, and Class in the Nineteenth-Century United States.* New Haven: Yale University Press, 1990.

Gordon, Michael, ed. *The American Family in Social–Historical Perspective.* 2d ed. New York: St. Martin's Press, 1978.

Greven, Philip. *The Protestant Temperament: Patterns of Child-Rearing, Religious Experience, and the Self in Early America.* New York: New American Library, 1977.

Handlin, David P. *The American Home: Architecture and Society, 1815–1915.* Boston: Little, Brown, 1979.

Hewitt, Nancy A. *Women's Activism and Social Change: Rochester, New York, 1822–1872.* Ithaca: Cornell University Press, 1984.

Kett, Joseph F. *Rites of Passage: Adolescence in America, 1790 to the Present.* New York: Basic Books, 1977.

Lystra, Karen. *Searching the Heart: Women, Men and Romantic Love in Nineteenth-Century America.* New York: Oxford University Press, 1989.

Marcus, Steven. *The Other Victorians: A Study of Sexuality and Pornography in Mid-Nineteenth-Century England.* 1964. Reprint. New York: New American Library, 1974.

McDannell, Colleen. *The Christian Home in Victorian America, 1840–1900.* Bloomington: Indiana University Press, 1986.

Mintz, Steven. *A Prison of Expectations: The Family in Victorian Culture.* New York: New York University Press, 1983.

Premo, Terri L. *Winter Friends: Women Growing Old in the New Republic, 1785–1835.* Urbana: University of Illinois Press, 1990.

Rosenberg, Rosalind. *Beyond Separate Spheres: Intellectual Roots of Modern Feminism.* New Haven: Yale University Press, 1982.

Rossi, Alice, ed. *The Feminist Papers: From Adams to Beauvoir.* New York: Bantam Books, 1973.

Rothman, Ellen K. *Hands and Hearts: A History of Courtship in America.* New York: Basic Books, 1984.

Ryan, Mary P. *Cradle of the Middle Class: The Family in Oneida County, New York, 1790–1865.* Cambridge University Press, 1981.

Sklar, Katherine Kish. *Catharine Beecher: A Study in American Domesticity.* New Haven: Yale University Press, 1973.

Smith, Daniel Scott. "Family Limitation, Sexual Control, and Domestic Feminism in Victorian America." In *Clio's Consciousness Raised: New Perspectives on the History of Women,* ed. Mary S. Hartman and Lois Banner. New York: Harper and Row, 1974.

Smith-Rosenberg, Carroll. *Disorderly Conduct: Visions of Gender in Victorian America.* New York: Knopf, 1985.

Ulrich, Laurel Thatcher. *Good Wives: Image and Reality in the Lives of Women in Northern New England, 1650–1750.* New York: Knopf, 1982.

　A Midwife's Tale: The Life of Martha Ballard. Based on Her Diary, 1785–1812. New York: Knopf, 1990.

6. Politics

Alexander, Thomas B., and Richard E. Beringer. *The Anatomy of the Confederate Congress: A Study of the Influences of Member Characteristics on Legislative Voting Behavior, 1861–1865.* Nashville: Vanderbilt University Press, 1972.

Baker, Jean H. *Affairs of Party: The Political Culture of Northern Democrats in the Mid-Nineteenth Century.* Ithaca: Cornell University Press, 1983.

　The Politics of Continuity: Maryland Political Parties from 1858 to 1870. Baltimore: Johns Hopkins University Press, 1973.

Beringer, Richard E. "The Unconscious 'Spirit of Party' in the Confederate Congress." *Civil War History* 18 (1972): 312–33.

Bogue, Allan. "Members of the House of Representatives and the Process of Modernization." *Journal of American History* 63 (1976): 275–302.

Cooper, William J., Jr. *The South and the Politics of Slavery, 1828–1856.* Baton Rouge: Louisiana State University Press, 1978.

Escott, Paul D. *Many Excellent People: Power and Privilege in North Carolina, 1850–1900.* Chapel Hill: University of North Carolina Press, 1985.

Foner, Eric. *Free Soil, Free Labor, Free Men: The Ideology of the Republican Party before the Civil War.* London: Oxford University Press, 1970.

Formisano, Ronald P. "Toward a Reorientation of Jacksonian Politics: A Review of the Literature, 1959–1975." *Journal of American History* 63 (1976): 42–65.

Freehling, William H. *The Road to Disunion: Secessionists at Bay, 1776–1854.* New York: Oxford University Press, 1990.

Gienapp, William E. *The Origins of the Republican Party, 1852–1856.* New York: Oxford University Press, 1987.

Greenberg, Kenneth S. *Masters and Statesmen: The Political Culture of American Slavery.* Baltimore: Johns Hopkins University Press, 1985.

Hofstadter, Richard. *The Idea of a Party System: The Rise of Legitimate Opposition in the United States, 1780–1840.* Berkeley: University of California Press, 1969.

Holt, Michael F. *The Political Crisis of the 1850s.* New York: John Wiley and Sons, 1978.

Howe, Daniel Walker. *The Political Culture of the American Whigs.* Chicago: University of Chicago Press, 1979.

Keller, Morton. *Affairs of State: Public Life in Late Nineteenth Century America.* Cambridge, Mass.: Harvard University Press, 1977.

Kleppner, Paul. *The Third Electoral System, 1853–1892.* Chapel Hill: University of North Carolina Press, 1979.

Kohl, Lawrence Frederick. *The Politics of Individualism: Parties and the American Character in the Jacksonian Era.* New York: Oxford University Press, 1989.

McCormick, Richard L. *The Party Period and Public Policy: American Politics from the Age of Jackson to the Progressive Era.* New York: Oxford University Press, 1986.

McGeer, Michael E. *The Decline of Popular Politics: The American North, 1865–1928.* New York: Oxford University Press, 1986.

McKitrick, Eric L. "Party Politics and the Union and Confederate War Efforts." In *The American Party Systems,* ed. William Nisbet Chambers and Walter Dean Burnham. 2d ed. New York: Oxford University Press, 1975.

Montgomery, David. *Beyond Equality: Labor and the Radical Republicans, 1862–72.* New York: Knopf, 1967.

Perman, Michael. *The Road to Redemption: Southern Politics, 1869–1879.* Chapel Hill: University of North Carolina Press, 1984.

Polsby, Nelson W. "The Institutionalization of the U.S. House of Representatives." *American Political Science Review* 62 (1968): 144–68.

Price, H. Douglas. "The Congressional Career: Then and Now." In *Congressional Behavior,* ed. Nelson W. Polsby. New York: Random House, 1971.

Shields, Johanna Nicol. *The Line of Duty: Maverick Congressmen and the Development of American Political Culture, 1836–1860.* Westport, Conn.: Greenwood Press, 1985.

Silbey, Joel H. *A Respectable Minority: The Democratic Party in the Civil War Era, 1860–1868.* New York: Norton, 1977.

Thompson, Margaret Susan. *The "Spider Web": Congress and Lobbying in the Age of Grant.* Ithaca: Cornell University Press, 1985.

Tocqueville, Alexis de. *Democracy in America.* 1835. Reprint. Ed. J. P. Mayer. 2 vols. in one. Garden City, N.Y.: Anchor Books, 1969.

Wilson, Major. "Republicanism and the Idea of Party in the Jacksonian Period." *Journal of the Early Republic* 8 (1988): 419–42.

THE CIVIL WAR ERA: SOCIETY AND CULTURE

Aaron, Daniel. *The Unwritten War: American Writers and the Civil War.* New York: Knopf, 1973.

Ambrose, Stephen E. *Duty, Honor, Country: A History of West Point.* Baltimore: Johns Hopkins University Press, 1966.

Barton, Michael. *Goodmen: The Character of Civil War Soldiers.* University Park: Penn State University Press, 1981.

Blassingame, John W. *The Slave Community: Plantation Life in the Antebellum South.* Rev. ed. New York: Oxford University Press, 1979.

Dearing, Mary R. *Veterans in Politics: The Story of the G.A.R.* Baton Rouge: Louisiana State University Press, 1952.

Faust, Drew Gilpin. "Altars of Sacrifice: Confederate Women and the Narratives of War." *Journal of American History* 76 (1990): 1200–28.

The Creation of Confederate Nationalism: Ideology and Identity in the Civil War South. Baton Rouge: Louisiana State University Press, 1988.

A Sacred Circle: The Dilemma of the Intellectual in the Old South, 1840–1860. Baltimore: Johns Hopkins University Press, 1977.

Foner, Eric. *Politics and Ideology in the Age of the Civil War.* Oxford: Oxford University Press, 1980.

Reconstruction: America's Unfinished Revolution. New York: Harper and Row, 1988.

Foster, Gaines M. *Ghosts of the Confederacy: Defeat, the Lost Cause, and the Emergence of the New South, 1865–1913.* New York: Oxford University Press, 1987.

Fredrickson, George M. *The Black Image in the White Mind: The Debate on Afro-American Character and Destiny, 1817–1914.* New York: Harper and Row, 1971.

The Inner Civil War: Northern Intellectuals and the Crisis of the Union. New York: Harper and Row, 1965.

Genovese, Eugene D. *Roll, Jordan, Roll: The World the Slaves Made.* New York: Vintage, 1972.

Hahn, Steven. *The Roots of Southern Populism: Yeoman Farmers and the Transformation of the Georgia Upcountry, 1850–1890.* New York: Oxford University Press, 1983.

Hanna, Alfred Jackson, and Kathryn Abbey Hanna. *Confederate Exiles in Venezuela.* Tuscaloosa, Ala.: Confederate Publishing Company, 1960.

Hesseltine, William B. *The Blue and the Gray on the Nile.* Chicago: University of Chicago Press, 1961.

Hill, Lawrence F. *The Confederate Exodus to Latin America.* Austin: University of Texas Press, 1936.

Hobson, Fred. *Tell about the South: The Southern Rage to Explain.* Baton Rouge: Louisiana State University Press, 1983.

Jimerson, Randall. *The Private Civil War: Popular Thought during the Sectional Conflict.* Baton Rouge: Louisiana State University Press, 1988.

Leonard, Thomas C. *Above the Battle: War-Making in America from Appomatox to Versailles.* New York: Oxford University Press, 1978.

Linderman, Gerald F. *Embattled Courage: The Experience of Combat in the American Civil War.* New York: Free Press, 1987.

Massey, Mary Elizabeth. *Bonnet Brigades.* New York: Knopf, 1966.

McPherson, James M. *Battle Cry of Freedom: The Civil War Era.* New York: Oxford University Press, 1988.

Mitchell, Reid. *Civil War Soldiers.* New York: Viking, 1988.

Oakes, James. *The Ruling Race: A History of American Slaveholders.* New York: Vintage, 1982.

Slavery and Freedom: An Interpretation of the Old South. New York: Knopf, 1990.

Paludan, Phillip Shaw. *"A People's Contest": The Union and the Civil War, 1861–1865.* New York: Harper and Row, 1988.

Powell, Lawrence N. *New Masters: Northern Planters during the Civil War and Reconstruction.* New Haven: Yale University Press, 1980.

Pressley, Thomas J. *Americans Interpret Their Civil War.* Princeton: Princeton University Press, 1954.

Rable, George C. *Civil Wars: Women and the Crisis of Southern Nationalism.* Urbana: University of Illinois Press, 1989.

Rolle, Andrew F. *The Lost Cause: The Confederate Exodus to Mexico.* Norman: University of Oklahoma Press, 1965.

Stowe, Steven M. *Intimacy and Power in the Old South: Ritual in the Lives of the Planters.* Baltimore: Johns Hopkins University Press, 1987.

Vinovskis, Maris A., ed. *Toward a Social History of the American Civil War: Exploratory Essays.* Cambridge University Press, 1990.

Wiley, Bell Irvin. *The Life of Billy Yank: The Common Soldier of the Union.* 1951. *The Life of Johnny Reb: The Common Soldier of the Confederacy.* 1943. Reprinted as *The Common Soldier in the Civil War.* 2 vols. in one. New York: Grosset and Dunlap, n.d.

Wilson, Charles Reagan. *Baptized in Blood: The Religion of the Lost Cause, 1865–1920.* Athens: University of Georgia Press, 1980.

Wilson, Edmund. *Patriotic Gore: Studies in the Literature of the American Civil War.* New York: Farrar, Straus and Giroux, 1962.

Woodward, C. Vann. *American Counterpoint: Slavery and Racism in the North–South Dialogue.* Boston: Little, Brown, 1971.

Wyatt-Brown, Bertram. *Southern Honor: Ethics and Behavior in the Old South.* New York: Oxford University Press, 1982.

Index

Abbott, Abby (or Abigail; wife of Lyman Abbott), and women's labor, 81–2
Abbott, Jacob (father of Lyman Abbott), 48n52
Abbott, Lyman: career choice, 39, 94, 96; and Henry Ward Beecher, 28, 93; memoirs of, 251; political discussion during the Civil War, 225; productivity of, 79; relationship with his father, 93, 94; religious experience, 26n17, 27–8, 39, 41, 46, 52n98; on religious toleration, 39, 40, 41; working relationship with his wife, 81–2
Abrams, M. H., 9
Adams, Henry, 197n7
Agassiz, Alexander: as a child, 178; courtship and marriage, 149, 160; leisure activities, 117, 124; as a widower, 152, 153
Akerman, Amos T., 227
Alcott, Louisa May, attitude toward women and careers, 83
Alexander, Thomas, 229
American Victorian culture: and Catholicism, 47–50; definition, 4–5, 7–9; and modernism, 10, 254; and Protestant fundamentalism, 10, 254; and Protestant liberalism, 26n17, 35, 39; in relation to British Victorianism, 7–8, 15; in relation to economic goals, 68–70; in relation to family, 145–7; in relation to the individual, 6–7, 13n16; in relation to leisure, 109–111; in relation to politics, 193–5, 203; in relation to religion, 3–4, 17–20; role of the Civil War in, 1–4, 59, 97–8, 234–5, 237; and romanticism, 9–10; as the viewpoint of a generation, 3, 235; see also northern Victorian culture, southern Victorian culture
Americanism controversy, 49, see also Catholicism
Anthony, Susan B., and Elizabeth Cady Stanton, 124
Arendt, Hannah, 103n83

Atkinson, Annie (daughter of George Atkinson), as a child, 173
Atkinson, George: conversion experience, 26n17; as a father, 172–3; as a husband, 162; as minister, 52n98, 57–8; and religious liberalism, 35; and temperance, 56
Atkinson, George, Jr. (son of George Atkinson), as a child, 172–3
autobiography: the American tradition of, 252–4; as the characteristic Victorian genre, 49, 245; views of the Civil War in, 235, 248–52

Barlow, Samuel, as friend of William Montague Browne, 128
Barnum, P. T., 121
Bartlett, George, 100
Beauregard, Pierre: as amateur politician, 204n25; career of, 80–1, 90; as a Catholic, 48–9n85; as friend of Augusta Evans, 129; influence of Napoleon on, 196; as patron of water cures, 114
Beecher, Henry Ward: and the Civil War, 64; influence on Lyman Abbott, 28, 93
Beecher, Lyman, 22
Beekman, James William: church attendance, 52n98; comparison of his piety to his father's, 37; as a nativist, 47
Bellows, Henry, and George Templeton Strong, 64
Beringer, Richard, 229
Bierce, Ambrose, view of the Civil War, 237
Blaine, James G., 204
Bonaparte, Napoleon, 196
Brady, Julia (wife of Mathew Brady), 171
Brady, Mathew: career of, 86, 105, 210; marriage and family life, 161, 171, 175, 182; photographs of war heroes, 105, 226–7; and politics, 210; during Reconstruction, 105

Garfield, James (*cont.*)
  natural religion, 54; as politician, 1, 206,
    208n36, 217, 218, 231–2; religious
    background, 24–5, 44; and religious
    toleration, 44, 45–6; on slavery, 216–17;
    and spiritual languor, 35–6, 37; wartime
    friendship with General William Rosecrans,
    64–6, 139, 140
Garfield, Lucretia (or Crete; wife of James
  Garfield): correspondence with her husband
    during the Civil War, 1; visiting
    her husband during the Civil War, 184,
    185–6
Garrison, Wendell, 152
Gibbons, James Cardinal: influenced by Isaac
  Hecker, 49; as a liberal Catholic, 49;
    memoirs of, 49, 251; as priest, 49, 52n98;
    relations with Protestants, 49
Gilman, Daniel Coit: attitude toward the
  ministry, 58, 95; career dilemma, 95; as
    president of Johns Hopkins University, 95
Godkin, Edwin: attitude toward political
  corruption, 209; attitude toward religious
    rituals, 57; as editor of the *Nation,* 57, 152,
    225; as a father, 172; as a widower, 152
Grant, Fred (son of Julia Grant and Ulysses
  Grant), visits to his father during the Civil
    War, 184, 187
Grant, Hannah (mother of Ulysses Grant),
  relationship with her son, 168–9
Grant, Jesse (father of Ulysses Grant): role in the
  Civil War, 184, 187–8; social background, 86
Grant, Julia (wife of Ulysses Grant): and leisure,
  127n50; memoirs of, 229, 248; as a soldier's
    wife, 184; and travel, 120
Grant, Ulysses: career of, 86, 91, 106; Civil
  War experience, 59, 63, 86, 98, 139, 140;
    deathbed baptism of, 57; as a father, 184,
    187; memoirs of, 241–2, 246, 247, 250;
    and political image-making, 226–7; as
    politician, 106, 208n36, 211, 226–7, 231;
    public deathwatch of, 232; relationship with
    his father, 184, 187–8; relationship with his
    mother, 168–9; and travel, 120
Green, Beriah, 196
Grinnell, Josiah: entrepreneurship of, 76; as
  minister, 52n98, 58; as politician, 211–12;
    and temperance, 56; as a young Whig, 198
Guignard, James Sanders: career of, 87; religious
  experience, 26n17, 37
Guignard, John Gabriel: communal ideas of labor,
  74; and importance of family in the postwar
    South, 191; religious experience, 26n17, 37;
    on the social utility of wealth, 72
Guignard, Sanders (father of James Sanders
  Guignard and John Gabriel Guignard):
    occupations, 87; political career, 89, 199

Hale, Edward Everett: attitude toward nature,
  115; career dilemma, 89–90, 91, 95; and his
    father's influence, 91; memoirs of, 250; as a
    minister, 52n98, 89–90; political activity,
    while at Harvard, 200; productivity of, 79;
    religious background, 22, 23
Hale, Edward Everett; *The Man without a
  Country,* 200, 225
Hale, Nathan (father of Edward Everett Hale):
  editor of the *Boston Daily Advertiser,* 91;
    influence on his son, 91
Hale, Sarah, and travel, 117n15
Hale, Sarah, *Northwood,* 190
Halleck, Henry, 246
Halttunen, Karen, 125
Hampton, McDuffie (son of Wade Hampton
  III), relationship with his father, 166–7
Hampton, Wade III: and his children, 163,
  166–7, 171, 191–2; and Civil War
    commemoration, 142; and family-centered
    leisure, 126; political career, 104–5,
    208n36; relationship with his sister during
    the Civil War, 184; religious attitudes, 42–
    3; and southern leisure, 112–13; and
    southerners' career goals, 81
Hays, Fanny, 160
Hecker, Isaac: and the Americanism controversy,
  49; conversion to Catholicism, 48; influence on
    James Cardinal Gibbons, 49; as priest, 52n98
Herndon, Anna (second wife of William
  Herndon), as a mother, 169
Herndon, William: and Abraham Lincoln, 93,
  105, 220, 221, 247–8; as an admirer of
    Theodore Parker, 54–5; and antislavery,
    215, 220–1; career of, 93, 96, 105; and the
    legal profession, 96; on political corruption,
    202; political impulsiveness, 202–3;
    relationship with his father, 25, 93, 94,
    215; relationship with his second wife, 169;
    schooling, 25, 94
Herndon, William, *Herndon's Life of Lincoln,* 93,
  248
Hewitt, Abram: as church administrator, 53; as
  an Episcopalian, 46; and his father's career in
    New York City, 89; and individualism and
    the family, 173; marriage and social
    advancement, 181; and Peter Cooper, 99,
    181; as professional politician, 208n36; and
    Victorian leisure, 125
Higginson, Henry Lee: and boardinghouses,
  175; career dilemma, 78, 99–100, 101,
    106–7; on Catholicism, 47–8; Civil War
    experience, 99–100; commemoration of the
    Civil War, 142; as founder of the Boston
    Symphony Orchestra, 106; leisure activities,
    117; on natural religion, 54; as a patron of
    water cures, 114; recollections of the Civil

Index

Index

Johnson, Andrew, 227
Johnston, Joseph, 246
Juarez, Benito, and Lew Wallace, 107, 108, 119
Judaism: George Templeton Strong on Jewish ritual, 45–6; Protestant interest in synagogues, 45; Zebulon Vance on the toleration of Jews, 44–5

Kent, James, 96
Kinkade, John: on Abraham Lincoln, 210; ambitions of, 76, 77; career of, 96; and his children's deaths, 162–3; courtship of, 148; political enthusiasm, 209

Lamar, Lucius, 101–2
language, issues in the interpretation of, 6, 8
Larcom, Lucy: childhood leisure activities, 124; and family size, 171; memoirs of, 21, 250; religious background, 21, 30, 33n36, 38; as an unmarried woman, 155n31
Larson, Henrietta, 169
Lee, Robert E., 189
leisure: clubs, 111, 130, 131–2, 137–8; in the Civil War armies, 138–9, 140–1; Civil War commemoration as a form of, 111, 131, 141–3; and correspondence, 128–9; definition, 111n3; in the family, 125; friendships cultivated in, 127–30, 139; and individualism, 122; and manners, 130–1, 140–1; and mass audiences, 121–2, 143; in natural settings, 112–15; private theatricals, 124–5; and routinization, 122, 143; in the South, 112–13, 132, 133–4, 139–40, 143; and travel, 112, 116–20; of Victorian men, 112–13, 130–1; of Victorian women, 111, 123–4, 130–1, 136–3; and voluntary associations, 131; water cures, 113–14
liberalism: in relation to Victorian Catholicism, 48–9, 49n86; in relation to Victorian Protestantism, 26n17, 35, 39; see also religion
Lincoln, Abraham: influence on William Herndon, 93, 220–1; second inaugural address, 13, 61–2; and Ulysses Grant, 63, 140
Little, Josiah (uncle of George Atkinson), 35
Lowe, Clovis (father of Thaddeus Lowe), in New Hampshire politics, 200
Lowe, Thaddeus: as a child, 179, 200; political activity, 211; as promoter of tourism, 116
Lynn, Kenneth, on William Dean Howells, 169, 174

McCullough, Samuel: as church administrator, 53; church attendance, 52n98; courtship of, 160n44; economic aspirations, 75; and political corruption, 212

McFeely, William: on Hannah Grant, 168; on Oliver Otis Howard, 63; on Ulysses Grant, 120, 139
Maclay, Charles: attitude toward black suffrage, 223; attitude toward political corruption, 208–9; and church administration, 52–3; conversion experience, 26n17; as minister, 52n98, 52–3, 58; and political self-interest, 211
Mannheim, Karl, 103n83
Marx, Karl, 103n83, 122n32
Melville, Herman: Civil War poetry of, 245n28; *The Confidence Man*, 122
memoirs: as instrument of Victorian self-definition, 236; list of retrospective writings by Victorians, 248–49n33; and optimism, 239–41; philosophical implications of, 49, 245; polemical intent of, 245–7; on race and racism, 237, 242–5; in relation to intellectual history, 8–9, 236; and self-mastery, 241–2, 247–8; and Victorian labor, 107–8; on wartime suffering, 237–41; *see also* autobiography
men: as bachelors, 154–5; and church attendance, 23–4; clubs for, 131–2, 137–8; as fathers, 164–8, 187; as husbands, 149–50, 184, 185–6; and opportunities to create identities in careers, 70; political opportunities of, 198–200; relationships of the Victorians with their fathers, 87–9, 91–4, 198–200; on sexuality, 155–6; and tests of character, 112–13, 115; as widowers, 152–3
Mexican War: as opportunity for advancement for soldiers, 87; and romantic attitudes toward war, 100n73
middle-class culture: rise of a national, 14–15; *see also* middle classes
middle classes: and bureaucracy, 52–4, 95–7; Catholics in the, 48–9; creating identities through careers, 108; definition, 3, 10–11; distinctive view of the Civil War, 237, 244–5; economic opportunities, 69–70, 84–7; and emotional families, 177–9; and the evangelical tradition, 26; and family capital, 180–2; inner crisis, 4–5, 9; and the leisure of working-class soldiers, 138–9; political roles of, 198, 202
military history, as a historical genre, 2
modernism: definition, 10, 254; modernists' views of Victorianism, 8, 254–5
Moore, William: marriage of, 157; on the social utility of labor, 72; and spiritualism, 51; as an unmarried man, 154–5
Moorhead, James, on Civil War religion, 61, 64
Morgan, Lewis Henry: as advocate of Native Americans, 42, 211; as amateur politician,